Ethnography
Principles in practice
Third edition

**Martyn Hammersley
and Paul Atkinson**

Routledge
Taylor & Francis Group

LONDON AND NEW YORK

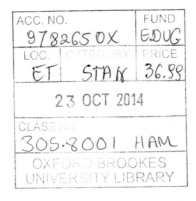
First edition published in 1983 by Tavistock Publications Ltd.
Reprinted in 1986 and 1987.

Second edition first published 1995
by Routledge
2 Park Square, Milton Park, Abingdon, Oxon OX14 4RN

Simultaneously published in the USA and Canada
by Routledge
711 Third Avenue, New York: NY 10017

Third edition published 2007

Routledge is an imprint of the Taylor & Francis Group, an informa business

© 2007 Martyn Hammersley and Paul Atkinson

Typeset in Times New Roman by
Florence Production Ltd, Stoodleigh, Devon
Printed and bound in Great Britain by
TJ International Ltd, Padstow, Cornwall

British Library Cataloguing in Publication Data
A catalogue record for this book is available from
the British Library

Library of Congress Cataloging in Publication Data
Hammersley, Martyn.
  Ethnography: principles in practice/Martyn Hammersley and
  Paul Atkinson. – 3rd ed.
    p. cm.
  1. Ethnology – Methodology. 2. Ethnology – Field work.
  3. Social sciences – Field work. I. Atkinson, Paul, 1947–
  II. Title.
  GN345.H35 2007
  305.8001–dc22   2007005419

ISBN10: 0–415–39604–2 (hbk)
ISBN10: 0–415–39605–0 (pbk)
ISBN10: 0–203–94476–3 (ebk)

ISBN13: 978–0–415–39604–2 (hbk)
ISBN13: 978–0–415–39605–9 (pbk)
ISBN13: 978–0–203–94476–9 (ebk)

The more ancient of the Greeks (whose writings are lost) took up . . . a position . . . between the presumption of pronouncing on everything, and the despair of comprehending anything; and though frequently and bitterly complaining of the difficulty of inquiry and the obscurity of things, and like impatient horses champing at the bit, they did not the less follow up their object and engage with nature, thinking (it seems) that this very question – viz., whether or not anything can be known – was to be settled not by arguing, but by trying. And yet they too, trusting entirely to the force of their understanding, applied no rule, but made everything turn upon hard thinking and perpetual working and exercise of the mind.

(Francis Bacon 1620)

Contents

Prologue to the third edition

The first edition of this book, which appeared in 1983, was the result of a collaboration of several years' standing. In the late 1970s, when we started working together, there was only a small literature for us to draw on. Our book filled a very obvious gap. There were some influential texts, all deriving from the United States and reflecting the interactionist tradition in sociology. Key authors such as Anselm Strauss and John Lofland set the scene for our collective understanding of ethnography. There were also methodological appendices to well-known monographs, but there was little or nothing that combined general methodological principles with their practical applications. We consructed a shared approach to the appropriate research strategies and intellectual stances associated with ethnographic work, and brought together a wide range of sources and examples.

At the time of our first edition, there were influential strands of ethnographic research in key areas like deviance, education, medicine and studies of work. But in most of the social sciences (with the obvious exception of social anthropology) ethnography was a distinctly minority interest. Moreover, while anthropologists took its value for granted, or perhaps because of this, on the whole they paid singularly little attention to the documentation or discussion of research methods.

Much has changed since the early 1980s. The volume of methodological writing has expanded greatly and continues to do so unabated; though, of course, the pattern of this has varied in different countries, and rather different narratives concerning the history of ethnography and qualitative research have been provided (Burawoy *et al.* 2000: intro; Weber 2001; Denzin and Lincoln 2005: intro; McCall 2006). By the time we wrote our second edition, which appeared in 1995, the methodological landscape had already shifted. There were, by then, a great many methods texts and commentaries available. The social sciences seemed to have experienced a 'methodological turn'. Graduate students throughout the world were receiving more training in the techniques of social research. There was an increasing awareness of research methods as an area of special interest, as well as being the core of practising social scientists' craft skills. That trend has continued, fuelled by a virtuous circle of research funding, postgraduate and postdoctoral opportunities, and the interests of commercial publishers. The sheer number of methodology texts and papers has become quite overwhelming. The domain of what is broadly labelled 'qualitative research' now spans a wide range of disciplines and sub-fields, and incorporates a variety of research styles and strategies. Work of this kind has become a central feature of sociology, cultural and media studies, cultural geography, educational research, health and nursing research, business and organization studies; involving the use of participant observation, individual and group interviews, focus groups, visual methods, conversation- and discourse-analytic techniques, and so on. Qualitative researchers have developed specialist literatures devoted to quite specific techniques – photographic and other visual methods (Pink 2006), narrative-analytic methods (Riessman 1993), interviewing of many sorts (Gubrium and Holstein 2002), the qualitative analysis of documentary sources (Prior 2003), and the exploration of virtual social realities (Hine 2000).

There are now available numerous major works on the variety of qualitative research methods and perspectives (e.g. Gubrium and Holstein 1997; Seale *et al.* 2004; Silverman 2004). The fashionable status of qualitative research has been encouraged by its alleged alignment with various tendencies within the social and cultural disciplines: such as 'critical' research, postmodernism, feminism and postfeminism, or postcolonialism. Qualitative inquiry has been promoted as having intrinsic political and ethical value, in giving voice to marginalized and otherwise muted groups and/or in challenging the powerful. The development and dissemination of qualitative research has been accompanied by recurrent announcements of innovation, renewal and paradigm-change *within* qualitative research itself.

Confronted with this exponential growth in writing about qualitative research, its increasing popularity, and the heady claims entered on its behalf, there is clearly a need for us to try to locate this third edition of our book within the broader method-ological terrain. First, we need to reaffirm that it focuses on *ethnography*, rather than qualitative research in general; even though there are no hard and fast boundaries. This means that it is primarily concerned with field research involving a range of methods, with participant observation being given particular emphasis. It is not necessary to think naively in terms of naturally occurring communities or isolated populations, nor do we need to entertain romantic visions of social exploration, in order to insist on the continued importance of participant observation in, and first-hand engagement with, social worlds (Delamont 2004b).

As many reviews of ethnography reveal, this is a variegated approach that is amenable to different emphases and nuances (see, for instance, Atkinson *et al.* 2001). We are not in the business of trying to impose a single orthodoxy here. It is, after all, a particular virtue of ethnographic research that it remains flexible and responsive to local circumstances. We do, however, emphasize the importance of the tradition of ethno-graphic research, and what guidance can be drawn from it.

In restating the importance of the ethnographic tradition we remain sceptical about many claims for innovation and novelty in research methods. Some readers might assume that, in producing a third edition of a work that first appeared in 1983, we would have removed all 'old' sources and references in the process of 'updating'. We have not done so, even though we have included more recent examples and developments. We are frequently disturbed by the widespread misapprehension that qualitative research in general, and ethnographic research in particular, are somehow novel approaches in the social sciences, or that research strategies that were current for most of the twentieth century are now redundant. Research communities that overlook their own past are always in danger of reinventing the wheel, and of assuming novelty when all that is really revealed is collective ignorance or amnesia (Atkinson *et al.* 1999). The collective memory of many research networks is far too shallow, in our view. We have, therefore, retained material that spans the first and second editions of our book.

The most visible preachers of novelty and change have been Norman Denzin and Yvonna Lincoln (Denzin and Lincoln 2005). They have helped to shape the current landscape of qualitative research more than most. The successive editions of their monumental *Handbook* have been remarkable not just for their scale and scope, but also for promoting a view of the history of qualitative research (and, by implication, of ethnography) as marked by a series of revolutionary transformations. They construct a developmental narrative of qualitative research that portrays sharp discontinuities and an increasing rate of change, following a broad trajectory from 'modernist' to 'postmodernist' standpoints.

Now there is no doubt that change has occurred and will continue to take place. And some of it has been of great value. The original influences of anthropology have been challenged and supplemented, and there has been major change within that discipline as well. The interactionist foundations of ethnographic work in sociology have been enriched by ideas stemming from many other sources. But we believe that current narratives of radical transformation are overstated, and sometimes simply wrong. Differences between past and current principles and practices are often exaggerated, and distorted views about the past are promoted. Equally important, in the championing of 'new' approaches, there has been a failure, often, to recognize the difficulty and complexity of the methodological issues that face ethnographers, along with other social scientists.

Recent trends, in some research fields, towards a re-emphasis on the importance of experimental method, and quantitative techniques more generally, sometimes labelled as a form of methodological fundamentalism, should not be met with an equivalent fundamentalism, in which the virtues of qualitative research are blindly extolled. Whatever the future has in store, in order to deal with it we must learn from the past as well as taking account of current circumstances and new ideas. In producing this third edition, we have tried to strike a balance between preserving the past and nurturing the new.

Acknowledgements

We thank the following colleagues for much help in clarifying our ideas over the long period during which the first and second editions of this book were produced: Sara Delamont, Anne Murcott, and other members of the School of Social and Administrative Studies, Cardiff University; Andy Hargreaves, Phil Strong, Peter Woods, John Scarth, Peter Foster, and Roger Gomm. We must also express our thanks to Meryl Baker, Stella Riches, Myrtle Robins, Lilian Walsh, Aileen Lodge, and June Evison for typing various drafts of the manuscript.

1   What is ethnography?

Ethnography is one of many approaches that can be found within social research today. Furthermore, the label is not used in an entirely standard fashion; its meaning can vary. A consequence of this is that there is considerable overlap with other labels, such as 'qualitative inquiry', 'fieldwork', 'interpretive method', and 'case study', these also having fuzzy semantic boundaries. In fact, there is no sharp distinction even between ethnography and the study of individual life histories, as the example of 'auto/ethnography' shows; this referring to an individual researcher's study of his or her own life and its context (Reed-Danahay 1997, 2001; Holman Jones 2005). There is also the challenging case of 'virtual ethnography', whose data may be restricted entirely to what can be downloaded from the internet (Markham 1998, 2005; Hine 2000; Mann and Stewart 2000). While, for the purposes of this opening chapter, we will need to give some indication of what we are taking the term 'ethnography' to mean, its variable and sometimes contested character must be remembered; and the account we provide will inevitably be shaped by our own views about what form ethnographic work *ought to take*.

The origins of the term lie in nineteenth-century Western anthropology, where an ethnography was a descriptive account of a community or culture, usually one located outside the West. At that time 'ethnography' was contrasted with, and was usually seen as complementary to, 'ethnology', which referred to the historical and comparative analysis of non-Western societies and cultures. Ethnology was treated as the core of anthropological work, and drew on individual ethnographic accounts which were initially produced by travellers and missionaries. Over time, the term 'ethnology' fell out of favour because anthropologists began to do their own fieldwork, with 'ethnography' coming to refer to an integration of both first-hand empirical investigation and the theoretical and comparative interpretation of social organization and culture.

As a result of this change, since the early twentieth century, ethnographic fieldwork has been central to anthropology. Indeed, carrying out such work, usually in a society very different from one's own, became a rite of passage required for entry to the 'tribe' of anthropologists. Fieldwork usually required living with a group of people for extended periods, often over the course of a year or more, in order to document and interpret their distinctive way of life, and the beliefs and values integral to it.

Moreover, during the twentieth century, anthropological ethnography came to be one of the models for some strands of research within Western sociology. One of these was the community study movement. This involved studies of villages and towns in the United States and Western Europe, often concerned with the impact of urbanization and industrialization. A landmark investigation here was the work of the Lynds in documenting life in Muncie, Indiana, which they named 'Middletown' (Lynd and Lynd 1929, 1937).

In a parallel development, many sociologists working at the University of Chicago from the 1920s to the 1950s developed an approach to studying human social life that was similar to anthropological research in some key respects, though they often labelled it 'case study'. The 'Chicago School' was concerned with documenting the range of different patterns of life to be found in the city, and how these were shaped by the developing urban ecology.

From the 1960s onwards, forms of sociological work influenced by these developments, especially by Chicago sociology, spread across many sub-fields of the discipline, and into other disciplines and areas of inquiry as well; and they also migrated from the United States to Europe and to other parts of the world. Furthermore, for a variety of reasons, an increasing number of anthropologists began to do research within Western societies, at first in rural areas but later in urban locales too.[1] Another relevant development in the latter half of the twentieth century was the rise of cultural studies as an area of investigation distinct from, but overlapping with, anthropology and sociology. Work in this field moved from broadly historical and textual approaches to include the use of ethnographic method, notably in studying audiences and the whole issue of cultural consumption. Furthermore, in the later decades of the twentieth century, ethnography spread even further, for example into psychology and human geography. Indeed, it tended to get swallowed up in a general, multidisciplinary, movement promoting qualitative approaches; though the term 'ethnography' still retains some distinctive connotations.[2]

This complex history is one of the reasons why 'ethnography' does not have a standard, well-defined meaning. Over the course of time, and in each of the various disciplinary contexts mentioned, its sense has been reinterpreted and recontextualized in various ways, in order to deal with particular circumstances. Part of this remoulding has arisen from the fact that ethnography has been associated with, and also put in opposition to, various other methodological approaches. Furthermore, it has been influenced by a range of theoretical ideas: anthropological and sociological functionalism, philosophical pragmatism and symbolic interactionism, Marxism, phenomenology, hermeneutics, structuralism, feminism, constructionism, post-structuralism and postmodernism. Increasingly, it has been compared and contrasted not just with experimental and survey research but also with interview-based studies, macro-historical analysis, political economy, conversation and discourse analysis, and psycho-social approaches.

In short, 'ethnography' plays a complex and shifting role in the dynamic tapestry that the social sciences have become in the twenty-first century. However, this term is by no means unusual in lacking a single, standard meaning. Nor does the uncertainty of sense undermine its value as a label. And we can outline a core definition, while recognizing that this does not capture all of its meaning in all contexts. In doing this we will focus, initially, at a fairly practical level: on what ethnographers actually do, on the sorts of data that they usually collect, and what kind of analysis they deploy to handle those data. Later we will broaden the discussion to cover some of the ideas that have informed, and continue to inform, ethnographic practice.

1 For an account of the development and reconfiguration of ethnographic work within British anthropology, see Macdonald (2001).
2 Diverse strands and trends of the qualitative research movement are exemplified in the various editions of the *Handbook of Qualitative Research*: Denzin and Lincoln (1994, 2000, 2005).

What ethnographers do

In terms of data collection, ethnography usually involves the researcher particu, overtly or covertly, in people's daily lives for an extended period of time, watching what happens, listening to what is said, and/or asking questions through informal and formal interviews, collecting documents and artefacts – in fact, gathering whatever data are available to throw light on the issues that are the emerging focus of inquiry. Generally speaking ethnographers draw on a *range* of sources of data, though they may sometimes rely primarily on one.[3]

In more detailed terms, ethnographic work usually has most of the following features:

1   People's actions and accounts are studied in everyday contexts, rather than under conditions created by the researcher – such as in experimental setups or in highly structured interview situations. In other words, research takes place 'in the field'.
2   Data are gathered from a range of sources, including documentary evidence of various kinds, but participant observation and/or relatively informal conversations are usually the main ones.
3   Data collection is, for the most part, relatively 'unstructured', in two senses. First, it does not involve following through a fixed and detailed research design specified at the start. Second, the categories that are used for interpreting what people say or do are not built into the data collection process through the use of observation schedules or questionnaires. Instead, they are generated out of the process of data analysis.
4   The focus is usually on a few cases, generally fairly small-scale, perhaps a single setting or group of people. This is to facilitate in-depth study.
5   The analysis of data involves interpretation of the meanings, functions, and consequences of human actions and institutional practices, and how these are implicated in local, and perhaps also wider, contexts. What are produced, for the most part, are verbal descriptions, explanations, and theories; quantification and statistical analysis play a subordinate role at most.

As this list of features makes clear, as regards what is referred to in methodological texts as 'research design', ethnographers typically employ a relatively open-ended approach (see Maxwell 2004b). They begin with an interest in some particular area of social life. While they will usually have in mind what the anthropologist Malinowski – often regarded as the inventor of modern anthropological fieldwork – called 'foreshadowed problems', their orientation is an exploratory one. The task is to investigate some aspect of the lives of the people who are being studied, and this includes finding out how these people view the situations they face, how they regard one another, and also how they see themselves. It is expected that the initial interests and questions that motivated the research will be refined, and perhaps even transformed, over the course of the research; and that this may take a considerable amount of time. Eventually, through this process, the inquiry will become progressively more clearly focused on a specific set of research questions, and this will then allow the strategic

3   These methods can include those that are 'unobtrusive': Lee (2000). There has been some dispute about whether ethnographic studies can rely entirely on interview or documentary data, without complementary participant observation. See Atkinson and Coffey (2002).

collection of data to pursue answers to those questions more effectively, and to test these against evidence.

Collecting data in 'natural' settings, in other words in those that have not been specifically set up for research purposes (such as experiments or formal interviews) also gives a distinctive character to ethnographic work. Where participant observation is involved, the researcher must find some role in the field being studied, and this will usually have to be done at least through implicit, and probably also through explicit, negotiation with people in that field. Access may need to be secured through gatekeepers, but it will also have to be negotiated and renegotiated with the people being studied; and this is true even where ethnographers are studying settings in which they are already participants. In the case of interviewing, too, access cannot be assumed to be available automatically, relations will have to be established, and identities co-constructed.

The initially exploratory character of ethnographic research means that it will often not be clear where, within a setting, observation should be begin, which actors need to be shadowed, and so on. Sampling strategies will have to be worked out, and changed, as the research progresses. Much the same is true of the use of interviews. Here, decisions about whom to interview, when, and where, will have to be developed over time, and the interviewing will normally take a relatively unstructured form, though more structured or strategic questioning may be used towards the end of the fieldwork. Furthermore, as already noted, the data will usually be collected in an unstructured form, by means of fieldnotes written in concretely descriptive terms and also through audio- or video-recordings, plus the collection of documents. Given the nature of these data, a considerable amount of effort, and time, will need to go into processing and analysing them. In all these respects, ethnography is a demanding activity, requiring diverse skills, including the ability to make decisions in conditions of considerable uncertainty.

This is true despite the fact that, as a set of methods, ethnography is not far removed from the means that we all use in everyday life to make sense of our surroundings, of other people's actions, and perhaps even of what we do ourselves. What is distinctive is that it involves a more deliberate and systematic approach than is common for most of us most of the time, one in which data are specifically sought to illuminate research questions, and are carefully recorded; and where the process of analysis draws on previous studies and involves intense reflection, including the critical assessment of competing interpretations. What is involved here, then, is a significant *development* of the ordinary modes of making sense of the social world that we all use in our mundane lives, in a manner that is attuned to the specific purposes of producing research knowledge.

In the remainder of this chapter we will explore and assess a number of methodological ideas that have shaped ethnography. We shall begin by looking at the conflict between quantitative and qualitative method as competing models of social research, which raged across many fields in the past and still continues in some even today. This was often seen as a clash between competing philosophical positions. Following some precedent we shall call these 'positivism' and 'naturalism': the former privileging quantitative methods, the latter promoting ethnography as the central, if not the only legitimate, social research method.[4] After this we will look at more recent

---

4 'Naturalism' is a term which is used in a variety of different, even contradictory, ways in the literature: see Matza (1969). Here we have simply adopted the conventional meaning within the ethnographic literature.

ideas that have shaped the thinking and practice of ethnographers, some interp[r]
of which are at odds with the earlier commitment to naturalism.

Positivism versus naturalism

Positivism has a long history in philosophy, but it reached its high point in the 'logical positivism' of the 1930s and 1940s (Kolakowski 1972; Halfpenny 1982; Friedman 1991; Hammersley 1995: ch. 1). This movement had a considerable influence upon social scientists, notably in promoting the status of experimental and survey research and the quantitative forms of analysis associated with them. Before this, in both sociology and social psychology, qualitative and quantitative techniques had generally been used side by side, often by the same researchers. Nineteenth-century investigators, such as Mayhew (1861), LePlay (1879) and Booth (1902–3), treated quantitative and qualitative data as complementary. Even the sociologists of the Chicago School, often portrayed as exponents of participant observation, employed both 'case-study' and 'statistical' methods. While there were recurrent debates among them regarding the relative advantages and uses of the two approaches, there was general agreement on the value of both (Bulmer, 1984; Harvey 1985; Hammersley 1989a; Deegan 2001). It was only later, with the rapid development of statistical methods and the growing influence of positivist philosophy, that survey research came to be regarded by some of its practitioners as a self-sufficient methodological tradition.[5]

Today, the term 'positivism' has become little more than a term of abuse among social scientists, and as a result its meaning has become obscured. For present purposes, the major tenets of positivism can be outlined as follows:

1 *The methodological model for social research is physical science, conceived in terms of the logic of the experiment.* While positivists do not claim that the methods of all the physical sciences are the same, they do argue that these share a common logic. This is that of the experiment, where quantitatively measured variables are manipulated in order to identify the relationships among them. This logic is taken to be the defining feature of science.

2 *Universal or statistical laws as the goal for science.* Positivists adopt a characteristic conception of explanation, usually termed the 'covering law' model. Here events are explained in deductive fashion by appeal to universal laws that state regular relationships between variables, holding across all relevant circumstances. However, it is the statistical version of this model, whereby the relationships have only a high probability of applying across relevant circumstances, that has generally been adopted by social scientists; and this has encouraged great concern with sampling procedures and statistical analysis, especially in survey research. Here, a premium is placed on the generalizability of findings.

3 *The foundation for science is observation.* Finally, positivists give priority to phenomena that are directly observable, or that can be logically inferred from what is observable; any appeal to intangibles runs the risk of being dismissed as metaphysical speculation. It is argued that scientific theories must be founded upon, or tested by appeal to, descriptions that simply correspond to the state of

---

5 In social psychology this process started rather earlier, and it was the experiment which became the dominant method.

the world, involving no theoretical assumptions and thus being beyond doubt. This foundation could be sense data, as in traditional empiricism, or it may be the realm of the 'publicly observable': for example, the movement of physical objects, such as mercury in a thermometer, which can be easily agreed upon by all observers. Great emphasis is therefore given to the standardization of procedures of data collection, which is intended to facilitate the achievement of measurements that are stable across observers. If measurement is reliable in this sense, it is argued, it provides a sound, theoretically neutral base upon which to build. This is sometimes referred to as procedural objectivity.

Central to positivism, then, is a certain conception of scientific method, modelled on the natural sciences, and in particular on physics (Toulmin 1972). Method here is concerned with the testing of theories or hypotheses. A sharp distinction is drawn between the context of discovery and the context of justification (Reichenbach 1938, 1951). The question of how theoretical ideas are generated belongs to the former and is outside the realm of scientific method. It is the procedures employed in the context of justification that are held to mark science off from common sense, since they involve the rigorous assessment of alternative theories from an objective point of view.

Thus, for positivists, the most important feature of scientific theories is that they are open to, and are actually subjected to, test: that they can be confirmed, or at least falsified, with certainty. This requires the exercise of control over variables, which can be achieved through physical control, as in experiments, or through statistical control, as in survey research. Without any control over variables, it is argued, one can do no more than speculate about causal relationships, since no basis for testing hypotheses is available. So, the process of testing involves comparing what the theory says should occur under certain circumstances with what actually does occur – in short, comparing it with 'the facts'.

These facts are collected by means of methods that, like the facts they collect, are regarded as theory-neutral; otherwise, it is assumed, they could not provide a conclusive test of the theory. In particular, every attempt is made to eliminate the effect of the observer by developing an explicit, standardized set of data elicitation procedures. This also allows replication by others so that an assessment of the reliability of the findings can be made. In survey research, for example, the behaviour of interviewers is typically specified down to the wording of questions and the order in which they are asked. In experiments the conduct of the experimenter is closely defined. It is argued that if it can be ensured that each survey respondent or experimental subject in a study and its replications is faced with the same set of stimuli, then their responses will be comparable. Where such explicit and standardized procedures are not employed, as in participant observation, so the argument goes, it is impossible to know how to interpret the responses since one has no idea what they are responses *to*. In short, positivists argue that it is only through the exercise of physical or statistical control of variables, and their rigorous measurement, that science is able to produce a body of knowledge whose validity is conclusive; and thus can justifiably replace the myths and dogma of traditional views or common sense.

Ethnography, and many kinds of qualitative research, do not match these positivist canons.[6] As a result, especially in the middle part of the twentieth century, they came

---

6 At the same time it is worth noting that the anthropological work of Malinowski was influenced by early positivist ideas: see Leach (1957) and Strenski (1982).

under criticism as lacking scientific rigour. Ethnography was sometimes dismissed as quite inappropriate to social science, on the grounds that the data and findings it produces are 'subjective', mere idiosyncratic impressions of one or two cases that cannot provide a solid foundation for rigorous scientific analysis. In reaction, ethnographers developed an alternative view of the proper nature of social research, which they often termed 'naturalism' (Lofland 1967; Blumer 1969; Matza 1969; Denzin 1971; Schatzman and Strauss 1973; Guba 1978). Like positivism, this appealed to natural science as a model, but the latter's method was conceptualized differently, and the exemplar was usually nineteenth-century biology rather than twentieth-century physics.

Naturalism proposes that, as far as possible, the social world should be studied in its 'natural' state, undisturbed by the researcher. Hence, 'natural' not 'artificial' settings, like experiments or formal interviews, should be the primary source of data. Furthermore, the research must be carried out in ways that are sensitive to the nature of the setting and that of the phenomena being investigated. The primary aim should be to describe what happens, how the people involved see and talk about their own actions and those of others, the contexts in which the action takes place, and what follows from it.

A key element of naturalism is the demand that the social researcher should adopt an attitude of 'respect' or 'appreciation' towards the social world. In Matza's (1969: 5) words, naturalism is 'the philosophical view that remains true to the nature of the phenomenon under study'. This is contrasted with the positivists' primary and prior commitment to a conception of scientific method reconstructed from the experience of natural scientists:

> Reality exists in the empirical world and not in the methods used to study that world; it is to be discovered in the examination of that world . . . . Methods are mere instruments designed to identify and analyze the obdurate character of the empirical world, and as such their value exists only in their suitability in enabling this task to be done. In this fundamental sense the procedures employed in each part of the act of scientific enquiry should and must be assessed in terms of whether they respect the nature of the empirical world under study – whether what they signify or imply to be the nature of the empirical world is actually the case.
> (Blumer 1969: 27–8)

A first requirement of social research according to naturalism, then, is fidelity to the phenomena under study, not to any particular set of methodological principles, however strongly supported by philosophical arguments or by the practice of natural scientists.

Moreover, naturalists regard social phenomena as quite distinct in character from physical phenomena. In this respect, naturalism drew on a wide range of philosophical and sociological ideas, but especially on symbolic interactionism, phenomenology, and hermeneutics (these sometimes being collectively labelled 'interpretivism'). From different starting points, these traditions all argue that the social world cannot be understood in terms of simple causal relationships or by the subsumption of social events under universal laws. This is because human actions are based upon, or infused by, social or cultural meanings: that is, by intentions, motives, beliefs, rules, discourses, and values.

For example, at the heart of symbolic interactionism is a rejection of the stimulus-response model of human behaviour, which is built into the methodological arguments of positivism. In the view of interactionists, people *interpret* stimuli, and these interpretations, continually under revision as events unfold, shape their actions. As a result, the 'same' physical stimulus can mean different things to different people – and, indeed, to the same person at different times.[7] Many years ago, Mehan (1974) provided a striking example that relates directly to the sort of data collection method supported by positivism:

> A question from [a] language development test instructs the child to choose 'the animal that can fly' from a bird, an elephant, and a dog. The correct answer (obviously) is the bird. Many first grade children, though, chose the elephant along with the bird as a response to that question. When I later asked them why they chose that answer they replied: 'That's Dumbo'. Dumbo (of course) is Walt Disney's flying elephant, well known to children who watch television and read children's books as an animal that flies.
>
> (Mehan 1974: 249)

Such indeterminacy of interpretation undermines attempts to develop standard measures of human behaviour. Interpretations of the same set of experimental instructions or interview questions will undoubtedly vary among people and across occasions; and, it is argued, this undermines the value of standardized research methods.[8]

Equally important, naturalists argue that because people's behaviour is not caused in a mechanical way, it is not amenable to the sort of causal analysis and manipulation of variables that are characteristic of the quantitative research inspired by positivism. Any hope of discovering *laws* of human behaviour is misplaced, it is suggested, since human behaviour is continually constructed, and reconstructed, on the basis of people's interpretations of the situations they are in.

According to naturalism, in order to understand people's behaviour we must use an approach that gives us access to the meanings that guide their behaviour. Fortunately, the capacities we have developed as social actors can give us such access. As participant observers we can learn the culture or subculture of the people we are studying. We can come to interpret the world more or less in the same way that they do. In short, we not only can but also *must* learn to understand people's behaviour in a different way from that in which natural scientists set about understanding the behaviour of physical phenomena.[9]

The need to learn the culture of those we are studying is most obvious in the case of societies other than our own. Here, not only may we not know why people do what they do, but often we may not be able to recognize even *what* they are doing. We are in much the same position as Schutz's (1964) stranger: Schutz notes how, in the weeks and months following an immigrant's arrival in a host society, what he or she previously took for granted as knowledge about that society turns out to be unreliable, if not obviously false. In addition, areas of ignorance previously of no importance come to

---

7 For useful accounts of interactionism, see Maines (2001), Atkinson and Housley (2003) and Reynolds and Herman-Kinney (2003).

8 Cooper and Dunne (2000) provide a similar and more developed analysis of the processes of interpretation involved in mathematical tests.

9 This form of understanding social phenomena is often referred to as *Verstehen*. See Truzzi (1974) for a discussion and illustrations of the history of this concept, and O'Hear (1996) for a more recent discussion of its role across the social sciences and humanities.

take on great significance; and overcoming them is necessary for the pursuit of important goals, perhaps even for the stranger's very survival in the new environment. In the process of learning how to participate in the host society, the stranger gradually acquires an inside knowledge of it, which supplants his or her previous 'external' knowledge. But Schutz argues that by virtue of being forced to come to understand a culture in this way, the stranger acquires a certain objectivity not normally available to culture members. The latter live inside the culture, and tend to see it as simply a reflection of 'how the world is'. They are often not conscious of the fundamental presuppositions that shape their vision, many of which are distinctive to their own culture.

Schutz's (1964) account of the experience of the stranger matches most obviously the work of anthropologists, who typically study societies very different from their own. However, the experience of the stranger is not restricted to those moving to live in another society. Movement among groups within a single society can produce the same effects; generally, though not always, in a milder form. There are many different layers or circles of cultural knowledge within any society. Indeed, this is particularly true of modern industrial societies with their complex divisions of labour, multifarious lifestyles, ethnic diversity, and deviant communities; and the subcultures and perspectives that maintain, and are generated by, these social divisions. This was, of course, one of the major rationales for the research of the Chicago School sociologists. Drawing on the analogy of plant and animal ecology, they set out to document the very different patterns of life to be found in different parts of the city of Chicago, from the 'high society' of the so-called 'gold coast' to slum ghettos such as Little Sicily. Later, the same kind of approach came to be applied to the cultures of occupations, organizations, and social groups of various kinds.

According to the naturalist account, the value of ethnography as a social research method is founded upon the existence of such variations in cultural patterns across and within societies, and their significance for understanding social processes. Ethnography exploits the capacity that any social actor possesses for learning new cultures, and the objectivity to which this process gives rise. Even where he or she is researching a familiar group or setting, the participant observer is required to treat this as 'anthropologically strange', in an effort to make explicit the presuppositions he or she takes for granted as a culture member. In this way, the culture can be turned into an object available for study. Naturalism proposes that through marginality, in social position and in perspective, it is possible to construct an account of the culture under investigation that both understands it from within and captures it as external to, and independent of, the researcher: in other words, as a natural phenomenon. Thus, the description of cultures becomes the primary goal. The search for universal laws is downplayed in favour of detailed accounts of the concrete experience of life within a particular culture and of the beliefs and social rules that are used as resources within it. Indeed, attempts to go beyond this, for instance to *explain* particular cultural forms, are sometimes discouraged. Certainly, as Denzin (1971: 168) noted, 'the naturalist resists schemes or models which over-simplify the complexity of everyday life'; though some forms of theory, especially those which are believed to be capable of capturing social complexity, are often recommended, most notably the kind of grounded theory proposed by Glaser and Strauss.[10]

10 See Glaser and Strauss (1968); Strauss and Corbin (1998); Pidgeon and Henwood (2004); for critical commentaries, see Williams (1976) and Dey (1999).

Over the last decades of the twentieth century, the influence of positivism waned and with it, in many areas, the dominance of quantitative method; though there are currently some signs of a revival.[11] At the same time, various aspects of naturalism came under attack from within the ranks of qualitative researchers. In the next section we shall explore the ideas that stimulated this.

Anti-realist and political critiques of naturalism

The field of social research methodology nowadays is a complex one. There has been considerable diversification in qualitative research, including the rise of discourse and narrative analysis, of various kinds of action research, of autoethnography and performance studies, and so on. At the same time, there have been growing calls to combine qualitative methods with quantitative techniques.[12] These have often been met with charges that this neglects the conflicting philosophical and political presuppositions built into qualitative and quantitative approaches (Smith and Heshusius 1986; Smith 1989; Guba 1990; Hodkinson 2004). Along with this, there has been criticism of older forms of ethnographic work on the grounds that these still betray the influence of positivism and scientism. What is pointed to here is that, despite their differences, positivism and naturalism share much in common. They each appeal to the model of natural science, albeit interpreting it in different ways. As a result, both are committed to trying to understand social phenomena as objects existing independently of the researcher. And they therefore claim that research can provide knowledge of the social world that is superior in validity to that of the people being studied. Equally important, they both regard practical and political commitments on the part of the researcher as, for the most part, extraneous to the research process – indeed, as a source of potential distortion whose effects have to be guarded against to preserve objectivity.

Many ethnographers have begun to question the commitment to naturalism, challenging these assumptions. Doubts have been raised about the capacity of ethnography to portray the social world in the way that naturalism claims it does. Equally, the commitment of the older kinds of ethnography to some sort of value neutrality has been questioned, and politically interventionist forms of ethnography have been recommended. We shall look at these two aspects of the critique of naturalism separately, though they are sometimes closely related.

Questioning realism

Many critics of naturalism today reject it on the grounds that, like positivism, it assumes that the task of social research is to represent social phenomena in some literal fashion: to document their features and explain their occurrence. What is being questioned here is sometimes referred to as realism. In part, criticism of realism stems from a tension within ethnography between the naturalism characteristic of ethnographers' methodological thinking and the constructionism and cultural relativism that shape their understanding of the perspectives and behaviour of the people they study (Hammersley 1992: ch. 3). As we saw, ethnographers portray people as constructing

---

11 See Smith and Hodkinson (2006); Denzin and Giardina (2006).
12 Some have argued that mixed methods research can be a new paradigm that transcends the distinction between the other two: see, for example, Tashakkori and Teddlie (2003).

the social world, both through their interpretations of it and through actions based on those interpretations. Furthermore, those interpretations sometimes reflect different cultures, so that there is a sense in which through their actions people create distinct social worlds (Blumer 1969: 11). But this constructionism and relativism is compatible with naturalism only so long as it is not applied to ethnographic research itself. Once we come to see ethnographers as themselves constructing the social world through their interpretations of it, thereby producing incommensurable accounts that reflect differences in their background cultures, there is a conflict with the naturalistic realism built into older ethnographic approaches.

This internal source of doubts about realism was reinforced by the impact of various external developments. One was changes in the field of the philosophy of science. Whereas until the early 1950s positivism had dominated this field, at that time its dominance began to be undermined, eventually producing a range of alternative positions, some of which rejected realism. A sign of this change was the enormous influence of Thomas Kuhn's book *The Structure of Scientific Revolutions* (Kuhn 1996; first published in 1962). Kuhn argued against views of the history of science that portray it as a process of cumulative development towards the truth, achieved by rational investigation logically founded on evidence. He, and others, showed that the work of those involved in the major developments of scientific knowledge in the past was shaped by theoretical presuppositions about the world that were not themselves based on empirical research, and many of which are judged by scientists today as false. Kuhn further claimed that the history of science, rather than displaying the gradual build-up of knowledge, is punctuated by periods of revolution when the theoretical presuppositions forming the 'paradigm' in terms of which scientists in a particular field have previously operated are challenged and replaced. An example is the shift from Newtonian physics to relativity theory and quantum mechanics in the early part of the twentieth century. The replacement of one paradigm by another, according to Kuhn, does not, because it cannot, occur on the basis simply of the rational assessment of evidence. Paradigms are incommensurable, they picture the world in incompatible ways, so that the data themselves are interpreted differently by those working within different paradigms. This implies that judgements of the validity of scientific claims is always relative to the paradigm within which they operate are judged; they are never simply a reflection of some independent domain of reality.[13]

Kuhn's work embodied most of the arguments against positivism that had become influential: that there is no theory-neutral observational foundation against which theories can be tested, and that judgements about the validity of theories are never fully determined by any evidence. He also proposed an alternative conception of science that contrasted sharply with the positivist model. However, his critique counted as much against naturalism, against the idea of the researcher getting into direct contact with reality, as it did against positivism. On his account, all knowledge of the world is mediated by paradigmatic presuppositions. Furthermore, the alternative view he offered made natural scientists look very similar to the people that ethnographers had long portrayed in their accounts as constructing diverse social worlds. And sociologists of science have subsequently produced ethnographies of the work of natural scientists and technological innovators along these lines (see Hess 2001). In this way, natural

---

13 There is some ambiguity in Kuhn's work, and this has led to disputes about its interpretation. For a
    detailed discussion see Sharrock and Read (2002).

science moved from being primarily a methodological model for social research to being an object of sociological investigation; and in many ways this brought the conflict between naturalism and constructionism to a head.

As important as developments within the philosophy of science for the generation of doubts about realism was the influence of various continental European philosophical trends. Naturalism had been influenced by nineteenth-century ideas about hermeneutics, about the interpretation of historical texts, notably the work of Dilthey (see Makkreel 1975). This was the source of the idea, mentioned earlier, that socio-cultural under-standing takes a different form from how natural scientists go about understanding physical phenomena. In the twentieth century, however, this earlier hermeneutic tradition came to be challenged by a new form of 'philosophical hermeneutics', developed by Gadamer (see Howard 1982; Warnke 1987; Dostal 2002). Where, previously, under-standing human texts had been presented as a rigorous task of recovering the meaning intended by the author and locating it within relevant cultural settings, philosophical hermeneutics viewed the process of understanding as inevitably reflecting the 'preju-dices', the pre-understandings, of the interpreter. Interpretation of texts, and by extension understanding of the social world too, could no longer be seen as a matter of capturing social meanings in their own terms; the accounts produced were regarded as constructions that inevitably reflected the socio-historical position and background assumptions of the researcher.

Another powerful influence on ethnography has been post-structuralism and post-modernism. These labels refer to a diverse set of ideas and work, but we shall mention just two of the most influential figures: Derrida's 'deconstruction' and the work of Foucault.[14] Like philosophical hermeneutics, deconstruction has also led to a ques-tioning of the idea that ethnographers can capture the meanings on the basis of which people act. It does this because it argues that meanings are not stable; nor are they properties of individuals. Rather, they reflect the shifting constitutive role of language. Also important has been deconstruction's undermining of the distinctions between different genres of writing: its advocates have sought to erase the differentiation between fiction and non-fiction, indeed between literary and technical writing generally. This has led to recognition of the fact that the language used by ethnographers in their writing is not a transparent medium allowing us to see reality through it, but rather a construction that draws on many of the rhetorical strategies used by journalists, travel writers, novelists, and others. Some commentators have drawn the conclusion from this that the phenomena described in ethnographic accounts are created in and through the rhetorical strategies employed, rather than being external to the text; in short, this concern with rhetoric has often been associated with forms of anti-realism.[15]

Foucault's work is also based on a rejection of realism: he is not concerned with the truth or falsity of the ideas that he studies – for example about madness or sex – but rather with the 'regimes of truth' by which they are constituted and how they have structured institutional practices during the development of Western society.[16]

---

14 For an excellent account of the rise of these ideas in the context of French philosophy, see Gutting (2001).

15 See, for example, Tyler (1986), Ashmore (1989); Piper and Stronach (2004).

16 The statement that Foucault rejects realism, while not fundamentally misleading, does obscure both the, probably witting, ambiguities in his work in this respect, and its emergence out of the tradition of rationalist epistemology: see Gutting (1989). On Foucault more generally, see Gutting (1994).

He stresses the fact that the psychological and social sciences are socio-historical in character, and claims that they function as part of the process of surveillance and control, which he sees as the central feature of modern society. Their products reflect this social character, rather than representing some world that is independent of them. Foucault argues that different regimes of truth are established in different contexts, reflecting the play of diverse sources of power and resistance. Thus, what is treated as true and false, in social science as elsewhere, is constituted through the exercise of power.[17]

The reception of post-structuralist and postmodernist ideas in the context of Anglo-American qualitative research has involved diverse readings and responses to what was, of course, by no means a coherent set of texts; these extending well beyond those of Derrida and Foucault. Typically, these readings and responses have reinforced tendencies towards anti-realism of some kind, encouraged the adoption of non-Marxist Leftist political orientations, and involved the idea that some discourses/voices are suppressed and that the function of research should be to liberate them. Much less commonly, this influence has also led to the subversion of conventional ethnographic textual strategies.

While realism has not been completely abandoned by most ethnographers, the idea that ethnographic accounts can represent social reality in a relatively straightforward way (for example, through the ethnographer getting close to it) has been widely rejected; and doubt has been thrown on the claims to scientific authority associated with realism. Moreover, in the work of Foucault especially, we have a direct link with the second criticism of naturalism: its neglect of the politics of social research.

The politics of ethnography

Naturalists shared with positivists a commitment to producing accounts of factual matters that reflect the nature of the phenomena studied rather than the values or political commitments of the researcher. Of course, both recognized that, in practice, research is affected by the researcher's values, but the aim was to limit the influence of those values as far as possible, so as to produce findings that were true independently of any particular value stance. Since the mid-1980s, any such striving after value neutrality and objectivity has been questioned, sometimes being replaced by advocacy of 'openly ideological' research (Lather 1986), 'militant anthropology' (Scheper-Hughes 1995), or research that is explicitly carried out from the standpoint of a particular group, for example women, those suffering racism, indigenous peoples, or people with disabilities (see Denzin and Lincoln 2005).

In part this has resulted from the continuing influence of Marxism and 'critical' theory, but equally important has been the impact of feminism and of post-structuralism. From a traditional Marxist point of view the very distinction between facts and values is a historical product, and one that can be overcome through the future development of society. Values refer to the human potential that is built into the unfolding of history. In this sense values are facts, even though they may not yet have been realized in the social world. Moreover, they provide the key to any understanding of the nature of current social conditions, their past, and their future. From this point of view, a science

---

17 For discussions of the implications of Foucault's work for ethnography, see Gubrium and Silverman (1989); Kendall and Wickham (2004).

of society should provide not only abstract knowledge but also the basis for action to transform the world so as to bring about human self-realization. On this argument, ethnography, like other forms of social research, cannot but be concerned simultaneously with factual and value matters, and its role inevitably involves political intervention (whether researchers are aware of this or not).

A similar conclusion about the political character of social research has been reached in other ways, for example by those who argue that because research is always affected by values, and always has political consequences, researchers must take responsibility for their value commitments and for the effects of their work. It has been suggested that ethnography and other forms of social research have had too little impact, that their products simply lie on library shelves gathering dust, and that as a result they are worthless. To be of value, it is suggested, ethnographic research should be concerned not simply with understanding the world but with applying its findings to bring about change (see, for example, Gewirtz and Cribb 2006).

There are differences in view about the nature of the change that should be aimed at. Sometimes the concern is with rendering research more relevant to national policy-making or to one or another form of professional practice (see, for example, Hustler *et al.* 1986; Hart and Bond 1995; Healy 2001; Taylor *et al.* 2006). Alternatively, or as part of this, it may be argued that research should be emancipatory. This has been proposed by feminists, where the goal is the emancipation of women (and men) from patriarchy (Fonow and Cook 1991; Lather 1991; Olesen 2005); but it is also to be found in the writings of critical ethnographers and advocates of emancipatory action research, where the goal of research is taken to be the transformation of Western societies so as to realize the ideals of freedom, equality, and justice (Gitlin *et al.* 1989; Kemmis and McTaggart 2005). Similar developments have occurred in the field of disability studies (Barnes 2003) and in the context of queer theory (Plummer 2005).

Of course, to the extent that the very possibility of producing knowledge is undermined by the sort of anti-realist arguments we outlined earlier, a concern with the practical or political effects of research may come to seem an essential alternative goal to the traditional concern with truth. This too has led to the growth of more inter-ventionist conceptions of ethnography. In this way post-structuralism and postmodern-ism have contributed to the politicization of social research, though in a far from unambiguous way because they seem simultaneously to undermine all political ideals (Dews 1987). For example, they threaten any appeal to the interests or rights of Humanity; and in the context of feminist research they challenge the concept of woman.

Reflexivity

The criticisms of naturalism we have outlined are sometimes seen as arising from what has been called the reflexive character of social research.[18] It is argued that what both positivism and naturalism fail to take into account is the fact that social researchers are part of the social world they study. A sharp distinction between science and common

---

18 'Reflexivity' is a term that has come to be used in a variety of different ways, and the meaning we are giving to it here is by no means uncontested, see Lynch (2000). For discussions of some of the problems with reflexivity, see Troyna (1994); Paechter (1996); Adkins (2002); Finlay (2002); Haney (2002).

sense, between the activities and knowledge of the researcher and those of the researched, lies at the heart of both these positions. It is this that leads to their joint concern with eliminating the effects of the researcher on the data. For positivism, the solution is the standardization of research procedures; for naturalism, it is getting into direct contact with the social world, and in extreme form the requirement that ethnographers 'surrender' themselves to the cultures they wish to study (Wolff 1964; Jules-Rosette 1978a, 1978b). Both positions assume that it is possible, in principle at least, to isolate a body of data uncontaminated by the researcher, by turning him or her either, in one case, into an automaton or, in the other, into a neutral vessel of cultural experience. However, searches for empirical bedrock of this kind are futile; all data involve presuppositions (Hanson 1958).

The concept of reflexivity acknowledges that the orientations of researchers will be shaped by their socio-historical locations, including the values and interests that these locations confer upon them. What this represents is a rejection of the idea that social research is, or can be, carried out in some autonomous realm that is insulated from the wider society and from the biography of the researcher, in such a way that its findings can be unaffected by social processes and personal characteristics. Also, it is emphasized that the production of knowledge by researchers has consequences. At the very least, the publication of research findings can shape the climate in which political and practical decisions are made, and it may even directly stimulate particular sorts of action. In fact, it may change the character of the situations that were studied. Moreover, the consequences of research are not neutral in relation to what are widely felt to be important values, nor are they necessarily desirable. Indeed, some commentators see social research as playing an undesirable role in supporting one or another aspect of the political status quo in Western societies. As we saw, for Foucault, the social sciences were part of a modern apparatus of surveillance.

There is no doubt that reflexivity, in the sense just outlined, is a significant feature of social research. Indeed, there is a sense in which all social research takes the form of participant observation: it involves participating in the social world, in whatever role, and reflecting on the products of that participation. However, it is not necessary to draw conclusions from the reflexivity of social research of the kind that critics of naturalism have done. In our view, recognition of reflexivity implies that there are elements of positivism and naturalism which must be abandoned; but it does not require rejection of all the ideas associated with those two lines of thinking. Thus, we do not see reflexivity as undermining researchers' commitment to realism. In our view it only undermines naive forms of realism which assume that knowledge must be based on some absolutely secure foundation.[19] Similarly, we do not believe that reflexivity implies that research is necessarily political, or that it should be political, in the sense of serving particular political causes or practical ends. For us, the exclusive, immediate goal of all research is, and must remain, the production of knowledge.

Reflexivity and realism

It is true that we cannot avoid relying on 'common-sense' knowledge nor, often, can we avoid having an effect on the social phenomena we study. In other words, there

---

19 For an influential epistemological analysis that recognizes the fallible character of any evidence but retains a commitment to realism, see Haack (1993). See also Hammersley (2004).

is no way in which we can escape the social world in order to study it. Fortunately, though, this is not necessary from a realist point of view. There is as little justification for rejecting all common-sense knowledge out of hand as there is for treating it as all 'valid in its own terms': we have no external, absolutely conclusive standard by which to judge it. But we can work with what we currently take to be knowledge, while recognizing that it may be erroneous; and engaging in systematic inquiry where doubt seems justified. And in doing this we can still make the reasonable assumption that we are able to describe phenomena as they are, and not merely how we perceive them or how we would like them to be (Hammersley 1992: ch. 3). All of us, in our everyday activities, rely on presuppositions about the world, few of which we have subjected to test ourselves, and none of which we could fully and independently test. Most of the time this does not and should not trouble us, and social research is no different from other activities in this respect. We need to reflect only on what seems – or can be shown to be – problematic, while leaving open the possibility that what currently is not problematic may in the future become so.

It is also important to recognize that research is an active process, in which accounts of the world are produced through selective observation and theoretical interpretation of what is seen, through asking particular questions and interpreting what is said in reply, through writing fieldnotes and transcribing audio- and video-recordings, as well as through writing research reports. And it is true that some aspects of this process have not been given the attention they deserve until recently. However, to say that our findings, and even our data, are *constructed* does not automatically imply that they do not or cannot represent social phenomena. To believe that this is implied is to assume that the only true form of representation would involve the world imprinting its characteristics on our senses without any activity on our part, a highly implausible account even of the process of perception (Gregory 1970).

Similarly, the fact that as researchers we are likely to have an effect on the people we study does not mean that the validity of our findings is restricted to the data elicitation situations on which we relied. We can minimize reactivity and/or monitor it. But we can also exploit it: how people respond to the presence of the researcher may be as informative as how they react to other situations. Indeed, rather than engaging in futile attempts to eliminate the effects of the researcher completely, we should set about understanding them, a point that Schuman (1982) made in relation to social surveys:

> The basic position I will take is simple: artifacts are in the mind of the beholder. Barring one or two exceptions, the problems that occur in surveys are opportunities for understanding once we take them seriously as facts of life. Let us distinguish here between the simple survey and the scientific survey. . . . The simple approach to survey research takes responses literally, ignores interviewers as sources of influence, and treats sampling as unproblematic. A person who proceeds in this way is quite likely to trip and fall right on his artifact. The scientific survey, on the other hand, treats survey research as a search for meaning, and ambiguities of language and of interviewing, discrepancies between attitude and behaviour, even problems of non-response, provide an important part of the data, rather than being ignored or simply regarded as obstacles to efficient research.
>
> (Schuman 1982: 23)

In short, 'what is an artifact if treated naively reflects a fact of life if taken seriously' (Schuman 1982: 24). In order to understand the effects of the research and of research procedures, we need to compare data in which the level and direction of reactivity vary. Once we abandon the idea that the social character of research can be standardized out or avoided by becoming a 'fly on the wall' or a 'full participant', the role of the researcher as active participant in the research process becomes clear. As has long been recognized by ethnographers, he or she is the research instrument par excellence. The fact that behaviour and attitudes are often not stable across contexts and that the researcher may influence the context becomes central to the analysis. Indeed, it can be exploited for all it is worth. Data should not be taken at face value, but treated as a field of inferences in which hypothetical patterns can be identified and their validity tested. Different research strategies can be explored and their effects compared with a view to drawing theoretical conclusions. Interpretations need to be made explicit and full advantage should be taken of any opportunities to test their limits and to assess alternatives. Such a view contrasts sharply with the image of social research projected by naturalism, though it is closer to some other models of ethnographic research such as 'grounded theorizing', 'analytic induction', and the strategy model to be found alongside naturalism in the work of Schatzman and Strauss (1973). And in this way the image of the researcher is brought into parallel with that of the people studied, as actively making sense of the world, yet without undermining the commitment of research to realism.

Reflexivity and the political character of research

Positivism and naturalism, in the forms we have discussed them, tend to present research as an activity that is done for its own sake and in its own terms. By contrast, as we have seen, some critics insist that research has a social function, for instance serving to legitimize and preserve the status quo. And on this basis they argue that researchers must try to make their research serve a different function, such as *challenging* the status quo, in some respect. Often, this point of view is organized around the question: whose side is the researcher on? (Becker 1967b; Troyna and Carrington 1989; but see Hammersley 2000: ch. 3).

As we saw earlier, others argue that what is wrong with ethnography is its lack of impact on policy-making and practice, its limited payoff in the everyday worlds of politics and work. Here it is dismissed as an idle pastime, a case of fiddling while the world burns; one that is engaged in by intellectual dilettantes who live off the taxes paid by hard-working citizens.

These criticisms of naturalist ethnography seem to us to involve an overestimation of the actual and potential contribution of research to policy and practice, and an associated failure to value the more modest contributions it offers (Rule 1978; Hammersley 2002). It is also worth pointing out that one may believe that the only justification for research is its contribution to policy and practice, and recognize that it inevitably has effects on these, without concluding that it should be directed towards the achievement of particular political or practical goals. Indeed, there are good reasons for research not being directed towards such goals. The most important one is that this would increase the chances of the findings being distorted by ideas about how the world *ought to be*, or by what it would be politic for others to believe. When we are engaged in political or practical action, the truth of what we say is not always our principal concern, even though we may prefer to be honest. We are more interested in the practical effects of our actions, and sometimes this may lead us to be 'economical' with the truth, at the very least; perhaps even in relation to ourselves (Benson and Stangroom 2006: ch. 1). Moreover, even where the truth of our beliefs is the main issue, in practical activities judgement of factual and value claims as more or less reliable will be based on somewhat different considerations than in research directed towards producing knowledge: we will probably be concerned above all with whether the information is sufficiently reliable for our current purposes. Of course, if one believes, as Marx and others did and do, that (ultimately at least) the true and the good are identical, one might deny the significance of this difference in orientation between research and other practical activities. But this view relies on an elaborate and unconvincing philosophical infrastructure (Hammersley 1992: ch. 6, 1993).

It is worth emphasizing that to deny that research should be directed towards political goals is not to suggest that researchers could, or should, abandon their political convictions. It is to insist that as researchers their primary goal must always be to produce knowledge, and that they should try to minimize any distortion of their findings by their political convictions or practical interests. Nor are we suggesting that researchers should be unconcerned about the effects of their work on the world. The point is that acknowledging the reflexivity of research does not imply that it must be primarily directed towards changing (or for that matter preserving) the world in some way or other. And, as we have indicated, there are good reasons why it should not be so directed.

Conclusion

We began this chapter by examining two contrasting accounts of the logic of social research and their implications for ethnography. Neither positivism nor naturalism provides an adequate framework. Both neglect its fundamental reflexivity: the fact that we are part of the social world we study, and that there is no escape from reliance on common-sense knowledge and methods of investigation. All social research is founded on the human capacity for participant observation. We act in the social world and yet are able to reflect upon ourselves and our actions as objects in that world. However, rather than leading to doubts about whether social research can produce knowledge, or to the desire to transform it into a political enterprise, for us this reflexivity provides the basis for a reconstructed logic of inquiry that shares much with positivism and naturalism but goes beyond them in important respects. By including our own role within the research focus, and perhaps even systematically exploiting our participation in the settings under study as researchers, we can produce accounts of the social world and justify them without placing reliance on futile appeals to empiricism, of either positivist or naturalist varieties.

Reconstructing our understanding of social research in line with the implications of its reflexivity also throws light on the relationship between quantitative and qualitative approaches. Certainly there is little justification for the view, associated with naturalism, that ethnography represents a superior, alternative paradigm to quantitative research. On the other hand, it has a much more powerful contribution to make to social science than positivism allows. And, while combining different methods, for particular purposes, may often be of value, this should not be done at the expense of forgetting the important methodological ideas associated with ethnography, and with qualitative research more generally.

Reflexivity is an aspect of all social research. It is one that has been given increasing attention by ethnographers and others in recent years, notably in the production of 'natural histories' of particular studies.[20] The remainder of this book is devoted to spelling out what we take to be the implications of reflexivity for ethnographic practice.

---

20 For a listing of examples of natural histories of social research, see Hammersley (2003b).

2 Research design

Problems, cases and samples

The conduct of ethnography can seem deceptively simple, by contrast for example with the pursuit of quantitative research. It may appear to require only that one 'act naturally', putting aside any methodological rules and constraints. Perhaps for this reason, in the past, new ethnographers were sometimes given little or no research advice before they set out on their fieldwork. Nader (1986), for example, tells how this was a tradition among North American anthropologists:

> Before leaving Harvard I went to see Kluckhohn. In spite of the confidence I had gained from some of my training at Harvard, this last session left me frustrated. When I asked Kluckhohn if he had any advice, he told the story of a graduate student who had asked Kroeber the same question. In response Kroeber was said to have taken the largest, fattest ethnography book off his shelf, and said, 'Go forth and do likewise.'
>
> (Nader 1986: 98)

Here we have a model of learning ethnography that does not even amount to apprenticeship. Rather, each new researcher must discover for him or herself what is required in order to produce an ethnographic study. At the other end of the spectrum, today 'research training' is a major enterprise in which key skills and essential knowledge are identified and must be inculcated before novices enter the field. Where the first approach leaves them frustrated, uncertain, if not panic-stricken, the second can turn learning how to do research into a chore. Even more importantly, in the case of ethnography especially, it can present a quite distorted picture of what is involved.

While even in the early twentieth century there were attempts to provide training for ethnographic fieldwork (Fowler and Hardesty 1994: 6–7), and while this later became standard practice, there remains some ambivalence about what is required. To a large extent this probably derives from awareness of the fact that ethnographic research cannot be programmed, that its practice is replete with the unexpected, as any reading of the many published research biographies now available will confirm (see Hammersley 2003b). Indeed, there is an important sense in which all research is a practical activity requiring the exercise of judgement in context; it is not a matter of following methodological rules, nor can all the problems be anticipated, or for that matter resolved.

So, we must recognise that, even less than other forms of social research, the course of ethnographic work cannot be predetermined, all problems anticipated, and ready-made strategies made available for dealing with them. However, this neither eliminates the need for pre-fieldwork preparation nor means that the researcher's behaviour in the field can be haphazard, merely adjusting to events by taking 'the line of least resistance'. Indeed, we shall argue that research design is crucial to ethnography, but that it is a reflexive process that operates throughout every stage of a project (see Maxwell 2004b).

Foreshadowed problems

Research always begins with some problem or set of issues, at the very least it starts from what Malinowski (1922) referred to as 'foreshadowed problems':

> Good training in theory, and acquaintance with its latest results, is not identical with being burdened with 'preconceived ideas'. If a man sets out on an expedition, determined to prove certain hypotheses, if he is incapable of changing his views constantly and casting them off ungrudgingly under the pressure of evidence, needless to say his work will be worthless. The more problems he brings with him into the field, the more he is in the habit of moulding his theories according to facts, and of seeing facts in their bearing upon theory, the better he is equipped for the work. Preconceived ideas are pernicious in any scientific work, but foreshadowed problems are the main endowment of a scientific thinker, and these problems are first revealed to the observer by his theoretical studies.
>
> (Malinowski 1922: 8–9)

Sometimes the starting point for research is a well-developed theory from which a set of hypotheses can be derived. It is rare for ethnographic research to follow this pattern, though there is at least one classic participant observation study with this character: Festinger and his colleagues tested cognitive dissonance theory by investigating the response of members of an apocalyptic religious group to the fact that the world did not end on the day predicted by their leader (Festinger *et al.* 1956).

Most ethnographic research, however, has been concerned with producing descriptions and explanations of particular phenomena, or with *developing* theories, rather than with testing existing hypotheses. A number of authors, most notably advocates of grounded theorizing, have pointed to the advantages to be gained from developing theory through systematic empirical investigation rather than by relying on 'armchair theorizing'.[1] Nevertheless, as Strauss (1970) himself showed, considerable progress can sometimes be made in clarifying and developing research problems before fieldwork begins. To illustrate this, he examined Davis's (1961b) research on 'the management of strained interaction by the visibly handicapped':

> Davis's theory is about (1) *strained* (2) *sociable* interaction (3) in *face-to-face* contact between (4) *two persons*, one of whom has a (5) *visible handicap* and the other of whom is (6) *normal* (no visible handicap). . . . The underlined terms in the above sentence begin to suggest what is explicitly or implicitly omitted from Davis's theoretical formulation. The theory is concerned with the visibly (physically) handicapped, not with people whose handicaps are not immediately visible, if at all, to other interactants. The theory is concerned with interaction between two people (not with more than two). . . . The interaction occurs in situations termed

---

1   For recent accounts of grounded theorizing, see Dey (2004) and Pidgeon and Henwood (2004).

'sociable'; that is, the relations between interactants are neither impersonal nor intimate. Sociable also means interaction prolonged enough to permit more than a fleeting exchange but not so prolonged that close familiarity ensues.

(Strauss 1970: 47–8, original emphases)

Strauss goes on to show that by varying these different elements of the theory new research questions can be generated.

Often, the relevant literature is less developed even than in the case discussed by Strauss. However, the absence of detailed knowledge of a phenomenon or process itself represents a useful starting point for research. And this is a very common rationale provided for ethnographic studies. Here, for example, is the beginning of Mary Pattillo-McCoy's Introduction to her book *Black Picket Fences*: 'The goal . . . is to richly describe the neighbourhood-based social life of a population that has received little scholarly or popular attention – the black middle class' (Pattillo-McCoy 1999: 1).

It is equally common for studies to begin from dissatisfaction with the accounts of some phenomenon currently found in the research literature. Edensor (1998: 1–6) reports that his investigation of how tourists 'consume' symbolic sites was stimulated in this way, but also by a visit he had made as a young backpacker to the Taj Mahal. He was struck by the fact that most existing theories of tourism had been developed by studying Western tourists and/or Western tourist sites, and that insufficient attention had been paid to cultural differences.

Alternatively, the stimulus may be a surprising fact or set of facts. Thus, Measor (1983) noted that not only did girls tend to fare worse than boys in science examinations, but also the gap was even greater in the case of Nuffield science, a course emphasizing discovery learning. She set out to discover why this was so, through participant observation in Nuffield science lessons and by interviewing both boys and girls about their attitudes to these lessons.

As this example illustrates, the significance of the initial problem may be not so much theoretical as political or practical. Even where the starting point is not current social theory, however, elaboration of the problem soon draws such theory in, as with the classic case of Freilich's (1970b) work on 'Mohawk heroes':

> New Yorkers sometimes read in their newspapers about a unique phenomenon in their midst: the Mohawk Indians who work on the steel structures of various buildings in and around their city. Articles, at times accompanied by pictures of smiling Indians, discuss these 'brave' and 'sure-footed' Mohawks. The question of why so many Mohawks work in structural steel is one that is often researched by students enrolled in colleges located in and around New York. In 1956, this problem was, in fact, my first professional research assignment. I used A.F.C. Wallace's paper 'Some Psychological Determinants of Culture Change in an Iroquoian Community' as the foil in my proposal for research support. Wallace's paper suggested that Mohawks lack a fear of heights, and that this lack of fear explains their involvement with the steel industry. I argued that a negative trait (lack of fear) cannot have specific positive consequences (lead a tribe into steel work). I argued further that there is no functional value in a lack of fear of heights for steel work, and that in actuality the opposite is true: a normal fear of high places leads to caution that saves lives. A more plausible argument seemed to be that Mohawks frequently act as if they have no fear of heights. In presenting a

subsidiary problem, 'Why these acts of daredevilry?', I put forth my theoretical belief that socio-cultural factors explain social and cultural phenomena better than do psychological factors. I had a vague notion that Mohawks in steel work represented some kind of cultural continuity. Thus, the questions I posed were (1) why is it good, culturally, for a Mohawk male to be a structural steel worker? and (2) How does such a cultural 'goodness' relate to Mohawk cultural history?

(Freilich 1970b: 185–6)

Social events themselves may also stimulate research, providing an opportunity to explore some unusual occurrence or to test an explanatory idea. Notable here are what are sometimes called 'natural experiments': organizational innovations, natural disasters, or political crises that promise to reveal what happens when the limiting factors normally constraining social life in a particular context are breached. At such times, social phenomena that are otherwise taken for granted become visibly problematic for the participants themselves, and thus for the observer. Schatzman and Strauss (1955) provided an example, many years ago, in their discussion of the problems of inter-class communication arising subsequent to a tornado. Studying the origins and consequences of organizational innovations is even more common. An example is Walford and Miller's study of Kingshurst School, the first City Technology College in Britain, established as part of the educational reforms of the late 1980s (Walford 1991; Walford and Miller 1991). Similarly, the political crisis sparked by the student revolt in Tiananmen Square in 1989 gave Pieke (1995) an important research opportunity.

Even chance encounters or personal experiences may provide motive and opportunity for research. Henslin (1990) came to do research on the homeless as a result of meeting someone for whom the problem of homelessness had become a consuming passion:

> When [he] found out that I was a sociologist and that I was writing a textbook on social problems, he asked me to collaborate on a book about the homeless. He felt that my background might provide an organizing framework that would help sort out his many experiences and observations into a unified whole. During our attempt at collaboration, he kept insisting that as a sociologist I owed it to myself to gain first-hand experience with the homeless. Although I found that idea somewhat appealing, because of my heavy involvement in writing projects I did not care to pursue the possibility. As he constantly brought up the topic, however, I must admit that he touched a sensitive spot, rubbing in more than a little sociological guilt. After all, I was an instructor of social problems, and I did not really know about the homeless. . . . With the continued onslaught, I became more open to the idea. (Or perhaps I should say that I eventually wore down.) When he invited me on an expense-paid trip to Washington, DC, and promised that I would see sights hitherto unbeknownst to me – such as homeless people sleeping on the sidewalks in full view of the White House – firing my imagination, he had pierced my armor through. With the allure of such an intriguing juxtaposition of power and powerlessness, of wealth and poverty, how could I resist such an offer?

(Henslin 1990: 52)

By contrast, Currer (1992: 4–5) began her research on Pathan mothers in Britain as a result of her own experience as an English mother in Peshawar, Pakistan. Her research questions arose initially from what she saw as the parallels between her former position and that of the people she chose to study, and from her sympathy for them.

It is also common for research to be stimulated by previous experience in temporary or permanent jobs. Thus Olesen traces the origins of her research on temporary clerical workers to her own experience supporting herself as a student by working in a typing pool (Olesen 1990: 214). Of course, research interest may equally arise from difference, conflict, and negative feelings. Van Maanen (1991: 33) reports that his long career investigating police culture began in part because he had been 'subject to what I regarded as more than my fair share of police attention and hence viewed the police with a little loathing, some fear, and considerable curiosity'.

Up to now, we have assumed that ethnographers are relatively free to decide for themselves what to investigate, but of course it is increasingly true that they have to select topics for study in terms of what is likely to gain funding, or what is in line with the strategic priorities of the institution in which they work. Indeed, they may be specifically recruited to investigate a particular issue. Even here, though, there is usually some leeway for remaking rather than simply 'taking' the research focus as defined by sponsors or research directors.

Whatever the origins of the inquiry, there is always a need to work the research problem up into a worthwhile and viable form. To some degree this is a task that is carried out over the course of the whole project, but reflection and reading in the early stages are advisable. While there are no hard-and-fast rules for deciding how far initial ideas can be clarified and elaborated before the collection of data begins, exploring them and their implications with the help of whatever secondary literature is available is certainly a wise first step. Relevant here are not only research monographs and journal articles but also official reports, journalistic exposés, autobiographies, diaries, and 'non-fiction novels' (see Chapters 6 and 10).

The development of research problems

The aim in the pre-fieldwork phase, and one of the tasks in the early stages of data collection, is to turn the foreshadowed problems into a set of questions to which an answer could be given, whether this is a narrative description of a sequence of events, a generalized account of the perspectives and practices of a particular group of people, or a more abstract theoretical formulation. Sometimes in this process the original problems are transformed or even completely abandoned in favour of others. For instance, one study began from an interest in the organization of a housing association, how it had been established and changed in character over time, then shifted to focus on the conflicting stories that members of the association told about its history, and was finally transformed into an investigation of the 'confused' talk of people suffering from dementia (Shakespeare 1994, 1997).

Change in research problems can derive from several sources. It may be discovered that the original formulation was founded on mistaken assumptions. Equally, it could be concluded that, given the current state of knowledge, the problem selected is not tractable. This is a possibility that arises across the whole field of human inquiry. Medawar (1967) comments, in relation to natural science:

Good scientists study the more important problems they think they can solve. It is, after all, their professional business to solve problems, not merely to grapple with them. The spectacle of a scientist locked in combat with the forces of ignorance is not an inspiring one if, in the outcome, the scientist is routed. That is why some of the most important biological problems have not yet appeared on the agenda of practical research.

(Medawar 1967: 7)

Periodically, methodologists rediscover the truth of the old adage that finding the right question to ask is more important, and sometimes more difficult, than answering it (Merton 1959). What are viable research problems depends, of course, on the resources available to the researcher; and what are relevant here are not just external resources like time and funds but also personal ones such as background knowledge, social characteristics and circumstances. Moreover, these can change during the course of research, perhaps forcing a refocusing of inquiry.

Much of the effort that goes into early data analysis is concerned with formulating and reformulating the research problem in ways that make it more fruitful and/or more amenable to investigation. Problems vary in their degree of abstractness. Some, especially those deriving from practical or political concerns, will be 'topical' (Lofland 1976), being concerned with types of people and situations readily identified in everyday language. Others have a more 'generic' cast. Here the researcher is asking questions such as 'Of what abstract sociologically conceived class of situation is this particular one an instance?' and 'What are the general features of this kind of situation?' This distinction between topical and generic research problems is closely related to the distinction between substantive and formal analyses outlined by Glaser and Strauss in their account of grounded theorizing:

> By substantive theory, we mean that developed for a substantive, or empirical, area of sociological inquiry, such as patient care, race relations, professional education, delinquency, or research organizations. By formal theory, we mean that developed for a formal, or conceptual, area of sociological inquiry, such as stigma, deviant behavior, formal organization, socialization, status incongruency, authority and power, reward systems, or social mobility.
>
> (Glaser and Strauss 1967: 32)

In ethnographic research there is usually a constant interplay between the topical and the generic, or the substantive and the formal. One may, for instance, begin with some formal analytic notion and seek to extend or refine its range of application in the context of a particular new substantive application. This can be illustrated by reference to the work of Hargreaves *et al.* (1975) on deviance in school classrooms. Starting from the formal concepts of 'labelling theory', Hargreaves and his colleagues sought to extend the use of this analytic framework to, and examine its value for, the study of student deviance in secondary schools. They were able to derive from it a sort of 'shopping list' of issues. This list of topics moves the focus of concern from the formal towards the substantive, from the generic towards the topical. Their list reads:

> *Rules.* What are the rules in schools and classrooms? Which rules are allegedly broken in imputations of deviance? Who makes the rules? Are the rules ever negotiated? How are the rules communicated to members? What justifications are given for the rules, by whom, to whom, and on what occasions? Do teachers and pupils view the rules in the same way? Are some rules perceived as legitimate by some teachers and some pupils? How do members know that certain rules are

relevant to (i.e. are 'in play' in) a given situation? How do members classify the rules? What differences do members see between different rules? For example, do rules vary in importance?

Deviant acts. How do members link an act to a rule to permit the imputation of deviance? How do teachers know that a pupil has broken a rule? That is, what is the interpretive work undertaken by teachers to permit the categorization of an act as deviant? Similarly, how do pupils know that their acts are deviant? . . .

Deviant persons. How do teachers link deviant acts to persons so that persons are defined as deviant? What is the relationship between different labels? Why is one label used rather than another? . . .

Treatment. What treatments are made by teachers in relation to acts or persons defined as deviants? On what grounds and with what justifications do teachers decide on one treatment rather than another? . . .

Career of the deviant. What is the structure of the career of the deviant pupil? What are the contingencies of such careers? How are such careers initiated and terminated?

(D. Hargreaves *et al.* 1975: 23–4)

Such a list of problems clearly draws on the authors' prior knowledge of sociological work on schools and deviance, and reflects an interplay between formal and substantive interests. Of course, these questions do not constitute a research design as such. Similarly, one would not expect such a list to be a definitive one: in some ways it will probably prove to be overambitious, and in others it will undoubtedly omit unforeseen issues.

Just as one can formulate research problems by moving from the formal to the substantive, so one can move from the substantive to the formal or generic. This can be illustrated in part from a research project in which one of us was involved (Atkinson 1981b). It was concerned with the investigation of 'industrial training units' designed to ease the transition from school to working life for 'slow learners'. The research included a number of strands, including participant observation in two such industrial units, interviews with a range of officials, documentary sources, and so on. The project was not simply a 'one-off' case study, but one of a number of similar pieces of research being undertaken in Britain. These other projects were also investigating innovative interventions to facilitate the transition from school to work.

The research began with foreshadowed problems that were primarily substantive or topical in origin. In an exploratory orientation, the research team started the fieldwork phase with general interests of this sort: How is the day-to-day work of the unit organized? How are the students selected and evaluated? What sort of work do they do, and what sort of work are they being prepared for?

During the course of the fieldwork a number of issues were identified with more precision, and new categories were developed. At the same time, it became apparent that there was a need to reformulate these ideas in terms that were more general than their local manifestations in our own project. A more pressing reason for this was the desirability of generating concepts that would provide principles for, and systematic comparison between, the different research projects in Britain. A research memorandum put the issue in this way:

During our last meeting ... we talked about the possibility of developing and working with some general analytic categories. The idea I was putting forward ... was that evaluation projects were doomed to be little more than one-off, local affairs, unless we were able to work with ideas and frameworks of more general applicability. Such 'generalization' would not imply that all projects should work within 'the same' research design, or collect 'the same' data by 'the same' technique. Clearly, particular evaluations must remain sensitive to local conditions and responsive to changing circumstances. Nor should such a suggestion be interpreted as a plea for a straitjacket of predetermined questions and categories. Such categories should only be thought of as 'sensitizing' concepts indicating some broad dimensions for comparison between projects, and for the development of general frameworks to tie together disparate projects and evaluation.

(Atkinson 1981b)

We shall not attempt to detail all the ideas drawn on and alluded to in this particular project, but the following extracts from the same research memorandum are illustrative of how these ideas were used to categorize some key issues in the research, and to stimulate the posing of further topical questions:

Gatekeepers. By gatekeepers I mean actors with control over key sources and avenues of opportunity. Such gatekeepers exercise control at and during key phases of the youngster's status passage(s). Such gatekeepers' functions would actually be carried out by different personnel in the different organizational settings.

...

The identification of the general class of 'gatekeepers' would then allow us to go on to ask some pertinent questions of a general nature. For instance: What resources do gatekeepers have at their disposal? What perceptions and expectations do gatekeepers have of 'clients'? Are these perceptions mutually compatible or are there systematic differences of opinion? Do gatekeepers believe that their expectations of clients are met or not? Do they have an implicit (or even an explicit) model of the 'ideal client'?

What is the information-state of gatekeepers? For example, what sort of model of the labour market are they operating with? What views of working life do they bring to bear? How accurate are their assessments of the state of local labour markets?

What sort of routines and strategies do gatekeepers employ? For instance, what criteria (formal and informal) are used to assess and categorize 'clients'? What bureaucratic routines are used (if any)? What record-keeping procedures are used, and how are such data interpreted in practice?

(Atkinson 1981b)

Closely allied with this outline of 'gatekeepers' as a general sensitizing device, the memorandum also included the following:

Labelling. This general category clearly overlaps with the gatekeepers' practical reasoning, and with some issues in definitions of client populations. To what extent is there a danger of self-fulfilling prophecies, as a result of the identification of target populations? To what extent do projects themselves help to crystallize racial, gender or ability categorizations and stereotypes?

Do employers and potential employers operate with stigmatizing stereotypes? Do projects overcome, or do they help to confirm, such stereotypes? What particular aspects of projects and the youngsters do 'gatekeepers' such as employers seize on and react to?

Do the youngsters label themselves and each other in accordance with formal or informal labels attached to them? Are the professionals involved in projects themselves subject to stigma in the views of other professionals and agencies?

(Atkinson 1981b)

While many of the questions that are posed here are fairly concrete or topical in content, the general tenor of the document draws attention to generic concepts such as gatekeepers, labelling, stigma, routines, strategies, practical reasoning, and self-fulfilling prophecies.

This research memorandum, then, gives some sense of the process of problem formulation during the intermediate stage of a research project. The initial fieldwork had suggested a number of potentially important aspects to be identified more thoroughly, and some potentially useful analytic ideas. Thus, over the course of inquiry, research problems are identified more precisely. At the same time, such identifications permit new research questions to be posed, or for them to be formulated more systematically. Hence guidelines for further data collection are also laid down.

One must beware of oversimplifying the distinction between topical and generic levels of analysis. One does not simply progress in a unidirectional way from one to the other. There will normally be a constant shuttling back and forth between the two analytic modes. Particular substantive issues may suggest affinities with some formal concept that will, in turn, indicate substantive issues as deserving new or further attention, and so on.

Selecting settings and cases

There is another factor that often plays a significant role in shaping the way in which research problems are developed in ethnography: the nature of the setting or settings chosen for study. Sometimes the setting itself comes first – an opportunity arises to investigate an interesting situation or group of people; and foreshadowed problems spring from the nature of that setting. This is true, for example, in the case of studying 'natural experiments' or where ethnographers are specifically employed to investigate particular settings, or where they are carrying out 'part-time' ethnography in their own places of work. Such 'opportunistic research' (Riemer 1977) also includes situations where sudden events provide the chance of studying history-in-the-making or unusual circumstances. For example, Pieke (1995) recounts how, five months into his fieldwork in Beijing, he witnessed the emergence of the 1989 Chinese People's Movement, which even at the time clearly represented an important research opportunity.

Where a setting is selected on the basis of foreshadowed problems, the nature of the setting may still shape the development of the research questions. This arises because, as we noted earlier, in ethnographic research the development of research problems is rarely completed before fieldwork begins; indeed, the collection of primary data often plays a key role in that process of development. Furthermore, it is often found that some of the questions into which the foreshadowed problems have been translated are not open to investigation in the setting selected. The researcher is then faced with the choice of either dropping these questions from the investigation or restarting the research in a setting where they *can* be investigated, if that is possible. While, on occasion, the importance of a problem may lead to the latter decision, generally researchers stay where they are and select problems that can be investigated there. After all, more questions are usually generated than can be tackled in a single study. Moreover, not only does moving to another setting involve further delay and renewed problems of access, but also there is no guarantee that the new setting will turn out to be an appropriate one in which to investigate the preferred problem. The Chicago sociologist Everett Hughes is reported to have remarked, only half jokingly, that the researcher should select the research problem for which the setting chosen is the ideal site!

All this does not mean that the selection of settings for study is unimportant, simply that the ethnographer is rarely in a position to specify the precise nature of the setting required. At best, it is a matter of identifying the sorts of location that would be most appropriate for investigation of the research problem, as currently formulated. And, when a type of setting has been decided on, it is advisable (if possible) to 'case' possible research sites with a view to assessing their suitability, the feasibility of carrying out research there, and how access might best be accomplished should they be selected. This involves collecting and subjecting to preliminary analysis any documentary evidence available about the setting, interviewing anyone who can be easily contacted who has experience or knowledge of it, and perhaps making brief visits there, covertly or overtly. It may be possible to combine this with carrying out pilot research, trying out some of the methods that one plans to use; though sometimes it is better to use a setting for this purpose that one knows one will *not* be using for the main data collection.[2]

'Casing the joint' in this fashion not only will provide information about potential settings in which the research could be carried out, but also feeds into the development and refinement of the research problem. It may be discovered that what had been assumed to be a homogeneous category of sites must be broken down into a number of sub-types which have significantly different characteristics. Equally, assumptions about the categories of people associated with different sites may need to be revised. Warren (1972) provides an example:

> The first decision that must be made by a researcher who wishes to study the gay community – unless he has unlimited time and money to spend – is which 'gay community' he wishes to study: the world of exclusive private gay clubs for businessmen and professionals? or the dope addict transvestites so vividly depicted in *Last Exit to Brooklyn*? or the sado-masochistic leather boys? Any extended preliminary observation will make it objectively obvious that 'the' gay community is divided – fairly loosely at the boundaries – into a hierarchy linked to some extent with status and class criteria in the 'real' world.
>
> (Warren 1972: 144)

2   For an illuminating discussion of the role of pilot research in qualitative research, see Sampson (2004).

The role of pragmatic considerations must not be underestimated in the choice of a setting. While by no means absent in hypothesis-testing research, these are likely to play an especially important role in ethnographic work. This is because here the criteria specifying suitability are usually much less determinate: there is generally a very wide range of settings that could be relevant. Furthermore, the data collection process is usually very intensive, and this has implications for what is and is not viable. As a result, contacts with personnel promising easy access, the scale of the travel costs likely to be involved, and the availability of documentary information, etc. are often major considerations in narrowing down the selection.[3] Sampson and Thomas (2003) provide a variation on this theme from their ethnographic work on board ships. They write:

> In the course of our research we deliberately selected a high proportion of ships with long sea passages and few port calls. This was the result of our finding that seafarers tend to have little free time in port and some, for example chief officers, have many demands made on their time in port and therefore become very fatigued. Seafarers with time 'off' generally go ashore and may be unavailable to researchers who may find that research opportunities are limited aboard ships engaged in what are termed short-sea trades, where port calls are very frequent and close together. Our choice of ship was thus driven by our assessment of the optimum conditions for data collection.
>
> (Sampson and Thomas 2003: 170)

Sometimes, the search for an appropriate setting can take unpredictable turns, as Campbell's (1992) account of his research in Greece in the 1950s illustrates. He set out to study one of the villages in a mountain region north-east of Jannina. However, he found the populations of the villages much depleted as a result of civil war, and that his English background led to suspicions that he was a spy. A fortuitous event transformed his research plans. Sarakatsan transhumant shepherds lived on the hills above the village, and relations between them and the villagers were uneasy:

> Our own contacts with them had not gone beyond formal greetings when one day in the heat of summer a young shepherd-boy returning from school had stopped at the village spring to drink, and was there set upon by larger village boys. . . . At this point, the anthropologist's wife entered indignantly to rescue the victim. This small adventure had its consequences. We received an invitation to visit a Sarakatsan encampment and the relationship prospered. When some weeks afterwards the time arrived for the Sarakatsani to take their flocks and families down to the plains of Thesprotia for the winter, one family sent us a peremptory message. We were to accompany them and they would build us a hut.
>
> (Campbell 1992: 152)

This example also illustrates how occasionally researchers find that they have effectively been chosen to research a setting by one or more of the people involved in it, though usually with rather more strings attached than in this case. In such circumstances, the

---

3   See, for example, Fox's (1964) discussion of her choice of Belgium as the site for a study of European medical research.

ethnographer must balance the ease of initial access offered against the desirability of the site in other respects, as well as against any problems that such direct sponsorship by a gatekeeper might cause.

Usually ethnographers study only one or a small number of settings, and sometimes these are ones that are geographically close to where they are based. Often this is forced by the cost of using more remote sites and the limited resources available. This is not always the case, however. One exception is Henslin's (1990) study of homeless people. He decided to do a study that covered various parts of the United States, but found that setting off with his family in a motor home to combine research with sight-seeing led to little fieldwork being done. Fortunately, an alternative arose:

> I heard about a 'fly-anywhere-we-fly-as-often-as-you-want-for-21-days' sales gimmick from Eastern Airlines. I found their offer was legitimate, that for $750 I could pack in as many cities as I could stand – actually more than I could stand as it turned out. . . . It was the method itself, participant observation, that became the key for making this research affordable. Obviously, the homeless spend very little money, which dovetailed perfectly with my situation and desires. I was able to stay in the shelters at no financial cost. (The shelters, however, exacted a tremendous cost in terms of upsetting my basic orientational complacencies.) In addition to a free bed and a shower, the shelters usually provided morning and evening meals. Although those meals were not always edible, I was able to count on the noon meal being of quality, and that was already included in the price of my airline ticket . . . I primarily focused on major cities in the Western part of the United States, later adding cities in other areas during subsequent travels. My purpose was to obtain as good a 'geographical spread' as I could.
>
> (Henslin 1990: 55)

Generally speaking, of course, the more settings studied the less time can be spent in each. The researcher must make a trade-off here between breadth and depth of investigation.

It is important not to confuse the choice of settings with the selection of cases for study. The vocabulary of studying 'fields' and 'settings' is widely used in talking and writing about ethnography. The main source of this tendency to regard natural settings as the object of study is the kind of naturalism that was characteristic, for example, of the work of the Chicago School:

> [The sociological study of Chicago] was nursed as a cartographic exercise studying Little Sicily, the Jewish ghetto, Polonism, the Gold Coast, the slums, Hobohemia, roominghouse districts and the gangs of the city. Each of these areas was treated as a symbolic world which created and perpetuated a distinctive moral and social organization. Each was subjected to an interpretative analysis which attempted to reproduce the processes by which that organization was brought into being. They were collectively identified as natural areas: 'natural' because they were themselves part of the natural evolution and selection which shaped society; because they were different from the structures produced by planning and science; and because they represented a unit which allegedly framed American thinking on social and political life.
>
> (Rock 1979: 92)

In other sociological contexts, too, similar appeals are made to models of relatively self-contained groups of 'communities'. In the past, the anthropological tradition, for instance, tended to lay stress on the investigation of small-scale 'face-to-face' societies and local collectivities (such as 'the village'). This, and the cognate tradition of 'community studies', has often rested on a Gemeinschaft-like view of the local society, emphasizing its internal stability and its relative discreteness. The more recent concept 'community of practice' (see Lave and Wenger 1991), which was originally developed through an anthropological study of Liberian tailors, also encourages this tendency (Hammersley 2005b).

However, settings are not naturally occurring phenomena, they are constituted and maintained through cultural definition and social strategies Their boundaries are not fixed but shift across occasions, to one degree or another, through processes of redefinition and negotiation.

There is another reason, too, why it is potentially misleading to talk of 'studying a setting'. It is not possible to give an exhaustive account of any locale. In producing descriptions we always rely on criteria of selection and inference. There is an important sense, then, in which even in the most descriptively oriented study the case investigated is not isomorphic with the setting in which it is located. A setting is a named context in which phenomena occur that might be studied from any number of angles; a case is those phenomena seen from one particular angle. Some features of the setting will be given no attention at all, and even those phenomena that are the major focus will be looked at in a way that by no means exhausts their characteristics. Moreover, any setting may contain several cases. Thus, for example, in a study of the effects of various kinds of external assessment on secondary school teaching, it was particular courses within the school that constituted the cases under investigation rather than the school as a whole (Scarth and Hammersley 1988). Conversely, a case may not be contained within the boundaries of a setting; it may be necessary to go outside to collect information on important aspects of it. In studying gangs among male prisoners (Jacobs 1974), it may be necessary to explore their links with groups outside if the manner in which the gangs came to be formed and in which they continue to recruit new members is to be understood. While it may seem innocent enough, then, the naturalistic conception of studying fields and settings discourages the systematic and explicit selection of aspects of a setting for study, as well as movement outside of it to follow up promising theoretical leads. And, of course, the process of identifying and defining the case under study must proceed side by side with the refinement of the research problem and the development of the analysis.

One of the limitations often raised in connection with ethnographic work is that because only a single case, or at any rate a small number of cases, is studied, the representativeness of the findings is always in doubt. This can be an important point, but it is not always so. Sometimes, ethnographic research is concerned with a case that has intrinsic interest, so that generalization is not the primary concern. This is most obviously true with action research and evaluation studies, where the target is the characteristics of the particular situations investigated. And, occasionally, ethnographic work involves the study of a relatively large number of cases, thereby often providing a substantial basis for generalization. Thus, Strong (2001) studied 1000 cases of paediatric consultation in three hospitals, two in Britain and one in the United States. However, even where generalization is a goal of ethnographic research but only a small number of cases is studied, various strategies can be used to deal with the problem, more or less adequately. How it should be dealt with depends upon whether the research is directed towards the development and testing of a theory or whether the aim is generalization about a finite population of cases, actually existing or possible in the future (Schofield 1990).

Where the concern is theory development and testing, the strategic selection of cases is particularly important. This can take a variety of forms. One is what Glaser and Strauss (1967) called 'theoretical sampling'. The primary concern of these authors was the generation and elaboration of theory, and they argued that the selection of cases should be designed to produce as many categories and properties of categories as possible, and to facilitate the emergence of relations among categories. They recommended two complementary strategies: minimizing the differences between cases to highlight basic properties of a particular category; and then subsequently maximizing the differences between cases in order to increase the density of the properties relating to core categories, to integrate categories and to delimit the scope of the theory. As an illustration they cite their research on the awareness contexts surrounding patients dying in hospital:

> Visits to the various medical services were scheduled as follows: I wished first to look at services that minimized patient awareness (and so first looked at a premature baby service and then a neurosurgical service where patients were frequently comatose). I wished next to look at dying in a situation where expectancy of staff and often of patients was great and dying was quick, so I observed on an Intensive Care Unit. Then I wished to observe on a service where staff expectations of terminality were great but where the patient's might or might not be, and where dying tended to be slow. So I looked next at a cancer service. I wished then to look at conditions where death was unexpected and rapid, and so looked at an emergency service. While we were looking at some different types of services, we also observed the above types of services at other types of hospitals. So our scheduling of types of service was directed by a general conceptual scheme – which included hypotheses about awareness, expectedness and rate of dying – as well as by a developing conceptual structure including matters not at first envisioned. Sometimes we returned to services after the initial two or three or four weeks of continuous observation, in order to check upon items which needed checking or had been missed in the initial period.
>
> (Glaser and Strauss 1967: 59)

Strategic selection of cases can also be employed in testing theoretical ideas. Here the aim is to select cases for investigation that subject theories to a relatively severe test. An example is the sequence of studies by Hargreaves, Lacey and Ball (Hargreaves 1967; Lacey 1970; Ball 1981; see also Abraham 1989). They argue that the way in which schools differentiate students on academic and behavioural grounds – especially via streaming, tracking, and banding – polarizes them into pro- and anti-school subcultures. These subcultures, in turn, shape students' behaviour inside and outside school, and affect their levels of academic achievement. This theory was developed and tested in examples of three types of secondary school in the United Kingdom: secondary modern (Hargreaves), grammar (Lacey), and comprehensive (Ball). Moreover, in the case of the grammar school, because the students entering it had been strongly committed to school values at their junior schools, variables at the heart of competing explanations for the process of polarization – such as attitude to school, aspects of home background, etc. – are partially controlled. Similarly, in his study of Beachside Comprehensive, Ball examines the effects of a shift from banding to mixed ability grouping within a single case (some factors thereby remaining constant), this representing a weakening of differentiation.[4]

Where the aim is generalization to some finite set of cases, rather than the development and testing of theory, it may be possible to assess the typicality of the case or cases studied by comparing their relevant characteristics with information about the target population, if this is available in official statistics or from other studies. Thus, in his investigation of religious intermarriage in Northern Ireland, Lee (1992) sought to check the representativeness of his snowball sample of couples by comparing some of their characteristics with a special tabulation of the census data. This revealed that his sample 'showed a sharp bias towards young, recently married couples, mostly without children and with relatively high levels of educational attainment' (Lee 1992: 133). While he was not able to correct this sampling bias, because of the problem of gaining access to couples whose position was so delicate in the Northern Ireland situation, he was able to allow for it in his analysis.

It may even sometimes be possible to carry out a small-scale survey on a larger sample of the population to gather information to assess the typicality of the cases being studied. Thus, in his study of students at Rutgers University, Moffatt used a survey to assess the extent to which they had a vocational orientation; and he was also able to compare the results with those of a national study (Moffatt 1989: 331). Another possibility is to combine in-depth investigation of a small number of cases with more superficial checks on other cases. For example, in his study of law enforcement agencies, Skolnick (1966) concentrated on those in one city, but he made a brief investigation of agencies in another to check the likely generalizability of his findings.

The appropriate strategy to adopt in selecting cases may vary over the course of the research. In the early phases, which cases are chosen for investigation may not matter greatly. Later on, it may come to acquire considerable importance. Certainly, initial decisions may have to be revised. Klatch (1988) reports how in her research on women involved in right-wing political organizations she began with 'a neat fourfold table comparing four organizations: two Old Right groups and two New Right groups; two "religious" and two "secular organizations"'. However, she soon faced some problems. In particular, she discovered that:

> the chosen organizations for my original design did not in fact divide along secular versus religious lines. . . . Furthermore, I noticed a general pattern developing between the 'homemaker' type of woman active in many religious/pro-family groups. . . . and the 'professional' type of women active in the more secular conservative groups . . . . The final design continued to rely on in-depth interviews, participant observation, and a textual analysis of right-wing literature, but I broadened the sample to include a much wider range of conservative groups in order to increase the variation among the female activists, thereby gaining a better understanding of the broader divisions within the Right.
>
> (Klatch 1988: 73)

---

4   For further discussion of the process of theory development and testing involved in this sequence of studies, see Hammersley (1985).

Research design in ethnography, both as it relates to the selection of cases for study and in other respects too, is a continuous process. The match between research problems and cases selected must be continually monitored.

Sampling within the case

Selecting cases for investigation is not the only form of sampling involved in ethnography. Equally important, often, is sampling *within* cases. At least this is true where cases are not so small that they can be subjected to exhaustive investigation, as for example in Strong's (2001) study of paediatric consultations. Decisions must be made about where to observe and when, who to talk to and what to ask, as well as about what to record and how. In this process we are not only deciding what is and is not relevant to the case under study but also usually sampling from the data available in the case. Very often this sampling is not the result of conscious deliberation, but it is important to make any criteria employed as explicit and as systematic as possible, so as to try to ensure that data about the case have been adequately sampled, and to reflect on any inadvertent sampling that has taken place. There are three major dimensions along which sampling within cases occurs: time, people, and context.

Time

Time may seem a dimension of obvious importance in social life, but it has often been neglected. Attitudes and activities frequently vary over time in ways that are highly significant for social theory. Berlak *et al.* provide an example from their research on English 'progressive' primary schools in the early 1970s:

> During our first weeks in the English schools we gradually began to understand that the images of the schools conveyed in the literature were to some extent distorted. The way in which this understanding developed is exemplified by our experience during the first weeks of our study of Mr Thomas's classroom. In his classroom, in a school in an affluent suburban area, we observed thirty children on a Wednesday morning who, after a brief discussion with the teacher, went about their work individually: some began to work on 'maths', others to study spelling or to write original stories in much the way [that the literature describes]. We observed no teacher behavior on that morning which appeared to direct the children to what they were to do. It appeared that the children were pursuing their own interests. However, during the following days, we observed events and patterns which appeared to account for the behavior observed on that Wednesday morning. On the following Monday morning we observed Mr Thomas set work minimums in each subject for the week. . . . On the following Friday morning we saw him collect the children's work 'diaries' where each child had recorded in detail the work he had completed during the week. Over the weekend, Mr Thomas and, as we were to later discover, sometimes the head, checked each record book and wrote comments in the diaries such as 'good', 'more maths', or the ominous 'see me'. Such items, which explained some of the apparently spontaneous classroom behavior, had not appeared in the literature.
>
> (Berlak *et al.* 1975: 218)

The general issue of the social construction and distribution of time is quite beautifully demonstrated in Zerubavel's (1979) hospital study. Here, the organization of time is not an incidental feature or a background to a substantive focus on other organizational matters. Rather, it is an exercise, in the tradition of Simmel, on the formal category of time itself:

> Following the methodological guidelines which I derived from Simmel's formal sociology, I focused my observations on only one aspect of hospital life, namely, its temporal structure, deliberately ignoring – for analytical purposes – the history of the hospital, its national reputation, the quality of its patient care, its architectural design and spatial organization, its finances, the religious and ethnic makeup of its staff, and so on.
>
> (Zerubavel 1979: xvii)

Zerubavel's is thus an unusually sparse ethnography. Yet the single-mindedness of his observations and his formal analyses enable him to reveal the complex patterning of temporal orders within the organization of daily life in the hospital. He foreshadows their diversity in the introduction:

> The list of sociological aspects of temporality which can be discussed within the context of hospital life is almost endless: the temporal structure of patients' hospital careers; the relations between time and space; deadlines and strategies of beating the schedule; the temporal relations among the various hospital units; the impact of organizational time on hospital personnel's life outside the hospital; and so on.
>
> (Zerubavel 1979: xxi)

Following Zerubavel's example, we can think hypothetically about the accident and emergency department of an urban general hospital. Any systematic study here would almost certainly reveal different patterns of work and activity according to the time of day or night, and according to the day of the week. The nature of the referrals and emergency presentations would vary too. Saturday nights would probably be characterized by very different rates and patterns of admission from Monday nights, and so on. Study of temporal patterns in this department would also relate to changing shifts of nursing staff, rotations among junior doctors, and so forth. Very similar considerations apply in many other settings: in factories, bars, cafés, prisons, educational settings, and residential homes, for example.

It should be apparent, therefore, that any attempt to represent the entire range of persons and events in the case under study will have to be based on adequate coverage of temporal variation. On the other hand, it is impossible to conduct fieldwork round the clock, and some degree of time sampling must usually be attempted. It may be possible to undertake the occasional period of extended fieldwork, but these are hard to sustain. In any event, long uninterrupted periods of fieldwork are not always to be encouraged. The production of decent fieldnotes, transcribing audio- or video-recordings, the indexing and filing of material, writing memoranda and reflexive notes are all essential, as well as time-consuming and demanding, activities. Very long periods of observation will thus become quite unmanageable. The longer the time between observation and recording, the more troublesome will be the recall and recording of

adequately detailed and concrete descriptions. Long bursts of observation, unin
by periods of reflexive recording, will thus tend to result in data of poor qua

Hence, all ethnographers have to resist the very ready temptation to try
hear, and participate in everything that goes on. A more selective approach will no
result in data of better quality, provided the periods of observation are complen ...u
by periods of productive recording and reflection. Rather than attempting to cover the
entire working day, for instance, one may be able to build up an adequate representation
by following the sort of strategy outlined by Schatzman and Strauss (1973):

> If the researcher elects to observe work around the clock, he can first observe a
> day shift for several days, then evenings and then nights, for a period of consecutive
> days until he is reasonably familiar with all three shifts. Or he may cover events
> at any given sub-site by 'overlapping' time on consecutive dates – for example,
> 7:00 a.m. to 9:00 a.m., 8:00 a.m. to 10:00 a.m., 9:00 a.m. to 11:00 a.m. – and
> over a period of days cover the organization around the clock.
>
> (Schatzman and Strauss 1973: 39)

Over and above these procedures for establishing adequate coverage, the researcher
will probably identify particularly salient periods and junctures: the change-over between
shifts, for instance, might prove crucial in the organization of work and the sharing
of information in some settings, for example. Such crucial times should then come in
for particular attention.

Similar considerations to those outlined above will also apply to larger-scale temporal
dimensions, such as seasonal or annual cycles, and patterns of recruitment of new
cohorts; although overall constraints of time and resource will obviously prove limiting
here.

Up to now we have referred primarily to issues relating to fieldwork in organizations
and the like. It should also be apparent that similar considerations might apply to
fieldwork in less formally defined settings. The patterns of urban life, 'relations in
public', the use of public settings, and patterns of deviant activity all follow temporal
dimensions: the seasons, the days of the week, and the time of day or night all play
their part. Likewise, it may be important to pay some attention to special occasions,
such as seasonal festivals and carnivals, ceremonies and rituals, rites of passage, and
social markers of status passage.

In organizing the sampling of time, it is as important to include what is routine as
it is to observe the extraordinary. The purpose of such systematic data collection
procedures is to ensure as full and representative a range of coverage as possible, not
just to identify and single out the superficially 'interesting' events.

People

No setting will prove socially homogeneous in all relevant respects, and the adequate
representation of the people involved in a particular case will normally require some
sampling (unless the whole population of relevant actors can be studied in sufficient
depth). The sampling of persons may sometimes be undertaken in terms of fairly standard 'face-sheet' demographic criteria. That is, depending on the particular context,
one may sample persons by reference to categories of gender, 'race', ethnicity, age,

occupation, educational qualifications, and so on. Thus, in selecting people to interview in her study of black middle-class neighbourhoods, Pattillo-McCoy sought to represent different age groups and segments of the middle class; though she was aware that upwardly mobile young adults were under-represented in her sample because they had moved out of the neighbourhood (Pattillo-McCoy 1999: 222).

However, these face-sheet categories are of importance only as they relate to the emerging analysis or to rival theories, or to ensuring representation in terms of some larger population; and they will usually need to be complemented by other categories of analytic relevance. Such emergent categories may be either 'member-identified categories' or 'observer-identified categories' (Lofland 1976). The term 'member-identified categories' refers to typifications that are employed by members themselves, that is, they are 'folk' categories that are normally encapsulated in the 'situated vocabularies' of a given culture. By contrast, 'observer-identified categories' are types constructed by an observer.

Some cultures are particularly rich in member-generated categories. For instance, in her study of a women's prison, Giallombardo (1966) documents the following collection of labels that the prisoners themselves use to categorize themselves: snitchers, inmate cops, and lieutenants; squares, jive bitches; rap buddies, homeys; connects, boosters; pinners; penitentiary turnouts, lesbians, femmes, stud broads, tricks, commissary hustlers, chippies, kick partners, cherries, punks, and turnabouts. These labels are applied on the basis of 'the mode of response exhibited by the inmate to the prison situation and the quality of the inmates' interaction with other inmates and staff', including styles of sexual orientation (Giallambardo 1966: 270).

While member-identified types will often be essential to analysis, the observer may also construct hypothetical categories, on the basis of the fieldwork. In a study of waiting behaviour, for instance, Lofland (1966) identified the following key types:

1   *The Sweet Young Thing.* (Generally a female.) Once having taken a position, normally a seated one, she rarely leaves it. Her posture is straight; potentially suggestive or revealing 'slouching' is not dared.
2   *The Nester.* Having once established a position, such persons busy themselves with arranging and rearranging their props, much in the manner of a bird building a nest.
3   *The Investigator.* Having first reached a position, the investigator surveys his surroundings with some care. Then . . . he leaves his position to begin a minute investigation of every inanimate object in sight.
4   *The Seasoned Urbanite* . . . is easy and relaxed . . . within the confines of legitimate setting use and proper public behavior.
5   *The Maverick* . . . is a non-style . . . . Its users are those who either do not know, are not able, or do not care to protect themselves in public settings. . . . There are three types . . . : *children* . . . ; the *constantly stigmatised* . . . ; and *eccentrics.*
                        (Lofland 1966; cited in Lofland *et al.* 2006, original emphases)

Whether the sampling of persons takes place on the basis of member-identified or observer-identified categories (and often both are used), the process is inextricably linked with the development of analytical ideas and strategies for the collection of data.

Context

Taking account of variations in context is as important as sampling across time and people. Within any setting people may distinguish between a number of quite different contexts that require different kinds of behaviour. Some of these will be fairly obvious, others less so. In schools, for example, it is well known that the behaviour of teachers often differs sharply between classrooms and staffrooms (Woods 1979; Hammersley 1980). This contrast is an example of a more abstract distinction between frontstage and backstage regions developed by Goffman (1959):

> A back region or backstage may be defined as a place, relative to a given performance, where the impression fostered by the performance is knowingly contradicted as a matter of course. There are, of course, many characteristic functions of such places. It is here that the capacity of a performance to express something beyond itself may be painstakingly fabricated; it is here that illusions and impressions are openly constructed. Here stage props and items of personal front can be stored in a kind of compact collapsing of whole repertoires of actions and characters. Here grades of ceremonial equipment, such as different types of liquor or clothes, can be hidden so that the audience will not be able to see the treatment accorded them in comparison with the treatment that could have been accorded them. Here devices such as the telephone are sequestered so that they can be used 'privately'. Here costumes and other parts of personal front may be adjusted and scrutinized for flaws. Here the team can run through its performance, checking for offending expressions when no audience is present to be affronted by them; here poor members of a team, who are expressively inept, can be schooled or dropped from the performance. Here the performer can relax; he can drop his front, forgo speaking his lines, and step out of character.
>
> (Goffman 1959: 114–15)

Goffman illustrates his argument by reference to a wide range of settings from hotel restaurants to shipyards.

It is important, however, not to mistake places for contexts. We must remember, again following Goffman (1963), that architectural structures are merely props used in the social drama; they do not determine behaviour in a direct fashion. What we think of, for example, as 'staffroom behaviour' may also occur in other parts of a school where conditions are right, or even in the bar of a local public house. Conversely, behaviour typical of the staffroom may not occur while visitors are there, or even while the head teacher is there. If we are to ensure that we are not led into false generalizations about attitudes and behaviour within a case through contextual variability, we must identify the contexts in terms of which people in the setting act, recognizing that these are social constructions not physical locations, and try to ensure that we sample across all those that are relevant to our focus of inquiry. One way of doing this is through shadowing particular participants; observing them as they move, over time, between different contexts that form part of their lives or their work (see McDonald 2005).

Up to this point we have talked for the most part as though it were simply up to the researcher to select the settings and cases for study, and to sample them appropriately. But, of course, the cases we might wish to select may not be open to study, for one reason or another; and, even if they are, effective strategies for gaining access to the necessary data will need to be developed. Similarly, not all the people we wish to observe or talk to, nor all the contexts we wish to sample, may be accessible – certainly not at the times we want them to be. The problem of gaining access to data is particularly serious in ethnography, since one is operating in settings where the researcher generally has little power, and people have pressing concerns of their own which often give them little reason to cooperate. It is to this problem that we turn in the next chapter.

3   Access

The problem of obtaining access to the data looms large in ethnography; and Feldman *et al.* (2003: vii) suggest that it often comes 'as a rude surprise' to researchers who have not anticipated the difficulties that could be involved.[1] It is often at its most acute in initial negotiations to enter a setting and during the 'first days in the field'; but the problem, and the issues associated with it, persist, to one degree or another, throughout the data collection process. For example, Sampson and Thomas (2003) found that, in gaining access to carry out fieldwork on board ship, obtaining permission from the owners was only the very first step: the captain was an even more important gatekeeper; and, despite the sharply hierarchical character of ship life, even his support was far from sufficient. They comment that 'negotiating access is something of a full-time occupation in a shipboard context' (Sampson and Thomas 2003: 173). To one degree or another, this is true of most settings.

In many ways, gaining access is a thoroughly practical matter. As we shall see, it involves drawing on the intra- and inter-personal resources and strategies that we all tend to develop in dealing with everyday life. But achieving access is not merely a practical concern. Not only does its achievement depend upon theoretical understanding, often disguised as 'native wit', but also the discovery of obstacles to access, and perhaps of effective means of overcoming them, itself provides insights into the social organization of the setting or the orientations of the people being researched.

Thus, in negotiating access for a study of public commemoration of a terror attack at the Bologna railway station, Tota (2004) found that key figures in the Bolognese Victims' Association suspected her of being an infiltrator on behalf of the Italian secret service (Tota 2004: 134). And in trying to contact victims of punishment beatings in Northern Ireland, Knox (2001) discovered that doing this through community organizations had limited success because these organizations were suspected by victims of having links with the paramilitary groups that were responsible for their treatment. Instead, it turned out that a more productive route was through probation officers, whose cases included young people who had been punished for 'anti-social' behaviour by the paramilitaries (Knox 2001: 209).

The work of Barbera-Stein (1979) also illustrates how negotiating access can generate important knowledge about the field. She sought to investigate several different therapeutic or daycare centres for preschool children, but the original research design

---

1 Feldman *et al.*'s (2003) book provides a general discussion of access problems, and a collection of accounts from particular projects, focused mainly on gaining access to individuals rather than to institutions.

foundered because access was denied to several settings. She writes in retrospect of her experience: 'The access negotiations can be construed as involving multiple views of what is profane and open to investigation vs what is sacred or taboo and closed to investigation unless the appropriate respectful stance or distance is assumed' (Barbera-Stein 1979: 15). She ties this observation to particular settings and particular activities in them:

> I had requested the permission to observe what the psychoanalytic staff considered sacred. In their interactions with emotionally disturbed children, they attempted to establish effective bonds modelled after the parent-child bond. This was the first step in their attempts to correct the child's faulty emotional development. This also was the principal work of the social workers at the day-care centre. Formal access to the day-care centre initially was made contingent upon my not observing on Tuesdays and Thursdays when the social workers engaged the children in puppet play sessions. Puppet play was used as a psychological projective technique in monitoring and fostering the emotional development of the children.
>
> (Barbera-Stein 1979: 15)

Even after eight months of fieldwork, and after some renegotiation, access to such 'sacred' puppet-play sessions was highly restricted. The researcher was allowed to observe only three sessions and was forbidden to take notes.

In contrast, Barbera-Stein herself assumed that interactional data on families in the home would be highly sacred, and did not initially request access to such information. In fact it turned out that this was not regarded as problematic by the social workers, as they viewed working with families as their stock-in-trade, and it was an area in which they were themselves interested. Her experience illustrates, incidentally, that while one must remain sensitive to issues of access to different domains, it is unwise to allow one's plans to be guided entirely by one's own presuppositions concerning what is and is not accessible.

Negotiating access also involves ethical considerations, for example to do with whose permission *ought* to be asked, as well as whose *needs* to be obtained if initial access is to be granted. This issue arises most obviously in relation to those who occupy subordinate positions within the settings investigated, for example children or prisoners. But it often applies to all members within many organizations.

Equally important is what people are told about the research in the process of negotiating access, both as regards its purpose and what it will involve for them, including possible consequences stemming from the publication of findings. As we shall see, fully informed consent is often neither possible nor desirable in ethnographic (or, for that matter, other) research.[2] However, this does not mean that issues of consent and the provision of information are unimportant.

Dealing with these issues is increasingly complex in practical terms today, not least because very often permission has to be sought from relevant ethics committees or institutional review boards (one or more) before the research can go ahead. Informed consent is one of the key guiding principles on which such committees operate; and, at the present time at least, their deliberations are typically based on a biomedical, psychological, or survey research model; in which the researcher is presumed to be

---

2 The complexity of the ethical issues surrounding ethnographic research will be addressed in Chapter 10.

dealing with individual cases. Since ethnographers frequently study situations and groups, many of the guidelines on which ethics committees operate, such as opt-in consent and the right of withdrawal at any time, are inapplicable. These problems can often be overcome, but usually this is not without considerable, time-consuming negotiation; and it may involve ethnographic work being subjected to a greater degree of surveillance than other kinds of research – for example being subjected to continual review (Economic and Social Research Council (ESRC) 2005: section 2.2, pp. 22–3). It may also lead, sometimes, to research plans being altered simply to ensure smooth passage through the ethics committee procedures.

The rights and wrongs of ethical committees, in principle and in relation to their particular current orientation, are the subject of considerable, and continuing, dispute, but the task of dealing with them is a necessity for many researchers today. This arises both because universities increasingly police research done by their employees, and because the requirements associated with gaining access for research purposes to some settings or informants (particularly in the health field) demand compliance with local ethics committee procedures.[3]

Approaching the field

Access is not simply a matter of physical presence or absence. It is far more than the granting or withholding of permission for research to be conducted. Perhaps this can be illustrated by reference to research where too literal a notion of access would be particularly misleading. It might be thought that problems of access could be avoided if one were to study 'public' settings only, such as streets, shops, public transport vehicles, bars, and similar locales. In one sense this is true. Anyone can, in principle, enter such public domains; that is what makes them public. No process of negotiation is required for that. On the other hand, things are not necessarily so straightforward. In many settings, while physical presence is not in itself problematic, appropriate activity may be so.

Among other things, public domains may be marked by styles of social interaction involving what Goffman (1971) terms 'civil inattention'. Anonymity in public settings is not a contingent feature of them, but is worked at by displays of a studied lack of interest in one's fellows, minimal eye contact, careful management of physical proximity, and so on. There is, therefore, the possibility that the fieldworker's attention to and interest in what is going on may lead to infringements of such delicate interaction rituals. Similarly, much activity in public settings is fleeting and transient. The fieldworker who wishes to engage in relatively protracted observations may therefore encounter the problem of managing 'loitering', or having to account for himself or herself in some way.

Some examples of these problems are provided in Karp's (1980) account of his investigation of the 'public sexual scene' in and around Times Square in New York, particularly in pornographic bookshops and cinemas. Admittedly, this is a very particular sort of public setting, in that a good deal of what goes on may be 'disreputable' and the behaviour in public correspondingly guarded. Karp tried various strategies for achieving access and initiating interaction. He tried to negotiate openly with some bookshop managers, but failed. Similarly, after a while, regulars on the street interpreted

3 For arguments about current ethical regulation regimes, see Lincoln (2005) and Hammersley (2006a).

his hanging around in terms of his being a hustler, or a cop. He also reports failure to establish relationships with prostitutes, although his fieldnotes display what seems a rather clumsy and naive approach to this.

Karp (1980) resolved his problems to some extent by realizing that they directly paralleled the interactional concerns of the participants themselves, and he was able to draw on his access troubles for analytical purposes in that light. He quotes a research note to this effect:

> I can on the basis of my own experience substantiate, at least in part, the reality of impression-management problems for persons involved in the Times Square sexual scene. I have been frequenting pornographic bookstores and movie theatres for some nine months Despite my relatively long experience I have not been able to overcome my uneasiness during activity in these contexts. I feel, for example, nervous at the prospect of entering a theatre. This nervousness expresses itself in increased heartbeat. I consciously wait until few people are in the vicinity before entering; I take my money out well in advance of entering; I feel reticent to engage the female ticket seller in even the briefest eye contact.
>
> (Karp 1980: 94)

In the face of such interactional constraints, Karp decided to resort to observation alone, with minimal participation beyond casual conversation. He concludes by pointing out that such public settings may be as constraining for a researcher as any organizational setting.

To a considerable extent Karp's is an account of relative failure to establish and maintain working 'presence' and relationships, although he learns from his problems. One should not conclude from his experience, however, that 'loitering' can never lead to workable research conditions. West (1980) writes about the value of such apparently casual approaches: he 'met both ... referred delinquents and others by frequenting their hangouts, such as stores, pool halls, restaurants, and alleys, and by trying to strike up casual acquaintanceship'; though he comments that 'some boldness and a tough-skinned attitude to occasional personal rejection were helpful, in addition to skills in repartee, sports, empathy, and sensitivity'. He reports that 'after a few visits or perhaps a couple of weeks, I became recognized as something of a regular, and usually had managed to strike up conversations with a few youngsters' (West 1980: 34).

Anderson (2006) reports a rather more protracted process in gaining access to Jelly's bar on the Southside of Chicago, and illustrates the difference between being in a place and having access to the social relations that take place there. He provides a fieldnote from his first visit:

> As I entered, sat down at the bar, and ordered my first drink, I drew the attention, direct and indirect, of most of the other patrons. Their eyes followed me, they lowered their voices and stopped interacting so freely with one another, as they listened attentively to what I was saying to the barmaid, even observing the way I said it. They desired information about me, and I gave it, however unwittingly, through my interactions with them. . . . As the barmaid brought my beer, I promptly paid her, just as the sign ('Please pay when served') on the large mirror in front of me directed. She eagerly accepted my payment. As a stranger, I had to pay

when served, while the people around me, presumably regular customers, received round after round on credit. It was clear that the rule was for outsiders like me.

(Anderson 2006: 40)

So, individuals and groups whom one might want to study may be available in public settings, but they are not always welcoming to researchers, or indeed to outsiders of any kind. Sometimes very extensive 'hanging about', along with lucky breaks, is necessary before access is achieved, as Wolf's (1991) experience illustrates:

> As a new graduate student in anthropology at the University of Alberta, Edmonton, I wanted to study the 'Harleytribe'. It was my intent to obtain an insider's perspective of the emotions and the mechanics that underlie outlaw bikers' creation of a subcultural alternative . . . I customised my Norton, donned some biker clothing, and set off to do some fieldwork. My first attempts at contacting an outlaw club were near-disasters. In Calgary I met several members of the Kings Crew MC in a motorcycle shop and expressed an interest in 'hanging around'. But I lacked patience and pushed the situation by asking too many questions. I found out quickly that outsiders, even bikers, do not rush into a club, and that anyone who doesn't show the proper restraint will be shut out.

Following this, Wolf bought himself a new bike, and approached a new group, the Rebels, in a 'final make-it-or-forget-it attempt'. He writes that he sat in a bar watching them and working out how to approach them:

> I discovered that I was a lot more apprehensive than I thought as I sat at the opposite end of the Kingsway Motor Inn and watched the Rebels down their drinks. The loud thunder of heavy-metal rock music would make initiating a delicate introduction difficult, if not impossible, and there were no individual faces or features to be made out in the smoky haze, only a series of Rebel skull patches draped over leather jackets in a corner of the bar that outsiders seemed to avoid warily. . . . I decided to go outside and devise an approach strategy, including how I would react if one of the Rebels turned to me and simply said 'Who invited you?'. I had thought through five different approaches when Wee Albert of the Rebels MC came out of the bar to do a security check on the 'Rebel iron' in the parking lot. He saw me leaning on my bike and came over to check me out. For some time Wee Albert and I stood in the parking lot and talked about motorcycles, riding in the wind, and the Harley tradition. He showed me some of the more impressive Rebel choppers and detailed the jobs of customizing that members of the club had done to their machines. He then checked out my 'hog', gave a grunt of approval, and invited me to come in and join the Rebels at their tables. Drinking at the club bar on a regular basis gave me the opportunity to get to know the Rebels and gave them an opportunity to size me up and check me out on neutral ground. I had made the first of a long sequence of border crossings that all bikers go through if they hope to get close to a club.

(Wolf 1991: 212–15)

Making contact in public settings with people one wishes to study can be a difficult and protracted process, then; though Wolf's experience is undoubtedly extreme. Also sometimes involved is a testing out of the researcher to see whether he or she is genuine and can be trusted, and perhaps also whether being researched will be interesting or boring. Ryan (2006) provides an example from a life history study of Irish gay men:

> Darren . . . would not discuss the prospect of a series of interviews until we both had a number of drinks together. I recorded the incident afterwards in a journal:
>
>> I talked briefly again about the research but he wondered if I had seen Channel Four's *Queer as Folk* on Tuesday? It had made him horny and he wondered if it had made me horny? I said I thought it was daring. I'm embarrassed and my face has reddened. I again start to talk about the research but he interrupts to ask what my longest relationship was? Where did I go to school and what age was I when I had my first sexual encounter? I said it was one of those drunken things but this was in fact a lie, the first one that I told . . . I considered that he was trying to 'test' me with more and more sexually explicit conversation to gauge my reaction and I was determined to see it through to the end. He tells me that I'm a very open person, an honest man that he'd have no difficulty in talking with. If it was a test, I appear to have passed.
>>
>> (Ryan 2006: 155–6)

Sometimes, initial contacts may completely transform research plans. In his classic study, Liebow (1967) reports that on his first day he fell into conversation with some of the onlookers present at a scuffle between a policeman and a woman. This led into several hours of talk with a young man, which he subsequently wrote up. In retrospect he comments:

> I had not accomplished what I set out to do, but this was only the first day. And, anyway, when I wrote up this experience that evening, I felt that it presented a fairly good picture of this young man and that most of the material was to the point. Tomorrow, I decided, I would get back to my original plan – nothing had been lost. But tomorrow never came.
>
> (Liebow 1967: 238)

The 'original plan' that Liebow had was to do several small studies, 'each covering a strategic part of the world of the low-income male': a neighbourhood study, a labour union, and a bootleg joint, perhaps supplemented by some life histories and genealogies. In the event, however, in the first neighbourhood he tried,

> I went in so deep that I was completely submerged and any plan to do three or four separate studies, each with its own neat, clean boundaries, dropped forever out of sight. My initial excursions into the street – to poke around, get the feel of things, and to lay out the lines of any fieldwork – seldom carried me more than a block or two from the corner where I started. From the very first weeks, or even days, I found myself in the middle of things: the principal lines of my field work were laid out, almost without my being aware of it. For the next year or so, and intermittently thereafter, my base of operations was the corner carry-out across the street from my starting point.
>
> (Liebow 1967: 236–7)

On the second day of his fieldwork, Liebow returned to the scene of his first encounter. Again he fell into conversation, with three 'winos' in their forties, and a younger man 'who looked as if he had just stepped out of a slick magazine advertisement' (Liebow 1967: 238–9). This younger man was Tally Jackson, who subsequently acted as Liebow's sponsor and confidant, and on whose social circle the research came to be focused.

Now Liebow's study is an impressive and important contribution to urban ethnography, but there are danger signals in his account of the fieldwork. It may or may not have been a good idea to abandon his original intentions of conducting several small, related projects. Equally, it may not have been such a good idea to have, as it appears, surrendered himself so thoroughly to the chance meeting with Tally and its consequences. As Liebow himself remarks, 'the principal lines of my fieldwork, were laid out, *almost without my being aware of it*' (1967: 237; our emphasis). Here, rather than the research problem being transformed in response to opportunities arising in the course of the research, and the research design being modified accordingly, Liebow seems to have abandoned systematic research design altogether.

Nevertheless, Liebow's research illustrates the significance of informal 'sponsorship'. Tally vouchsafed for him, introduced him to a circle of friends and acquaintances, and so provided access to data. The most famous of such 'sponsors' in the field is undoubtedly 'Doc', who helped in Whyte's study of 'corner boys' (Whyte 1981). Whyte's methodological appendix is a classic description of the serendipitous development of a research design, and the influence of Doc was a major determinant in its evolution. Doc agreed to offer Whyte the protection of friendship, and coached him in appropriate conduct and demeanour.

Liebow's and Whyte's contacts with their sponsors were quite fortuitous. However, sponsorship of a similar kind may be gained through the mobilization of existing social networks, based on acquaintanceship, kinship, occupational membership, and so on. This is not always straightforward, however. Cassell (1988) reports the difficulties she had in negotiating access in a study of surgeons, and her reliance on personal and occupational networks:

> When I decided to study surgeons, I negotiated for the better part of a year with a representative of the Department of Surgery, at a hospital where my ex-husband was an attending physician, before the Chief of Surgery definitively refused to allow me access to his department.
>
> At the same time, after spending six months obtaining an interview with a representative of the American College of Surgeons, I flew to Chicago to ask for advice and possible sponsorship from this prestigious group. After a charming Southern surgeon, in his sixties, indulged in an hour of small talk, I broke in and asked if he thought my study was worth doing. Silence. 'Your husband is a doctor?' he finally inquired. When I assented, he said: 'Have you ever thought of . . . I mean, with your background, you'd be such an asset . . . has it ever occurred to you to become active in the Ladies Auxiliary of your husband's hospital?' This was the only advice I received.
>
> Eventually, at almost the last minute, when a reviewer for the agency that eventually funded my study asked for proof that I had access to surgeons, a friend of my ex-husband said that I could do research in the hospital where he was Chief of Surgery (and wrote a letter to that effect).
>
> (Cassell 1988: 94)

Hoffman (1980) also provides insight into the way in which personal networks can be used, while drawing attention once more to the relationship between problems of access and the quality of the data subsequently collected. Her research was concerned with a locally influential elite: members of boards of hospital directors in Quebec. In the first place she notes a general problem of access to such an elite:

> Introducing myself as a sociology graduate student, I had very limited success in getting by the gatekeepers of the executive world. Telephone follow-ups to letters sent requesting an interview repeatedly found Mr X 'tied up' or 'in conference'. When I did manage to get my foot in the door, interviews rarely exceeded a half hour, were continually interrupted by telephone calls (for 'important' conferences, secretaries are usually asked to take calls) and elicited only 'front work' (Goffman 1959), the public version of what hospital boards were all about.
>
> (Hoffman 1980: 46)

During one interview, however, Hoffman's informant discovered that he knew members of her family. This gave rise to a very different sort of interview, and more illuminating data:

> The rest of the interview was dramatically different than all my previous data. I was presented with a very different picture of the nature of board work. I learned, for example, how board members used to be recruited, how the executive committee kept control over the rest of the board, how business was conducted and of what it consisted, and many other aspects of the informal social organization of board work.
>
> (Hoffman 1980: 46–7)

Abandoning her original research design based on interviewing a representative sample from different institutions, Hoffman therefore started to select informants on the basis of social ties. She began with direct personal contacts, and then asked those acquaintances to refer her to other informants, and so on. This strategy, she concludes, produced 'more informative and insightful data'.

Hoffman graphically juxtaposes typical responses to illustrate the point:

Response to an Unknown Sociologist
Board Member A

Response to a Known Individual
Board Member B

Q. How do you feel in general about how the board has been organized?

I think the basic idea of participation is good. We need better communication with the various groups. And I think they probably have a lot to offer.	This whole business is unworkable. It's all very nice and well to have these people on the board, they might be able to tell us something here and there, or describe a situation, but you're not going to run a hospital on that!

Q. How is the new membership working out? Do they participate? Any problems?

... oh yes, Mr. X (orderly) participates. He asked something today, now what was it? Sometimes they lack skill and experience, but they catch on. There is no problem with them. We get along very well.

Mr. X (orderly) hasn't opened his mouth except for a sandwich. ... But what can he contribute? ... You could rely on the old type of board member ... you knew you could count on him to support you. You didn't have to check up all the time. But these new people, how do you know how they will react? Will they stick behind you? And there is the problem of confidentiality. Everything you say you know will be all over the hospital ten minutes after the meeting. You can't say the same things anymore. You have to be careful in case someone interprets you as being condescending or hoity-toity.

(Hoffman 1980: 48–9)

Hoffman tends to portray the issue of access here in terms of 'penetrating informants' fronts', and clearly contrasts the two varieties of data in terms of aiming for 'better' and more truthful accounts. This is important, but it can also be problematic: 'frankness' may be as much a social accomplishment as 'discretion', and we shall return to the problem of the authenticity of accounts later. But Hoffman's discussion dramatically focuses attention on the relationships between 'access', the fieldworker's perceived identity, and the data that can be gathered.

In this context it is perhaps worth acknowledging that sometimes the problems can be such that the attempt to gain access to a particular setting, or to a particular informant or group of informants, may fail completely. For example, Ryan reports from his study of Irish gay men how his attempt to engage with one informant failed both because the latter was suspicious about the sort of story the research would tell, and because of personal dislike on both sides (Ryan 2006: 157).

Gatekeepers

Cassell's and Hoffman's accounts take us towards those 'formal', 'private' settings where boundaries are clearly marked, are not easily penetrated, and may be policed by 'gatekeepers'. In formal organizations, for example, initial access negotiations may be focused on official permission that can legitimately be granted or withheld by key personnel. Although not necessarily the case, such gatekeepers are often the ethnographer's initial point of contact with such research settings.

It should be said, though, that identifying the relevant gatekeepers is not always straightforward. Indeed, the distinction between sponsors and gatekeepers is by no means clear-cut. Even in formal bureaucratic organizations it is not always obvious whose permission needs to be obtained, or whose good offices it might be advisable to secure. Much the same is true in studying local communities. In his study of violence in Northern Ireland, Knox (2001) recognized that his research 'required the imprimatur of paramilitaries, or, at the very least, making them aware that fieldwork of this nature was being undertaken and its purpose'. He comments that 'their "approval" was secured by contacts with key political representatives in both communities [republican and loyalist], ostensibly to "keep them informed" of our work, in reality it amounted to securing their unofficial endorsment' (Knox 2001: 212).

There are sometimes several possible routes by which access might be achieved, and some judgement needs to be made about the viability, advantages and disadvantages of each. Sanders (2006: 203) discusses the various means by which researchers concerned with prostitution have sought to overcome the 'problem of locating and contacting sellers, buyers and organizers, who are cleverly hidden in the urban landscape'. These range from making contact with those who have been imprisoned, gaining an 'assisted passage' via the police or specialist health and welfare services, or capitalizing on personal contacts.

Equally, there will sometimes be a need for negotiation with multiple gatekeepers, as Gouldner (1954) notes on the basis of his research at the Oscar Center gypsum plant. He recounts that the research team

> made a 'double-entry' into the plant, coming in almost simultaneously by way of the Company and the Union. But it soon became obvious that we had made a mistake, and that the problem had not been to make a double-entry, but a triple entry; for we had left out, and failed to make independent contact with a distinct group – the management of that particular plant. In a casual way, we had assumed that main office management also spoke for the local plant management and this, as a moment's reflection might have told us, was not the case. In consequence our relations with local management were never as good as they were with the workers or the main office management.
>
> (Gouldner 1954: 255–6)

Sampson (2004) reports a similar problem in her research aboard ship: 'my presence was not welcomed by the Captain (again despite full access being granted by the company) and this resulted in an extremely unpleasant and personally threatening experience that lasted for a period of 16 days isolated from the land' (Sampson 2004: 390).

Knowing who has the power to open up or block off access, or who consider themselves and are considered by others to have the authority to grant or refuse access, is, of course, an important aspect of sociological knowledge about the setting. However, this is not the catch-22 situation it might appear. For one thing, as we argued in Chapter 1, research never starts from scratch; it always relies on common-sense knowledge to one degree or another. We may already know sufficient about the setting to be able to judge what the most effective strategy is likely to be for gaining entry. If we do not, we may be able to 'case' the setting beforehand, for example by contacting people with knowledge of it or of other settings of a similar type. This will often solve the problem, though as Whitten (1970) found out in his research on black communities in Nova Scotia, there is no guarantee that the information provided is sound. He was told by local people that he should phone the councillor for the largest settlement, that to try to meet him without phoning would be rude. He did so, 'with disastrous results':

> I introduced myself as an anthropologist from the United States, interested in problems encountered by people in rural communities in different parts of the

Americas. Following procedures common in the United States and supported by educated Nova Scotians, I said that I was particularly interested in Negro communities kept somewhat outside of the larger social and economic system. I was told, politely, but firmly, that the people of the rural Dartmouth region had had enough of outsiders who insulted and hurt them under the guise of research, that the people of the region were as human as I, and that I might turn my attention to other communities in the province. I was asked why I chose 'Negroes' and when I explained that Negroes, more than others, had been excluded from full participation, I was again told that the people of rural Nova Scotia were all alike, and that the colored people were tired of being regarded as somehow different, because there were no differences.

(Whitten 1970: 371)

Whitten discovered that he had made two basic mistakes:

First, when Nova Scotians tell one to first call the official responsible for a community, they are paying due respect to the official, but they do not expect the investigator to take this advice. They expect that the investigator will establish an enduring contact with someone who can introduce him to the official. Crucial to this procedure is that the investigator be first known to the person who will make the introduction, for the middleman may be held responsible for the investigator's mistakes. . . . Second, it is not expected that one will use the term 'Negro' in referring to Nova Scotians ethnically identified as colored. The use of ethnic terminology (including the term 'colored') is reserved for those who are already a part of the system. . . .

The most effective way to approach an official, we found, is to cognize no ethnic distinctions whatsoever, thereby forcing the official to make the preliminary distinction (e.g. between colored community and white community). By so doing the investigator is in a position to immediately inquire as to the significance of ethnicity. Had we acted a bit more slowly, and ignored ethnic differences, we might have succeeded in gaining early entrée, but we erred by assuming that we knew the best way to do things in Anglo-America. By talking too much, and not reflecting carefully on the possible connotations attached to our 'instructions', our work bogged down for a time.

(Whitten 1970: 371–2)

Whether or not they grant entry to the setting, gatekeepers will generally, and understandably, be concerned as to the picture of the organization or community that the ethnographer will paint, and they will usually have practical interests in seeing themselves and their colleagues presented in a favourable light. At least, they will wish to safeguard what they perceive as their legitimate interests. Gatekeepers may therefore attempt to exercise some degree of surveillance and control, either by blocking off certain lines of inquiry, or by shepherding the fieldworker in one direction or another.

Bogdan and Taylor (1975) provide an example of one way in which gatekeepers may try to influence things:

We know one novice who contacted a detention home in order to set up a time to begin his observation. The supervisor with whom he spoke told him that he wouldn't be interested in visiting the home that day or the next because the boys would just be making Hallowe'en decorations. He then suggested which times of the day would be best for the observer to 'see something going on'. The observer allowed himself to be forced to choose from a limited number of alternatives when he should have made it clear that he was interested in a variety of activities and times.

(Bogdan and Taylor 1975: 44–5)

Although Bogdan and Taylor report this as happening to a novice, it often remains a problem for even the most experienced fieldworker. In this instance, the ethnographer needs to explain that he or she is willing or even eager to sample the mundane, the routine, or perhaps the boring aspects of everyday life. But, nevertheless, the source of the problem is that it is often precisely the most sensitive things that are of most prima facie interest. Periods of change and transition, for example, may be perceived as troublesome by the participants themselves, and they may wish, therefore, to steer observers away from them: the conflict of interest arises from the fact that such disruptions can be particularly fruitful research opportunities for the fieldworker.

The issue of 'sensitive' periods is something that Ball (1980) explicitly remarks on in the context of a discussion of initial encounters in school classrooms. He notes that researchers have tended to devote attention to classrooms where patterns of interaction are already well established. Hence there is a tendency to portray classroom life in terms of fixed, static models. The pictures of classroom interaction with which we are familiar, Ball argues, may be artefacts of the preferred research strategy. He goes on to note:

The problem is that most researchers, with limited time and money available to them, are forced to organise their classroom observations into short periods of time. This usually involves moving into already established classroom situations where teachers and pupils have considerably greater experience of their interactional encounters than does the observer. Even where the researcher is available to monitor the initial encounters between a teacher and pupils, the teacher is, not unreasonably, reluctant to be observed at this stage.

But the reasons for the teacher's reluctance are exactly the reasons why the researcher should be there. These earlier encounters are of crucial significance not only for understanding what comes later but in actually providing for what comes later.

(Ball 1980: 143–4)

Here, then, Ball neatly draws attention to a particular problem of access, and shows how this is not simply a practical matter of organizing the fieldwork (though it is that too), but also bears on issues of descriptive accuracy and analytical adequacy.

What is required of the researcher by gatekeepers in order to grant access may not be simply a matter of their judgement and power but may be covered by institutional regulations and even the law; though, of course, these regulations and laws are also resources that gatekeepers can use for their own, and for institutional, purposes. For example, it is common today, in some countries, that research in schools, especially that focusing on the students, requires parents' consent for their children to be included in the study. Thus, it is necessary to send home consent forms with the students and (as far as is possible) to restrict the focus of inquiry to those students whose parents have agreed. One problem here is that the return rates of such forms are not usually high: and this is not always because parents are unwilling to give consent but rather that the forms get forgotten or lost. In her study of a large English urban comprehensive school, Hudson (2004) adopted an effective (if not entirely politically correct) strategy in dealing with this problem: she set up a raffle with a prize of McDonald's vouchers into which all students who brought back their forms (whether with consent agreed or refused) would be entered (Hudson 2004: 267).

To deceive or not to deceive?

Sometimes, of course, it may be judged that the relevant gatekeepers will almost certainly block entry altogether. Here, resort may be made to secret research.[4] This was the case, for example, with Calvey's (2000) research on 'bouncers'. He judged that entry would almost certainly be barred or that his relations with bouncers would be undermined if his research identity were known; though his choice of a covert strategy was also informed by an ethnomethodologically-inspired concern with minimizing reactivity and gaining access to the spontaneous lived experience of the people he was studying (Calvey 2000: 46–7). A very similar justification was offered by Graham for her covert study of a Japanese car factory in the United States (Graham 1995).

Covert research does not always involve an outsider entering the field by 'passing' or by formally taking on a job there. It may also be carried out by those who are already participants in the relevant context. A case in point is Holdaway's (1982) study of the police. As a serving officer who was seconded to university to read sociology and returned to the force wishing to do research on it, he reports that he was faced with six options:

A. Seek the permission of the chief officer to research, giving full details of method and intention.
B. Seek permission as above, so phrasing the research description that it disguised my real intentions.
C. Seek permission of lower ranks, later requesting more formal acceptance from senior officers.
D. Do no research.
E. Resign from the police service.
F. Carry out covert research.

I chose the final option without much difficulty. From the available evidence, it seemed the only realistic option; alternatives were unrealistic or contained an element of the unethical which bore similarity to covert observation. I believe that my senior officers would have either refused permission to research or obstructed me. Option B is as dishonest a strategy as covert research, if the latter is thought dishonest. For example, if I were a Marxist and wanted to research the police and declared my Marxism, I know that I would be denied research access; yet to 'front' myself in a different research guise is surely dishonest. Option C could not have been managed. D denies the relevance of my studies, and Option E would have been its logical progression – yet I felt an obligation to return to the police who had financed my [university studies].

(Holdaway 1982: 63)

4 We discuss the ethical issues surrounding covert research in Chapter 10.

Holdaway knew the setting he wanted to research, and the gatekeepers who would have had to be approached to get permission, very well indeed. Often, however, judgements to the effect that access to a setting is impossible are less well founded. There are some settings to which one might expect entry to be blocked but that have nevertheless been shown to be accessible, at least to some degree. For example, Fielding (1982) approached an extreme right-wing political organization in the United Kingdom, the National Front, for permission to carry out research on their organization, and received it; though he felt it necessary to supplement official access with some covert observation. Some years later, Back (2004) discovered that, despite his own associations with anti-racist work, it was possible to gain an interview with the leader of a similar organization, the British National Party.

Indeed, there is often a considerable amount of uncertainty and variation in the scope for negotiating access. Shaffir (1985) was told that the Tasher Hassidic community he was interested in studying would not agree to be researched. He was advised to get a job in the community and do covert research, which he did:

> Since I suspected that members of the community would not sanction my sociological investigation, I did not inform the Tasher that I was collecting data about them. (Neither did I tell them about my connection with the Lubavitcher, a community they disapproved of because of the involvement of its members with non-Orthodox Jews.) I did, however, tell those who were interested that I was a sociology student at McGill University. Invariably, I was asked to explain the meaning of 'sociology', a term that was entirely foreign to the Tasher.
>
> But I was able to define it sufficiently to use my interest in sociology to add legitimacy to the kinds of questions I regularly asked about the organization of the community. . . . Some people were surprised at my curiosity about topics unconnected with my clerical duties. However, others seemed convinced by my explanations and volunteered information about themselves which they believed might interest an outsider. But several members looked at me so oddly that I felt they considered me an intruder and were (quite rightly!) suspicious of my presence.
>
> (Shaffir 1985: 126)

Shaffir found his covert role a severe constraint on his research, and experienced great difficulty in combining a full-time clerical job with his research. He decided to reduce his hours of work, explaining this to his Tasher employers on the grounds that:

> my commitments at the university required me to conduct research and to write a thesis. That thesis, I explained, would probably be about pool halls. 'Pool hall, what is that?', asked the rabbi in Yiddish. The other man, who had graduated from university before becoming a Tasher Hassid, gave his version of a pool hall, 'It's a place where you play with balls on a table', and turning to me, he asked: 'How can I describe a pool hall to him? He's never been'. Then he elaborated: 'It's a dirty place that attracts the criminal element. It's suitable for Gentiles, not for Jews.'
>
> They both quickly agreed that I ought to be discouraged from pursuing that research and suddenly the rabbi said, 'Look, you know us. Why don't you write about us and we could help you . . . I'm telling you, you'll win a prize. I'll help you and so will the others and you'll win an award. . . . When do you want to

start? Let's set a time.' The other man seemed to be of the same opinion. Stunned, I managed to say calmly that I would consider the suggestion and meet them the next day to pursue it further.

Of course, I intended to tell them that I would do as they advised. By the following afternoon, however, both men had changed their mind. . . . That was the end of my first attempt at fieldwork among the Tasher.

I was to be more successful a few years later in the same Tasher community. There were new administrators in charge of the community's day-to-day affairs who were quite receptive to my request to visit and chat about matters of community life that interested me. I candidly explained my research interests to them . . . . The chief administrator appeared to adopt a 'We have nothing to hide' attitude.

(Shaffir 1985: 128–9)

Rather surprisingly, perhaps, Chambliss (1975) recounts a more straightforward process of gaining access to the world of organized crime, but once again one relying on an initial covert approach:

I went to the skid row, Japanese, Filipino, and Black sections of Seattle dressed in truck driver's clothes. . . . Sitting in the bar of a café one day I noticed several people going through a back door. I asked the waitress, Millie – a slight, fortyish ex-prostitute and sometime-drug-user with whom I had become friends – where these people were going:

> MILLIE: To play cards.
> ME: Back there?
> MILLIE: Yes, that's where the poker games are.
> ME: Can I play?
> MILLIE: Sure. Just go in. But watch your wallet.

So I went, hesitantly, through the back door and into a large room which had seven octagonal, green felt covered tables. People were playing five-card stud at five of the tables. I was immediately offered a seat by a hand gesture from the cardroom manager. I played, all the time watching my wallet as I had been advised.

I went back every day for the next week. . . . In conversation with the cardroom manager and other players I came to realize (discover?) what any taxicab driver already knew: that pornography, gambling, prostitution, and drugs were available on practically every street corner. So I began going to other cafés, card-rooms, and bars. I played in many games and developed a lot of information just from casual conversation.

Within a week I was convinced that the rackets were highly organized. The problem became one of discovering how, and by whom. I was sitting talking to Millie on the 30th of the month when a man I recognized as a policeman came through the door and went into the manager's office. I asked Millie what he was doing:

> MILLIE: He's the bag man.
> ME: The what?
> MILLIE: The bag man. He collects the payoff for the people downstairs
> ME: Oh.

I spent the next two months talking informally to people I met at different games, in pornography shops, or on the streets. I soon began to feel that I was at a dead end . . . I had discovered the broad outlines of organized crime in Seattle, but how it worked at the higher level was still a mystery. I decided it was time to 'blow my cover'.

I asked the manager of the cardroom I played in most to go to lunch with me. I took him to the faculty club at the University of Washington. This time when he saw me I was shaven and wore a shirt and tie. I told him of my 'purely scientific' interests and experience and, as best I could, why I had deceived him earlier. He agreed to help. Soon I began receiving phone calls: 'I understand you are interested in Seattle. Did you ever think to check Charles Carroll's brother in law?' And there was one honest-to-God clandestine meeting in a deserted warehouse down at the wharf.

Over the next ten years I pursued this inquiry, widening my contacts and participating in an ever larger variety of rackets. As my interest in these subjects and my reliability as someone who could be trusted spread, I received more offers to 'talk' than I had time to pursue.

(Chambliss 1975: 36–8)

The work of Calvey, Graham, Holdaway, Fielding, Shaffir, and Chambliss raises the question of deception in negotiations over access. Where the research is secret to all those under study, and to gatekeepers too, the practical problem of access may be 'solved' at a stroke, providing the deception is not discovered. Nor need the covert researcher be restricted to a single role, and adopting more than one may improve the quality of the data. In the initial stages of her research on shop work, Pettinger (2004) took a job as a part-time store assistant, which enabled her to discover something of what went on behind the scenes, even while she realized that it was not providing the full story. To complement these data, she subsequently engaged in covert observation as a shopper. This

entailed visiting stores on a regular basis and looking at how many people were working, their gender, ethnic backgrounds, class and age, the tasks being done and by whom. I did not only observe, I also tried to manipulate events. I 'tested' customer service provision by demanding customer services, as any other shopper might, seeing how stores had different norms and regulations.

(Pettinger 2005: 356)

She comments that whereas 'taking the role of the worker involved a continual need to be active in order to avoid the condemnation of colleagues and customers',

as a shopper, I had the cultural freedom to be a 'flaneur', an activity that intrinsically involves looking. Thus, the social role of the customer provided a different form and style of data gathering that could add new layers of meaning.

(Pettinger 2005: 356)

Even when 'cover' is successfully maintained, the researcher engaging in covert research has to live with the moral qualms, anxieties, and practical difficulties to which the use of this strategy may lead. However, research carried out without the knowledge of anyone in, or associated with, the setting is quite rare. Much more common is that some people are kept in the dark while others are taken into the researcher's confidence, at least partly. Thus, for example, in studying 'the role of faculty senates in shared governance', Labaree sought to protect his 'insiderness' by operating in a covert way, but found it necessary to share the information that he was researching the situation with some senate colleagues (Labaree 2002: 98).

What is at issue here, though, is not just whether permission to carry out the research is requested, and from whom, but also what those concerned are told about it. Some commentators recommend that an explicit research bargain, spelling out in full the purposes of the research and the procedures to be employed, be made with all those involved, right from the start. This is often seen as essential to the requirement of 'informed consent'. Often, though, in ethnographic work, this is neither possible nor desirable. As a result of the way in which research problems may change over the course of fieldwork, the demands likely to be made on people in the setting and the policy implications and political consequences of the research are often a matter for little more than speculation at the outset. There is also the danger that the information provided will influence the behaviour of the people under study in such a way as to invalidate the findings. While often it may be judged that the chances of this are small, given the other pressures operating on these people, there are instances where it may be critical. Had Festinger *et al.* (1956) informed the apocalyptic religious group they were studying not only that the research was taking place but also about the hypothesis under investigation, this would almost certainly have undermined the validity of their research.

The other argument for not always trying to provide a 'full' account of one's purposes to gatekeepers and others at the beginning of the research is that, unless one can build up a trusting relationship with them relatively rapidly, they may refuse access in a way that they would not do later on in the fieldwork. Wolf's study of bikers, in which he spent three years hanging out with them before he raised the question of doing research, is an extreme but instructive example (Wolf 1991). Once people come to know the researcher as a person who can be trusted to be discreet in handling information within the setting, and who will honour his or her promises of anonymity in publications, access may be granted that earlier would have been refused point blank. On this argument it is sometimes advisable not to request at the outset the full access to data one may eventually require but to leave negotiation of what seem to be the more delicate forms of access until field relationships have been established – though we should perhaps reiterate that assumptions about what is and is not delicate may not always prove reliable.

Nevertheless, while telling the 'whole truth' in negotiating entry for research, as in most other social situations, may not always be a wise or even a feasible strategy, deception should be avoided wherever possible; not just for ethical reasons but also because it can rebound badly later on in the fieldwork. Indeed, sometimes it may be necessary to insist that gatekeepers or sponsors recognize possible consequences of the research to avoid problems subsequently, as Geer notes from her research on American colleges:

> In colleges of high prestige, the researcher may be hampered in his negotiations because the administrators cannot imagine that anything harmful to the college could be discovered. In this case, it is up to the researcher to explain the kinds of

things that often turn up. . . . The administrator can sometimes be drawn into a scientific partnership. By treating him as a broadminded and sophisticated academic, one gradually works him around to a realization that although the study may be threatening, he and his college are big enough to take it. It may seem unnecessary to prepare administrators for the worst in this fashion, but it prepares the ground for the shock they may get when they see the manuscript at the end of a study. Administrators may attempt to prevent publication or feel that the college has been exploited and similar research should not be authorized. However, the administrator who has committed himself to a generous research bargain is more likely to be proud of the results.

(Geer 1970: 83)

Negotiating access is a balancing act, then. Gains and losses now and later, as well as ethical and strategic considerations, must be traded off against one another in whatever manner is judged at the time to be most appropriate, given the purposes of the research and the circumstances in which it is to be carried out. Moreover, changes in judgement about what is best may need to be made as the research progresses.

Obstructive and facilitative relationships

Seeking the permission of gatekeepers or the support of sponsors is often an unavoidable first step in gaining access to the data. Furthermore, the relationships established with such people can have important consequences for the subsequent course of the research. Berreman (1962), discussing his research on a Pahari village in the Himalayas, reports:

We were introduced [to the villagers] by a note from a nonPahari wholesaler of the nearest market town who had long bought the surplus agricultural produce of villagers and had, as it turned out, through sharp practices of an obscure nature, acquired land in the village. He asked that the villagers treat the strangers as 'our people' and extend all hospitality to them. As might have been expected, our benefactor was not beloved in the village and it was more in spite of his intercession than on account of it that we ultimately managed to do a year's research in the village.

(Berreman 1962: 6)

Equally, though, one can be fortunate in one's associations with gatekeepers:

The impression I received of people's attitudes to me was that they were very curious and very friendly. As I walked along country paths I was constantly being bothered by inquisitive peasants who had no inhibitions in talking about their problems, especially in relation to the land. It took at least an hour to cross from one side of the village to the other due to the constant need to stop and converse. This contrasts markedly to reports I had received from anthropologists who have worked in Quechua speaking areas of Peru and have found people dour and uncommunicative. I believe one reason for this is that my introductions into the area were exceptionally good. On the one hand, my official introductions through the Ministry of Agriculture had come through the one official who was not distrusted.

He was referred to as 'a good person, he didn't try to cheat us like the other officials'. On the other hand, I had introductions through, and for a time lived in the same building as, members of the progressive Catholic Church. They also happened to be Europeans. Their identification with the peasants, and people's identification of me with them, was extremely valuable.

(Rainbird 1990: 89)

However, even the most friendly and cooperative of gatekeepers or sponsors will shape the conduct and development of the research. To one degree or another, the ethnographer will be channelled in line with existing networks of friendship and enmity, territory and equivalent 'boundaries'. Having been 'taken up' by a sponsor, the ethnographer may find it difficult to achieve independence from such a person, discovering that his or her research is bounded by the social horizon of a sponsoring group or individual. Such social and personal commitments can, like gatekeepers' blocking tactics, close off certain avenues of inquiry. The fieldworker may well find him- or herself involved in varieties of 'patron–client' relationship with sponsors, and in so doing discover influence exerted in quite unforeseen ways. The ambiguities and contingencies of sponsorship and patronage are aptly illustrated by two similar studies from rural Spain (Barrett 1974; Hansen 1977).

Barrett (1974) reports that the members of his chosen village, Benabarre, were initially reserved. This was partially breached when a village baker started to take Barrett round and introduce him to others. However, the big breakthrough came when the village was visited by a Barcelona professor who was descended from a Benabarre family. The professor was interested in Barrett's work and spent a good deal of time with him:

Nothing could have had a more beneficial effect on my relations with the community. Don Tomás enjoys immense respect and popularity among the villagers, and the fact that he found my work significant was a behavioural cue to a great many people. The reasoning was apparently that if I were someone to beware of, Don Tomás would not be fooled; if he believed I was the genuine article, then I must be! The response was immediate. Doors which until then had been closed to me opened up; new people greeted me on the streets and volunteered their services.

(Barrett 1974: 7)

Barrett realized that this was not simply a lucky breakthrough; it was also an important clue to social relationships in the village. Hierarchical relationships were of fundamental importance. Initially, Barrett had avoided close association with the 'upper crust' families:

I thought that if there were polarization between the social strata this might make it more difficult later to win acceptance among the peasants. It was virtually the opposite! The fact that I was not associating with those who were considered my peers was simply confusing, and made it vastly more difficult to place me in the social order. Once Don Tomás extended his friendship, and introduced me to other families of similar social rank, this served almost as a certificate of respectability.

(Barrett 1974: 8)

Hansen's (1977) experiences in rural Catalonia are equally revealing about the hierarchical assumptions of village life:

> Initially, the interviewing process went very slowly because I was overly polite and solicitous about seeking interviews with people I hardly knew. I made the error of being too formal, which made these people suspicious of me. My mistake was brought home to me forcefully by one of the few nobles remaining in the Alto Panadés, whom I had interviewed by chance. He explained in no uncertain terms that I was behaving like a servant or client to these individuals when my own wealth, looks and education meant that I was superior to them. He proceeded to accompany me to more than twenty bourgeois landholders, and ordered them to give me what I wanted, on the spot, including details of business scandals, etc. All complied, some with obeisance towards the Count, and all with both deference and expansiveness toward me. The Count checked all their answers to see if they were concealing vital information. Astonished and embarrassed as I was, the Count had a point. After these twenty interviews, I was swamped by volunteers. It had suddenly become fashionable to be interviewed by *el distinguido antropólogo norteamericano*.
>
> (Hansen 1977: 163–4)

Gatekeepers, sponsors, and the like (indeed, most of the people who act as hosts to the research) will operate in terms of expectations about the ethnographer's identity and intentions. As the examples of Hansen and Barrett make clear, these can have serious implications for the amount and nature of the data collected. Many hosts have highly inaccurate, and lurid, expectations of the research enterprise, especially of ethnographic work. Two closely related models of the researcher tend to predominate in this context, 'the expert' and 'the critic'. Both images can conspire to make gatekeepers and sponsors uneasy as to the likely consequences of the research, and the effects of its conduct.

The model of the 'expert' often seems to suggest that the social researcher is, or should be, a person who is extremely well informed as to 'problems' and their 'solutions'. The expectation may be set up that the ethnographer seeking access is claiming such expertise, and is expecting to 'sort out' the organization or community. This view therefore leads directly to the second image, that of the 'critic'. Gatekeepers may expect the ethnographer to try to act as an evaluator.[5]

Under some circumstances, these expectations may have favourable connotations. Evaluation by experts, leading to improvements in efficiency, interpersonal relations, planning, and so on, may have at least the overt support of those at the top (though not necessarily of those in subordinate positions). On the other hand, the expectation of expert critical surveillance may create anxieties, on the part of gatekeepers and others. Even if permission for the research is not withheld altogether, gatekeepers may, as we have suggested, attempt to guide the research in directions they prefer, or away from potentially sensitive areas.

---

5 Sometimes, of course, the ethnographer may be officially engaged in evaluation: see Fetterman (1984); Fetterman and Pittman (1986); Shaw (1999); McKie (2002). However, even in this situation, it may still be advisable to try to distance oneself from the roles of both expert and critic.

At the same time, it may be very difficult for the ethnographer to establish credibility if hosts expect some sort of 'expertise'. Such expectations may clash with the fieldworker's actual or cultivated ignorance and incompetence. Smigel (1958), for example, has commented on the propensity of lawyers to try to 'brush off' researchers who appear to be legally ill-informed, a point confirmed to some extent by Mungham and Thomas (1981). Ethnographers are sometimes conspicuous for an apparent lack of activity as well. This, too, can militate against being treated seriously by their hosts.

From a variety of contexts researchers report hosts' suspicions and expectations as often proving barriers to access. Such suspicions may be fuelled by the very activities of the fieldworker. Barrett (1974), for instance, remarks on how the inhabitants of his Spanish village interpreted his actions. He was not sensitive to the possibility that villagers might be frightened by someone making notes, when they did not know what was being written down. Rumours about him included beliefs that he was a communist spy, a CIA agent, a Protestant missionary or a government tax agent. Relatedly, in her fieldwork in Brazil in the late 1930s, Landes (1986) was accused of seeking 'vigorous' men to do more than carry her luggage. She was labelled a prostitute during her research because she inadvertently broke the local rules about the proper behaviour of a woman (Landes 1986: 137). As might be expected, this created problems for her research and for her personal relationships in the field. Scourfield and Coffey (2006) report a similar experience in which a male researcher was negotiating access to a UK local authority social services department: questions were raised as to whether he might be a paedophile wanting to make contact with others of a similar persuasion. Suspicions may also sometimes arise as a result of events in the society being studied. Owens (2003) reports how a political crisis in Zanzibar led to him being identified as a spy and ordered out of the country without warning.

Equally, though, it is possible to misread the responses of gatekeepers and participants as more negative than they are. In the case of his research on Hasidic Jews, Shaffir comments:

> My suspicion that I was not fully welcomed resulted from a basic misinterpretation: I mistook an indifferent reaction for a negative one. As much as I wished for people to be curious and enthusiastic about my research, the majority could not have cared less. My research did not affect them, and they had more important matters to which to attend.

> (Shaffir 1991: 76)

Such indifference is not uncommon, nor is a tendency towards paranoia on the part of the ethnographer.

As we noted early on in this chapter, the problem of access is not resolved once one has gained entry to a setting, since this by no means guarantees access to all the relevant data available within it. Not all parts of the setting will be equally open to observation, and not everyone may be willing to talk. Moreover, even the most willing informant will not be prepared, or perhaps even able, to divulge all the information available to him or her. If the data required are to be obtained, negotiation of access is therefore likely to be a recurrent preoccupation for the ethnographer. Negotiation here takes two different but by no means unrelated forms. On the one hand, explicit discussion with those whose activities one wishes to study may take place, much along the lines of that with sponsors and gatekeepers. But the term 'negotiation' also refers to the much more wide-ranging and subtle process of manoeuvring oneself into a position from which the necessary data can be collected. Patience and diplomacy are often at a premium here, though sometimes boldness is also required. The ethnographer's negotiation of a role in the setting, and the implications of different roles for the nature of the data collected, will be examined in the next chapter.

4   Field relations

Ethnographic research can take place, and has taken place, in a wide variety of types of setting: villages, towns, inner-city neighbourhoods, factory shop floors, deep-shaft mines, ships, farms, retail stores, business offices of various kinds, hospital wards, operating theatres, prisons, public bars, churches, schools, colleges, universities, welfare agencies, courts, morgues, funeral parlours, etc. These settings vary from one another in all manner of respects that are relevant to the nature of the relationships that are possible and desirable with the people who live and/or work in them. Furthermore, there is much variation within each category of setting. Generalizations about field relations are therefore always subject to multiple exceptions. No set of rules can be devised which will produce good field relations. All that can be offered is discussion of some of the main methodological and practical considerations surrounding ethnographers' relations in the field.

Initial responses

Where the research is overt, as with gatekeepers and sponsors, people in the field will seek to place or locate the ethnographer within the social landscape defined by their experience. Some individuals and groups have little or no knowledge of social research; and, as we saw in the previous chapter, field researchers are frequently suspected, initially at least, of being spies, tax inspectors, missionaries, or of belonging to some other group that may be perceived as undesirable. Thus, Kaplan reports that the New England fishermen she studied initially believed her to be either a government official or an insurance investigator (Kaplan 1991: 233).

Generally, such suspicions quickly dissipate as contact increases; but this is not always the case. And, sometimes, given the nature of the research, it may be difficult to distance oneself from such labels. Hunt (1984: 288) reports that the police officers she studied suspected that she was an undercover agent for the Internal Affairs Bureau or the Federal Bureau of Investigation (FBI), a suspicion encouraged by officials in the police department in which she was working. But, over and above this, she was, and was known to be, a consultant hired by the city to evaluate the police, a role that could easily be seen as spying by those subject to the evaluation. Despite this, Hunt (1984) was able to build trust among the police officers she studied by proving herself reliable in emergencies on the street, and by explicitly criticizing the higher echelons of the police department.

By contrast, Den Hollander (1967) provides an example of an apparently more favourable initial identification that nevertheless proved to be an insurmountable obstacle to his research:

> In a town in southern Georgia (1932) it was rumoured after a few days that I was a scout for a rayon concern and might help to get a rayon industry established in the town. My denial reinforced the rumour, everyone tried to convince me of the excellent qualities of the town and its population – the observer had turned into a fairy godmother and serious work was no longer possible. Departure was the only solution.
>
> (Den Hollander 1967: 13)

Even where people in a setting are familiar with social research, there may be a serious mismatch between their expectations of the researcher and his or her intentions. Like gatekeepers, they too may view the researcher as expert or critic; and, here again, a balancing act may need to be achieved between these roles and that of someone who is unacceptably ignorant or naive. Thus, Atkinson 'found it necessary to manage . . . contrasting impressions of expertise and ignorance' (Atkinson 1997: 65) during the course of his fieldwork in a medical school. The students tended to assume his ignorance, but there were also some who came to recognize that he had picked up quite a bit of medical knowledge in the course of the research and resented 'my ability to gain some passing acquaintance with their subject, without the background training in the basic and medical sciences' (1997: 62).

Occasionally, participants may be, or consider themselves to be, very sophisticated in their knowledge of research methodology; and/or they may have a negative attitude towards research. Anderson, for example, found that his whole way of investigating environmental activism was challenged by those he studied, leading him radically to restructure his approach (Anderson 2002).

This problem of resistance may be especially acute, of course, where the people being studied are academics, or even sociologists, themselves (Platt 1981). Scott (1984) provides an example from research on the experience of postgraduate students in British universities. Along with her co-researcher, she was asked to present a paper at a graduate seminar in a sociology department in which they had conducted interviews:

> Almost before we had finished speaking the professor leapt to his feet and began a diatribe, during which he evinced not simply disagreement with our presentation and methodology, but anger. He took us to task for writing an article in the British Sociological Association's magazine Network, because this 'made our research worthless' since we had published before completing the research . . . . We felt that we had been set up as an example of the 'dangers' of ethnographic research so that this professor could play the big man and knock us down in front of his graduate students. We found out later that the professor had been one of those most vociferous in preference for a large-scale survey when our project had first been mooted.
>
> (Scott 1984: 175)

Resistance, or at least reluctance to participate, may also arise because of fears of retaliation by others. Baez (2002) reports how, in his study of minority ethnic group staff in a private US university, one tenured African-American professor within the sociology department refused to allow his interview to be audio-recorded, 'suggesting that to do so would place him at risk of retaliation from his colleagues' (Baez 2002: 39).

Outside academia there may be less knowledge but equal or greater hostility. The comment of a constable in the Royal Ulster Constabulary (RUC), cited by Brewer (1991: 16), provides an example: 'If anything gets me down it's bloody sociology. I think it's the biggest load of shite, simple as that.' Brewer notes that for many police officers the word 'sociologist' sounds too much like 'socialist'. But this is not the only source of problems; he quotes a senior police officer:

> I think most policemen can't relate to sociology at all, because, you see, the way we're taught everything is black and white: those who do bad should be punished, those who do good should be rewarded. Sociology just seems to turn all that on its head. It would seem to say that all those who are right and honest are wrong. Just to say a man doesn't earn as much money as me and he has to steal to keep his family, well, sociology says that's OK. Another thing, sociology would seem to be saying that those who have wealth and do well do so at the expense of the poor unfortunate.

Where such attitudes prevail, people may challenge the legitimacy of the research and the credentials of the researcher, as Brewer's colleague Kathleen Magee found in their research on the RUC:

> PC 1. Look, just hold on a wee minute. What gives you the right to come here and start asking us these personal questions about our families and that? . . . You're not going to learn anything about the police while you're here. They're not going to tell you anything. . . . And you know why? Because you're always walking around with that bloody notebook writing everything down, and you're not getting anywhere near the truth. . . . Like, what use is this research you're doing anyway? Is it going to do me or my mates any good? What you doing it for? 'Cos let me tell you, the only people who are going to be interested in your bloody research are the authorities.

This verbal assault continued for some time, but it ended on a less hostile note:

> PC 1. . . . Maybe the police has made me this way, but do you not see that if you're going to come in here asking me questions about my family, if you're going to want to know all these things, I've got to be able to trust you? Like, after this tonight, I'd let you come out in a vehicle with me.

(Brewer 1991: 21–2)

As this example shows, whether or not people have knowledge of social research, and whatever attitude they take towards it, they will often be more concerned with what kind of person the researcher is than with the research itself. They will try to gauge how far the ethnographer can be trusted, what he or she might be able to offer as an acquaintance or friend, and perhaps also how easily he or she could be manipulated or exploited.[1] The management of 'personal front' (Goffman 1955) is important here. As in other situations where identities have to be created or established, much thought must be given by the ethnographer to 'impression management'. Impressions that pose an obstacle to access must be avoided or countered as far as possible, while those which facilitate it must be encouraged, within the limits set by ethical considerations.

1 For a striking analysis of this process, see Edgerton (1965).

Impression management

Personal appearance can be a salient consideration. Sometimes it may be necessary for the researcher to dress in a way that is very similar to the people to be studied. This is most obviously true in the case of covert research, where the fieldworker will be much more sharply constrained to match his or her personal front to that of the other participants. Patrick's (1973) research on a Glasgow gang reveals what 'passing' in this way can involve:

> Clothes were another major difficulty. I was already aware of the importance attached to them by gang members . . . and so, after discussion with Tim, I bought [a midnight-blue suit, with a twelve-inch middle vent, three-inch flaps over the side pockets and a light blue handkerchief with a white polka dot (to match my tie) in the top pocket]. Even here I made two mistakes. Firstly, I bought the suit outright with cash instead of paying it up, thus attracting both attention to myself in the shop and disbelief in the gang when I innocently mentioned the fact. Secondly, during my first night out with the gang, I fastened the middle button of my jacket as I was accustomed to. Tim was quick to spot the mistake. The boys in the gang fastened only the top button – 'ra gallous wae'.
>
> (Patrick 1973: 15)

Much the same sort of attention to dress is often required in research that is destined to be overt, especially where an initial period of gaining trust is necessary. In the case of Wolf's (1991) research on 'outlaw bikers', it was important not only that he looked like a biker – shoulder-length hair and a heavy beard, leather jacket and studded leather wrist bands, a cut-off denim jacket with appropriate patches, etc. – but also that he had a 'hog', a bike, that would stand scrutiny by experts (Wolf 1991: 214).

Even where the research is overt, the researcher's appearance can be an important factor in shaping relationships with people in the field. Van Maanen (1991) reports that, having done participant observation as a student at the police academy, in studying the police on the street he:

> still carried a badge and a gun. These symbols of membership signified to others my public commitment to share the risks of the police life. Aside from a few special events, parades, and civic ceremonies where uniformed bodies were in short supply, I was, as the police said, out of the bag. I dressed for the street as I thought plainclothes officers might – heavy and hard-toed shoes, slit or clip-on ties, and loose-fitting jackets that would not make conspicuous the bulge of my revolver. I carried with me chemical Mace, handcuffs, assorted keys, extra bullets, and sometimes a two-way portable radio and a concealed two-inch revolver loaned to me by co-workers who felt that I should be properly prepared.
>
> (van Maanen 1991: 37–8)

He reports that his 'plainclothes but altogether coplike appearance' caused some confusion for citizens, who tended to assume he was a high-ranking police officer.

Similar considerations, but a rather different outfit, were involved in Henslin's (1990) research on homeless people. He sought to dress in a way that would allow him to 'blend in' with the inhabitants of the skid rows he visited. This was necessary both to facilitate rapport and to avoid marking himself out as a target for muggers. At the same time, he needed to look sufficiently like a researcher to have his announcement of that identity believed by people working in shelters for homeless people whom he wished to interview. He solved this problem by carrying an old briefcase that was cheap-looking and whose stitching had unravelled at one corner 'making it look as though I had just snatched it up out of the trash'. He reports:

> When I would announce to shelter personnel that I was a sociologist doing research on the homeless, they immediately would look me over – as the status I had announced set me apart from the faceless thousands who come trekking through the shelters – making this prop suddenly salient. To direct their attention and help them accept the announced identity, I noticed that at times I would raise the case somewhat, occasionally even obtrusively setting it on the check-in counter (while turning the side with the separating stitching more toward myself to conceal this otherwise desirable defect).
>
> (Henslin 1990: 56–8)

In her research on an elite girls' school in Edinburgh, Delamont (1984) recounts a similar concern with dressing in a way that enabled her to preserve relationships with multiple audiences:

> I had a special grey dress and coat for days when I expected to see the head and some pupils. The coat was knee-length and very conservative-looking, while the dress was mini-length, to show the pupils I knew what the fashion was. I would keep the coat on in the head's office, and take it off before I first met pupils.
>
> (Delamont 1984: 25)

While those engaged in overt research do not have to copy closely the dress and demeanour of the people they are researching, they may need to alter their appearance and habits a little in order to reduce any sharp differences. In this way they can make people more at ease in their presence; but this is not the only reason for such adjustments, as Liebow (1967) notes:

> I came close in dress (in warm weather, tee or sport shirt and khakis or other slacks) with almost no effort at all. My vocabulary and diction changed, but not radically. . . . Thus, while remaining conspicuous in speech and perhaps in dress, I had dulled some of the characteristics of my background. I probably made myself more acceptable to others, and certainly more acceptable to myself. This last point was forcefully brought home to me one evening when, on my way to a professional meeting, I stopped off at the carry-out [his research site] in a suit and tie. My loss of ease made me clearly aware that the change in dress, speech, and general carriage was as important for its effect on me as it was for its effect on others.
>
> (Liebow 1967: 255–6)

In some situations, however, it may be necessary to use dress to mark oneself off from particular categories to which one might otherwise be assigned. Thus, in her research in Nigeria, Sudarkasa (1986) found that in order to be able to get answers to her questions in settings where the people did not already know her, she had to avoid dressing like a Yoruba woman: 'People were suspicious of the woman with the notebook, the more so because she did not look like the American student she claimed to be.' They suspected she was a Yoruba collecting information for the government:

> I was so often 'accused' of being a Yoruba that when I went to a market in which I was not certain I would find a friend to identify me, I made a point of speaking only American-sounding English (for the benefit of the English speakers there) and of dressing 'like an American'. On my first trip to such a market, I even abandoned my sandals in favour of moderately high heels and put on make-up, including lipstick.
>
> (Sudarkasa 1986: 175)

In overt participant observation, then, where an explicit research role must be constructed, forms of dress, can 'give off' the message that the ethnographer seeks to maintain the position of an acceptable marginal member, perhaps in relation to several audiences. They may declare affinity between researcher and hosts, and/or they may distance the ethnographer from constraining identities.

There can be no clear prescription for dress other than to commend a high degree of awareness about self-presentation. A mistake over such a simple matter can jeopardize the entire enterprise. Having gained access to the Edinburgh Medical School, for instance, Atkinson (1976, 1981a) went to see one of the influential gatekeepers for an 'informal' chat about the actual fieldwork. He was dressed extremely casually (as well as having very long hair). He had absolutely no intention of going on to the hospital wards looking like this. But the gatekeeper was taken aback by his informal appearance, and started to get cold feet about the research altogether. It took a subsequent meeting, after a hair-cut and the donning of a lounge suit, to convince him otherwise.

At the same time, there may be personal limits for the researcher in how far the strategic use of dress and other aspects of identity can and should be manipulated in order to establish good field relations. While Blackwood (1995) hid her lesbianism from her Indonesian hosts, she did not feel able to conform completely to the expectations made about her as an unmarried, and presumably heterosexual, woman. She writes:

> where the dress code was at odds with my lesbian self . . . I developed the most resistance in reconstructing my identity. I could not force myself to wear skirts as any proper Indonesian woman does, except very occasionally. My host sometimes remarked on this lapse because it raised deeper questions for her about my womanhood.
>
> (Blackwood 1995: 58; quoted in Coffey 1999: 26–7)

To some extent we have already touched on more general aspects of self-presentation. Speech and demeanour will require monitoring, though as we have seen it is not necessarily desirable for them to be matched to those of participants. The researcher must judge what sort of impression he or she wishes to create, and manage appearances accordingly. Such impression management is unlikely to be a unitary affair, however. There may be different categories of participants, and different social contexts, which demand the construction of different 'selves'. In this, the ethnographer is no different in principle from social actors generally, whose social competence requires such sensitivity to shifting situations.

The construction of a working identity may be facilitated in some circumstances if the ethnographer can exploit relevant skills or knowledge he or she already possesses. Parker (1974) illustrates the use of social skills in the course of his work with a Liverpool gang. He wrote that:

> blending in was facilitated by certain basic skills. One of the most important involved being 'quick': although I was regarded as normally 'quiet' and socially marginal, this placidity is not always a good idea. Unless you are to be seen as something of a 'divvy' you must be able to look after yourself in the verbal quickfire of the Corner and the pub. . . . Being able to kick and head a football reasonably accurately was also an important aspect of fitting into the scheme. Again, whilst I was 'no Kevin Keegan' and indeed occasionally induced abuse like 'back to Rugby Special', I was able to blend into a scene where kicking a ball around took up several hours of the week. I also followed The Boys' football team closely each week and went to 'the match' with them when I could. This helped greatly. Indeed when everyone realized I supported Preston (as well as Liverpool, of course) it was always a good joke since they were so often getting beaten. 'Why don't you play for them they couldn't do any worse?'; 'Is there a blind school in Preston?' (Danny).
>
> (Parker 1974: 217–19)

With covert research, of course, having relevant kinds of knowledge and skill will often be essential to playing particular roles. Calvey's employment as a bouncer depended to a large extent on his having studied martial arts for many years, and his taking a course in 'door supervision' (Calvey 2000: 44). Holdaway's (1982) covert study of the police required not just that he was already formally a member of the police force, but also that he had the knowledge, skills and experience to carry out the job and to protect his research identity. Graham's (1995) experience in previous factory work was probably essential for her to survive 'on the line' at Subaru-Isuzu Automotive.

Expertise and knowledge may also be of value in the field as a basis for establishing reciprocity with participants. Thus, in some contexts, anthropologists often find themselves trading on their superior technical knowledge and resources. Medical knowledge and treatment constitute one form of this. The treatment of common disorders, usually by simple and readily available methods, has long been one way in which anthropologists in the field have succeeded in ingratiating themselves. This can create problems, of course, as McCurdy (1976) found out, with 'surgery time' capable of taking up the whole day. Nevertheless, this is one way in which the fieldworker can demonstrate that he or she is not an exploitative interloper, but has something to give. Legal advice, the writing of letters, and the giving of 'lifts', for example, can perform the same role. Moreover, sometimes providing such services can directly aid the research. In his study of 'survivalists', Mitchell (1991):

> offered to compose a group newsletter on my word processor and, in doing so, became the recipient of a steady stream of members' written opinions and perceptions. Being editor of 'The Survival Times', as the newsletter came to be known,

in turn, legitimated the use of tape recorders and cameras at group gatherings, [and] provided an entrée to survivalist groups elsewhere around the country.

(Mitchell 1991: 100)

Participants sometimes come to expect the provision of services, and it may be costly to disappoint them. While in his study of a political campaign organization Corsino often helped out stuffing envelopes, delivering materials, clipping newspapers, etc., on one occasion he refused to scrub floors and help prepare someone's home for a fund-raising reception, on the grounds that he could more usefully spend his time observing the organizational preparations for the event. He describes the result:

The reactions of the campaign manager and volunteer director were more antagonistic than I expected. Over the next several days, I noticed a polite but unmistakable cooling in my relationship with these officials ... I began to feel more and more like an ingrate. . . . This, in turn, resulted in a rather barren period of fieldwork observations. . . . At best, I had to become a passive observer.

(Corsino; quoted in Adler and Adler 1987: 18)

This is not to say that all the expectations of those in the field are legitimate or should be honoured. Sometimes the ethnographer will have to refuse requests and live with the consequences. Indeed, one must take care not to offer too much, to the detriment of the research. Furthermore, being helpful to participants will not always be appreciated, as O'Reilly (2005) found in her study of British expatriates on the Costa del Sol. She writes:

A group within which I was doing participant observation used to run informal coffee mornings. Anyone was welcome to come along . . . . I volunteered to help . . . and was given the task of making the coffees for the other volunteers before the doors were opened to the public. One morning was particularly busy and I stayed on after the doors were opened to help out serving to the customers. I stayed an extra two hours and was quite pleased with myself for having worked so hard and been so helpful. However, the supervisor came to me later in the week and asked me if, at the next coffee morning, could I please simply serve coffees to the staff and then leave. It turned out that I had almost caused a strike amongst the other volunteers whose positions were hard-won and jealously guarded.

(O'Reilly 2005: 96–7; see also O'Reilly 2000: 130)

The value of pure sociability should not be underestimated as a means of building trust. Indeed, the researcher must often try to find ways in which 'normal' social intercourse can be established. This requires finding some neutral ground with participants where mundane small talk can take place. It may be very threatening to hosts if one pumps them constantly about matters relating directly to research interests. Especially in the early days of field negotiations it may be advantageous to find more 'ordinary' topics of conversation, with a view to establishing one's identity as a 'normal', 'regular', 'decent' person.

Hudson (2004) reports how, in studying pupils' perspectives in a large secondary school, she 'sat in on lessons and had as many informal conversations as possible with the young people, in peer groups and on a one-to-one basis'. Moreover, she comments that:

> What stands out from my research log is the range of conversations I was engaged in with the young people, often within a very short period of time. In one tutor time, for example, the subject of conversations . . . encompassed cars, hair dye, what clothes to wear for a party, Christmas shopping, sharing bedrooms, and animals. . . . I aimed to show my interest in the young people by referring, over time, to previous conversations with them, to demonstrate that I had remembered what they had told me on a previous occasion. For example, a group of boys and I developed a long running joke about how I could exchange my Nissan Micra for a car from one of the boy's father's garage.
>
> (Hudson 2004: 258)

Beynon (1983), also working in a school, was faced with a more recalcitrant set of participants: the teaching staff. He outlines the strategies he used to establish rapport with them:

> Although I did not consciously search these out, I stumbled upon topics in which they and I shared a certain degree of interest to serve as a backcloth, a resource to be referred to for 'starters', or for 'gap fillers' to keep the conversational door ajar.
>
> (Beynon 1983: 40)

Needless to say, such 'neutral' topics are not actually divorced from the researcher's interests at hand, since they can throw additional and unforeseen light on informants, and yield fresh sources of data. Beynon also lists as a 'way in' his own local connections: 'being regarded as "a local" was an important step forward, especially when it became known that I lived within comfortable walking distance of Victoria Road. This considerably lessened the sense of threat which some felt I posed' (Beynon 1983: 41).

This would not lessen such 'threats' in all cases, however. In some settings the participants might feel less threatened by a stranger, and feel more uneasy about the possible significance of an observer's local knowledge. The same applies to another of Beynon's 'ways in':

> More significant by far, however, was my own background in teaching and experience in secondary schools, which I unashamedly employed to show staff that I was no stranger to teaching, to classrooms, and to school life in general. I was too old to adopt the now-familiar ethnographic persona of 'naive student', and found it best to present myself as a former teacher turned lecturer/researcher.
>
> (Beynon 1983: 41)

Beynon goes on to quote the following exchange, which illustrates how such experience was a 'bonus' in his particular circumstances. At the same time, the extract illustrates a reaction to the attentions of a research worker typical of many settings:

MR. BUNSEN: Where did you teach in London?
J.B.: South London and then Hertfordshire.

MR. PIANO:	(who had been reading the staff notice board): Good Lord, I didn't realise you were one of us! I thought you were one of the 'experts' who never taught, but knew all about it.
J.B.:	I don't know all about it, but I have taught.
MR. PIANO:	How long?
J.B.:	Ten years, in a Grammar and then a Comprehensive.
MR. PIANO:	That's a fair stretch. Well, well, I can start thumping them now!

(Beynon 1983: 42)

We can note in passing the common resentment on the part of some occupational practitioners, and especially teachers, towards detached, often invisible, 'experts' – though a fieldworker's willingness to stay and learn can often overcome such hostilities, irrespective of prior membership or expertise.

Both Hudson and Beynon note that the employment of such strategies in establishing 'mutuality' was more than simply establishing field relations. Not only did such exchanges facilitate the collection of data, but also they were data in their own right. At the same time, ethnographers often experience some feelings of personal disquiet, wondering whether they are unduly exploitative in offering 'friendship' in return for data. There are no easy answers to such questions, they always depend upon the particular circumstances and personal judgement.

A problem that the ethnographer often faces in the course of fieldwork is deciding how much self-disclosure is appropriate or fruitful. It is hard to expect 'honesty' and 'frankness' on the part of participants and informants, while never being frank and honest about oneself. And feminists, in particular, have stressed the importance of this from an ethical point of view also (see, for example, Oakley 1981; see also Tang 2002). At the same time, just as in many everyday situations, as a researcher one often has to suppress or play down personal beliefs, commitments, and political sympathies. This is not necessarily a matter of gross deception. The normal requirements of tact, courtesy, and 'interaction ritual', in general (Goffman 1972), mean that in some ways 'everyone has to lie' (Sacks 1975). However, for the researcher this may be a matter of self-conscious impression management, and may thus become an ever-present aspect of social interaction in the field. One cannot bias the fieldwork by talking only with the people one finds most congenial or politically sympathetic: one cannot choose one's informants on the same basis as one chooses friends (for the most part). Indeed, it may be necessary to tolerate situations, actions, and people of which one dissaproves, or that one finds distasteful or shocking (Hammersley 2005a).

Particular problems arise where the researcher's own religious or political attitudes differ markedly from those of the people being studied. This is illustrated by Klatch's (1988) research on women involved in right-wing organizations. She comments:

> I often faced an uneasy situation in which the women concluded that because I did not challenge their ideas, I must agree with them. Nodding my head in understanding of their words, for example, was interpreted as acceptance of their basic beliefs. Thus, the women I interviewed often ended up thanking me for doing the study, telling me how important it was for a like-minded person to convey their perspective. As one pro-family activist told me, 'We need people like you, young people, to restore the faith.' Having successfully gained her trust, this woman

then interpreted that trust, and my enthusiasm for learning, as concurrence with her own beliefs.

(Klatch 1988: 79)

Sometimes, the fieldworker may find him- or herself being 'tested' and pushed towards disclosure, particularly when the group or culture in question is founded upon strong beliefs and commitments (such as religious convictions, political affiliations, and the like). Here the process of negotiating access and rapport may be a matter of progressive initiation. The fieldworker may find the management of disclosure a particularly crucial feature of this delicate procedure. The same can apply with particular force to the investigation of deviance, where members of stigmatized groups may require reassurance that the ethnographer does not harbour feelings of disapproval, nor intends to initiate action against them.

It is worth emphasizing the contingencies involved in these processes, however. For instance, Abell *et al.* (2006) report the divergent results on different occasions, and in different contexts, of their efforts to build relationships with young people through disclosing shared experience. What is expected to be recognized as commonality can sometimes be interpreted as marking significant difference. And this may, sometimes, damage the nature of the data that become available.

The personal characteristics of the researcher

There are, of course, aspects of personal front that are not open to 'management' and that may limit the negotiation of identities in the field, and these include so-called 'ascribed' characteristics. Although it would be wrong to think of the effects of these as absolutely determined or fixed, such characteristics as gender, age, 'race', and ethnic identification may shape relationships with gatekeepers, sponsors, and people under study in important ways. In the case of covert participant observation, these characteristics may of course be a barrier to doing the research that is difficult if not impossible to overcome. For example, going under cover as a 'bouncer' on a club or pub door (Calvey 2000) involves certain requirements, at the very least in terms of age and physique, that not everyone would meet.

Similarly, the researcher cannot escape the implications of gender: no position of genderless neutrality can be achieved, though the implications of gender vary according to setting (Roberts 1981; Golde 1986; Whitehead and Conaway 1986; Warren 1988; Westmarland 2000). Revealingly, most concern with the effects of gender has focused on the role of women fieldworkers: in particular, the way in which their gender bars them from some situations and activities, while opening up others that are not accessible to men. This has long been a theme in the methodological writings of anthropologists, where it has been noted that women may find themselves restricted to the domestic world of fellow women, children, elderly people, and so on. In Golde's (1986) study of the Nahua, the problem was exacerbated by other characteristics:

What was problematic was that I was unmarried and older than was reasonable for an unmarried girl to be, I was without the protection of my family, and I traveled alone, as an unmarried, virginal girl would never do. They found it hard to understand how I, so obviously attractive in their eyes, could still be single.

> ... Being an unmarried girl meant that I should not drink, smoke, go about alone at night, visit during the day without a real errand, speak of such topics as sex or pregnancy, entertain boys or men in my house except in the presence of older people, or ask too many questions of any kind.
>
> (Golde 1986: 79–80)

In much the same way, male researchers may find it difficult to gain access to settings that are reserved for women, especially in cultures where there is a strong division between the sexes; and even in public settings there may be rules about what they can and cannot do.

However, often, the anthropologist's status as a foreigner can allow some distance to be created from such restrictions. Reflecting on her experience in studying purdah, Papanek (1964) points out that as a woman she had access to the world of women, which no man could ever attain, while her own foreignness helped to remove her from the most restricting demands of female modesty. Rainbird's (1990) experience was similar:

> Being female affected my relations in the field insofar as certain activities were exclusive to one sex or the other. Nevertheless, the fact that I towered over most peasants, wore trousers and was an outsider of high social status placed me in a rather ambiguous category that allowed me to attend meetings and visit people freely around the countryside as men did, but not to drink with the men unless other women were present .... On the other hand, I had good access to women's activities and gossip networks, their warmth and affection.
>
> (Rainbird 1990: 78–9)

Similar problems and freedoms tied to gender can also arise in research within Western societies. Easterday *et al.* (1977) note that in male-dominated settings women may come up against the male 'fraternity', from which they are excluded; that women may find themselves the object of 'hustling' from male hosts; that they may be cast in the role of the 'go-fer' runner of errands, or may be adopted as a sort of mascot. These possibilities all imply a lack of participation, or non-serious participation, on the part of the woman – which may, or may not, be a problem in research terms. Not only may the female researcher sometimes find it difficult to be taken seriously by male hosts, but also other females may display suspicion and hostility in the face of her intrusions. Of course, female researchers may also find advantageous trade-offs. The 'hustling' informant who is trying to impress the researcher may prove particularly forthcoming to her; males may be manipulated by femininity. Similarly, in so far as women are seen as unthreatening, they may gain access to settings and information with relative ease. Thus, common cultural stereotypes of females can work to their advantage in some respects. Warren (1988) provides illustrations of both the restrictions and the leeway that can arise from being a woman researcher:

> When I did my dissertation study of a male secretive gay community during the late 1960s and early 1970s, I was able to do fieldwork in those parts of the setting dedicated to sociability and leisure – bars, parties, family gatherings. I was not, however, able to observe in those parts of the setting dedicated to sexuality – even

quasi-public settings such as homosexual bath houses ... and 'tearooms'. ...
Thus, my portrait of the gay community is only a partial one, bounded by the
social roles assigned to females within the male homosexual world.

She contrasts this with research in a drug rehabilitation centre:

> This institution was open to both male and female residents. But as a female
> researcher, and over several months of observation, I found that men were generally
> much more ready to talk to me than women. Furthermore, I was generally perceived
> as harmless by the males, and afforded access bordering on trespass. I vividly
> remember one day deciding to go upstairs, an action expressly forbidden to anyone
> not resident in the facility. Someone started to protest; the protest was silenced
> by a male voice saying, 'aah, what harm can she do, she's only a broad'. Upstairs
> I went.
>
> (Warren 1988: 18)

There is often some scope, then, both for capitalizing on gender roles and for
renegotiating some aspects of them for the purposes of the fieldwork. This is part of
the more general process of impression management. Thus, in her study of the police,
Westmarland had to contend with 'protectiveness' on the part of male police officers,
but this related to her outsider status as well as to her gender. Moreover, by passing
various tests and 'showing bottle', good field relations were established (Westmarland
2000). Of course, gaining respect and trust may take considerable time for any
ethnographer, and there will always be limits to how far this is achieved.

'Race', ethnicity, and religious affiliation, like gender, can also set limits and pose
problems. 'Race' is, of course, not merely a matter of physical appearance, but is also
defined in terms of culture, power, and personal style. Keiser (1970), reflecting on his
work with the 'Vice Lords', a Chicago street gang, notes that it was difficult for him,
as a white man, to establish relationships with black informants. While some were
willing to accept him as a 'white nigger', others displayed strong antagonisms. Similar
problems may arise, however, even where both researcher and researched are black.
Whitehead (1986) was seen by the Jamaicans he studied as a 'big', 'brown', 'pretty-
talking man'. 'Big' referred not to his size, but to his status as an educated foreigner,
and 'pretty-talking' indicated his use of standard rather than dialect English. 'Brown'
was the term used by local Jamaicans to refer to a combination of light skin colour
and desirable economic and social characteristics. He reports that one of the effects
of his being seen in this way was that:

> when I tried to hold casual conversations or formal interviews with a number of
> low-income men, they avoided looking me in the face and often suggested that I
> talk to someone else who was considered a bigger man than they. Frequently they
> answered me with meaningless 'yes sirs' and 'no sirs'.
>
> (Whitehead 1986: 215)

Peshkin's (1985) experience researching a fundamentalist Protestant school shows
also that the ethnicity and religious affiliation of the ethnographer can be an important
factor in the establishment of field relations:

At Bethany I wanted to be the non-Christian scholar interested in learning about the fundamentalist educational phenomenon that was sweeping the country. [But] I discovered . . . that being Jewish would be the personal fact bearing most on my research; it became the unavoidably salient aspect of my subjectivity. Bethanyites let me define my research self, but could never rest easy with my unsaved self. I became forcibly aware that the threats to my identity as a Jew were not just a matter of history.

For in the course of inculcating their students with doctrine and the meaning of the Christian identity, Bethany's educators taught us both that I was part of Satan's rejected, humanist world; I epitomized the darkness and unrighteousness that contrasts with their godly light and righteousness. They taught their children never to be close friends, marry, or to go into business with someone like me. What they were expected to do with someone like me was to proselytize.

(Peshkin 1985: 13–15)

While this did not force Peshkin out of the setting, it did shape the whole character of the fieldwork.

A similar problem was faced by Magee, a Catholic woman, studying the (predominantly Protestant) Royal Ulster Constabulary in Northern Ireland; but she too managed to establish good relations with many of those in the field:

Over a twelve-month period a field-worker's persistent inquisitiveness is bound to become something of an irritant . . . . But leaving aside instances of momentary irritation, of which there were many, . . . most respondents became confident enough in the field-worker's presence to express what were undoubtedly widely held fears about the research. Sometimes these concerns were expressed through humour and ribaldry. The field-worker became known as 'Old Nosebag', and there were long-running jokes about spelling people's names correctly in Sinn Fein's Republican News.

(Brewer 1991: 21)

Sometimes, belonging to a different ethnic or national group can even have distinct advantages. Hannerz (1969), discussing his research on a black ghetto area in the United States, points out that, while one of his informants jokingly suggested that he might be the real 'blue-eyed blond devil' that the Black Muslims talked about, his Swedish nationality usefully distanced him from other whites.

Age is another important aspect of the fieldworker's persona. Although it is by no means universally true, there appears to be a tendency for ethnography to be the province of younger research workers. In part this may be because the younger person has more time to commit to the fieldwork; in part it may suggest that junior people find it easier to adopt the 'incompetent' position of the 'outsider' or 'marginal' person. This is not to imply that ethnography is properly restricted to younger investigators, but one must at least entertain the possibility that age will have a bearing on the kinds of relationships established and the data collected. The junior research student may well establish quite different working relationships from those available to, say, the middle-aged professor.

Age can also have an effect on the researcher's modus operandi, as Henslin (1990) illustrates, comparing his research on cab drivers, at age 29, with that on the homeless, at age 47:

> [In the participant observation study of cab drivers] I gave little thought to danger, as I was caught up in the excitement of the sociological pursuit. Although two or three cabbies were stabbed the first week that I drove a cab, certain that such a thing would not happen to me, I gave the matter little thought.
>
> Now, however, I was once again face to face with street realities, and at this point in my life things no longer looked the same. Age had accomplished what it is rumored to accomplish: It had brought with it a more conservative . . . approach to street experiences. I found myself more frequently questioning what I was doing, and even whether I should do it.

He goes on to describe his hesitation in approaching a group of runaways:

> Down the block I saw about half a dozen or so young males and two females clustered in front of a parking lot. Somehow they did not look like the midwestern suburban youth I had come to know. What was most striking about this group was the amount of 'metal' they were displaying, notably the studs protruding from various parts of their bodies.
>
> A few years back those youths would have struck me as another variant group that likely had engrossing experiences to relate. No longer. They now impressed me as a group that discretion would indicate as being better off left alone.
>
> (Henslin 1990: 69–70)

He did in fact make contact with them. They told him that they slept in abandoned buildings, and he immediately began to wonder about how they found these, how they protected themselves from other intruders, etc. However, despite his curiosity, he decided that to stay with them at night would be too dangerous.

Being the 'wrong' age, or generation, can be a particular problem in covert research, in that it may lead to the researcher engaging in 'inappropriate' behaviour. In the covert phase of his research on college students, Moffatt (1989: 7) found that he had to control both his tendency towards 'high' or academic talk and the use of 'low' talk about sex. Much the same sort of problem can arise, though, in overt research, where behaving in what are judged to be inappropriate ways may damage relations with some participants (though it may improve relations with others!).

Age and its associated features can also affect the way people react to the researcher, along with what he or she is and is not allowed to do. An extreme example is provided by Corsaro's (1981) research on nursery school children:

> Two four-year-old girls (Betty and Jenny) and adult researcher (Bill) in a nursery school:
>
> BETTY: You can't play with us!
> BILL: Why?
> BETTY: Cause you're too big.
> BILL: I'll sit down. (sits down)

> JENNY: You're still too big.
> BETTY: Yeah, you're 'Big Bill'!
> BILL: Can I just watch?
> JENNY: OK, but don't touch nuthin!
> BETTY: You just watch, OK?
> BILL: OK.
> JENNY: OK, Big Bill?
> BILL: OK

(Later Big Bill got to play.)

(Corsaro 1981: 117)

Very often researchers working with children have sought to adopt the 'least adult' role in this manner. This can/may work well, but it can create its own limitations (Fine and Sandstrom 1988; Mandell 1988; Epstein 1998).

We have restricted our discussion here to some of the standard face-sheet characteristics of the ethnographer and their implications for research relationships. It is perhaps worth emphasizing that this discussion has not exhausted the personal characteristics that can make a difference. Oboler (1986) provides a striking example of this, discussing her husband's acceptance among the Nandi of Kenya:

> His first trip to the river to bathe was a crucial test. In a spirit of camaraderie, as same-sex communal bathing is customary, he was accompanied by a number of young men. Tagging along was an enormous group of curiosity-seeking children and younger adolescents . . . everyone wanted to know the answer. . . . Was Leon circumcised? In Nandi, male initiation involving adolescent circumcision is the most crucial event in the male life-cycle, without which adult identity, entry into the age-set system, and marriage are impossible. It is also viewed as an important ethnic boundary marker . . . . Fortunately Leon, a Jew by ancestry and rearing, passed the test. I believe that an uncircumcised husband would have made fieldwork in Nandi extremely difficult for me.
>
> (Oboler 1986: 37)

This example also illustrates the fact that it is not just ethnographers' own personal or social characteristics that can be crucial: so may be those of partners who accompany them into the field. And, occasionally, research may be done in a field in which a partner already has an established role. Hudson (2000) studied a school in which her husband was employed, and in the course of the fieldwork he moved from being a teacher to being assistant principal in charge of discipline. Not surprisingly, this had an influence on how the students perceived her, but it did not have the damaging results that might be anticipated. At the outset, she decided 'not to introduce the subject of being married to a teacher' but at the same time that 'if the young people raised the subject, then I would answer their questions openly'. She reports that 'it was not long before the subject arose'. Initially, they confused her husband with another teacher:

> Girls crowded round in a flurry of sympathy. Anna exclaimed: 'What not that tall bloke! Poor you! What's he like at home?' (Research Log, 24.1.97). Her remark suggests some sympathy for my perceived position, rather than constructing Richard

and myself as a couple, separate from the young people. Indeed, over fieldwork, the young people's comments tended to suggest they had a much stronger sense of my relationship with them, rather than any relationship I might have with my husband. For instance, later in the fieldwork, when Sara was reading the school newsletter in December 1997, she turned to me and exclaimed: 'Miss! Did you know your husband's been made Assistant Principal?' (Research Log, 12.12.97). When Sara telephoned me at school during the summer holidays, my husband answered the phone. . . . Despite the explicit reminder that I was married to someone official, when I asked how she was, [she] immediately launched into a diatribe about a boy she had 'shagged' and described the prospect of returning to school as 'crap'.

(Hudson 2004: 264)

In the course of fieldwork, then, people who meet, or hear about, the researcher will cast him or her into certain identities on the basis of 'ascribed characteristics', as well as other aspects of appearance and manner, and relationships. This 'identity work' (Goffman 1959) must be monitored for its effects on the kinds of data collected. At the same time, the ethnographer will generally try to shape the nature of his or her role, not least through adaptation of dress and demeanour, in order to facilitate gaining the necessary data.

Field roles

In the early days of fieldwork, the conduct of the ethnographer is often little different from that of any layperson faced with the practical need to make sense of a particular social setting. Consider the position of the novice or recruit – a student fresher, a military rookie, a person starting a new job – who finds him- or herself in relatively strange surroundings. How do such novices get to 'know the ropes' and become 'old hands'? Obviously, there is nothing magical about this process of learning. Novices watch what other people are doing, ask others to explain what is happening, try things out for themselves – occasionally making mistakes – and so on. But, in an important sense, the novice is also acting like a social scientist: making observations and inferences, asking informants, constructing hypotheses, and acting on them.

When studying an unfamiliar setting, the ethnographer is necessarily a novice. Moreover, wherever possible they must put themselves into the position of being an 'acceptable incompetent', as Lofland (1971) neatly describes it. It is only through watching, listening, asking questions, formulating hypotheses, and making blunders that the ethnographer can acquire a good sense of the social structure of the setting and begin to understand the culture(s) of participants.

Styles (1979) provides an example of the early stages of learning to be a participant observer in his research on gay baths. He comments that before he started he assumed that as a gay man he was 'among the "natural clientele" of the baths. It never occurred to me that I might not understand what was going on' (Styles 1979: 151). Before going to the bath house he consulted a gay friend who frequented it:

From this conversation, I saw no major problems ahead and laid some tentative research plans. I would first scout out the various scenes of sexual activity in the bath and diagram the bath's physical and sexual layout. After observing the interaction in the various areas, I would start conversations with one or two of the customers, explaining that I was a first-time visitor, and ask them questions about their bath-going. To write fieldnotes, I could use the isolation of some of the downstairs toilets, described by my friend, which had doors that could be locked to ensure privacy.

As might be expected, his plans did not work out as intended:

> The bath was extremely crowded, noisy, and smelly. My first project – scouting out the layout of the bath itself – consisted of twenty or thirty minutes of pushing my way between, around, and beside naked and almost-naked men jamming the hallways . . . I gave up on field notes when I saw the line to the downstairs toilets had half a dozen men in it . . . more lining up all the time. I did identify the major sexual arenas . . . but these were, for the most part, so dimly lit that I could see few details of behavior and gave up on the orgy room when, after squeezing through a mass of bodies, I stumbled around in the dark, bumped into a clutch of men engaging in group sexual activity, and had my towel torn off while one of them grabbed for my genitals. I gave up on the steam room after the steam poured in and my glasses fogged over. The blaring rock Muzak, the dour looks of the customers, and the splitting headache I developed (from what I later learned was the odor of amylnitrite, a drug inhaled to enhance the sexual experience) effectively killed any desire I had for conversation.
>
> (Styles 1979: 138)

He comments that it was 'only through a slow trial-and-error process [that] I gradually came to understand some of the patterns of behavior in the bath' (Styles 1979: 139).

The crucial difference between the 'lay' novice and the ethnographer in the field is that the latter attempts to maintain a self-conscious awareness of what is learned, how it has been learned, and the social transactions that inform the production of such knowledge. As we saw in Chapter 1, it is an important requirement of ethnography that we suspend a wide range of common-sense and theoretical knowledge in order to minimize the danger of taking on trust misleading preconceptions about the setting and the people in it.

'Strange' or 'exotic' settings quickly demolish the ethnographer's faith in his or her preconceptions, just as Schutz's (1964) stranger discovers that what he or she knows about the new country will not suffice for survival in it. Laura Bohannon (under the pen name Elenore Bowen) wrote a vivid, semi-fictionalized account of her own initial encounters with an African culture. She captures the sense of alienation and 'strangeness' experienced by the fieldworker, and a feeling of being an 'incompetent':

> I felt much more like a backyard child than an independent young woman. My household supported me, right or wrong, against outsiders, but made their opinions known after the fact, and so obviously for my own good that I could not be justifiably angry. I felt even less like a trained and professional anthropologist pursuing his researches. I was hauled around from one homestead to another and scolded for my lack of manners or for getting my shoes wet. Far from having docile informants whom I could train, I found myself the spare-time amusement

of people who taught me what they considered it good for me to know and what they were interested in at the moment, almost always plants or people.

(Bowen 1954: 40–1)

She documents the personal and emotional difficulties of coming to terms with such estrangement, but it is apparent from her account that this is integral to the process of learning.

This experience of estrangement is what is often referred to as 'culture shock' and it is the stock-in-trade of social and cultural anthropology. Confrontation of the ethnographer with an 'alien' culture is the methodological and epistemological foundation of the anthropological enterprise, whether it be from the point of view of a romantically inspired search for exotic cultures, or the less glamorous sort of encounter described by Chagnon (1997) from his fieldwork among the Yanomamö. He reports, with engaging frankness, how he set off into the field with a mixture of assumptions. On the one hand, he confesses to Rousseau-like expectations about the Yanomamö; that they would like him, even adopt him, and so on. At the same time, by virtue of his seven years of training as an anthropologist, he carried with him a considerable load of social-scientific assumptions: as he puts it, he expected to encounter 'social facts running about altruistically calling each other kinship terms . . ., each waiting and anxious to have me collect [their genealogies]'. In contrast to his romantic fantasies, and his social-scientific assumptions, he did not encounter a collection of social facts, nor indeed were his chosen people the noble or welcoming savages of his imagination. Quite the reverse:

> I looked up and gasped when I saw a dozen burly, naked, filthy, hideous men staring at us down the shafts of their drawn arrows! Immense wads of green tobacco were stuck between their lower teeth and lips making them look even more hideous, and strands of dark green slime dripped or hung from their noses . . . . I was horrified. What sort of welcome was this for the person who came here to live with you and learn your way of life, to become friends with you?
>
> (Chagnon 1997: 11–12)

It is worth noting in passing that Chagnon's account shows not only the 'culture clash' of the Westerner encountering an 'exotic' culture, but also the problem of the social scientist who expects to uncover social facts, rules, institutions, organizations, and so on by direct observation of the social world. This is perhaps one of the hardest lessons to learn at the outset. One does not 'see' everyday life laid out like a sociology or anthropology textbook, and one cannot read off analytic concepts directly from the phenomena one experiences in the field. Some researchers, setting out on fieldwork, may even feel a sense of betrayal when they discover this, or alternatively experience a panic of self-doubt, believing themselves to be inadequate research workers because their observations do not fall neatly into the sorts of categories suggested by the received wisdom of 'the literature'.

In researching settings that are more familiar, it can be much more difficult to suspend one's preconceptions, whether these derive from social science or from everyday knowledge. One reason for this is that what one finds is so obvious, it may be necessary to 'fight familiarity' (Delamont and Atkinson 1995). Becker (1971) provides a classic statement of the problem, in the context of research on educational institutions:

We may have understated a little the difficulty of observing contemporary class-rooms. It is not just the survey method of educational testing or any of those things that keeps people from seeing what is going on. I think, instead, that it is first and foremost a matter of it all being so familiar that it becomes impossible to single out events that occur in the classroom as things that have occurred, even when they happen right in front of you. I have not had the experience of observing in elementary and high school classrooms myself, but I have in college classrooms and it takes a tremendous effort of will and imagination to stop seeing only the things that are conventionally 'there' to be seen. I have talked to a couple of teams of researchers and it is like pulling teeth to get them to see or write anything beyond what 'everyone' knows.

(Becker 1971: 10)

Another problem with settings in one's own society is that it may not be possible to take on a novice role. We noted in Chapter 3 how researchers are sometimes cast into the role of expert or critic. Moreover, ascribed characteristics, notably age, and latent identities, may reinforce this. In studying such settings the ethnographer is faced with the difficult task of rapidly acquiring the ability to act competently, which is not always easy even within familiar settings, while simultaneously privately struggling to suspend for analytic purposes precisely those assumptions that must be taken for granted in relations with participants.

The 'acceptable incompetent' is not, then, the only role that ethnographers may take on in the field; and, indeed, even where it is adopted it is often abandoned, to one degree or another, as the fieldwork progresses. There have been several attempts to map out the various roles that ethnographers may adopt in settings (Adler and Adler 1991, 1994). In their classic accounts, Junker (1960) and Gold (1958), for example, distinguish between the 'complete participant', 'participant-as-observer', 'observer-as-participant', and 'complete observer', these representing points on a dimension from 'external' to 'internal'.

In the 'complete participant' role, the ethnographer's activities are wholly concealed. Here the researcher may try to 'pass' as an ordinary participant in a scene (Karp 1980; Pettinger 2005) or will join covertly an organization or group – Alcoholics Anonymous (Lofland and Lejeune 1960), Pentecostalists (Homan 1980), an army unit (Sullivan *et al.* 1958), a mental hospital (Rosenhahn 1973), bouncers on a club door (Calvey 2000), the staff of a shop (Pettinger 2005). Complete participation is also involved where the putative researcher is already a member of the group or organization that he or she decides to study. This was the case with Holdaway's (1982) research on the police, and Dalton's (1959) work on 'men who manage'. An extreme example is Bettelheim's (1970) account of life in German concentration camps.

What 'complete participation' means will vary, of course; but it is approximated in some circumstances. Some commentators have suggested that it is the ideal to which researchers should aim (Jules-Rosette 1978a, 1978b; Ferrell and Hamm 1998). Jules-Rosette, for instance, argued for the necessity of 'total immersion' in a native culture: in other words, not simply pretending to be a member but actually committing oneself, body and soul. In her case this was accompanied by conversion to the Apostolic Church of John Maranke, an indigenous African movement. This indeed is the criterion Jules-Rosette demands for what she calls 'reflexive ethnography': a usage of the term 'reflexive' that is somewhat different from our own.

'Complete participation' may perhaps seem very attractive. Such identification and immersion in the setting appear to offer safety: one can travel incognito, obtain 'inside' knowledge, and avoid the trouble of access negotiations. There is some truth in this, and indeed in some settings covert participation may be the only strategy by which the data required can be obtained. However, when carried out over a protracted period it usually places great strain on the fieldworker's dramaturgical capacities. Moreover, however successfully the research is pursued in these terms, various contingencies may lead to one's cover being blown. Calvey's (2000) covert research on bouncers was endangered by the following item in the local student newspaper:

> Conscientious as ever, members of staff at the Sociology Department have been doing undercover research into the life of those much-maligned guardians of the door, Bouncers. At least, Biteback presumes that's why some tutors have been working on the door at Pub X in town. They wouldn't be moonlighting would they?
>
> (*Mancunian* issue no. 13, 29 January 1996;
> quoted in Calvey 2000)

While in this case no serious consequences followed, the effect can be disastrous for the completion of the fieldwork project, and perhaps also for the researcher personally. Severe embarrassment is the least of the problems that can be expected:

> Athena appeared again, and excitedly told me some people wanted to talk to me . . . and she led me into a room where five members of the Council were gathered – the Priests Armat and Wif, and the Masters Firth, Huf and Lare. The latter was the chairman of the Council.
>
> At first, as I walked in, I was delighted to finally have the chance to talk to some higher-ups, but in moments the elaborate plotting that had taken place behind my back became painfully obvious.
>
> As I sat down on the bed beside Huf, Lare looked at me icily. 'What are your motives?' she hissed.
>
> At once I became aware of the current of hostility in the room, and this sudden realization, so unexpected, left me almost speechless.
>
> 'To grow', I answered lamely. 'Are you concerned about the tapes?'
>
> 'Well, what about them?' she snapped.
>
> 'It's so I can remember things,' I said.
>
> 'And the questions? Why have you been asking everyone about their backgrounds? What does that have to do with growth?'
>
> I tried to explain. 'But I always ask people about themselves when I meet them. What's wrong with that?'
>
> However, Lare disregarded my explanation. 'We don't believe you,' she said.
>
> Then Firth butted in. 'We have several people in intelligence in the group . . . We've read your diary.'
>
> At this point . . . I couldn't think of anything to say. It was apparent now they considered me some kind of undercover enemy or sensationalist journalist out to harm or expose the Church, and they had gathered their evidence to prove this.
>
> Later Armat explained that they had fears about me or anyone else drawing attention to them because of the negative climate towards cults among 'humans'.

So they were afraid that any outside attention might lead to the destruction of the Church before they could prepare for the coming annihilation. However, in the tense setting of a quickly convened trial, there was no way to explain my intentions or try to reconcile them with my expressed belief in learning magic. Once Firth said he read my diary, I realized there was nothing more to say.

'So now, get out,' Lare snapped. 'Take off your pentagram and get out.'

As I removed it from my chain, I explained that I had driven up with several other people and had no way back.

'That's your problem,' she said. 'Just be gone by the time we get back.' Then, threateningly, she added: 'You should be glad that we aren't going to do anything else.'

(Scott 1983: 132–3)

Fortunately, Scott had already collected a substantial amount of data before her identity as a researcher was discovered, and the group she was involved with decided against violent reprisals.

Even if successfully maintained, the strategy of 'complete participation' will normally prove rather limiting. The range and character of the data that can be collected will often be quite restricted. The participant will, by definition, be implicated in existing social practices and expectations in a far more rigid manner than the known researcher. The research activity will therefore be hedged round by these pre-existing social routines and realities. It will therefore normally prove hard for the fieldworker to arrange his or her actions in order to optimize data collection possibilities. Some potentially fruitful lines of inquiry may be rendered practically impossible, in so far as the complete participant has to act in accordance with existing role expectations. At the same time, of course, others may be opened up that might not have been available to someone researching overtly.

There are also issues to do with the sheer time and energy that can be taken up with participation. During the early days of fieldwork in a Brazilian Indian village, Gregor and his wife attempted – in the interests of 'good public relations' – to live out their lives as villagers:

Unfortunately we were not learning very much. Each day I would come back from treks through the forest numb with fatigue, ill with hunger, and covered with ticks and biting insects. My own work was difficult to pursue, for fishing and hunting are serious business and there is no time to pester men at work with irrelevant questions about their mother's brothers. Meanwhile, my wife was faring little better with the women.

(Gregor 1977: 28)

Hence the Gregors stopped 'pretending' that they were 'becoming' Brazilian villagers, and turned to systematic research activity.

In contrast to the 'complete participant', the 'complete observer' has no contact at all with those he or she is observing. Thus, Corsaro (1981) complemented his participant observation with nursery school children by observing them through a one-way mirror. Covert observation of public behaviour in the street from a window (Lofland 1973) also falls into this category, and perhaps also research like that by Karp (1980) on the 'public sexual scene' in Times Square or Pettinger's (2005) adoption of the role of shopper in department stores.

Paradoxically, complete observation shares many of the advantages and disadvantages of complete participation. In their favour they can both minimize problems of reactivity: in neither case will the ethnographer interact as a researcher with the people being studied. On the other hand, there may be severe limits on what can and cannot be observed, and questioning of participants may be impossible. Adopting either of these roles alone would usually make it very difficult to generate and test accounts in a rigorous manner, though both may be useful strategies to adopt during particular phases of the fieldwork, and in some situations may be the only options possible.

Most field research involves roles somewhere between these two poles. And Junker (1960) and Gold (1958) distinguish two midway positions: participant-as-observer and observer-as-participant. Whether this distinction is of any value is a moot point. Indeed, it runs together several dimensions of variation that are by no means necessarily related. One of these, touched on earlier, is the question of secrecy and deception. Another is the issue of whether the ethnographer takes on a role already existing in the field or negotiates a new one – though no hard-and-fast distinction can be made here, and indeed we should beware of treating the roles already established in the setting as completely fixed in character. Another important issue concerns how central to proceedings within the setting is any established role taken on by the ethnographer.

Of course, in secret research one has little option but to adopt an existing role, though it may be possible to extend and modify it somewhat to facilitate the research. And sometimes even in open research there may be no choice but to adopt an established role, as Freilich (1970a, 1970b) found out in his research on Mohawk steelworkers in New York. Having become friends with one of the Mohawks, he tried to revert to the role of anthropologist. As he remarks:

> It was soon clear that any anthropological symbol was taboo . . . I could use no pencils, notebooks or questionnaires. I even failed in attempts to play the semi-anthropologist. For example I tried saying, 'Now that is really interesting; let me write that down so that I don't forget it.' Suddenly my audience became hostile, and the few words I jotted down cost me much in rapport for the next few days.
>
> (Freilich 1970b: 193)

Currer (1992) reports much the same experience in negotiating access to Pathan women informants:

> Once permission to visit was given, the visits were on social terms: my agenda and public domain purpose were never referred to. When once I did so, the women concerned were very offended and our relationship was jeopardized. Yet the women, no less than the men, knew of my research purpose. Only in two cases did the relationship more closely combine the personal and the professional. In these cases I was able to take notes and to lead the exchange.

She concludes that she 'had to choose between insisting on my rules and being denied any real access or [visiting] on the women's terms' (Currer 1992: 17–18).

Generally, though, in open research the ethnographer has some choice over whether or not to take on one of the existing roles in the field. Thus, for example, in research on schools, ethnographers have sometimes adopted the role of teacher (see, for example, Aggleton 1987; Mac an Ghaill 1991), but sometimes they have not (Brown 1987; Walker 1988; Stanley 1989; Riddell 1992). Perhaps not surprisingly, they have rarely taken on the role of school student (but see Llewellyn 1980), although in studies of higher education ethnographers do sometimes enrol as students (Moffatt 1989; Tobias 1990).

Reflecting on her research into how families with school-age children use television and other media in their homes, Jordan (2006) explores the limitations on the role of researcher in this context, and how these are co-constructed. The fact that the setting was very much a private one made the task of negotiating access and treading a path that was both ethically defensible and ethnographically productive a delicate matter. She draws attention to the subtle changes in ascription and adoption of roles that the people she studied engaged in, and the implications of this for her own behaviour. She traces her movement among the roles of 'researcher as student', 'researcher as person', 'researcher as guest', and 'researcher as negative agent'. The last of these ascribed and felt roles arose where the researcher's presence seemed to exacerbate tensions within families (Jordan 2006: 179–80).

Decisions about the sort of role to try to adopt in a setting will depend on the purposes of the research and the nature of the setting. In any case, anticipation of the likely consequences of adopting different roles can rarely be more than speculative. Fortunately, shifts in role can often be made over the course of fieldwork. Indeed, there are strong arguments in favour of moving among roles so as to allow one to discount their effects on the data. Thus, Sevigny (1981), studying art classes in a college, collected data by surreptitiously taking on the role of student, and by acting as tutor, as well as adopting a variety of researcher roles. Different roles within a setting can be exploited, then, in order to get access to different kinds of data, as well as to acquire some sense of the various kinds of bias characteristic of each.

Managing marginality

Another dimension of variation associated with the typology of research roles developed by Junker (1960) and Gold (1958) concerns the perspective adopted. In crude terms, this can range from the 'external' view of an observer to an 'internal' view from the position of one or more participants. However, this dimension is surrounded by what Styles (1979) refers to as outsider and insider myths:

> In essence, outsider myths assert that only outsiders can conduct valid research on a given group; only outsiders, it is held, possess the needed objectivity and emotional distance. According to outsider myths, insiders invariably present their group in an unrealistically favourable light. Analogously, insider myths assert that only insiders are capable of doing valid research in a particular group and that all outsiders are inherently incapable of appreciating the true character of the group's life.
>
> Insider and outsider myths are not empirical generalizations about the relationship between the researcher's social position and the character of the research findings.

They are elements in a moral rhetoric that claims exclusive research legitimacy for a particular group.

(Styles 1979: 148)

Indeed, the very distinction between outsider and insider is problematic (Merton 1972; Labaree 2002; Kusow 2003). In her study of African-American communities on the Sea Islands of South Carolina, Beoku-Betts was able to draw on her racial background to build rapport with the Gullah women, but as an educated professional and university academic she was also sometimes positioned as an outsider (Beoku-Betts 1994).

At the same time, the insider/outsider distinction does capture something important about the different sorts of roles that ethnographers can play in the field, and the perspectives associated with them. Broadly speaking, those defined as outsiders or insiders are likely to have immediate access to different sorts of information. And they are also exposed to different kinds of methodological dangers. The danger that attends the role of complete observer is that of failing to understand the orientations of participants. Where this strategy is used alone, participant perspectives have to be inferred from what can be observed plus the researcher's background knowledge, without any possibility of checking these interpretations against what participants would say in response to questions. The risk here is not simply of missing out on an important aspect of the setting, but rather of seriously misunderstanding the behaviour observed. Indeed, Labaree (2002) suggests that even in research where an insider role is taken on, there is a danger of 'going observationalist'.

A more common danger in ethnographic research, one that is associated with the other three roles in Junker's and Gold's typology, is 'going native'. Not only may the task of analysis be abandoned in favour of the joys of participation, but also, even where it is retained, bias may arise from 'overrapport'. In a classic discussion, Miller (1952) outlines the problem in the context of a study of local union leadership:

> Once I had developed a close relationship to the union leaders I was committed to continuing it, and some penetrating lines of inquiry had to be dropped. They had given me very significant and delicate information about the internal operation of the local [union branch]: to question closely their basic attitudes would open up severe conflict areas. To continue close rapport and to pursue avenues of investigation which appeared antagonistic to the union leaders was impossible. To shift to a lower level of rapport would be difficult because such a change would induce considerable distance and distrust.

(Miller 1952: 98)

Having established friendly relations, Miller found the possibilities of data collection limited. Indeed, he suggests that the leaders themselves might have fostered such close relationships as a strategy to limit his observations and criticisms. Miller also notes that over-rapport with one group leads to problems of rapport with others: in his study, his close contact with union leaders limited his rapport with rank-and-file members.

The question of rapport applies in two senses, both of which may be glossed as issues of identification. In the sort of case outlined by Miller (1952), one may be identified with particular groups or individuals so that one's social mobility in the field and relationships with others become impaired. More subtle, perhaps, is the danger of personally identifying with such members' perspectives, and hence of failing to treat these as problematic.

One very well-known British ethnography that is flawed by such partial perspectives is Paul Willis's (1977) study of working-class adolescent boys. Willis's work is based primarily on conversations with twelve pupils who displayed 'anti-school' attitudes. These particular working-class boys describe themselves as 'lads' and distinguish themselves from those they call 'ear'oles', who subscribe to the values of the school. The 'lads' not only see little chance of obtaining middle-class jobs but also have no desire for them, enthusiastically seeking working-class employment. Willis argues that their school counterculture fits with the culture of the workplace for manual workers, even suggesting that the more conformist pupils are less well adapted to the culture of working-class jobs.

There are two senses in which over-rapport appears to be indicated in Willis's treatment of these youngsters. In the first place he seems to have devoted his attention almost entirely to the 'lads', and to have taken over their views in the analysis, where these did not conflict with his own. Hence, the book becomes, in many ways, a celebration of their lifestyle: Willis appears unable or unwilling adequately to distance himself from their accounts. Second, the 'lads' are endorsed by Willis, since he treats them more or less as spokesmen for the working class. While he explicitly recognizes that working-class culture is variable, he nonetheless seems to identify the views held by the 'lads', or those of some of them, as representative in important respects of true working-class consciousness. Since the 'ear'oles' or conformists are also from working-class backgrounds, this is problematic, to say the least. To a large extent, Willis is guilty of identifying with his chosen twelve, and his theoretical description of schooling is affected by this.

In a striking parallel, from some years earlier, Stein (1964) provides a reflexive account of his own identification with one set of workers, the miners in the gypsum plant he studied with Gouldner (1954):

> Looking back now I can see all kinds of influences that must have been involved. I was working out authority issues, and clearly I chose the open expression of hostile feelings that was characteristic in the mine rather than the repression that was characteristic on the surface. I came from a muddled class background which involved a mixture of lower-, upper-, and middle-class elements that I have not yet been able to disentangle fully. The main point is that I associate working-class settings with emotional spontaneity and middle-class settings with emotional restraint. I never quite confronted the fact that the surface men were as much members of the working class as were the miners.
>
> The descriptive writing became an act of fealty since I felt that writing about life in this setting was my way of being loyal to the people living in it. This writing came more easily than most of my other writing. But the efforts at interpreting the miners' behavior as a product of social forces, and especially seeing it as being in any way strategic rather than spontaneous, left me with profound misgivings.
>
> (Stein 1964: 20–1)

While ethnographers may adopt a variety of roles, the usual aim throughout is to maintain a more or less marginal position, thereby providing access to participant perspectives but at the same time minimizing the dangers of over-rapport. As Lofland (1971: 97) points out, the researcher can also generate creative insight out of this marginal position of being simultaneous insider-outsider. The ethnographer needs to be intellectually poised between familiarity and strangeness; and, in overt participant observation, socially he or she will usually be poised between stranger and friend (Powdermaker 1966; Everhart 1977). As the title of the collection edited by Freilich (1970a) suggests, the ethnographer is typically a 'marginal native'.

The strains and stresses of fieldwork

Marginality is not an easy position to maintain, however, because it engenders a continual sense of insecurity. It involves living simultaneously in two worlds, that of participation and that of research. In covert research there is the constant effort to maintain one's cover and at the same time to make the most of whatever research opportunities arise. And the consequences of being discovered to be a researcher could in some cases be dire, as for example in Scheper-Hughes's (2004) covert investigation of illegal trade in body organs. In overt participant observation there is the strain of living with the ambiguity and uncertainty of one's social position on the margin, and doing so in a way that serves the research but is also ethically acceptable. To one degree or another, as Thorne (1983: 221) puts it, one is often 'running against the grain' of the settings in which one works. And the stress will be particularly great where one is researching a setting from which one cannot escape at the end of each day, in which one must remain for days at a time; as, for example, in ethnographic research carried out on board ship (Sampson 2004).

   Johnson (1975) recorded in some detail his emotional and physical reactions to the stresses of fieldwork. Some of his fieldnotes document his response with notable frankness:

> Every morning around seven forty-five, as I'm driving to the office, I begin to get this pain in the left side of my back, and the damn thing stays there usually until around eleven, when I've made my daily plans for accompanying one of the workers. Since nearly all of the workers remain in the office until around eleven or twelve, and since there's only one extra chair in the two units, and no extra desks as yet, those first two or three hours are sheer agony for me every damn day. Trying to be busy without hassling any one worker too much is like playing Chinese checkers, hopping to and fro, from here to there, with no place to hide.
>
> (Johnson 1975: 152–3)

The physical symptoms that Johnson describes are perhaps rather extreme examples of fieldwork stress. But the phenomenon in general is by no means unusual: many fieldworkers report that they experience some degree of discomfort by virtue of their 'odd', 'strange', or 'marginal' position. Some flavour of this can be gleaned from Wintrob's (1969) psychological appraisal of the anxieties suffered by anthropologists in the field: it is based on the experiences of a number of graduate students, along with published autobiographical accounts. He identifies various sources of stress, including what he glosses as the 'dysadaptation syndrome' which includes a wide range of feelings – incompetence, fear, anger, frustration. He cites one graduate student's account:

I was afraid of everything at the beginning. It was just fear, of imposing on people, of trying to maintain a completely different role than anyone else around you. You hem and haw before making a leap into the situation. You want to retreat for another day. I'd keep thinking: am I going to be rejected? Am I really getting the data I need? I knew I had to set up my tent but I'd put it off. I'd put off getting started in telling people about wanting to give a questionnaire. I was neatly ensconced in –'s compound (an area of tents comprising one kin group). Every-body there knew what I was doing. I found it hard to move over to the other camp (a few miles away). I rationalised that a field worker shouldn't jump around too much.

(Wintrob 1969: 67)

Malinowski's diaries reveal many indications of similar kinds of stress and anxiety: indeed they are a remarkable document for what they reveal about his ambivalent feelings towards the Trobriand Islanders, his own intense self-absorption, and his pre-occupation with his own well-being (Malinowski 1967). In a similar vein, Wax (1971) has provided an excellent account of her difficulties in working in a relocation centre for Japanese Americans after the Second World War. She describes her initial difficulties with collecting data, in the face of (understandable) suspicion and hostility: 'At the conclusion of the first month of work I had obtained very little data, and I was discouraged, bewildered and obsessed by a sense of failure' (Wax 1971: 70).

These problems are, of course, exacerbated where the fieldwork is carried out in a setting that involves dangerous activities or unusual risks. Here, sensible judgements have to be made about what to do and what not to do; and about what precautions to take. The problem is that these will both shape others' perceptions of the researcher, and the extent to which it is possible to gain both 'inside' and 'outside' perspectives (Lee 1995; Lee-Treweek and Linkogle 2000).

We do not wish to convey the impression that the experience of fieldwork is one of unrelieved stress and misery: for many it is often a matter of intense personal reward and satisfaction. At the same time, the stress experienced by the 'marginal native' is a very common aspect of ethnography, and it is an important one. In so far as he or she resists over-identification or surrender to hosts, then it is likely that there will be a corresponding sense of betrayal, or at least of divided loyalties. Lofland (1971: 108–9) draws attention to the 'poignancy' of this experience. There is a sense of split personality that the disengaged/engaged ethnographer may suffer. But this feeling, and equivalent feelings, should be managed for what they are. Such feelings are not necessarily something to be avoided, or to be replaced by more congenial sensa-tions of comfort. The comfortable sense of being 'at home' is a danger signal. From the perspective of the 'marginal' reflexive ethnographer, there can thus be no question of total commitment, 'surrender', or 'becoming'. There must always remain some part held back, some social and intellectual 'distance'. For it is in the space created by this distance that the analytic work of the ethnographer gets done. Without that distance, without such analytic space, the ethnography can be little more than the autobiographical account of a personal conversion. This would be an interesting and valuable document, but not an ethnographic study.

Ethnographers, then, must strenuously avoid feeling 'at home'. If and when all sense of being a stranger is lost, one may have allowed the escape of one's critical, analytic perspective. The early days of fieldwork are proverbially problematic, and may well be fraught with difficulties: tough decisions concerning fieldwork strategy have to be made; working relationships may have to be established quickly; and social embarrassment, or worse, is a real possibility. On the other hand, it would be dangerous to assume that this is just a temporary phase that the researcher can simply outgrow, after which he or she can settle down to a totally comfortable, trouble-free existence. While social relations and working arrangements will get sorted out, and gross problems of strangeness will be resolved, it is important that this should not result in too cosy a mental attitude. Everhart (1977) illustrates the danger from his research on college students and teachers:

> saturation, fieldwork fatigue, and just plain fitting in too well culminated, toward the end of the second year, in a diminishing of my critical perspective. I began to notice that events were escaping me, the significance of which I did not realize until later. For example, previously I had recorded in minute detail the discussions teachers had on categorizing students and those conversations students had on labelling other students. While these discussions continued and were especially rich because of the factors that caused these perspectives to shift, I found myself, toward the end of the study, tuning out of such discussions because I felt I had heard them all before when, actually, many dealt with dimensions I had never considered. On the one hand I was angry at myself for not recording and analyzing the category systems, on the other hand I was tired and found it more natural to sit with teachers and engage in small talk. The inquisitiveness had been drained from me.
>
> (Everhart 1977: 13)

This is not to deny that there will be occasions, many occasions, when one will need to engage in social interaction for primarily social and pragmatic reasons, rather than in accordance with research interests and strategies. Rather, the point is that one should never surrender oneself entirely to the setting or to the moment. In principle, one should be constantly on the alert, with more than half an eye on the research possibilities that can be seen or engineered from any and every social situation.

If one does start to feel at ease, and the research setting takes on the appearance of routine familiarity, then one needs to ask oneself some pertinent questions. Is this sense of ease a reflection of the fact that the research is actually finished? Have all the necessary data already been collected? Obviously, in principle, there is always something new to discover, unforeseen events to investigate, unpredictable outcomes to follow up, and so on; but the line has to be drawn somewhere. And there is no point in hanging on in the field to no good purpose, just for the sake of being there, just 'for interest', or from a lack of confidence that one has enough information.

Sometimes you will tell yourself that you are done: that you should either finish the fieldwork, or now move on to a new social setting. Alternatively, it may be the case that a sense of familiarity has been produced by sheer laziness. Further questions may be in order, if the research does not seem to be finished: Do I feel at ease because I am being too compliant? That is, am I being so 'nice' to my hosts that I never get them to confront any potentially troublesome or touchy topics? Likewise, does my social ease mean that I am avoiding some people, and cultivating others with whom I feel more comfortable? In many social contexts, we find ourselves in need of formal or informal sponsors, helpful informants, and so forth. But it is important not to cling to them. From time to time one should evaluate whether the research is being unduly limited by such a possibility. In general, it is well worth pausing to consider whether a sense of comfort and familiarity may be an artefact of laziness, and a limitation imposed on the research by a failure to go on asking new questions, by a reluctance ever to go against the grain, a fear of ever making mistakes, and an unwillingness to try to establish new or difficult social relationships. It is possible to carve out an inhabitable niche in the field during the early stages of a project: it is important not to stay there and never try one's wings in other contexts.

As we have already indicated, marginality is not the only source of strain and stress in fieldwork. Another is finding oneself in physical and social situations that one might not otherwise encounter and would normally avoid. Henslin (1990) provides an example from his participant observation research on homeless people:

> It was not the shelter's large size and greater impersonality . . . that brought culture shock. It was, rather, its radically different approach to the homeless. For example, at check-in each man was assigned a number. At the exact designated time the man located a bed marked with that number, one that held at its foot a similarly-numbered basket. Each man then undressed at his bedside and waited in the nude until his number was called. Still nude, he then had to parade in front of the other hundred and nine men, carrying his clothing . . . to a check-in center operated by clothed personnel.
>
> After showering, but still standing in the nude and surrounded by nude strangers, each man was required to shave, using the common razors laid out by the sinks. Finally, still nude, he took the long walk back to his assigned bed.
>
> This routine burst upon me as a startling experience. . . . For me . . . to parade nude in front of strangers . . . and to witness man after man parading nude was humiliating and degrading, a frontal assault on my sensibilities.
>
> Nor was that night spent peacefully. Gone now was my cuddly sleeping partner of the past dozen years. Gone were my familiar surroundings. And, especially, gone was the lock that protected me from the unknown . . .
>
> Then my mind insisted on playing back statements made by one of the directors of the shelter. Earlier that day, as I was interviewing him . . . he mentioned homosexual rapes that had occurred in the dormitories. Then during the interview two men had to be removed from the dining hall after they drew a knife and a pistol on one another. When I told him that I was planning to spend the night and asked him if it was safe, instead of the reassurance I was hoping for, he told me about a man who had pulled a knife on him and added, 'Nothing is really safe. You really have to be ready to die in this life.'
>
> That was certainly not the most restful night I have ever spent, but by morning I was sleeping fairly soundly. I knew that was so because in the early hours, at 5.35 to be exact, the numerous overhead lights suddenly beat onto my upturned face while simultaneously over the loudspeaker a shrieking voice trumpeted, 'Everybody up! Everybody up! Let's get moving!'
>
> (Henslin 1990: 60–1)

Women fieldworkers are sometimes thought to be especially vulnerable, particularly to sexual attack. As Warren (1988: 30) notes, the question of sexuality in fieldwork first arose in the context of safety from rape of 'white women' alone in 'primitive' societies. She argues for a wider perspective, noting the reports of fieldworkers' sexual participation in the field (see also Fine 1993; Kulick and Willson 1995; Coffey 1999; Goode 1999, 2002). Nevertheless, sexual harassment, at the very least, can be a problem. Warren (1988) reports the research of one of her students Liz Brunner among homeless people:

> During her fieldwork, Liz slept, drank, talked, and shared meals with the homeless on Los Angeles streets – almost all of whom were male. After several episodes of unwanted physical touching, she learned to avoid being alone with particular men, or going into dark areas of the street with those she did not know well. . . . These homeless men – some of them de-institutionalised mental patients – often did not share, or perhaps know about, Liz's middle class, feminist values and beliefs concerning sexual expression and male-female relationships.
>
> (Warren 1988: 33–4)

Such problems are not, of course, restricted to contacts with the homeless on the streets, as Gurney (1991) reports from her research on lawyers:

> One clear-cut example of a problem related to my gender was an instance of sexual hustling on the part of one of the prosecutors. He tried, on several different occasions, to get me to come over to his apartment on the pretense of having me use his computer. . . . When that failed, he asked me if I knew anyone who might be willing to come to his apartment to help him program his computer to analyze bank accounts in embezzlement cases. I said I did not know anyone, but offered to post an advertisement for him at the university. He rejected that idea and never raised the issue again.
>
> (Gurney 1991: 58–9)

Unpleasant fieldwork experiences do not arise solely from what may be done to the ethnographer, however. Even more distressing can be what the participant observer feels it necessary to do in order to maintain the participant role. This is a problem that is especially likely to occur where the complete participant observation role has been adopted, since here, as we noted earlier, there is usually less scope for manoeuvre. The situation is also exacerbated where the people with whom one is involved are prone to violence. In such circumstances, one may find oneself drawn deep into activities that are obnoxious and dangerous, as Mitchell (1991) found in his research on survivalists:

> Alone, two thousand miles away from home, on the third day of the Christian Patriots Survival Conference, I volunteered for guard duty. . . . The Aryan nations were there, with the Posse Comitatus, and the Klan. In the names of Reason and Patriotism and God they urged repudiation of the national debt, race revolution, economic assistance to small farmers, and genocide. . . . Four of us were assigned the evening gate watch. Into the dusk we directed late arriving traffic, checked passes, and got acquainted. The camp settled. Talk turned to traditional survivalist topics. First, guns: They slid theirs one by one from concealed holsters to be admired. 'Mine's in the car,' I lied. Then, because we were strangers with presumably a common cause, it was time for stories, to reconfirm our enemies

and reiterate our principles. We stood around a small camp fire. . . . Our stories went clockwise. Twelve O'clock told of homosexuals who frequent a city park in his home community and asked what should be done with them in 'the future'. His proposal involved chains and trees and long fused dynamite taped to body parts. Understand these remarks. They were meant neither as braggadocio nor excessive cruelty, but as a reasoned proposal. We all faced the 'queer' problem didn't we? And the community will need 'cleansing' won't it? In solemn agreement we nodded our heads. Three O'clock reflected for a moment, then proposed a utilitarian solution regarding nighttime and rifle practice. 'Good idea,' we mumbled supportively. . . . One more car passed the gate. It grew quiet. It was Nine O'clock. My turn. I told a story, too. As I began a new man joined us. He listened to my idea and approved, introduced himself, then told me things not everyone knew, about plans being made, and action soon to be taken. He said they could use men like me and told me to be ready to join. I took him seriously. Others did, too. He was on the FBI's 'Ten Most Wanted' list. If there are researchers who can participate in such business without feeling, I am not one of them nor do I ever hope to be. What I do hope is someday to forget, forget those unmistakable sounds, my own voice, my own words, telling that Nine O'clock story.

(Mitchell 1991: 107)

Here we are reminded that field researchers do not always leave the field physically and emotionally unscathed, and they rarely leave unaffected by the experience of research. But even where very distressing, the experience is rarely simply negative, as Cannon (1992) indicates on the basis of her research on women with breast cancer:

It would sound overdramatic to say that it 'changed my life' (although it has a lasting effect) but it certainly 'took over' my life in terms of emotional involve-ment in ways I was not altogether prepared for, and taught me a number of 'extra curricular' lessons about life and death, pain and endurance, and human relationships.

(Cannon 1992: 180)

Leaving the field

With all research there comes a time when the fieldwork needs to be terminated (Delamont 2004a). Often this is determined by the non-availability of further resources, or by the approach of deadlines for the production of written reports. With the exception of those who are doing research in a setting within which they normally live or work, ending the fieldwork generally means leaving the field – though sometimes the setting itself disintegrates, as Gallmeier (1991) found in his research on a professional hockey team:

Compared to some other field researchers I had a less difficult time disengaging from the setting and the participants. This was attributable largely to the fact that once the season is over the players rapidly disperse and return to summer jobs and families in the 'Great White North'. In late April the Rockets were eliminated in the third round of the playoffs and the season was suddenly over. In just a few days the majority of the Rockets left Summit City.

(Gallmeier 1991: 226)

Virtually overnight, the people he had been studying dispersed geographically, though he was able to follow up individuals subsequently.

Most ethnographers, however, must organize leaving the field, and this is not always a straightforward matter. Like all other aspects of field relations it usually has to be negotiated. Indeed, sometimes participants are reluctant to let the researcher go, for a variety of reasons. David Snow's first attempts at disengagement from a group of Nichiren Shosnu Buddhists were met with a flurry of reconversion activity:

> No sooner had I finished (telling my group leader about my growing disillusionment) than he congratulated me, indicating that (such feelings) were good signs. He went on to suggest that something is really happening in my life. . . . Rather than getting discouraged and giving up, I was told to chant and participate even more. He also suggested that I should go to the Community Center at 10: 00 this evening and get further guidance from the senior leaders. Later in the evening my group leader stopped by the apartment at 10: 00 unnannounced – to pick me up and rush me to the Community Center to make sure that I received 'guidance'.
>
> While I was thus trying to curtail my involvement and offer what seemed to be legitimate reasons for dropping out, I was yet being drawn back at the same time.
>
> (Snow 1980: 110)

Difficulty in leaving can also sometimes reflect the quality of the relationships that have been established with participants in the field: the more successful one has been in this respect, the harder it can be to extricate oneself from the setting. From the beginning, Hudson (2004) had told the young people she was studying when the research would end, and she reminded them of this at various points later. As the time approached, she explained that she would be spending her time writing her book, and 'talked through the ways they could keep in touch with me, if they wished'. But, at the beginning of the new school year, 'the young people demanded that the fieldwork should continue', and she reversed her decision on ethical grounds, feeling that not to do so showed disrespect for them and smacked of exploitation. Furthermore she found that 'the data were enriched because my relationships with the young people developed further during the unexpected extension to the fieldwork' (Hudson 2004: 265).

Leaving the field is not usually as difficult as this; it is generally more a matter of saying goodbye to those with whom one has established relationships, making arrangements for future contacts (for follow-up interviews or perhaps in order to feed data or findings back to them), and generally smoothing one's departure. And leaving does not necessarily mean breaking off completely all relationships with those one has come to know while working there. Most ethnographers retain friends and acquaintances from their periods of fieldwork, sometimes for a long time (Miller and Humphreys 2004). A sad exception is Cannon (1992), whose friends from her research were progressively depleted as they died from cancer.

However smoothly managed, though, leaving can be an emotionally demanding experience. It can sometimes be strange and disorienting for people in the setting to find that the ethnographer is no longer going to be a part of their everyday world. Informants must adjust to the fact that someone they have come to see as a friend is going to turn back into a stranger, at least to some degree. For the ethnographer too the experience may sometimes be traumatic. An extreme case is that of Young (1991), where the end of the fieldwork coincided with his retirement from the police:

> In the months since I retired and have been compiling the material for this book, I have become crucially aware that . . . I have been . . . involved in what I have decided can only be a deconstruction of an identity. Shedding the institutional framework and the heavy constraints of a disciplined organization after thirty-three years, like the snake sheds his skin, has been another culture shock. . . . During this time I have dreamed regularly (in full colour) of situations where I am in half or partial uniform, often, for example, in police tunic but civvy trousers, and without epaulettes on the jacket or buttons and badges of rank. In these dreams, in which I was often with ex-colleagues from the distant past, I somehow was aware that I was now standing outside my police identity, but had still to throw off the last vestiges of it.
>
> (Young 1991: 391)

Frequently, the ethnographer leaves the field with mixed feelings, and some sadness, but often with not a little relief.

Conclusion

In Chapter 1 we emphasized the importance of recognizing the role of the researcher in generating ethnographic data. Rather than seeking, by one means or another, to eliminate reactivity, its effects should be monitored and, as far as possible, brought under analytic control. As we have seen, there are a variety of strategies and roles the ethnographer may adopt in the field, carrying with them a range of advantages and disadvantages, opportunities and dangers. In addition, by systematically modifying field roles, it may be possible to collect different kinds of data whose comparison can greatly enhance interpretation of the social processes under study. However, field roles are not entirely under the control of the ethnographer; establishing and maintaining field relations can be a stressful as well as an exciting experience; and leaving the field may involve some difficulties. Furthermore, ethnographers must learn to cope with their own feelings if they are to sustain their position as marginal natives and complete their fieldwork.

   The various roles which ethnographers establish within settings are, of course, the bases from which data can be collected. One form of data is researchers' descriptions of people's behaviour, of what they do and say in various circumstances, and of their own experience of participation in settings. Equally important, though, are the accounts that people in the setting provide, while being observed or in interviews. In the next chapter we consider the role of such accounts in ethnographic research.

5 Oral accounts and the role of interviewing

It is a distinctive feature of social research that the 'objects' studied are in fact 'subjects', in the sense that they have consciousness and agency. Moreover, unlike physical objects or animals, they produce accounts of themselves and their worlds. Recognition of the significance of this has always been central to ethnographic thinking, though it has been interpreted in somewhat different ways over time and across different fields. Generally speaking, there has been a tension between treating the accounts of the people being studied as sources of information about themselves and the world in which they live, and treating those accounts as social products whose analysis can tell us something about the socio-cultural processes that generated them.

Differences in view about the methodological function, and importance, of participants' accounts have been generated by divergent methodological philosophies. From the point of view of positivism, common-sense accounts are subjective and must be replaced by scientific ones. On the strictest interpretation this leads to a behaviourist stance, to the effect that people's own accounts are simply epiphenomena that have no causal significance, and therefore little relevance in explaining their behaviour. By contrast, naturalism treats common-sense knowledge as constitutive of social reality; and, therefore, requires that it be appreciated and described, not ignored or explained away. More recent ethnographic critics of naturalism retain an interest in insider accounts, but they adopt a variety of attitudes towards them. Some regard the role of the ethnographer as to amplify the voices of those on the social margins; these being treated as having epistemological or ethical privilege. They therefore seek ways of representing insider accounts in ways that preserve their authenticity. Here, often, the ethnographer's role approaches advocacy. Others see the task as to deconstruct accounts in order to understand how they were produced and the presuppositions on which they are based. Here the ethnographer's role comes close to ideology critique. Slightly different again is the stance of those ethnographers, for example influenced by discourse analysis, for whom accounting practices, in interviews or in naturally occurring talk, are an important topic for investigation rather than the accounts being usable as sources of information. Associated with some of these latter views is a tendency to reject any concept of validity which implies even a potential correspondence between informants' accounts and the world (Murphy *et al.* 1998; Atkinson and Coffey 2002).

Our own position is a catholic one, fitting neatly into none of these categories. For us, there are two legitimate and complementary ways in which participants' accounts can be used by ethnographers. First, they can be read for what they tell us about the phenomena to which they refer. Second, we can analyse them in terms of the perspectives they imply, the discursive strategies they employ, and even the psychosocial dynamics they suggest.

We see no reason to deny (or for that matter to affirm) the validity of accounts on the grounds that they are subjective, nor do we regard them as simply constitutive of the phenomena they document. Everyone is a participant observer, acquiring knowledge about the social world in the course of participating in it. And, in our view, such participant knowledge on the part of people in a setting is an important resource for the ethnographer – though its validity should certainly not be accepted at face value, any more than should that of information from other sources.

However skilful a researcher is in negotiating a role that allows observation of events, some information will not be available at first hand. For this reason, ethnographers have usually cultivated or even trained people as informants. Indeed, at one time the use of informants seems to have been the staple research method in cultural anthropology. At that time, the central concern was the collection of specimens of 'primitive' life, whether material artefacts or myths and legends. An extract from the field diary of Franz Boas illustrates the implications of this:

> I had a miserable day today. The natives held a big potlatch again. I was unable to get hold of anyone and had to snatch at whatever I could get. Late at night I did get something (a tale) for which I had been searching – The Birth of the Raven' ... [Next day:] The big potlatches were continued today, but people found time to tell me stories.
>
> (Rohner 1969: 38; quoted in Pelto and Pelto 1978: 243)

As Pelto and Pelto remark: 'Most anthropologists today would be overjoyed at the prospect of observing a full-blown potlatch and would assume that crucially important structural and cultural data could be extracted from the details of the ceremony' (1978: 243). While in more recent times ethnographers have shown rather different priorities and have come to place more reliance on their own observations, considerable use is still made of informants, both to get information about activities that for one reason or another cannot be directly observed and to check inferences made from observations (Burgess 1985e).

At the same time, ethnographers have also seen accounts as important for what they may be able to tell us about the people who produced them and the intellectual and discursive resources on which they draw. We can use what people say as evidence about their perspectives, and perhaps about the larger subcultures and cultures to which they belong. Knowledge of these perspectives and cultures will often form an important element of the analysis. Here the approach is along the lines of the sociology of knowledge (Berger and Luckmann 1967; Curtis and Petras 1970); though we can also frame it in more current terms, where what is of interest is the forms of discourse through which accounts are constituted. Here, accounts are often treated as part of the world they describe, and as thus shaped by the contexts in which they occur (see, for instance, van den Berg *et al.* 2003).

Besides contributing to the analysis directly, this second approach to accounts can also aid our assessment of the validity of the information that is provided by particular informants. The more effectively we can understand an account and its context – the presuppositions on which it relies, how it was produced, by who, for whom, and why – the better able we are to anticipate the ways in which it may suffer from biases of one kind or another as a source of information. In this sense the two ways of reading accounts are complementary. The same account can be analysed from both angles, though in asking questions of informants we may have one or other concern predominantly in mind at different times.

Separating the question of the truth or falsity of people's accounts from the analysis of those accounts as social phenomena allows us to treat participants' knowledge as *both* resource and topic, and to do so in a principled way.

Unsolicited and solicited oral accounts

We shall focus on oral accounts in this chapter, leaving the discussion of written documents for Chapter 6. Not all oral accounts are produced by informants responding to an ethnographer's questions: they may be unsolicited. We find that in everyday life people continually provide accounts to one another: retailing news about 'what happened' on particular occasions, discussing each other's motives, moral character, abilities, and so on. Such talk sometimes occurs when some kind of misalignment is perceived between values, rules, or normal expectations and the actual course of events (Hewitt and Stokes 1976). The resulting accounts may be concerned with remedying the discrepancy or problem, or with finding some explanation for it, for example by categorizing people as 'stupid', 'immoral', 'unfortunate', or whatever. However, oral accounts are produced in many other situations as well, and can be stimulated by a variety of motives, including the obligation to relay news: gossip is integral to human social relations.

Ethnographers may find these 'naturally occurring' oral accounts a useful source both of direct information about the setting and of evidence about the perspectives, concerns, and discursive practices of the people who produce them. Furthermore, there are some sites where the exchange of accounts among participants is particularly likely to take place; and these are often rewarding locations for the ethnographer to visit. For instance, Hammersley found the staffroom of the school he was studying an extraordinarily rich source of teacher accounts, notably about particular students, their actions, 'moods', characters, and likely prospects, but also about the teachers' attitudes towards national political events. These accounts provided the basis for an analysis of the ideological framework on which teachers in the school drew in making sense of their world (Hammersley 1980, 1981, 1991).

Of course, oral accounts not only are provided by participants to one another, but also are sometimes given in an unsolicited way to ethnographers. Indeed, especially in the early stages of fieldwork, participants may be intent upon making sure that the researcher understands the situation 'correctly'. Very often, the aim is to counteract what it is assumed others have been saying, or what are presumed to be the ethnographer's likely interpretations of what has been observed.

Sometimes, ethnographers are unable to go much beyond observation and the collection of unsolicited accounts. Even the informal asking of questions may be interpreted as threatening or inappropriate, and where answers are provided they may be of little value; as Okely (1983) found in her research on Gypsies:

> The Gypsies' experience of direct questions is partly formed by outsiders who would harass, prosecute or convert. The Gypsies assess the needs of the questioner and give the appropriate answer, thus disposing of the intruder, his ignorance intact. Alternatively the Gypsies may be deliberately inconsistent ... I found the very act of questioning elicited either an evasive and incorrect answer or a glazed

look. It was more informative to merge into the surroundings than alter them as inquisitor. I participated in order to observe. Towards the end of fieldwork I pushed myself to ask questions, but invariably the response was unproductive, except among a few close associates. Even then, answers dried up, once it appeared that my questions no longer arose from spontaneous puzzlement and I was making other forms of discussion impossible.

(Okely 1983: 45)

Agar's (1980) experience was similar in his research on drug addiction, though the threatening nature of questions was not the only reason they had to be avoided:

In the streets, though, I learned that you don't ask questions. There are at least two reasons for that rule. One is because a person is vulnerable to arrest by the police, or to being cheated or robbed by other street people. Questions about behaviour may be asked to find out when you are vulnerable to arrest. Or they may be asked to find out when or in what way you can be parted from some money or heroin. Even if one sees no direct connection between the question and those outcomes, it might just be because one has not figured out the questioner's 'game' yet.

The second reason for not asking questions is that you should not have to ask. To be accepted in the streets is to be hip; to be hip is to be knowledgeable; to be knowledgeable is to be capable of understanding what is going on on the basis of minimal cues. So to ask a question is to show that you are not acceptable and this creates problems in a relationship when you have just been introduced to somebody.

(Agar 1980: 456)

While questioning may occasionally have to be avoided or abandoned, it is sometimes possible to overcome initial resistance through modification of the way in which questions are asked. Lerner (1957) reports the defensive reactions he met when he started interviewing members of French elites, and the strategy he developed to deal with them:

Our first approaches to interviewing were modest, tentative, apologetic. Trial-and-error, hit-and-miss (what the French love to call 'L'empiricisme anglo-saxon') finally produced a workable formula. To each prospective respondent, the interviewer explained that his Institute had undertaken a study of attitudes among the elite. As Frenchmen do not respond readily to questionnaire, he continued, we were seeking the counsel of specially qualified persons:

Would you be so kind as to review with us the questionnaire we propose to use and give us the benefit of your criticisms? In responding yourself, you could explain which questions a Frenchman would be likely to resist and why; which questions would draw ambiguous or evasive responses that could not be properly interpreted; and which questions could be altered in such a way as to require reflective rather than merely stereotyped answers.

By casting the interviewee in the role of expert consultant, we gave him the opportunity to indulge in a favourite indoor sport – generalizing about Frenchmen.

(Lerner 1957: 27)

As a result of the influence of naturalism, it is not uncommon for ethnographers to regard solicited accounts as less valid than those produced spontaneously. Thus, for example, Becker and Geer (1960) argued that it is important to ensure that conclusions about the perspectives of participants are not entirely reliant on solicited answers, otherwise we may be misled by reactivity, by the effects of the researcher's questions on what is said. Some discourse analysts have taken an even stronger naturalist line, emphasizing the extent to which interview data are co-constructed (Potter and Hepburn 2005). This has led to important debates about naturalism, its validity and implications (Speer 2002).

Naturalism has also led many ethnographers to favour non-directive interviewing, in which the interviewee is allowed to talk at length in his or her own terms, as opposed to more directive questioning. The aim here is to minimize, as far as possible, the influence of the researcher on what is said, and thus to facilitate open expression of the informant's perspective on the world.

Now it is certainly true that the influence of the researcher on the production of data is an important issue, but it is misleading to regard it simply as a source of bias that must be, or can be entirely, removed. For one thing, neither non-directive interviewing nor even reliance on unsolicited accounts avoids the problem entirely. Hargreaves *et al.* (1975) outline how they sought to develop a non-reactive way of eliciting teachers' accounts of classroom events:

> Our principal method was to observe a lesson and from these observations to extract those teacher statements and/or actions which consisted of a reaction to a deviant act. . . . We then reported the reaction back to the teacher at a later stage, asking for his commentary upon what he did. . . . We often merely quoted what the teacher had said, and the teacher was willing to make a commentary upon his action without any direct question from us. On other occasions we reported the teacher's statement back and then asked why the teacher had said or done something.
> (Hargreaves *et al.* 1975: 219)

They comment that even where no question was asked the teacher's account was still shaped by what he or she assumed would be seen as 'an appropriate, reasonable and meaningful answer to our unspoken question' (Hargreaves *et al.* 1975: 220). In fact, even where the researcher plays no role at all in generating the account, one can never be sure that his or her presence was not an important influence.[1] Sometimes this influence is made obvious, as the following fieldnote from Hammersley's study of staffroom talk (Hammerslay 1980, 1981, 1998) among secondary school teachers makes clear:

> (The researcher is sitting in an armchair reading a newspaper. Two teachers are engaged in conversation nearby, in the course of which the following exchange occurs.)
>
> > Larson: You ought to be official NUT [National Union of Teachers] convenor.
> > Walker: I'm only in the NUT for one reason.

1 Some discourse analysts rely on data from situations in which no researcher was involved. Even here, though, what is said may be shaped by people's knowledge that what they are saying is being recorded: see Hammersley (2003a).

> Larson   (looking significantly at the researcher): In case you get prosecuted for hitting someone.
> Walker: That's right.

Of course, the influence of the researcher (in the role of researcher) can be eliminated through adoption of the 'complete observer' or 'complete participant' role, but not only does this place restrictions on the data collection process, as we saw in Chapter 4, it also in no sense guarantees valid data. The problem of reactivity is merely one aspect of a more general issue: the effects of audience, and indeed of context generally, on what people say and do. All accounts must be interpreted in terms of the context in which they were produced. The aim is not to gather 'pure' data that are free from potential bias. There is no such thing. Rather, the goal must be to discover the best manner of interpreting whatever data we have, and to collect further data that enable us to develop and check our inferences.

Of course, in order to do this we may need to diversify the sorts of data on which we draw, so there is no suggestion that *how* we collect data, or *what* data we collect, is of no importance. The point is that minimizing the influence of the researcher is not the only, or always even a prime, consideration. Assuming we understand how the presence of the researcher may have shaped the data, we can interpret the latter accordingly and it can provide important insights, allowing us to pursue the emerging analysis.

There is no reason, then, for ethnographers to shy away from the use of interviews, where these are viable. Interviewing can be an extremely important source of data: it may allow one to generate information that it would be very difficult, if not impossible, to obtain otherwise – both about events described and about perspectives and discursive strategies. And, of course, some sorts of qualitative research rely very heavily if not entirely on interview data, notably life-history work (see Plummer 2000).

At the same time, it should be noted that there are distinct advantages in combining participant observation with interviews; in particular, the data from each can be used to illuminate the other. As Dexter (1970) notes from his research on the United States Congress, experience as a participant observer can have an important effect on how one interprets what people say in interviews:

> [In my research] I sometimes appear to rely chiefly upon interviews, but in fact I was living in Washington at the time, spent much of my 'free' time in a congressional office, saw a good deal of several congressional assistants and secretaries socially, worked on other matters with several persons actively engaged in relationships with Congress (lobbying and liaison), had participated in a number of congressional campaigns, had read extensively about congressional history and behaviour, and had some relevant acquaintance with local politics in several congressional districts. All these factors made my analysis of interviews somewhat credible. And, as I look back, interviews sometimes acquired meaning from the observations which I often made while waiting in congressional offices – observation of other visitors, secretarial staffs, and so forth. And, finally, most important of all, it happened that interviews with constituents, lobbyists, congressmen of different views and factions, could be and were checked and re-checked, against each other. Yet in the book we say little about all this; and in fact it is only now that I realize how much these other factors affected what I 'heard'.
>
> (Dexter 1970: 15)

The effect may also work the other way. What people say in interviews can lead us to see things differently in observation, as Woods (1981) illustrates, discussing his research on secondary school students. The way in which the students talked about boredom cued him into the experience of it:

> One of my outstanding memories from the enormous mass of experience at the school is that of pupils talking to me about boredom. They managed to convey, largely in a very few words, years of crushing ennui that had been ingrained into their bones. Great wealth of expression was got into 'boring, 'boredom', 'it's so bo-or-ring here'. The word, I realized now, is onomatopoeic. I could never view lessons in company with that group again without experiencing that boredom myself. They would occasionally glance my way in the back corner of the room with the same pained expression on their faces, and I knew exactly what they meant. This, then, provided a platform for my understanding of the school life of one group of pupils.
>
> (Woods 1981: 22)

Any decision about whether to use interviews, alone or in combination with other sources of data, must be made in the context of the purpose of one's research and the circumstances in which it is to be carried out. And here, as elsewhere, there are no right and wrong decisions, only better and worse ones; and, sometimes, these can only be recognized with hindsight. What is important to remember, though, is that different research strategies may produce different data, and thereby, perhaps, different conclusions.

At the same time, it must be said that there is an increasing tendency for qualitative research, even that labelled as ethnographic, to rely exclusively on interview data. And there are serious questions to be raised about this trend, and about how interview data are used. Moreover, there is a sense in which this usage reflects the character of the wider society; in which interviews designed to elicit 'the inside story', to lay bear people's feelings, and so on, are ubiquitous (Atkinson and Silverman 1997). Any tendency to assume that interviews are the default method for the ethnographer must be challenged.[2]

Ethnographic interviewing: selecting informants

A crucial issue that arises once the decision has been made to collect data via interviews is: who should be interviewed? Sometimes, particularly in the context of participant observation, people select themselves or others for interview, as Cannon (1992) found in her research on women with breast cancer:

> Liz told me that she thought Yvonne was ready for another interview, 'she's not stopped talking all weekend'. A number of times women rang me to ask me to see them because they 'needed someone to talk to' about a particular event.
>
> (Cannon 1992: 171)

2 For a range of views about interviewing, and discussion of a host of issues relating to them, see Gubrium and Holstein (2002) and Fielding (2003).

Here the driving force was the therapeutic value of the interviewing, but self-selection for interview can occur for other reasons. Most obviously, it may arise where ethnographers encourage informants to keep them updated, hoping that they will initiate contacts to report any news:

> One of my key informants, Sylvia Robinson, always came to tell me what was going on in the school. She told me what happened on days when I was outside school, she talked to me about aspects of school policy that had been discussed at school meetings that I did not or could not attend, attributing remarks to particular teaching staff. Furthermore, she always updated me and any other teacher within earshot of the latest gossip in the school.
>
> (Burgess 1985c: 149–50)

Such informants are of considerable use to an ethnographer, and interviews with them, formal and informal, may be initiated by either side.

Gatekeepers or other powerful figures in the field sometimes attempt to select interviewees for the ethnographer. This may be done in good faith to facilitate the research, or it may be designed to control the findings, as happened in Evans's (1991) study of a school for hearing-impaired children:

> In the course of time I learned from another administrator that Mr Gregory [the head of the school] would definitely require handling with kid gloves. This fact came to light when I asked the former if he could direct me to some key people on the high school campus. The naivete of the question, and the political dimensions of my work, were noted quickly by his response:
>
> 'No, I couldn't do that. Mr Gregory will send you to those he picks out. If you try to do any interviews without his approval and knowledge, then he will close it up tight.'
>
> . . . Days later Gregory met with me again and announced, 'We have selected for you the "cream of the crop".' That is, four teachers had been handpicked for interviews.
>
> (Evans 1991: 170–1)

While often welcoming self-selection, and perhaps even selection by others, the ethnographer must try to retain the leeway to choose people for interview. Otherwise there is a grave danger that the data collected will be misleading in important respects, and the researcher will be unable to engage in the strategic search for data that is essential to a reflexive approach. However, gaining access to informants can be quite complex, sometimes as difficult as negotiating access to a setting. Indeed, as we have seen, it may even be necessary to negotiate with gatekeepers before one can contact the people one wants to interview:

> If the sample of navy wives was to be broad, it was essential that the cooperation of the naval authorities was secured. The Royal Navy was approached to elicit its cooperation and support and to gain access to their personnel listings. . . . This was not some polite formality prior to being given a free hand, but a delicate series of negotiations.

Research on service personnel inevitably encounters security problems. Therefore, it was hardly surprising that the Royal Navy was apprehensive about any organization having access to personnel files. Access to such records was limited, even within the Royal Navy, and they were certainly not for outside eyes. There was an additional problem. The Ethics Committee of the Royal Navy had in the past developed regulations, it was claimed, to protect the civilian status of naval wives; they were not to be contacted by civilian or naval authorities without the prior permission of their husbands. Although the Navy was clearly interested in the consultative value of . . . outside research, initially these problems seemed to be major stumbling blocks. Eventually, however, a compromise was reached and a listing of all the personnel in the administrative region of Western Area was sent to the Family Services section of a local naval establishment. No names or addresses were permitted to be removed from these premises, but all replies to a questionnaire survey and later invitations to an interview were returned to the Polytechnic. This means of contacting women was cumbersome, but it protected their anonymity and fitted in with the Navy's regulations on security.

(Chandler 1990: 124)

Even where gatekeepers are not involved, identifying and contacting interviewees may not be straightforward, as Shaffir (1991) found in his research on people who had left ultra-Orthodox Jewish groups. His hope was that, having identified one or two *haredim*, they would be able to supply the names of others, so producing a 'snowball sample', but this plan was initially frustrated:

I quickly learned that there was no institutional framework within which to locate such persons. Thus I arranged a meeting with a journalist who recently had written a sensitive piece on the topic and who claimed that she located respondents through an ad in her newspaper inviting former *haredim* to contact her. The similar ad I inserted yielded only one individual who claimed to know of no others like himself. Although he did not lead me to further contacts, my conversation with him sensitized me to the pain, anguish, and desperation that characterized his departure from the ultra-Orthodox world – a theme that proved central in the account of every former *haredi* I was to meet.

The snowball technique that proved so effective for meeting Chassidic and newly observant Jews was largely unhelpful in the *haredi* project. Ex-*haredim* with whom I met suspected that there were others like themselves, but they did not know where to find them. Although at first I was suspicious of this claim, I gradually appreciated the extent to which former *haredim* were cut off from their previous circle such that they knew little, if anything, about other individuals who had defected recently. The important exception was Chaim. . . . At the end of my conversation with him, I asked whether he knew of others like himself with whom I might meet. 'Yes, I do,' he replied, 'I have names and telephone numbers. How many people do you want to meet?'

(Shaffir 1991: 76)

Sometimes the difficulty of getting access to informants determines who will and will not be interviewed. But usually there is a choice of potential interviewees, and then decisions have to be made about how many to interview and whom these should be. These are not decisions that have to be taken once and for all; usually in ethnographic work they will be made over a lengthy period of time. But, of course, in making them the researcher has to take account of the resources available, and of the opportunity costs of different decisions. In life-history work, there may be only a single informant, who is interviewed repeatedly. More usually, ethnographers interview a range of people, but some of these may need to be interviewed more than once, for example because the aim is to trace patterns of change over time, or because it is discovered that further information, or checking of previously supplied information, is required.

The criteria by which ethnographers choose people for interview can vary considerably, even over the course of the same research project. In survey research the aim, typically, is to achieve a representative sample. And, sometimes, this is the goal in ethnographic research too, though what is usually involved is sampling *within* rather than *across* cases (see Chapter 2).

When studying a large organization, one may not have the time and resources to interview *all* the occupants of a particular role, and may therefore try to select a sample of them that is representative. Doing this may be approached in much the same way as in survey research, selecting a suitably sized sample at random, or a stratified sample that takes account of known heterogeneity among the members of the population. However, such systematic sampling requires the existence of relatively clear boundaries around the population, and the availability of a full listing of its members. Such conditions may be met in some organizational contexts, but they will not be in others. Equally, often the time is simply not available to interview a large sample. In such circumstances, the researcher will have to select interviewees as best he or she can in order to try to achieve representativeness – though it may be possible to check the success of this by asking informants for their judgements about what are and are not representative views, and/or by comparing the characteristics of the sample with what is known about the population as a whole.

However, a representative sample of informants is by no means always what is required in ethnographic research. This is especially so where the primary concern is with eliciting information rather than with documenting perspectives or discursive practices. Here, the aim will often be to target the people who have the knowledge desired and who may be willing to divulge it to the ethnographer. Identifying such people requires that one draw on assumptions about the social distribution of knowledge and about the motives of those in different roles. Many years ago, Dean *et al.* (1967) provided a typology that illustrates the sort of thinking that can lie behind such strategic selection of interviewees:

1. *Informants who are especially sensitive to the area of concern.*
   The outsider who sees things from the vantage point of another culture, social class, community, etc.

   The rookie, who is surprised by what goes on and notes the taken-for-granted things that the acclimatized miss. And, as yet, he may have no stake in the system to protect.

   The nouveau statused, who is in transition from one position to another where the tensions of new experience are vivid.

   The naturally reflective and objective person in the field. He can sometimes be pointed out by others of this kind.

2. *The more-willing-to-reveal informants*

Because of their background or status, some informants are just more willing to talk than others:

> The naive informant, who knows not whereof he speaks. He may be either naive as to what the fieldworker represents or naive about his own group.
>
> The frustrated person, who may be a rebel or malcontent, especially the one who is consciously aware of his blocked drives and impulses.
>
> The 'outs', who have lost power but are 'in-the-know'. Some of the 'ins' may be eager to reveal negative facts about their colleagues.
>
> The habitué or 'old hand' or 'fixture', who no longer has a stake in the venture or is so secure that he is not jeopardized by exposing what others say or do.
>
> The needy person, who fastens onto the interviewer because he craves attention and support. As long as the interviewer satisfies this need, he will talk.
>
> The subordinate, who must adapt to superiors. He generally develops insights to cushion the impact of authority, and he may be hostile and willing to 'blow his top'.
>
> (Dean *et al.* 1967: 285)

Of course, some informants could fall into more than one of these categories.

Along the same lines, in his research on educational policy-makers, Ball (1994) reports how he discovered early on that there was limited value in interviewing government ministers currently in office, that a much more effective strategy was to concentrate on those who had left office, since they were much more likely to feel free to provide inside information. Informants may also be selected, of course, on the basis of what Glaser and Strauss (1967) call 'theoretical sampling', choosing those whose testimony seems most likely to develop and test emerging analytic ideas.

Who is interviewed, when, and how, will usually be decided as the research progresses, according to the ethnographer's assessment of the current state of his or her knowledge, and according to judgements about how it might best be developed further. Of course, not everyone whom one might wish to interview will be willing. And, even with those who are willing in principle, it may take a considerable time, and may involve some cost, to obtain an interview. Nor will the account obtained always be illuminating, as Thomas (1993) reports from his research on top business executives:

> Unless you have some sort of leverage with which to get their attention, chances are you will get it for only half the time you think you need. Journalists I know are pleased to get an hour with an executive; but journalists have a source of leverage most sociologists do not. A staff writer for the *Wall Street Journal* or *Fortune* magazine can at least imply that he won't say nice things – or he won't say anything at all (which can be worse) – if he does not get access to the executive he wishes to interview. Even then, if you do get the 30 minutes, you may find that an emergency or someone more important bumps you off the schedule. If you get in the door, you will find that the executive does not intend to answer your questions or has a script of her own that she'd like to repeat. All of this can happen (and has happened to me) after you've spent several months and hundreds of dollars to get to the executive's office in the first place.
>
> (Thomas 1993: 82–3)

As with any other data collection technique, the quality and relevance of the data produced by interviews can vary considerably, and is not always predictable. Selection of informants must be based on the best judgements one can make in the circumstances. However, one may need to revise these judgements on the basis of experience.

Interviews as participant observation

Interviews in ethnographic research range from spontaneous, informal conversations in the course of other activities to formally arranged meetings in bounded settings out of earshot of other people. In the case of the former, the dividing line between participant observation and interviewing is hard to discern. In the case of formal interviews it is more obvious. Here, the interview represents a distinct setting, and it follows from this that the participant understandings elicited there may not be those which underlie behaviour elsewhere (Silverman 1973; Murphy *et al.* 1998). This problem has been highlighted in research on teachers' typifications of students. Hargreaves *et al.* (1975), using observation and formal interviews, presented a picture of teachers' typifications as elaborate and individualized. Woods (1979) challenged their account, arguing, in part, that their data were a product of the interview situation and of their own analytical orientation. He claims that teachers would not be able to operate on the basis of such elaborate typifications in the secondary school classroom, given the sheer number of students they deal with each day, and the time pressures under which they worked. Whatever the merits of the arguments on each side, the fact that there is a problem about relating perspectives elicited in interviews to actions in other settings comes through clearly (Hargreaves 1977).

However, as we suggested earlier, the distinctiveness of the interview setting must not be exaggerated, and it can be viewed as a resource rather than as a problem. Just as the impact of the participant observer on the people observed is not simply a source of bias, so too with that of the interviewer. Indeed, it can be exploited through recognizing the active character of interviewing (Holstein and Gubrium 1995). To the extent that the aim in ethnography goes beyond the provision of a description of what occurred in a particular setting over a certain period of time, there may be positive advantages to be gained from subjecting people to verbal stimuli different from those prevalent in the settings in which they normally operate. In other words, the 'artificiality' of the interview, when compared with 'normal' events in the setting, may allow us to understand how participants would behave in other circumstances, for example when they move out of a setting or when the setting changes. Labov's (1969) work on 'the logic of non-standard English' illustrates this when he compares interviews in which the interviewer takes different roles. We might expect that the monosyllabic responses of some children in his formal interviews, while not an accurate indicator of their linguistic resources, may have been a genuine reflection of their behaviour in certain kinds of circumstances, such as interviews with counsellors and social workers, or lessons in school. It may be that by varying features of the interview situation in this way we can identify which aspects of the setting produce particular sorts of response. This more 'active' use of interviewing may also be worthwhile where the aim is to penetrate fronts, to overcome the kind of barriers that people put up to protect themselves and their activities (Douglas 1976).

Thus, while it is true that the perspectives elicited in interviews do not provide direct access to some cognitive and attitudinal base from which a person's behaviour in 'natural' settings is derived in an unmediated way, they may still be capable of illuminating that behaviour. Similarly, while we must not treat the validity of people's reports of their attitudes, feelings, behaviour, etc., as beyond all possible doubt – as a privileged source of information – there is no reason to dismiss them as of no value at all, or even to treat them as of value only as displays of perspectives or discourse strategies (Hammersley 2003c).

The differences between participant observation and interviewing are not as great as is sometimes suggested, then. In both cases we must take account of context and of the effects of the researcher. One issue here is: who is interviewing whom? Identities are initially attributed, whether these are indicated or not. But at the same time these may be revised or reconstructed over the course of the interview. While sharing a common identity, in some respect, is often seen as facilitating the process of building rapport, what is and is not shared, and its importance, is in an important sense defined, and perhaps redefined, during the course of the interview. For example, Riessman (1987) has noted that shared gender may not be enough to create rapport. Furthermore, difference can sometimes facilitate the interviewing process, rather than being a barrier.

The key point is that, like the participant observer, the interviewer will often need to work at building rapport. When interviewing people with whom one has already established a relationship through participant observation, little further work may be required. But where the research does not have a participant observation component, or where the ethnographer has had little or no previous contact with the person being interviewed, the task of building rapport is particularly important. Much of what we wrote in Chapter 4 about presentation of self applies here too. Measor (1985), for example, indicates the care she took with dressing appropriately when doing life-history interviews with teachers. This meant wearing very different clothes according, for example, to the age of the teacher concerned. She also reports drawing on shared interests and biographical experiences, and indeed developing some new interests, to facilitate the interview process. As in participant observation, so also in interviewing, it may be possible by careful self-presentation to avoid the attribution of damaging identities and to encourage ones that might facilitate rapport.

Ryan (2006) discusses another aspect of the interviewer's presentation of self: disclosure of personal information. It has often been argued, on both strategic and ethical grounds, that the researcher should provide information about him or herself to those being studied. However, there are questions about how much disclosure is appropriate, *and of what*. In discussing his narrative study of 'Irish male gay lives', Ryan reports that methodological texts about qualitative research had left him 'ill-prepared for the level of disclosure necessary' to create a relationship that would facilitate 'open and honest dialogue' (Ryan 2006: 155).

Building rapport is not the only concern, of course. Equally necessary may be establishing and maintaining the interview situation itself. This is especially likely to be a problem when one is interviewing relatively powerful people:

> Elites are used to being in charge, and they are used to having others defer to them. They are also used to being asked what they think and having what they think matter in other people's lives. These social facts can result in the researcher being too deferential and overly concerned about establishing positive rapport. ... I have found it important for the interviewer to establish some visible control of the situation at the very beginning, even if the elite subject is momentarily set

off balance. This came to my attention especially on one occasion when an elite board member of one of the family and child welfare agencies I was studying suggested that I meet him for our interview at 7:30 in the morning at an elegant downtown restaurant where he had a table in his name and breakfasted daily. I agreed and wondered aloud to a friend how I would convey the message from the outset – to myself as well as to him – that I was going to structure the social situation in which we found ourselves, even though we were clearly in his space and not mine. My friend suggested that I begin by arriving early and be sitting at his table when he came in. That would give me some time to get accustomed to the space and claim some of it as my own before he arrived. It worked like a charm. He appeared briefly taken aback and began by deferring to me and my research interests. It was a very successful interview, frank and substantive.

(Ostrander 1993: 19–20)

This problem of establishing the interview context may also arise outside the study of elites, as Currer (1992) found in her attempts to interview Pathan women, who insisted on treating the event as a social occasion. And it is a problem that is not always easy to resolve.

The initial few minutes of an interview can be particularly significant in establishing its nature and tone. At that point there may be some implicit, and perhaps even explicit, negotiation about the form the interview will take. One element of this will usually be information offered by the researcher about the reason for the interview, along with reassurances about confidentiality and the right of the interviewee to refuse to answer any question to which they would prefer not to respond. Small talk may also take place at this stage, perhaps while a decision is made about where to sit, where to put the audio-recorder (if one is being used), and so on.

The interviewer's manner while the informant is talking can also be very important. The latter will often be looking for some indication of whether the answers being provided are appropriate, and also perhaps for any sign of judgemental reaction. Generally, then, the interviewer needs to give clear indications of acceptance, especially at the beginning. Equally important, though, are signs that the ethnographer is following what is being said, and here appropriate responses on her or his part are essential. As Measor (1985) notes: 'God forbid that one should fail to laugh at an informant's joke!' This underlines an important feature of much ethnographic interviewing: that, within the boundaries of the interview context, the aim is to facilitate a conversation, giving the interviewee a good deal more leeway to talk on their own terms than is the case in standardized interviews.

Frequently, the researcher him- or herself is the only other person present at an interview, and the guarantee of confidentiality implies that no one else will ever hear what the informant has said in a way that is attributable. Under these circumstances, informants may be willing to divulge information and express opinions that they would not in front of others. However, this does not mean that this information is necessarily true; or that the opinions they present are more genuine, more truly reflect their perspectives, than what they say on other occasions. Whether or not this is the case, and in what senses it is true, will depend in part upon how their orientations towards others, including the researcher, are structured. Furthermore, informants are often aware that they are in some sense 'speaking for posterity', and this too will have an effect on what they say and how they say it. They may even doubt the ethnographer's assurances of confidentiality and seek to use him or her to 'leak' information to others.

Sometimes, of course, ethnographers conduct interviews where more than one other person is present, and here the question of audience is even more complex. On occasions, the presence of others cannot be avoided, as Lee (1992) reports:

> Where possible, couples were interviewed separately, but joint interviews were necessary in a number of cases. This was particularly so with some of the more recently married couples who lived in quite small flats. I found it embarrassing to ask one partner to wait in another room – usually the bedroom – while I interviewed the other.
>
> (Lee 1992: 136)

Chandler (1990) had the same problem in her study of navy wives, and it had a significant effect:

> Although appointments were made to interview only the women, on two occasions husbands were present. His presence transformed the interview; he altered the questioning, the woman's answers and sometimes he joined in. Even when he did not speak he communicated what he felt by means of what has come to be known as body language and his reactions were monitored by the women in their replies.
>
> (Chandler 1990: 127)

Such interventions need not always be counterproductive, of course. During an interview that Hunter (1993) was carrying out with a councillor at his home in a wealthy suburb of Chicago, the latter's wife came in:

> After listening briefly as an observer, she began to add asides and commentary on her husband's responses. Slowly, what had been heretofore a very focused and somewhat formal interview about issues and politics soon became transformed into a three-way conversation about particular persons among the elite. The wife was adding more 'social commentary' about people, who got along with whom, who was respected or not, and the interview was transformed into a very informative and revealing 'gossip situation'.
>
> (Hunter 1993: 48)

Sometimes, of course, ethnographers intentionally arrange interviews with more than one person at a time. In addition to the fact that group interviews allow a greater number of people to be interviewed in the same time, they also have the advantage that they may make the interview situation less threatening for interviewees, and thus encourage them to be more forthcoming. In particular, this may overcome the problem of the shy and retiring person, as in the case of Carol, quoted by Helen Simons (1981):

> Interviewer: Does the lesson help the shy ones or does it make them stand out more?
>
> Angela: They're so quiet and then all of sudden one of them'll speak and you think 'What's come over them?' I suppose they've got their opinion in their head and they hear everyone else talking so they think they will.

Patricia:	Carol's quiet.
Interviewer:	You didn't like speaking?
Carol:	I'd only talk when I was asked a question.
Angela:	Sort of speak when you're spoken to. I noticed that when I first met her, I thought she was quiet.
Interviewer:	But now you speak when you want to put your point of view.
Carol:	Yes. When I think someone's wrong, I'll say what I think.
Interviewer:	And how long did it take you to get to this stage?
Carol:	Well, it was more friendly, we sat in a circle and we could speak to each other. That was better and it didn't take long, only a few lessons.
Angela:	I noticed after three or four lessons Carol started speaking more.
Patricia:	I spoke the first lesson.
Angela:	So did I.
Carol:	It gets me mad when people say you're very quiet though. I enjoy other people's views as well.
Angela (to Patricia):	Probably the way you shout, you probably frighten them to death.

(Simons 1981: 40)

Of course, whether or not group interviews are successful in relaxing those who would find a one-to-one interview intimidating very much depends on the composition of the group. Frosh *et al.* (2002: ch. 1) compare the kinds of data generated in single and mixed gender, multi-ethnic and mono-ethnic, groups, as well as the differences between group and individual interviews with boys. They base their discussion, in part, on the boys' own comments on the experience of different interview formats. A key factor was, of course, topic, with discussions about bullying being very different in individual and group contexts. However, some of the biggest differences in how well the interviews 'flowed' was between first and follow-up individual interviews, with the latter being more relaxed.

Talking to more than one informant at a time can take a variety of forms. One of these is the focus group, and this technique is sometimes used by ethnographers. Jowett and O'Toole (2006) report contrasting experiences. While Jowett's focus group with young women about their attitudes towards feminism proved productive, O'Toole found the method much less successful in exploring the attitudes of mature students in further education towards participation in higher education. Indeed, in the face of 'worrying trends in terms of the group dynamic', she switched to what she describes as 'a more ethnographic style of research', 'casually chatting with the students in the common room' (Jowett and O'Toole 2006: 459, 461).

Whether a group or individual format is used is also likely to affect *what is said*, as well as *who speaks*. For example, in a group session the interviewer will usually find it more difficult to maintain control over topic. On the other hand, this may be all to the good in that informants can prompt one another – 'Go on, tell him', 'What about when you . . .?' – using information not available to the researcher and in ways which turn out to be productive. Douglas (1976) used an interesting variation on this strategy in his attempts to get an informant to 'spill the beans' about massage parlours:

We had long known that the ultimate insider in the massage parlors was a local lawyer who represented the massage parlor association and about 80 per cent of the cases. We wanted to open him up, so we tried to set him up for it. We wanted to make it manifest to the lawyer that we were on the inside and could thus be trusted. We knew it wouldn't do any good to give him verbal commitments – 'Hey, man, we're on your side, you can trust us.' He was used to every possible deception and double cross from all angles. It would have to be made manifest, physically real. . . . We got two young masseuses to go with [us] for the interview, showing by their presence and trust in [us] what angle [we were] coming from. As [we] were ushered into the lawyer's office, two employees at the parlor where one of the girls . . . worked came out and they had a grand reunion right there. (Researchers need luck as much as anyone else.) As the interview progressed, the two girls talked of their work. One of them, as we knew well, was under indictment for her work in a parlor. They talked about that. She was impressed by the lawyer and shifted her case to him. At the end of the interview, the lawyer told [us we] could use all his files, make xerox copies of them, use his name in doing [our] research, accompany him on cases, etc. We felt sure there were some things he wasn't telling us (and one of the girls later started working with him to get at more and check it out), but that seemed okay for the first hour.

(Douglas 1976: 174–5)

Some researchers have also found that using multiple interviewers can be effective in dealing with some types of informant, for example members of elites and white collar criminals (Kinkaid and Bright 1957; Bechofer *et al.* 1984; Dodge and Geis 2002).

At the same time, of course, the effects of audience must be monitored. Woods (1981) provides an illustration of the need for this from his group interviews with secondary school students:

For added ribaldry, the facts will probably have suffered some distortion. . . . Consider this example:

Tracy: Dianne fell off a chair first and as she went to get up, she got 'old of me skirt, she was having a muck about, and there was I in me petticoat, me skirt came down round my ankles and Mr. Bridge came in (great screams of laughter from girls). He'd been standing outside the door.

Kate: 'E told her she'd get suspended.

Tracy: He 'ad me mum up the school, telling her what a horrible child I was.

Kate: 'Nobody will marry you,' said Miss Judge.

Tracy: Oh yeah, Miss Judge sits there, 'n, nobody will want to marry you, Jones,' she said. I said, 'Well *you* ain't married, anyway.' (Shrieks of laughter from girls.)

(Woods 1981: 20)

The possibility of distortion is always present in participant accounts, since (as in the above example) they are often worked up for purposes where truth is probably not the primary concern. On the other hand, group discussions may provide considerable insight into participant culture: in other words, what is lost in terms of information may be compensated for by the illumination that the accounts provide into the perspectives, discursive repertoires, and rhetorical strategies of those being interviewed.

Pollard (1985) employed a further, novel variation on the manipulation of audience in the interviewing strategy he used in his research on a school:

> Children were invited to form a dinner-time interviewing team to help me, as I put it, 'find out what all the children think about school'. This group very quickly coined the name 'The Moorside Investigation Department' (MID) for themselves and generated a sense of self-importance. Over the next year the membership of MID changed gradually, but I always attempted to balance it by having members of a range of groups. Normally about six children were involved at any one time and the total number of children involved during the year was thirteen. . . . My intention in setting up a child interviewing team was to break through the anticipated reticence of children towards me as a teacher. I spent a lot of time with the MID members discussing the type of things I was interested in and establishing the idea of immunity to teacher-prosecution and of confidentiality. We then began a procedure of inviting groups of children – in twos, threes or fours to give confidence – to be interviewed by a MID member in a building which was unused at dinner-times. Sometimes the interviewers would interview their own friends, sometimes they would interview children whom they did not know well. Initially, I did not try to control this but left it very much to the children.
>
> (Pollard 1985: 227–8)

Here again, of course, the effects of audience need to be taken into account. And the data produced will have been affected not only by the particular children involved, but also by Pollard's background role.

As important as who is present at an interview, and who carries it out, often, is where and when it takes place. Again, though, the location of interviews is something which the ethnographer may not be able to control. Two of the couples Lee (1992) interviewed in his study of religious intermarriage in Northern Ireland agreed to meet him only

> on the condition that our initial contact was made in a public place, and that they would have a description of me but I would have no description of them. In this way they were able to 'look me over' and make a judgement about the possible threat I might pose before deciding whether or not to make themselves known to me. Obviously I passed the test since both couples did make themselves known and both were interviewed. In neither case, though, was I invited to the couple's home and each interview took place on 'neutral' territory, presumably so that the couples could ensure that their address remained unknown.
>
> (Lee 1992: 131)

Even where the ethnographer is able to decide where the interview will take place, finding a suitable locale is not always easy. Burgess notes that in his study of a secondary school he conducted interviews in classrooms and departmental workrooms, both of which were far from ideal. Others researching schools have ended up in broom cupboards; and Hammersley's (1980) most successful interview with a student took place at the bottom of a stairwell.

Where there is some choice of locale, several considerations have to be borne in mind. Dexter (1970) notes the need to take account of likely distractions:

One mistake which I have made on number of occasions is to try to carry on an interview in an environment unsuited for it. A legislator who is standing outside the legislative chamber, while half his attention is focused on buttonholing colleagues, is not a good subject for an interview; though one might learn something from observing him. I do not know whether, if confronted with such a situation again, I would have the nerve to say in effect, 'I need your full attention ...' but I hope I would ask whether I can arrange some time when he is less preoccupied. The most common difficulty is a man who really lacks a private office; for instance, state legislators or an executive assistant whose room is used as a passageway to his chief's. In all such cases, I shall in the future ask if there is a conference room or if we can have a cup of coffee, or, if worst comes to worst, even meet for a lunch.

(Dexter 1970: 54)

Whose 'territory' (Lyman and Scott 1970) it is can make a big difference to how the interview goes, as Skipper and McCaghy's (1972) research on strippers illustrates. They recount how one of the respondents asked them to come to the theatre, view her performance, and carry out the interview backstage:

On stage her act was highly sexual. It consisted primarily of fondling herself in various stages of undress while carrying on risqué banter with the audience. The act ended with the stripper squatting on the floor at the front of the stage, sans G-string, fondling her pudendum and asking a customer in the first row: 'Aren't you glad you came tonight? Do you think you can come again?'

Backstage, it was difficult for us to feign indifference over her appearance when she ushered us into her dressing room. As she sat clad only in the G-string she had worn on stage and with her legs on the dressing table, we became slightly mesmerized. We had difficulty in even remembering the questions we wanted to ask let alone getting them out of our mouths in an intelligible manner. To compound our difficulties, we felt it was obvious to the stripper what effect she was having on us. She seemed to enjoy the role. For over a half an hour she responded to our inquiries in what we perceived as a seductive voice, and her answers were often suggestive. After about forty minutes, she said very quickly, as if she had decided she had had enough, 'Doesn't it seem to be getting chilly in here? I'm freezing.' She rose, put on a kimono, and walked out of her dressing room and started talking to another stripper. When she did not return, we knew the interview had been concluded. . . . When we returned to our office to record our impressions, we discovered we had not collected as much of the data as we had intended. We either had forgotten to ask many questions or had obtained inappropriate answers to those asked. In short, we had not conducted an effective interview. Our sheltered backgrounds and numerous courses in sociological methodology simply had not prepared us for this kind of research environment. . . . It was very clear to us that the nudity and perceived seductiveness of the stripper, and the general permissiveness of the setting, had interfered with our role as researchers. The respondent, not we, had been in control of the interaction; we had been induced to play her game her way even to the point that she made the decision when to end the interview.

(Skipper and McCaghy 1972: 239–40)

In response to this experience the researchers arranged for future interviews with the strippers to take place in a restaurant.[3]

The physical features of a context and their arrangement can also have an effect on responses in interviews, as Burgess (1988a) notes:

> In the office of a head or a deputy head there are comfortable chairs as well as a desk and chair. Choosing to sit around a coffee table helps to break down the fact that the tape-recorded conversation did not occur spontaneously but was pre-set. In contrast, talking to a deputy head across a desk with a tape-recorder placed beside us may give the individual I am talking to some confidence, as he or she is surrounded by props: a filing cabinet that may be consulted, a file that can be opened. Yet it also adds to the formality and communicates something about the status of individuals and the way in which they perceived themselves.
>
> (Burgess 1988a: 142)

With many people, interviewing them on their own territory, and allowing them to organize the context the way they wish, is the best strategy. It allows them to relax much more than they would in less familiar surroundings, and it may also provide insight into their sense of themselves and their world (Herzog 2005). However, as we noted earlier, sometimes one may need to establish the interview as a distinct setting in which the *interviewer* is in control, and choice of locale and/or manipulation of its topography by the researcher can be an effective strategy for doing this.

Equally important in thinking about the context of interviews is to look at how the interview fits into the interviewee's life. There is a great temptation for the researcher to see interviews purely in terms of his or her own schedule, regarding them as time-out for participants from their everyday experience. However, they may not view them like this at all. This may well have been one source of the trouble that Skipper and McCaghy (1972) ran into. Equally, though, there are people of whom one might say that talk is their business, and indeed that being interviewed is a routine part of life for them. Dexter's (1970) senators and congressmen provide the obvious example. Their attitude to and behaviour in an interview will be very different from those who are unfamiliar with, or inexperienced in, this form of social interaction. Also, how people respond on any particular occasion may be affected by what else is going on in their lives, and how they currently feel. This was an important factor in Cannon's (1992) research:

> One day I had what I experienced as a particularly bad interview with Katherine, with whom I felt I had built a good deal of rapport and understanding . . . I felt that all my worst fears concerning interviewing sick people were being realized, that I was only serving further to upset her, that she was ill and tired and really only stayed in the hospital to talk to me out of politeness. She seemed remote and distant and the conversation was punctuated by long sighs and silences, yet when I asked her if she felt too tired to go on she said she wanted to continue . . . I worried about this encounter until the next time I saw her. . . . At the next interview I was able . . . to tell her how I had felt and the matter was resolved to both our

---

3 It is possible that this was a case of the researchers being put to the test. Sanders (2006: 211) reports a number of examples of researchers in the sex industry being tested out.

satisfaction. She said she had wanted to talk but had found herself to be too depressed and tired to be able to do so. We decided that in future if this happened we would simply have a cup of tea and make another appointment. In fact it did not happen again until she became very ill and bedridden when she would some-times say she would prefer to talk about matters other than her illness. This we would do, although the illness often emerged as the main topic of conversation in any case.

(Cannon 1992: 164)

In our discussion here, we have assumed that interviews involve face-to-face encounters. However, this is not always true. While ethnographers have perhaps made less use of telephone interviews than survey researchers, these can be of value: they may give access to people who could not otherwise be interviewed, and may even elicit information that would not otherwise have been forthcoming (Sturges and Hanraham 2004). Of course, nowadays, telephoning can take place via mobile phones or over the internet, and the particular mode adopted may introduce additional considerations. It is also possible to carry out interviews online, via email or through using chat rooms (see Mann and Stewart 2000; Markham 2005; James and Busher 2006). Here, as elsewhere, careful thought needs to be given to the implications of the particular strategy adopted, but there is also room for some trial and error, exploring the possibilities involved in different modes of communication.

Types of question

The main difference between the way in which ethnographers and survey interviewers ask questions is not, as is sometimes assumed, that one form of interviewing is 'structured' and the other is 'unstructured'. There is a sense in which all interviews, like any other kind of social interaction, are structured by both researcher and informant. The important distinction to be made is between prestructured and reflexive interviewing. Ethnographers do not usually decide beforehand the exact questions they want to ask, and do not ask each interviewee precisely the same questions, though they will usually enter the interviews with a list of issues to be covered. Nor do they seek to establish a fixed sequence in which relevant topics are covered; they adopt a more flexible approach, allowing the discussion to flow in a way that seems natural. Nor need ethnographers restrict themselves to a single mode of questioning. On different occasions, or at different points in the same interview, the approach may be non-directive or directive, depending on the function that the questioning is intended to serve; and this will usually be decided as the interview progresses (see Holstein and Gubrium 1995). In these senses, as we noted earlier, ethnographic interviews are closer in character to conversations than are survey interviews (Burgess 1984a, 1988a). However, they are never *simply* conversations, because the ethnographer has a research agenda and must retain some control over the proceedings.

This is true even in the case of non-directive questioning. Here, questions are designed as triggers that stimulate the interviewee into talking about a particular broad area:

Ordinarily, the questions should be of this nature: 'What do you hear from business?' (to the congressmen), 'What are they worrying you about?' not 'Do you hear from them about the tariff?'. Even better may be, 'What people do you hear from most?', 'Does anybody pressure you?'. Similarly, not 'How about the grants your agency is supposed to get from such-and-such a federal department?' but 'In what ways are you most affected in your work by national matters . . . ?' and if someone starts telling you, as an official of a racing commission told me, about ex-FBI agents who are employed by some national authority well and good, you have learned to redefine the impact of the federal government! A question which sharply defines a particular area for discussion is far more likely to result in omission of some vital data which you, the interviewer, have not even thought of.

(Dexter 1970: 55)

Non-directive questions, then, are relatively open-ended, rather than requiring the interviewee to provide a specific piece of information or, at the extreme, simply to reply 'yes' or 'no'. However, even here the interview format must be maintained, and this can be a problem where latent identities intrude, as Platt (1981) found in her research on fellow sociologists. Many of the respondents knew of Platt and her work, even if they did not know her personally. As a result, 'personal and community knowledge [was] used as a part of the information available to construct a conception of what the interview [was] meant to be about and thus affected what [was] said' (Platt 1981: 77). A particular problem was the tendency of respondents to invite her to draw on her background knowledge rather than spelling out what they were saying. As a result, she sometimes gained responses lacking the explicitness and/or detail necessary to bear her interpretations.

For this reason and others, in non-directive interviewing the interviewer must be an active listener; he or she must listen to what is being said in order to assess how it relates to the research focus and how it may reflect the circumstances of the interview. Moreover, this is done with a view to how the future course of the interview might be shaped. While the aim is often to minimize the influence of the researcher on what the interviewee says, some structuring is necessary in terms of what is and is not relevant. And even where what is said is highly relevant, it may be insufficiently detailed or concrete, or some clarification may be necessary if ambiguity is to be resolved. Whyte (1953) provides an illustration of the non-directive 'steering' of an interview in the questions he puts to Columbus Gary, a union official handling grievances in a steel plant:

> Whyte: I'm trying to catch up on things that have happened since I was last here to study this case. That was back in 1950. I think probably the best thing to start would be if you could give your own impressions as to how things are going now, compared to the past. Do you think things are getting better or worse, or staying about the same? . . .
>
> Whyte: That's interesting. You mean that it isn't that you don't have problems, but you take them up and talk them over before you write them up, is that it?
>   . . .
> Whyte: That's very interesting. I wonder if you could give me an example of a problem that came up recently, or not so recently, that would illustrate how you handled it sort of informally without writing it down. . . .
> Whyte: That's a good example. I wonder if you could give me a little more detail about the beginning of it. Did Mr. Grosscup first tell you about it? How did you first find out? . . .

Whyte: I see. He first explained it to you and you went to the people on the job
to tell them about it, but then you saw that they didn't understand it?

(Whyte 1953: 16–17)

As we indicated, interviewing in ethnography is by no means always non-directive.
Often one may wish to test inferences arising from the developing analysis, and here
quite directive and specific questions can be required, though of course one must bear
in mind that the answers may be deceptive. Such questions might also be necessary
if one suspects that informants have been lying, and this is important for the research
focus. Nadel (1939), a social anthropologist, reports that

> the expression of doubt or disbelief on the part of the interviewer, or the arrangement
> of interviews with several informants, some of whom, owing to their social position,
> were certain to produce inaccurate information, easily induced the key informant
> to disregard his usual reluctance and to speak openly, if only to confound his
> opponents and critics.
>
> (Nadel 1939: 323)

Confrontation of informants with what one already knows is another technique of
this kind, as Perlman (1970) illustrates from his research in Uganda:

> Christian [men] did not like to admit, for example, that they had at one time (or
> even still had) two or more wives. But in those cases where I had learned the truth
> from friends, neighbors, or relatives of the interviewee, I would confront him with
> the fact, although always in a joking manner, by mentioning, for instance, the first
> name of a former wife. At that point the interviewee – realizing that I knew too
> much already – usually told me everything for fear that his enemies would tell
> me even worse things about him. Although he might insist that he had lived with
> this woman for only six months and that he had hardly counted her as a real wife,
> he had at least confirmed my information. Later, I checked his story on the length
> of time, coming back to confront him again and again if necessary. Although I
> visited most people only once or twice – after first learning as much as possible
> about them from others – I had to go back to see some of them as many as five
> times until I was satisfied that all the data were accurate.
>
> (Perlman 1970: 307)

Of course, not all interviewees will tolerate such repeated and directive questioning.
As Troustine and Christensen (1982) indicate, from their study of community elites,
care is required:

> Respondents may be reluctant at first to offer candid views of their peers. . . .
> Sometimes a respondent will balk at virtually every question, finding it increasingly
> uncomfortable to share the inside views we are asking him or her to reveal. This
> won't happen often, but when it does we should be persistent but not belligerent.
> After all . . . the respondent could, if he or she is well-connected, make things
> difficult for us with just a phone call.
>
> (Troustine and Christensen 1982: 70, quoted in Hunter 1993: 45)

Researchers are often warned to avoid the use of leading questions. While the dangers of these must be borne in mind, they can be extremely useful in testing hypotheses and trying to penetrate fronts. What is important is to assess the likely direction of bias that the question will introduce. Indeed, a useful tactic is to make the question 'lead' in a direction opposite to that in which one expects the answer to lie, and thus avoid the danger of misleadingly confirming one's expectations – though one must take care that this does not undermine one's identity as a competent participant in the eyes of interviewees.

Directive questioning and non-directive questioning are likely to provide different kinds of data, and thus may be useful at different stages of inquiry. But whatever kinds of questioning are employed, ethnographers must remain aware of the likely effects of their questions on what is, and is not, said by informants.[4] Much the same is true of the use of various stimuli that can be used in the course of interviews, whether texts (Törrönen 2002); body mass index figures (Treseder 2006); elicited drawings (Kearney and Hyle 2004) or photographs (Allan 2005).

Conclusion

The accounts people provide can be an important source of data for ethnographers. These may be produced spontaneously or elicited by the researcher, in the course of participant observation or in formally defined interview situations. Whatever their form, interviews must be viewed as social events in which the interviewer (and for that matter the interviewee) is a participant observer. The ethnographer may be able to play a more dominant role than is the case in other contexts, and this can be capitalized upon, both in terms of when and where the interview takes place and who is present, as well as through the kinds of question asked. In this way different types of data can be elicited, as required by the changing demands of the research. While this feature of interviews heightens the danger of reactivity, this is only one aspect of a more general problem that cannot be avoided: the effects of audience and context on what is said and done.

The accounts produced by the people under study must neither be treated as 'valid in their own terms', and thus as beyond assessment and explanation, nor simply dismissed as epiphenomena or ideological distortions. They can be used both as a source of information about events, and as revealing the perspectives and discursive practices of those who produced them. Moreover, while it may sometimes be important to distinguish between solicited and unsolicited accounts, too much must not be made of this distinction. Rather, all accounts must be examined as social phenomena occurring in, and shaped by, particular contexts. Not only will this add to sociological knowledge directly, but also it can throw light on the kind of threats to validity that we may need to consider in assessing the information provided by an account.

In this chapter we have rather assumed that accounts take an exclusively oral form. While this may be true for non-literate societies, in many settings today paper-based and electronic documents are an important source of data, and so too are artefacts of various kinds, as we shall see in the next chapter.

---

4 For useful discussions of different question formats, and of other matters relating to ethnographic interviewing, see Spradley (1979: 83–91); and Lofland *et al.* (2006: ch. 5).

6   Documents and other artefacts, real and virtual

In the course of this chapter we consider two further kinds of data to which ethnographic researchers need to pay attention: documentary sources and material artefacts. Both are easily overlooked. In recent times, there has been so much emphasis, in some quarters, on the study of face-to-face interactions, on encounters and situations, that other key features of the social world could be forgotten. For example, many of the social settings we study are self-documenting, in the sense that that their members are engaged in the production and circulation of various kinds of written material. Government departments and many kinds of other organization generate and consume huge amounts of documentation. These include reports on 'cases', financial records, rule-books, organizational charts, timetables, memoranda, and so on. These may be on paper or in electronic form, or both. And, often, there are multiple sources of relevant documentation for any setting or group of people one might study. Given this, we need to think of contexts as involving *documentary constructions of reality* (Coffey and Atkinson 2004): documentary sources construct 'facts', 'records', 'diagnoses', 'decisions', and 'rules' that are crucially involved in social activities (see Prior 2003, 2004). Moreover, this is not just a matter of words: images can be involved in this process too, as Ball (2005) illustrates in relation to the practical work of the police and road users on public highways.

It is equally important to notice that the organization of collective social activity involves the creation, use and circulation of material artefacts. A great deal of practical mundane activity is concerned with the manipulation of objects of one kind or another. Social worlds are created out of material goods as well as from interpersonal relationships, and meaning inheres in them. They have often been given less attention even than written documents, but can be equally important.

In this chapter we will consider how these two kinds of material can be understood within the ambit of an ethnographic approach to the social world.

Documentary sources

Ethnographic work in its various guises has frequently been employed in the investigation of essentially oral cultures, or at least that is how they have been treated. Whether they were the non-literate cultures of much social anthropology, or the street cultures and demi-monde beloved of many sociological fieldworkers, the social worlds studied by ethnographers have often been largely devoid of written documents other than those produced by the fieldworkers themselves.

Although it was not the only rationale originally proposed for ethnographic fieldwork as a method, the fact that the 'exotic' societies studied by anthropologists had no written history was given as a major justification of the method, as well as of the synchronic functionalist analyses that initially went with it. Rather than attempt to reconstruct an essentially unknowable past, anthropologists were inclined to concentrate on the construction of working versions of the present. They turned their backs on conjectural history. There was, therefore, more than a coincidental relationship between ethnographic methods and the investigation of non-literate cultures.[1]

By contrast, sociologists of the Chicago School made rather more use of written materials, such as the records of social workers, diaries and letters. Indeed, they sometimes requested written life histories from those they were studying. For example, Thomas and Znaniecki (1927) in *The Polish Peasant in Europe and America* – generally regarded as an early classic of American sociology – relied substantially on written documents, mainly letters but also a life history. Thomas (1967) employed the same approach in *The Unadjusted Girl* (1924). He collected personal documentary accounts, in the belief that 'the unique value of the personal document is its revelation of the situations which have conditioned the behaviour' (Thomas 1967: 42). In both cases what we have is a dense accumulation of personal accounts, which were arranged thematically and juxtaposed in order to draw out the regularities and contrasts in 'definitions of the situation' (Thomas 1967: 42).

In a rather similar vein, early use of the term 'participant observation' designated the generation of documents by participants who might in contemporary parlance be called 'informants'. For instance, in the research that produced *The Gold Coast and the Slum*, Zorbaugh (1929) persuaded people who inhabited the exclusive society of Chicago's 'gold coast' to generate such 'inside' accounts. They were the participant observers as much as Zorbaugh himself.

Most of the settings in which contemporary sociologists and anthropologists work today are literate and contain a plethora of documents: not only are their members able to read and write, but this capacity is also an integral feature of their everyday life and work (Smith 1987, 1993). In many instances, therefore, ethnographers need to take account of documents as part of the social setting under investigation. Indeed, these documents may play a central role in the activities taking place there, in a way that they generally did not in the settings investigated by early Chicago School sociologists.

Documents can provide information about the settings being studied, or about their wider contexts, and particularly about key figures or organizations. Sometimes this information will be of a kind that is not available from other sources. On other occasions they may provide important corroboration, or may challenge, information received from informants or from observation.

Equally important, documents may be of value in stimulating analytic ideas. The development of generic concepts demands a broad and eclectic reading of textual sources (formal and informal, factual and fictional) on differing substantive topics. This means that there are rarely clear demarcations around what documents will and will not be of value. It also means that wide reading should inform the generation of

---

1   Of course, this is much less true today; indeed, anthropologists have taken a specific interest in literacy: Goody (1968, 1986, 1987); Street (1984); Gee (1996); Cook-Gumperz (2006).

concepts throughout the research process, rather than being limited either to the initial stage of planning or to that of writing up. By and large sociologists and anthropologists are not conspicuously good at this. The textual variety of an Erving Goffman is a rare accomplishment. His work shows how documents may play a key role in facilitating comparative analysis; both generating a sense of how the case(s) investigated are similar to and different from others, and indicating the limits to any generalizations that it may be tempting to make on the basis of the study. A much more recent example is provided by Gupta's use of 'a prize-winning novel written by an official of the Uttar Pradesh (U.P.) state government, and the accounts of corruption by one of the major social anthropologists of India, F. G. Bailey' to help make sense of the stories about corruption in his own fieldwork data (Gupta 2005).

In a literate culture, it is possible to draw on all sorts of documents, both those generated independently of the research as well as ones specifically elicited by the researcher. We shall begin with a discussion of documents as 'secondary' sources for the ethnographer, and then turn our attention to a more detailed examination of the ethnography of settings where the production and use of documents is an integral feature of everyday life.

Types of document and their uses

There is often a quite bewildering variety of documentary materials that might be of some relevance to the researcher. These may be distributed along a dimension ranging from the 'informal' to the 'formal' or 'official'. At the informal end of the spectrum there are many 'lay' accounts of everyday life that the enterprising and imaginative researcher can draw on for certain purposes. These include fictional literature, diaries, autobiographies, letters, and mass media products. Some of these will be produced in multiple copies and made widely available, some not.

There are, for example, numerous categories of persons in contemporary society who publish versions of their own life story:

> More than ever before in history, men of affairs, including politicians, military leaders, and business executives, are intent upon recording their experiences, personal as well as public, for posterity. In recent decades a number of American governmental leaders, including those in the military have, after resigning from their official posts, published their memories or personal accounts in which they seek public support for causes that the bureaucracy may have rejected during their period of office.
>
> (Sjoberg and Nett 1968: 163)

In the decades since that observation was made, nothing has changed. The output of memoirs continues unabated.

There are, too, a large number of first-hand accounts published by less politically eminent folk, including those drawn from the criminal underworld, and the realms of sports and entertainment. Similar personal accounts can be found in newspapers and magazines, or can be culled from radio and television documentaries and chat shows, or found on the web. These accounts by or about leading scientists, musicians, artists, celebrities, and others add to the list of contemporary social types represented in published documents.

Of course, such biographical and autobiographical accounts will rarely, if ever, be those of the actual people we are studying at first hand. They can, nevertheless prove valuable resources for the ethnographer. They can be a source of 'sensitizing concepts' (Blumer 1954): they can suggest distinctive ways in which their authors, or the people reported in them, organize their experiences, the sorts of imagery and 'situated vocabularies' (Mills 1940) they employ, the routine events, and the troubles and reactions, they encounter. Read in this light, they can be used to suggest potential lines of inquiry and refine 'foreshadowed problems'.

Documents of this sort have rather particular characteristics. Authors will have interests in presenting themselves in a (usually) favourable light; they may have axes to grind, scores to settle, or excuses and justifications to make. They are often written with the benefit of hindsight, and are thus subject to the usual problems of long-term recall. Authors have a sense of audience that will lead them to put particular glosses on their accounts. For some purposes, such considerations must be treated as potential sources of bias in accounts of this sort. But, looked at from another perspective, the sources of bias are data in themselves. As we noted in Chapter 5, as important as the accuracy or objectivity of an account is what it reveals about the teller's interests, perspectives, presuppositions, and discursive strategies.

Such accounts can be used, with appropriate caution, for comparative purposes. They can furnish information (albeit partial and personal) on groups and settings that are not available for first-hand observation. As a general category of data, published biographical and autobiographical sources are subject to a further sort of 'bias' in that they tend to over-represent the powerful, the famous, the extraordinary, and the articulate. But even that can also be a strength, since it is precisely people in such social categories who are often difficult to research directly.

Since the mid-1990s there has been a considerable resurgence of interest in the sociological analysis of biographical or autobiographical accounts. While that interest goes well beyond the scope of ethnographic research, ethnographers can incorporate many of the insights from this research field (Reed-Danahay 1997, 2001; Plummer 2001; Chase 2005). The growth in scholarly interest reflects a renewed emphasis on the study of narrative forms, temporality, and memory. It reflects too a focus on the intersection of the 'personal' and the 'social' (Erben 1993). As Stanley (1993) summarizes some of these concerns:

> I see a concern with biography and autobiography as fundamental to sociology, because I perceive the grounds of their sociological interest lying within the epistemological problematics concerning how we understand 'the self' and 'a life', how we 'describe' ourselves and other people and events, how we justify the knowledge-claims we make in the name of the discipline, in particular through the processes of textual production.
>
> (Stanley 1993: 50)

These sociological perspectives on 'lives' and 'documents' also often reflect commitments to a feminist standpoint. Documentary sources may be drawn on to recuperate the otherwise muted voices of women and other dominated groups, and feminist scholarship particularly affirms the intersection of the personal and the social (Stanley 1992; Evans 1993).

In the collection and investigation of 'informal' documentary materials, the fictional – even the most popular and ephemeral – can be used profitably. The most banal ('pulp' or 'pot-boiler') fiction is often replete with images, stereotypes, and myths bearing on a vast range of social domains. Indeed, the lack of literary merit characteristic of such genres reflects the fact that it unquestioningly trades on stocks of common knowledge and conventional wisdom. Here too, then, we can become sensitized to cultural themes pertaining to sex, gender, family, work, success, failure, class, mobility, regional variations, religious beliefs, political commitments, health and illness, the law, crime, social control, etc. These are not necessarily to be read at face value, as accurate representations of social reality, but can suggest themes, images, or metaphors. This is no less true of more 'serious' fiction: novels can suggest different ways of organizing experience, and alternative thematic models. We need not shy away from the careful use of literary sources. As various authors have pointed out, there is a long and complex set of relationships between literature and the social sciences (for example, Lepenies 1988; Cappetti 1993). As Davis (1974) noted in the mid-1970s, ethnographers and novelists alike find themselves telling 'stories'.[2]

Of course, by no means all informal documents are published, in the sense of being widely available via multiple copies. Unpublished personal diaries, or works of fiction, are sometimes available. There are also informal documents produced in the field that can illuminate key social relationships. In her study of girls' friendships, Hey (1997) made considerable use of the notes that the girls passed to one another in the course of lessons. She comments that they 'represented in their most condensed and dramatic form' some of the key themes of her book (Hey 1997: 2).[3]

At the other end of the spectrum are sources of a more 'formal' nature, and these include other published ethnographies. There is every reason for the sociologist interested in, say, hospitals or clinics to examine works on a variety of other institutional settings – schools, courts, welfare agencies, religious houses, police stations, university departments, or emergency services, for example. The precise selection of settings, and the lessons drawn from them, will depend on the analytic themes being pursued. Through such comparisons one might trace the variety of 'degradation ceremonies', the conditions of 'information control', or the moral evaluation of 'clients'. There is, in principle, no limit to such comparative work, and no prescriptions can be offered. The part played by serendipitous discoveries and unpredicted insights will be considerable here, as in all creative work. One must establish the right conditions for serendipity, however, and that includes attention to sources of many sorts. As Glaser and Strauss (1967) remark with characteristic enthusiasm:

> Theorizing begs of comparative analysis. The library offers a fantastic range of comparison groups, if only the researchers have the ingenuity to discover them. Of course, if their interest lies mainly with specific groups, and they wish to explore them in great depth, they may not always find sufficient documentation bearing on them. But if they are interested in generating theory, the library can be immensely useful especially . . . for generating formal theory. Regardless of which type of theory the theorist is especially interested in, if he browses intelligently

---

2 See Chapter 9 for further discussion of parallels between ethnography and literary analysis.
3 Nowadays, such data may no longer be available to the researcher; text messaging is probably used instead.

through the library (even without much initial direction), he cannot help but have his theorizing impulses aroused by the happily bewildering, crazy-quilt pattern of social groups who speak to him.

(Glaser and Strauss 1967: 179)

As in Goffman's work on topics like 'total institutions' (Goffman 1961; see also Perry 2007), the imaginative use of secondary documentary sources allows for the elaboration of 'perspective by incongruity' (Burke 1964; Lofland 1980; Manning 1980): that is, the juxtaposition of instances and categories that are normally thought of as mutually exclusive. Such sources and devices are ideal for heuristic purposes: they can rejuvenate jaded imaginations and spark off novel conceptualizations. In his or her imagination the researcher is free to wander at large among diverse social scenes, gathering ideas, insights, hypotheses, and metaphors.

In addition to the sorts of documentary source we have referred to up to now, in a literate culture it is possible to emulate researchers like Zorbaugh (1929) and draw on the ability of informants to generate written accounts specifically for research purposes. By such means one can gather information that complements other data sources in the field. Some versions of research have indeed drawn extensively on such indigenous written accounts. The entire tradition of 'mass observation' in Britain rested on the ability of literate volunteers to produce 'native' accounts of everyday life around them (see Stanley 2001). The revival of the Mass Observation Archive has again depended on such written documents:

> The writing has been generated in response to a call from the Mass-Observation Archive, repeated at intervals over the years, for people to take part in a form of collective autobiography. No special skills, knowledge or qualifications are required, only an enjoyment of writing and a willingness to put thoughts and experiences on paper in a discursive way.
>
> (Sheridan 1993: 27)

This emphasis on the collection of demotic accounts, characteristic of Mass Observation, is but one version of wide possibilities for the collection of documentary evidences. The use of diaries of different types is often an important adjunct to fieldwork. An influential version of this strategy was advocated by Zimmerman and Wieder (1977), who used a diary technique in their study of counter-cultural lifestyles. They comment that, while they were committed to participant observation, there were settings and activities that remained hard for them to observe directly. They therefore recruited insider informants, who kept detailed diaries over seven-day periods. Subsequently, the researchers subjected each informant to a lengthy and detailed interview, based on the diaries,

> in which he or she was asked not only to expand the reportage, but also was questioned on the less directly observable features of the events recorded, on their meanings, their propriety, typicality, connection with other events and so on.
>
> (Zimmerman and Wieder 1977: 484)

Narratives are also sometimes solicited by ethnographers. For example, Nygren and Blom (2001) collected short narratives from social work students dealing with problems that they had experienced. They note not only the advantages that such data can have, but also its drawbacks by comparison with interviews. Combining the two methods could, of course, overcome these.

Solicited written accounts, such as diaries and narratives, are especially useful ways of obtaining information about the personal and the private.[4] When carefully managed, and with suitable cooperation from informants, the diary, in particular, can be used to record data that might not be forthcoming in face-to-face interviews or other data collection encounters. Sexual behaviour is one obvious example. For instance, one major study among gay males made extensive use of personal diaries in order to obtain information on the types and frequencies of sexual practices (Coxon 1988, 1996).

Similarly, Davies used personal diaries in her study of student midwives (Davies and Atkinson 1991). Her research shows some of the anxieties and coping strategies associated with status passage, as experienced nurses became novice midwives. It is noticeable from the responses Davies obtained that the students were able to use the research diaries as a kind of personal confessional, often addressing the researcher directly about private anxieties, sources of anger, and frustrations. These personal accounts were complemented by interviews and observations.

Diaries of this sort can also be used to pick up the minutiae of day-to-day social action. Robinson (1971), in the course of an investigation of the experience of illness, persuaded a series of married women in South Wales to keep a diary on the health status of the members of their households. The diaries were kept over a four-week period. They enabled Robinson to gain some insight into the daily symptomatic episodes and health-related decisions characteristic of everyday living. Many of the episodes reported were minor, though by no means insignificant, and could easily have been overlooked in retrospective accounts produced in, say, interviews or questionnaires.

This sort of procedure has also been used in work on educational settings. Ball (1981), for instance, used diaries in combination with a range of other techniques, including sociometric questionnaires on friendship choices. He explicitly notes the value of combining such data sources:

> The sociometric questionnaires failed to pick up the casual friendships that existed between pupils outside school, and made it appear that they had no such contact. In addition, they failed to pick up the cross-sex friendships that were established at this time. Perhaps the notion of 'friendships' is too narrow and ill-defined to account for these other kinds of adolescent relationships. . . . The entries in the diaries that several of the pupils wrote for me did, however, refer to these contacts.
>
> (Ball 1981: 100)

Research-generated documents of this sort embody the strengths and weaknesses of all such personal accounts. They are partial, and reflect the interests and perspectives of their authors. They are not to be privileged over other sources of information, but nor are they to be discounted. Like other accounts, they should be read with regard to the context of their production, their intended or implied audiences, and the author's interests. Equally, one must note that a written account is not a debased version.

---

4 An alternative strategy, of course, is to provide informants with audio-recorders that they can use to record day-to-day events, their own thoughts and feelings, and so on. There is an interesting question about what differences there could be between written and oral diaries.

Given the historical and intellectual roots of ethnographic work, one can often detect a romantic legacy that privileges the oral over the literate. It is easy (but wrong) to assume that the spoken account is more 'authentic' or more 'spontaneous' than the written.[5]

We have discussed a range of documentary sources, but we have not yet paid attention to the investigation of social activities that directly involve generating documents. Fieldwork in literate societies – especially in formal organizations – is likely to encompass the production and use of documents of various kinds. In the following section we turn to such activities and their documentary products.

Documents in context

In some settings it would be hard to conceive of anything approaching an ethnographic account without some attention to documentary material in use. For instance, in his study of locomotive engineers, Gamst (1980) drew on a range of documentary sources:

> Some documents are published, for example: rule books, timetables, technical manuals for use of equipment, and instructional, regulating, and investigating publications of many kinds used by railroads, trade unions, government, and other firms. Unpublished documents include: official correspondence, reports in mimeographed and other forms, railroad operating bulletins and circulars, train orders, operating messages, and sundry other items.
>
> (Gamst 1980: viii)

Whether or not one would draw on all such sources, one would certainly expect an ethnography of work on the railway to make full reference to such features as operating schedules and timetables (whatever disgruntled passengers might feel). A similar instance is provided by Zerubavel (1979) in his formal analysis of time in hospitals; he necessarily draws on such sources as timetables, work rosters and clinical rotations, as embodied in organizational documents. In many organizational settings the use and production of such documents are an integral part of everyday life (Prior 2003).

Similarly, the ethnographic study of scientific work – especially the genre of 'laboratory studies' – cannot proceed adequately without acknowledgement of the work of writing. For instance, Latour and Woolgar (1979), in their classic study of a biomedical laboratory, document the centrality of written outputs. The scientific laboratory is fundamentally preoccupied with what these authors call 'inscriptions': that is, representations of natural phenomena, and the texts that are the products of the laboratory. Scientific papers are the currency that circulates within and between scientific research groups. One cannot address the complex social realities of scientific work, and the production of scientific knowledge, without paying serious attention to how and why scientific papers are written. The sociology of scientific knowledge is now replete with studies of written texts and other forms of representation (for example, Lynch and Woolgar 1990). And the same approach may be extended to all organizational and professional settings.

Douglas, writing in 1967, commented on the increasing importance of 'official' numerical data in contemporary society (see also Porter 1995; Power 1997), while

---

5 Derrida (1976) has identified this as a key theme in Western thought.

simultaneously regretting the relative failure of sociological commentators to address this as a topic:

> Throughout the Western world today there exists a general belief that one knows something only when it has been counted. . . . Considering the importance of such statistics for the formation and testing of all kinds of common-sense and scientific theories of human action, it is a remarkable fact that there is at present very little systematic knowledge of the functioning of official statistics-keeping organizations.
>
> (Douglas 1967: 163)

Since Douglas made those observations, there has been an increasing amount of work along the lines suggested (see Prior 2003, 2004). However, in comparison with the sheer volume of 'literate' record-keeping and documentation in contemporary society, the coverage remains at best patchy. There is still, apparently, a tacit assumption that ethnographic research can appropriately represent contemporary social worlds as essentially oral cultures. Many studies of medical settings, for instance, focus exclusively on spoken interaction between medical practitioners and their patients, or between health professionals, with relatively little attention to activities of reading and writing. As Rees remarks: 'Both medicine and medical sociology have to a large extent neglected the record. Indeed, so rarely is it mentioned that one could be forgiven for thinking that medicine is a purely oral discipline' (Rees 1981: 55).

Pettinari (1988) demonstrates the value of close attention to 'writing' in a medical setting. Here is provided a detailed account of how surgeons write their reports on operations, and in particular of how junior surgeons learn such occupational skills. There are ways in which the operation is represented competently in surgeons' reports, and the appropriate formulations are acquired over time with professional experience. The written account is a fundamental element in the everyday organization of surgical work. Its production and use are an important focus for an ethnographic account of surgery in general.

In a similar vein is Coffey's (1993) ethnography of accountants in training. Based on fieldwork in an office of an international accounting firm, she documented aspects of trainees' acquisition of accountancy expertise. She studied bookkeeping skills together with the trainees, and describes how they acquired skill and judgement in reading documentary sources such as balance sheets. It would clearly be absurd to represent the world of the corporate accountant as non-literate or as non-numerate – and a comprehensive ethnographic account must include reference to how organizational documents are read, interpreted, and used.

Because of the critique of 'official statistics', stemming largely from the ethno-methodological movement, some contemporary ethnographers may feel reluctant to engage in the systematic use of documentary data. We believe that they are right to treat seriously objections against employing 'official' data simply as a resource not a topic, but that they would be wrong to ignore such materials. The point of departure for critics of 'data from official sources' was the contention that, traditionally, the tendency had been for sociologists to treat such information at face value, and not to pay adequate attention to its character as a social product. This opens up an important area of investigation, rather than implying that official data should be ignored.

It is, of course, a long-standing concern of sociologists that data derived from official sources may be inadequate in some way: that they may be subject to bias or distortion, or that bureaucracies' practical concerns may mean that data are not formulated in accordance with sociologists' interests. The ethnomethodologists, on the other hand, proposed more radical problems. Cicourel (1976) remarks, for instance:

> for years sociologists have complained about 'bad' statistics and distorted bureaucratic record-keeping but have not made the procedures producing the 'bad' materials we label 'data' a subject of study. The basic assumption of conventional research on crime, delinquency and law is to view compliance and deviance as having their own ontological significance, and the measuring rod is some set of presumably 'clear' rules whose meaning is also ontologically and epistemologically 'clear'.

(Cicourel 1976: 331)

The argument is that rather than being viewed as more or less biased sources of data, official documents and enumerations should be treated as social products: they must be examined, not relied on uncritically as a research resource.

In this way attention is diverted towards the investigation of the socially organized practices whereby rates, categories, and statistics are produced by those whose job it is to generate and interpret such phenomena. An early example of work in this vein was that of Sudnow (1965) on the production of 'normal crimes' in a Public Defender's office. Sudnow details the practical reasoning that informs how particular crimes or misdemeanours become categorized in the course of organized activities such as plea bargaining. Thus, he looks 'behind' the categories of official designations and crime rates – based on convictions – to the work of interpretation and negotiation that generates such statistics. In addition to Sudnow's ethnographic study of crime rates, other studies of the same period included those of Cicourel (1967) on juvenile justice, and of Cicourel and Kitsuse (1963) on the organization of educational decision-making, the categorization of students, and their official biographies. More recent research in a similar vein includes a welter of constructionist accounts of social problems (see, for example, Holstein and Miller 1989, 1993). Similar in focus are Prior's studies of the social organization of death, with particular emphasis on the classification of causes, and of mental illness (Prior 1985, 1989, 1993). In this context one should also note the observations of Prior and Bloor (1993) on the life-table as a cultural and historical artefact.

The origins of the 'official statistics' debate in sociology were potentially misleading, important though the general perspective was. Issues became polarized quite unnecessarily. The problems associated with data from official sources were important, and they related directly to classic problems of sociological analysis, such as the explanation of suicide (Douglas 1967; Atkinson 1978); but they were by no means unique. The careful ethnographer will be aware that all classes of data have their problems, and all are produced socially; none can be treated as 'transparent' representations of 'reality'. The recognition of reflexivity in social research entails such an awareness (Holstein and Miller 1993). As a result, there is no logical reason to regard documents or similar information as especially problematic or totally vitiated. As Bulmer (1980) remarks in this context:

Firstly, there is no logical reason why awareness of possible serious sources of error in official data should lead to their rejection for research purposes. It could as well point to the need for methodological work to secure their improvement. Secondly, a great many of the more thorough-going critiques of official statistics relate to statistics of suicide, crime, and delinquency, areas in which there are special problems of reliable and valid measurement, notoriously so. The specific problems encountered in these fields are not, ipso facto, generalizable to all official statistics whatever their content. Thirdly, cases of the extensive use of official data – for example, by demographers – do not suggest that those who use them are unaware of the possible pitfalls in doing so. The world is not made up just of knowledgeable sceptics and naive hard-line positivists.

(Bulmer 1980: 508)

In other words, then, while drawing some inspiration from the ethnomethodological critique of 'official statistics' and similar documentary sources, we by no means endorse a radical view which suggests that such sources are of no value as a resource. Data of this kind raise problems, to be sure, but they provide information as well as opening up a range of analytic problems that are worth investigation. The ethnographer, like any other social scientist, may well draw on such documents and representations. Furthermore, he or she may be particularly well placed to engage in principled and systematic research bearing on their validity and reliability as data, through first-hand investigation of the contexts of their production and use.

Rees (1981), in his work on medical records, indicates the situated significance of readership and authorship within a professional setting:

What the House Officer writes, and the way in which he goes about constructing the history and examination, is one way his seniors can make inferences about the standard of his other activities. The supposition others make is that a House Officer who writes an organized and clearly thought out account of his work will be well organized in the way he carries out those activities. By paying attention to the construction of the account, and by ensuring that it conforms to the accepted model, the House Officer is able to influence one of the ways in which he will be judged by his seniors.

(Rees 1981: 58–9)

This reflects Garfinkel's (1967) remarks on records, where he suggests that they should be thought of as 'contractual' rather than as 'actuarial'. That is, they are not literal accounts of 'what happened' but are tokens of the fact that the relevant personnel went about their business competently and reasonably (see also Prior 2003). This is something that was taken up by Dingwall (1977b) in his study of the education of health visitors. He writes about the students' production of records of their visits to clients, and notes that since the actual conduct of the work is invisible to the supervisor, the record is the main focus of administrative control. Likewise, the record constitutes a major means of self-defence for these 'face-workers'. And, of course, the role of documents, of various kinds, in regimes of 'transparent' accountability has increased substantially in recent decades, with the rise of the 'audit society' (Power 1997).

In various ways, then, records have considerable importance in certain social settings. In some, the production of 'paperwork' is a major preoccupation. Even in organizations that have people-processing functions, this usually involves the translation of events into records of those events which can be filed, stored, and manipulated. Such files are a primary resource for members of the organization in getting through their everyday work. Often, the exigencies of record-making can play an important part in organizing the work that gets done, and the routines used to accomplish it. Records of previous encounters with clients can be used to formulate appropriate objectives and activities for a current consultation. As Dingwall (1977b) writes of his student health visitors:

> The good health visitor can derive sufficient data from the face sheet to identify the relevant areas of her knowledge about clients and the tasks she should be accomplishing in a visit. Unusual events are flagged in various ways. Thus, a child who is at risk may be marked by a red star on the card. Particular social problems may be pencilled on the cover.
>
> (Dingwall 1977b: 112)

Heath (1981) has also commented on this sort of use of medical records in the context of doctor–patient encounters. He explains how general practitioners use their record cards to open the encounter with the patient:

> It is often through the elaboration of the appropriate record's contents, prior to the initiation of first topic, that the doctor is able to render the relevant characteristics of the patient, and thereby design a 'successful' first topic initiator.
>
> (Heath 1981: 85)

Records, then, are used to establish actors as 'cases' with situated identities, which conform to 'normal' categories or deviate from them in identifiable ways. Records are made and used in accordance with organizational routines, and depend for their intelligibility on shared cultural assumptions. Records construct a 'documentary reality' that, by virtue of its very documentation, is often granted a sort of privilege. Although their production is a socially organized activity, official records have a certain anonymity which leads to their treatment by members as objective, factual statements rather than as mere personal belief, opinion, or guesswork. (It is, of course, the case that some records may contain specific entries, such as differential medical or psychiatric diagnoses, that are explicitly flagged as tentative or contested.)

It should be apparent from what we have outlined already that there are many locales where literate social activity is of some social significance, and may indeed be of major importance. Modern industrial and administrative bureaucracies, and professional or educational settings, are obvious cases in point. It requires little reflection to remind oneself of how pervasive are the activities of writing and reading written documents. And even in the case of settings where documents are not a central feature there is often an enormous amount of written material available that can be an invaluable research resource.

The presence and significance of documentary products provide the ethnographer with a rich vein of analytic topics, as well as valuable sources of data and information. Such topics include: How are documents written? How are they read? Who writes them? Who reads them? For what purposes? On what occasions? With what outcomes? What is recorded, and how? What is omitted? What does the writer seem to take for granted about the reader(s)? What do readers need to know in order to make sense of them? The list can be extended readily, and the exploration of such questions would lead the ethnographer inexorably towards a systematic examination of each and every aspect of everyday life in the setting in question.

The ethnographer who takes no account of such matters, on the other hand, ignores at his or her peril these features of a literate culture. There is nothing to be gained, and much to be lost, by representing such a culture as if it were an essentially oral tradition. In the scrutiny of documentary sources, the ethnographer thus recognizes and builds on his or her socialized competence as a member of a literate culture. Not only does the researcher read and write, but also he or she reflects on the very activities of reading and writing in social settings. Thus, such everyday activities are incorporated into the ethnographer's topics of inquiry as well as furnishing analytic and interpretative resources.

We have concentrated here for the most part on written documents, but it is perhaps worth stressing that materials containing images of various kinds, whether plans, drawings, photographs, or sounds are also often available. The mass media are a major source here, but by no means the only one. Images of various kinds are often part of the documents that are generated via organizational work, for example prospectuses for schools and universities, brochures of various kinds, the pictures (in print and online) that play a key role in the buying and selling of houses, etc. Many of the same questions need to be asked about these materials as about written documents; though the kinds of analysis used are likely to be distinctive (Emmison and Smith 2000; Pink 2004b).

Heath's work on technologically mediated action provides a series of key examples. Heath and Luff, for instance, analyse collaborative work and interaction in control rooms of the London Underground system, where visual data on screen is a key feature of everyday work (Heath and Luff 2000). In settings of scientific and medical work, visual culture may also be of fundamental importance, with data themselves being constructed in visual terms. Dumit's ethnography of brain-imaging is but one recent example: the striking images of brain scans he reproduces do not just illustrate the text. The visualization of brain function is what the bioscientists *do*, and their scientific work is intensely visual in character. Consequently, what is important here is not just the 'visual analysis' of scientific work, but the analysis of scientific visual work. There is, in other words, a direct homology between the social action under investigation and its ethnographic representation (Dumit 2004).

Artefacts

Just as ethnographers can sometimes overlook the literate quality of many social settings, they often seem to ignore the role of material artefacts. While the rise in studies of material culture has brought some of the relevant issues to the fore, there remains a tendency for material goods and objects to be neglected in ethnographic work, being left within a circumscribed boundary of specialist interests. Our (all too brief) account here is intended merely to remind ethnographers that the 'fields' in which they conduct fieldwork are populated not only with social actors, but with 'things' of many sorts.

Of course, the ethnographic gaze has encompassed material culture since the earliest days. Malinowski's classic anthropological research among the Trobrianders included a close reading of the building of a canoe, and how the practical construction work simultaneously evoked and aligned cooperative social relations. Likewise, his account of reciprocity and exchange relationships in the *kula* system necessarily involved some attention to the *material* goods that are circulated among exchange-partners across the archipelago. However, this focus on material artefacts is not very common in present-day ethnographic studies.

Rather than treating the analysis of such artefacts as a separate domain, we wish to stress that material goods, objects and traces need to be analysed in their broad ethnographic contexts. Moreover, the ethnography of everyday life demands attention to its material features, and how social actors engage with physical things. This is much more than just applying attention to physical surroundings and material context. There are many social phenomena that are impossible without the use of material goods. There are many social relationships that are crystallized and embodied in material objects. There are many forms of work that necessarily imply the competent and skilled manipulation of physical resources, whether as an official part of the job or in the production of 'homers', artefacts for personal use (Anteby 2003).

For instance, Atkinson's publications on haematologists highlight some of the material work that goes into the production of medical facts and opinions. Haematologists spend a lot of time *talking* about their patients, and transforming those patients into 'cases', 'opinions' and 'diagnoses' (Atkinson 1995). But their work is not just accomplished through talk. They also have to manipulate the physical traces of the body: the blood and bone-marrow have to be collected and read for signs of disease. This involves their physical manipulation, through techniques such as staining, in order to render them visible and legible. The preparation of a slide for microscopic inspection demands a certain physical and perceptual dexterity, as does use of the microscope itself. The skilful activities of inspecting physical traces of peripheral blood or bone-marrow are embedded in the exchange of talk between professional colleagues, or in teaching encounters. Objects, traces, skills and talk are mutually implicated, and the ethnography of professional knowledge-production has to take account of them.

These observations in a medical setting parallel a more general interest in ethnographic studies of scientific sites, such as laboratories and scientific networks. While a great deal of the sociology of scientific knowledge has been disproportionately concerned with the cultural-cognitive aspects of scientific controversy and discovery, some studies have explicitly incorporated an interest in the material circumstances of scientific work. Actor-network theory takes such an interest to an extreme (occasionally absurd) length. It makes no principled distinction between human and material actants within a complex of interrelationships. Hence, technical *equipment* can be analysed in terms of the theories of knowledge it embodies, and the active part it plays in shaping scientific knowledge. However, it is not necessary to engage in fully fledged actor-network theory in order to recognize the significance of materials in the *production* of scientific and technological knowledge. The ethnographer in this field needs to acquire some degree of technical expertise and an understanding of how material artefacts are made and used. This includes an appreciation of the physical qualities of things. A contemporary oral history of the Moog synthesizer, which played a significant part in the development of rock music, includes an appreciation of its technical qualities as well as the biographical relations in which it was embedded (Pinch and Trocco 2002). Ethnography and the archaeology of the present also converge in the analysis of computing and information technology (Finn 2001; English-Lueck 2002).

The 'thing-ness' of things in their material and social contexts needs to be understood by ethnographers. We are attentive to the nuances of social interaction, and we devote a considerable amount of time and effort to the analysis of social action. We need to give equally appropriate attention to things. They have material qualities, based on their physical composition, they have surface texture, shape and colour. Ethnographers have not been particularly good at exploring the significance of *appearance* in the material world about them. The social worlds that many of them describe have been oddly empty spaces, with little or no attention paid to the physical surroundings. Those ethnographic worlds are often flat and monochrome, in that aesthetic qualities, such as colour, are ignored. Yet, if we want to make sense of many social worlds, we ought to take account of how they are physically constituted. It would, for instance, seem odd to describe work in a modern office setting without paying heed to its physical layout (walled rooms or open plan, number of floors, connections to other buildings, etc.), its colour schemes, its furnishings and the like. Such places are *designed* and their design embodies corporate interests and implicit values. These features both constrain the social relations of work in distinctive ways and are resources that are used and even 'redesigned' by workers.

Atkinson's (2006a) ethnography of the Welsh National Opera Company gives central attention to several aspects of its material context. The production and performance of an opera depend not just on singing and acting, and the key features of an opera go beyond the work of the director and the conductor. The realization of music theatre involves the creation of *material* circumstances, such as the design and construction of the set. Moreover, once the set has been created, it in turn poses *physical* constraints on but also provides material opportunities to producers and performers. Atkinson's monograph includes graphic accounts of how performers had to grapple (literally as well as metaphorically) with recalcitrant aspects of the set: walls that move unpredictably (*Simon Boccanegra*), or boats that are difficult to manhandle *(Peter Grimes)*. Atkinson (n.d.) writes about how the props department in the opera company used their craft skills to engage in 'bricolage' to create the physical objects required for a new production. This department was also a physical archive of past productions, and a source of situated 'ethno-archaeology' through which the past achievements of the opera company could be traced. Individual pieces that had required particular ingenuity for their construction, or that have particular aesthetic value, are treasured by the props department as trophies of their own past 'operatic' triumphs.

Any theatrical performance, not least that of the opera, depends on material objects. However, as Erving Goffman showed many years ago, we all depend upon 'props' of various kinds in more mundane settings. Furthermore, there are ethnographic accounts that are explicitly focused on the collection and display of material artefacts. Macdonald's (2002) ethnography of London's Science Museum is an excellent case in point. She narrates the processes that went into the creation of a major museum exhibit on food. Such ethnographic examinations of the curating and display of material goods do more than documenting what happens in such esoteric places as museums and art galleries – important though those topics are in their own right. They also draw attention to more mundane aspects of material culture. The collection and display of objects is an important feature of mundane home cultures, for instance. Homes can be thought of as having 'museum-like' qualities, in that individual memorabilia or collections of objects can be self-consciously displayed. Hurdley's (2006, 2007) multimedia ethnography of mantelpieces in British homes is a useful case in point. The mantelpiece – the traditional structure over an open fireplace, still incorporated in modern homes that have central heating – is a key place for the display of ornaments, gifts, photographs and the like. There is a situated aesthetic that informs many of these displays, and the mantelpiece arrangement is often a focus of the living room. Moreover, the objects themselves embody their owners' memories: memory is not a mental state from this perspective, but is inscribed in material objects, and in the autobiographical narratives that they evoke. Mantelpiece objects can also embody the personal ties and mutual obligations of gift relationships. A deceptively trivial space such as the mantelpiece thus provides a microcosm of everyday domestic, aesthetic and interpersonal arrangements. The homespun example of the mantelpiece also directs ethnographic attention towards the more self-conscious cultural phenomenon of 'collecting' art and other material artefacts (see Painter 2002; Belk 1995; Pearce 1994).

The physicality of social phenomena can be extended to incorporate an appreciation of the built environment and physical space. While it is by no means a universal failing, it is undeniable that many ethnographic accounts seem to lack a sense of *places and spaces*. This is not just a matter of putting things into a 'context'. Rather, we ought to pay serious attention to the material circumstances that constrain social activity, how a sense of place is reflected in individual and collective identities, and how places are *used* by social actors, just as they use any material and symbolic resources. There are, of course, some clear examples that can be drawn on for inspiration. Pierre Bourdieu's (1979) classic analysis of the Kabyle house is a case in point. He analyses the house not merely as a physical locus of everyday life, but also as a site of symbolic ordering.[6] In a similar vein, anthropological accounts of Mediterranean societies stress the significance of the house, and its relationship to the street, as a physical coding of respectability – especially as regards the women of the household – and as an affirmation of strongly differentiated gender roles.

The house as a physical embodiment of identity, and its material decoration, are explored by Gregory (2003) in her exploration of householders' aesthetic work on late Victorian houses. These include the house-owners' need to purify the house of traces of previous occupants (carpets and soft furnishings, décor and colour schemes, bathroom suites and fittings etc.), often expressed in quite violent terms ('ripping out' fireplaces, for instance). The *material* decoration and furnishing of the house are not simply backdrops to the everyday performance of identity and biography. They are deeply implicated in the joint construction of a household by (for instance) couples who transform an older house into their own domestic space. These issues of personal identity are often informed by a sense of the identity of the house itself: the 'authenticity' of the material fabric of an older house is an important aspect of such reconstruction. Fireplaces, doors, windows and other 'features' may – for some house-owners at least – need to be in period if their personal, emotional investment in the house is to be adequately rewarding. These are partly aesthetic judgements, of course. They are also partly reflections of collective taste: in previous generations, the 'modernization' of the home would have been a far more common goal than its restoration. But they are profoundly dependent on the ethno-aesthetic of the social actors themselves, and depend upon the values attached to material goods (see Reid and Crowley 2000; Valis 2003).

The ethnographic appreciation of things should also extend to their creation and manufacture. As we have already noted, the rise of cultural studies and the associated emphasis on material culture have given rise to a rich vein of sources and analytic

---

6 For a critical assessment of his argument, see Silverstein (2004).

perspectives that can be drawn into the ethnographic imagination (see Miller 1998, 2001a, 2001b; Buchli 2002). They include the ethnographic analysis of processes of *design*, an aspect of contemporary material culture that has attracted considerable interest on the part of social scientists.[7] This includes ethnographic analysis of the design process (e.g Henderson 1998; Salvador *et al.* 1999) and the creation of visual culture itself (Frosh 2003). The same is true of architecture, urban design or the analysis of spaces and places (e.g. Dodds and Tavernor 2001; Borden 2002; Podalsky 2002; Crowley and Reid 2002; Butler and Robson 2003). We are now more than ever aware of the significance of the 'environment', as simultaneously shaped and shaping in the performance of individual and collective identities.

We repeat here a caveat. We are not referring to these issues simply in the interests of documenting the 'contexts' of social activity. These are not epiphenomenal issues either. Ethnographic research needs to pay close and serious attention to the material goods and circumstances that are integral to the organization of everyday social life. People do not act in a vacuum. Not only do they do things with words, but also they do things with things. The sort of issues that researchers sometimes lump together as 'experience', 'biography' or 'memory' are often embodied in material goods and personal possessions. The performance of work involves a sustained engagement with material means. The enactment of ritual normally involves the manipulation of objects charged with special significance. These and similar kinds of social action all call for a systematic ethnographic attention to the material world. We do not need a separate specialism or subdiscipline of 'material culture' in order to address these issues. On the contrary, they should be incorporated into the fabric of ethnographic inquiry, just as they contribute to the fabric of social life.

Finally, we should note that while physical space and objects have always been important for human behaviour, in recent times the virtual spaces created through fixed and mobile communication devices and the internet have gained increasing significance. While some ethnographers have given much attention to 'online cultures', there has perhaps been rather less awareness of how these virtual spaces shape more ordinary forms of social interaction, how virtual interaction intertwines with that which is face-to-face, and so on (Franklin and Lowry 2001). Here, too, there is a danger involved in specialization, that these issues will be ignored where they are not the main focus of inquiry. Moreover, of course, this is a field of expanding significance.

Ethnography in digital spaces

Digital technology has expanded our very notion of what constitutes a 'field'. Virtual fields and virtual fieldwork are now possible, and are assuming increasing significance in a social world that is simultaneously global and digital for some populations. Virtual communities and networks present particular challenges and opportunities for ethnographic research. Likewise, ethnographies of digital life itself are important aspects of contemporary social research. In addition, there are many opportunities to exploit digital technologies to reach particular research populations.

There are many kinds of informant who can be usefully accessed via the internet. For example, Stewart's research on people with irritable bowel disease included online access to sufferers. This is a very good example of how a potentially embarrassing or

---

7 See Julier (2000) for a useful introduction.

stigmatizing condition can be studied 'at a distance' when face-to-face interviewing and personal recruitment to a study might prove more troublesome (Stewart and Williams 2005). In much the same way Susie Scott conducted an interactionist project on shy people and constructions of shyness. She was able to contact and interact with shy people through internet access. Shyness is another prime example of the sort of personal quality or characteristic that lends itself especially well to internet research. Contrary to what one might initially and naively believe, shy people can be very willing to talk at length about themselves, and they are extremely reflective about their own interactional style. Indeed, their behaviour is often shy precisely because they have a heightened sense of self, are alert to the interactional niceties of dialogic interaction and group dynamics. Scott found that informants could and would produce very full, self-aware accounts of shyness, and that they could find the impersonal channel of communication of the internet quite amenable (Scott 2004).

Such research does not necessarily study 'naturally occurring' communities that exist in cyberspace, although in the course of setting up noticeboards and chat rooms researchers can create temporary, research-situated groupings that approximate to online focus groups. Their advantage over face-to-face focus groups is that they can persist more or less indefinitely, and actors can be enrolled on a rolling basis, while participation is not restricted by constraints of time and travel. Equally, however, we recognize that, increasingly, there are 'naturally occurring' communities in virtual, digital space. Researchers who use online means of accessing informants and participants are often tapping into existing networks of social actors who maintain 'virtual' communities through sustained interaction by digital means. It is clear that, for some participants at least, this is a prime social reality, and a major source of identity (Gatson and Zweerink 2004; Hammersley and Treseder 2007).

Our historical preferences for face-to-face communities and intense, local sites of interaction should not blind us to the fact that contemporary forms of communication can transform our sense of what is 'local' into widely distributed networks, and that 'communities' can (and do) exist in many different forms. We should also not forget that, as we noted earlier, one of the earliest inspirations for Chicago sociology was *The Polish Peasant*. The starting point of this was the exchange of communications, by letter, between Polish settlers in Chicago and relatives and friends living in Poland. There is no intrinsic difference between the slow exchange of written communication and the instant exchange of electronic messages. The density and speed of the latter, however, can create a more intense sense of shared experience and of a shared social world.

There do exist, therefore, 'virtual communities' that operate only in cyberspace, and can only be studied ethnographically through the same medium. Cyber-ethnography deals with social action and social organization in such virtual settings. Matthew Williams (2006), for instance, has undertaken an ethnographic study of multi-user domains (MUDs) in which participants can take on virtual identities ('avatars'), and interact with one another in virtual worlds. Williams paid particular attention to mechanisms of social control within such domains, which are explicitly 'policed' and are also subject to less formal forms of social control. Williams acted as a virtual participant observer within these virtual worlds. His research amply demonstrates that the proper preoccupations of ethnographic fieldwork can be brought to bear in such settings. There are issues of identity, of community and of social control that are vibrantly relevant to virtual worlds as much as they are to any other kind. The processes of negotiation, interaction and identity-formation are just as 'real' also. There is no fundamental distinction between 'virtual'; and 'real' environments in social terms, and research in the digital age needs to take account of that.[8]

Conclusion

In this chapter we have focused on the role that the study of documents, physical objects and virtual communication can play in ethnographic work. These have not always been given the attention they deserve within ethnographic work, the primary emphasis usually being on data from interviews and participant observation in face-to-face rather than virtual settings. We have tried to show the potential offered by these sources of data in the context of work that also draws on the more usual sources.

In the next chapter we will look at issues surrounding the recording and preparation of data for analysis.

8 For useful discussions of virtual methods, see Markham (2004) and Hine (2005).

7 Recording and organizing data

In previous chapters we have examined the main sources of data that ethnographers use: observation and participation; participants' oral accounts, both those that are 'naturally occurring' and those elicited in interviews; plus documents and artefacts of various kinds. In this chapter we want to look at how these data may need to be preserved or recorded, and organized, in preparation for the process of analysis. What is involved here varies considerably depending upon the nature of the data. In the case of documents and material objects, relatively little processing may sometimes be required, though these data will need to be catalogued in ways that make them available for analysis. By contrast, in the case of observing patterns of social interaction and collecting participant accounts, the task of recording the data is much more significant and time-consuming.

Technological developments have had a major impact upon the sort of data available to ethnographers, on how it can be recorded, and on the task of organizing it so as to facilitate analysis. CDs, DVDs and the internet represent relatively new sources of data, and ethnographers have made increasing use of them. Going a little further back into the past, the production of relatively cheap and portable audio-, and then video-, recorders transformed much ethnographic data collection. And, in relation to organizing data, the availability of cheap but very powerful personal computers, and of word-processing programs and specialized software for handling textual data, has been very significant. In recent years, the rise of digital audio-recorders and cameras, and the increased capacity of computers to handle pictures and sound as well as text, have opened up new possibilities.

We will begin by discussing what may be involved in processing documentary and physical data, then examine the methods available for recording observational and interview material, including transcription. Attention will be given to how the analytic process must carry on alongside data processing. Finally, we will move on to strategies for data organization.

Documents and other materials

We often need to collect and use documentary material from the research setting, as well as employing that from elsewhere. As we have noted, this kind of data can take a wide variety of forms (see Chapter 6). Some documents or material objects are freely available and can be retained by the ethnographer for later use. This is often true, for example, of such items as promotional material, guides, and circulars. Other documents can be bought or otherwise acquired. For example, material on the internet can often be downloaded and printed out.

Even when documentary sources are not produced in large numbers and are unavailable in electronic form, the researcher may be able to produce copies for retention (though here, and elsewhere, copyright issues need to be borne in mind). Photocopiers are available in some settings where research is carried out, and the ethnographer may be allowed access to them. The availability of relatively cheap and portable scanners also eases the problem considerably. However, what is produced by this latter means where text has been inputted into a word-processor, will almost always require considerable tidying up, correction, and filling in; much depends here upon the nature of the texts being scanned. It may also be possible to take digital photographs of posters and of other short texts.

Sometimes, there is no alternative to note-taking in recording the data from documents, or that pertaining to material objects. Here copying documents *in toto* may be necessary, but it is not always the most effective recording strategy. While it may reduce the danger of omitting something important, or losing the context, those advantages have to be set against the cost in time. It may be necessary to make judgements about which documents, and what parts of documents, are and are not to be copied. One can index a document so that the relevant sections can be consulted, as appropriate, at later stages of the research. This can be done relatively quickly, but it may only be of value if there will be easy future return access to the documentary sources concerned. One may also summarize relevant sections or copy them out by hand: by summarizing one can cover much more material, thus releasing scarce time for work of other kinds, but it will involve some loss of information and introduces an additional layer of interpretation.

These three modes of note-taking – copying by hand, indexing, and summarizing – are not mutually exclusive, of course, and each should be used according to the likely future accessibility of the documents and the anticipated use to which the notes will be put. Of particular importance here is whether they relate to central themes of the study or provide background information. These considerations may vary across different documents or even sections of documents, and judgements about them may change over time. It should also be remembered that written notes need not necessarily be made on the spot: where access to documents is restricted it may be more efficient to read indexes, summaries, or relevant sections into a portable audio-recorder, where this is possible, and then transcribe the recording later.

In the case of material objects, as with documents, copies or pictures may be readily available. Alternatively, it may be necessary to take photographs or make video-recordings, or perhaps to produce hand-drawn sketches. The use of photography and video-recording is discussed below.

Recording observations and interviews: fieldnotes

Fieldnotes are the traditional means in ethnography for recording observational and interview data. Originally, these were handwritten, but now they can sometimes be inputted directly into a handheld or laptop. Whether fieldnotes can be written at all, how, and covering what issues, depends on the nature of the research, the setting(s) in which fieldwork occurs, and the role(s) taken on by the ethnographer.[1]

---

1 For detailed guidance about the production of fieldnotes, see Emerson *et al.* (1995). Sanjek (1990) offers illuminating discussions of various aspects of fieldnotes, in the context of anthropology.

The writing of fieldnotes is not something that is (or should be) shrouded in mystery. It is not an especially esoteric activity. On the other hand, it does often constitute a central research activity, and it should be carried out with as much care and self-conscious awareness as possible. A research project can be as well organized and as theoretically sophisticated as you like, but with inadequate note-taking the exercise could be like using an expensive camera with poor quality film. In both cases, the resolution will prove unsatisfactory, and the results will be poor. Only foggy pictures result.

Fieldnotes are always selective: it is not possible to capture everything. And there is a trade-off between breadth of focus and detail. What is recorded will depend on one's general sense of what is relevant to the foreshadowed research problems, as well as on background expectations (Wolfinger 2002). Moreover, as we shall see, the character of fieldnotes may well change, in terms of focus and detail, over the course of the research. The completion of fieldnotes is not an entirely straightforward matter, then. Like most aspects of intellectual craft, some care and attention to detail are prerequisites: satisfactory note-taking needs to be worked at. It is a skill demanding repeated assessment of purposes and priorities, and of the costs and benefits of different strategies. Thus, the standard injunction, 'write down what you see and hear', glosses over a number of important issues. Among other things, the fieldworker will want to ask *what* to write down, *how* to write it down, and *when* to write it down.

The making of fieldnotes has been part of the invisible oral tradition of craft knowledge, and many who embark on their first project have to find their own way of doing things. So let us try to deal with some of the practical questions raised above. First, when to write notes? In principle, one should aim to make notes as soon as possible after the observed action. Most fieldworkers report that, while they can train themselves to improve recall, the quality of their notes diminishes rapidly with the passage of time; the detail is quickly lost, and whole episodes can be forgotten or become irreparably muddled. The ideal would be to make notes during actual participant observation. But this is not always possible, and even when it *is* possible the opportunities may be very limited. There are often restrictions arising from the social characteristics of the research setting, as well as from the ethnographer's role(s) in the field.

If the research is covert, then note-taking in the course of participation will often be practically impossible. In many settings, participants do not carry around notebooks (paper or electronic), and are not visibly engaged in a continual process of jotting down notes. In many circumstances, such activity would prove very disruptive either preventing 'natural' participation or generating distraction and distrust. It is unlikely, for example, that Calvey (2000) could take copious notes while acting as a 'bouncer' on the door of a club.

In a few contexts, of course, writing may be such an unremarkable activity that covert note-taking *is* possible. Rather surprisingly, Graham (1995) was able to take fieldnotes while working on a car assembly line. She writes:

> Luckily, the station that I worked during my last few months required that I carry a clipboard for noting damage to the car bodies as they entered our area; hence it was not unusual to see me jotting down notes. However, even before I was assigned to that particular station, I was able to stand next to one of my parts racks and take down notes. Each team member had paper and pencil for noting

parts shortages and for keeping daily records on car numbers and various other assigned duties. It was not out of the ordinary to observe people writing.

(Graham 1995: 16–17)

And observers in a covert study of patient life in mental hospitals found that they could take notes, since staff simply took this as a further sign of their mental illness (Rosenhahn 1973)!

Of course, note-taking is not always possible or easy even in overt research. To some extent our comments concerning covert participation apply here as well. The conduct of note-taking must be broadly congruent with the social setting under scrutiny. In some contexts, however 'well socialized' the hosts, open and continuous note-taking will be perceived as inappropriate or threatening, and will prove disruptive. In other contexts fairly extensive notes can be recorded without undue disruption. A classic example is Whyte (1981), who took on the role of secretary to the Italian Community Club because it enabled him to take notes unobtrusively in their meetings.

However, even in situations where note-taking is a 'normal' kind of activity, such as educational settings, care must be exercised if disruption is to be avoided. Olesen and Whittaker's (1968) research on student nurses is a case in point:

> I feel it much easier to write when the students write, and listen when they do; I have noticed that when I attempt to write when the students are not, I attract [the tutor's] attention and on a few occasions she seems to falter in what she is saying. . . . Similarly when all the students are writing and I am not, but rather looking at her, I again seem to 'put her off'. And so it is that I've become a student, sometimes slightly at the loss of my self-esteem when I find myself lazily inserting a pencil in my mouth. (Fieldnotes: February, third year.)
>
> (Olesen and Whittaker 1968: 28)

For a variety of reasons, many of the initial fieldnotes that ethnographers take are jottings, snatched in the course of observed action. A common joke about ethnographers relates to their frequent trips to the lavatory where such hasty notes can be scribbled in private. Even the briefest of notes can be valuable aids in the construction of a more detailed account. As Schatzman and Strauss suggest: 'A single word, even one merely descriptive of the dress of a person, or a particular word uttered by someone usually is enough to "trip off" a string of images that afford substantial reconstruction of the observed scene' (Schatzman and Strauss 1973: 95). Moreover, it is important to record even things that one does not immediately understand, because these may turn out to be important later.

Even if it proves possible to make fairly extensive notes in the field, they – like brief jottings – will need to be worked up, expanded on, and developed. Many social activities have a timetable of their own, and it may prove possible within these to match phases of observation with periods of writing up fieldnotes. For instance, Atkinson's work on haematologists in American and British hospitals was structured by regular schedules of clinical 'rounds', 'grand rounds', 'conferences', 'mortality and morbidity reviews', and similar occasions for medical talk. The pattern of data collection was fitted into the rhythm of the hospital, which allowed for periods of time in the canteen or the library, or back at the university, or at home, when detailed notes could be constructed (Atkinson 1992a, 1995).

In other settings, the phasing of observation and writing will be much less straight-forward to organize, but there are usually times when participants are engaged in activities that are not relevant to the research. At the very least they will usually sleep at regular times and, at the risk of fatigue, notes can be written up then. Carey (1972) reports a rare exception: that of 'speed freaks' (amphetamine users) who, under heavy doses, stay awake for several days in a hyperactive state:

> The peculiar round of life wherein people stay up for three, four or five days at a time and then sleep for several days posed enormous practical difficulties for the research. Our conventional commitments (family, friends, teaching responsibilities) had to be put aside for a time so that we could adapt ourselves more realistically to this youthful scene. As we became more familiar with this particular universe, we developed a crude sampling plan that called for observations at a number of different gathering spots, and this relieved us somewhat from a very exacting round of life. If we were interested, however, in what happened during the course of a run when a small group of people started shooting speed intravenously, it meant that one or two fieldworkers had to be present at the beginning and be relieved periodically by other members of the team until the run was over. Fatigue was a constant problem and suggests that more than one fieldworker is required in this type of research.
>
> (Carey 1972: 82)

Clearly, in such cases, finding time to write up fieldnotes poses particularly severe problems. The problem remains serious, however, even with less exhausting schedules. But some time for writing up fieldnotes must always be set aside, especially where this is the main means of data recording. There is no advantage in observing social action over extended periods if inadequate time is allowed for the preparation of notes. The information will quickly trickle away, and the effort will be wasted. There is always the temptation to try to observe everything, and the consequent fear that in withdrawing from the field one will miss some vital incident. Understandable though such feelings are, they must, in most circumstances, be suppressed in the interests of producing good-quality notes. Nevertheless, the trade-off between data collection and data recording must be recognized and resolved, in accordance with the overall research strategy and purpose. Thus, for example, the organization of periods of observation, with alternating periods of writing and other work, must be done with a view to the systematic sampling of action and actors (see Chapter 2).

It is difficult to overemphasize the importance of meticulous note-taking where this is the main means of data recording. The memory should never be relied on entirely, and a good maxim is 'if in doubt, write it down'. Furthermore, it is absolutely essential that one keep up to date in processing notes. Without the discipline of daily writing, the observations will fade from memory, and the ethnography will all too easily become incoherent and muddled.

What of the form and content of fieldnotes? As noted earlier, one can never record everything; social scenes are truly inexhaustible in this sense. Some selection has to be made. However, the nature of this is likely to change over time. During the early days of a research project, the scope of the notes is likely to be fairly wide, and one will probably be reluctant to emphasize any particular aspects. Indeed, one will probably not be in a position to make such a selection of topics. As the research progresses, and emergent issues are identified, the notes will become more restricted and more focused in subject matter. Moreover, features that previously seemed insignificant may come to take on new meaning, a point that Johnson (1975) illustrates from his research on social workers:

> Gradually I began to 'hear different things said' in the setting. This happened through a shift in attention from *what* was said or done to *how* it was said or done. The following excerpts from the fieldnotes illustrate several instances of my changing awareness. From the notes near the end of the sixth month of the observations:
>
>> Another thing that happened today. I was standing by Bill's desk when Art passed by and asked Bill to cover the phone for a couple of minutes while he walked through a request for County Supp over to Bess Lanston, an EW supervisor. Now I don't know how many times I've heard a comment like that; so many times that it's not even problematic any more. In fact, it's so routine that I'm surprised that I even made a note to remember it. The striking feature about this is that in my first days at Metro [the social work agency] I would have wanted to know all about what kind of form he was taking over there, what County Supp was, why and how one used it, got it, didn't get it, or whatever, who and where Bess Lanston was, what she did and so on. But all the time I've missed what was crucial about such a comment, the fact that he was walking it through. Before I would have only heard what he was doing or why, but today, instead, I began to hear the how.
>
> (Johnson 1975: 197)

So, as analytical ideas develop and change, what is 'significant' and what must be included in the fieldnotes change. Over time, notes can also change in *character*, in particular becoming more concrete and detailed. Indeed, the preservation of concreteness is an important consideration in fieldnote writing. For most analytic purposes, compressed summary accounts will prove inadequate for the detailed and systematic comparison or aggregation of information across contexts or across occasions. As far as possible, therefore, speech should be rendered in a manner that approximates to a verbatim report and represents nonverbal behaviour in relatively concrete terms; this minimizes the level of inference and thus facilitates the construction and reconstruction of the analysis.

The actual words people use can be of considerable analytic importance. The 'situated vocabularies' employed provide us with valuable information about the ways in which members of a particular culture organize their perceptions of the world, and so engage in the 'social construction of reality'. Situated vocabularies and folk taxonomies incorporate the typifications and recipes for action that constitute the stock-of-knowledge and practical reasoning of the members. Arensberg and Kimball (1968) provide an example from their study of interpersonal relations among family members in rural Ireland around the turn of the twentieth century. They note how the terms 'boy' and 'girl' are used by parents to refer to their children irrespective of age, indicating the sharply hierarchical character of parent–child relations: 'Sociological adulthood has little to do with physiological adulthood. Age brings little change of modes of address and ways of treating and regarding one another in the relationships within the farm family' (Arensberg and Kimball 1968: 59).

The potential significance and detail of the connotations of such members' terms apply equally to the use of argot. American hospital speech includes the term 'gomer', which is part of the rich and colourful vocabulary characteristic of most medical settings. George and Dundes (1978) summarize its use:

> What precisely is a 'gomer'? He is typically an older man who is both dirty and debilitated. He has extremely poor personal hygiene and he is often a chronic alcoholic. A derelict or down-and-outer, the gomer is normally on welfare. He has an extensive listing of multiple admissions to the hospital. From the gomer's standpoint, life inside the hospital is so much better than the miserable existence he endures outside that he exerts every effort to gain admission, or rather readmission, to the hospital. Moreover, once admitted, the gomer attempts to remain there as long as possible Because of the gomer's desire to stay in the hospital he frequently pretends to be ill or he lacks interest in getting well on those occasions when he is really sick.
>
> (George and Dundes 1978: 570)

Of course, this brief account glosses over a wide range of uses and connotations associated with this one folk term. In practice, the research worker will not be content to generate such a composite or summary definition. The important task is to be able to document and retrieve the actual contexts of use for such folk terms.

Kondo's (1990) ethnography of the production of identities in Japan provides an exemplary documentation of the terms and idioms of identity in various social contexts. She examines, for instance, the idiomatic use of Shitamachi and Yamanote: literally, different parts of Tokyo, used to convey different orientations, lifestyles and identities. Likewise, she explores the subtle usages and connotations of 'ie' and 'uchi'. Both terms have flexible, context-dependent meanings. The former refers to the inter-generational continuity of the group, the latter to the 'ingroup' as defined on any particular occasion, whether 'company, school, club, or nation' (Kondo 1990: 141). The ability to trace the social contexts of such idioms is dependent on the delicacy of one's ethnographic data: usage and social context must be identified with precision.

Making fieldnotes as concrete and descriptive as possible is not without its cost, however. Generally, the more closely this ideal is approximated, the more restricted the *scope* of the notes. Unless the focus of the research is extremely narrow, some concreteness and detail will have to be sacrificed for increased scope. Whatever the level of concreteness of fieldnotes, however, it is essential that direct quotations are clearly distinguished from summaries in the researcher's words, and that gaps and uncertainties in the record are clearly indicated. If speakers' original words cannot be reconstructed adequately, then indirect speech may be used to indicate the style and content. When we refer back to the notes there should be no ambiguity concerning the 'voices' that are represented there. One should not have to puzzle over 'Is that what they themselves said?' The observer's own descriptive glosses should be kept clearly distinct.

It is equally important that records of speech and action should be located in relation to who was present, where, at what time, and under what circumstances. When it comes to the analysis stage, when one will be gathering together, categorizing, comparing, and contrasting instances, it may be crucial that 'context' (participants, audience, setting, etc.) can be identified.

Fieldnotes cannot possibly provide a comprehensive record of the research setting. The ethnographer acquires a great deal more tacit knowledge than is ever contained in the written record. He or she necessarily uses 'head notes' or memory to fill in and recontextualize recorded events and utterances. One should not become totally wedded to the fieldnotes, as if they were the sum total of available information. Despite the scepticism of some commentators (for example, Agar 1980), however, the collection and maintenence of fieldnotes remain a major method of ethnographic recording.

Up to now, we have discussed fieldnotes in relation to observation, but they may also be used to record data from interviews. Sometimes, interviewees will refuse to allow the discussion to be audio-recorded; sometimes the ethnographer may judge that such recording will dissuade frankness or increase nervousness to an unacceptable level. Where fieldnotes are relied on in interviews, much the same considerations apply as in observation: decisions must be made about when they are to be written, what is to be noted, and how. It is important, incidentally, to have some record of the interviewer's questions, as well as of the answers. Once again, reliance will most likely have to be placed on jotted notes, and the dilemma of summarizing versus verbatim reporting is just as acute. Similarly, note-taking in interviews can prove disruptive, much as in the tutorial cited by Olesen and Whittaker (1968), with the interviewee becoming self-conscious about what is being written down. Furthermore, the need to take notes makes very difficult the kind of interviewing we advocated in Chapter 5. Much of the interviewer's attention will be taken up with recording what has been said rather than thinking about it. Nevertheless, combining interviewing and note-taking is a skill that can be learned with practice.

In light of the problems associated with writing fieldnotes, particularly in the context of interviews, the advantages of audio-recording, and perhaps even video-recording, are obvious. However, valuable though these are, they too involve difficulties and limitations.

Digitally recording observations and interviews

It is very easy to demonstrate the major differences – in volume and detail – between a permanent recording and an observer's reconstruction of a strip of spoken action in fieldnotes. Since the technology of permanent recording is now readily available, in small and reliable formats, there are many possibilities for better quality data in key respects. The uses of video or film, still photography, and audio-recording offer various options for data collection and storage. At the same time, their use is not always possible, may sometimes have unwelcome disadvantages, and can shape the process of ethnographic work in ways that are undesirable. No means of data recording should be simply adopted as a matter of routine: reflexive awareness is required here as much as anywhere else.

Audio-recording

For the reasons we have suggested, if possible the ethnographer will usually wish to audio-record interviews rather than to rely on fieldnotes. And, occasionally, the use of video-recording may even be necessary for this purpose. There are also often considerable advantages in using these methods in recording observational data; though the practicalities and reactive effects must be remembered.

We should also note that, despite its advantages over fieldnotes, the use of audio-recording does not provide a perfect and comprehensive record; and audio-recording processes of social interaction that are 'on the move' can be challenging, to say the least. In some cases background noise may make the recording virtually unintelligible. Also, any recording will be highly selective. Decisions have to be made about whether to use a single microphone or more than one, and where to place them; and these decisions are likely to determine what talk is and is not recorded. Furthermore, not only is non-verbal behaviour not captured in audio-recordings, but even such matters as who is being addressed, or how the talk relates to any material objects being used, are often not preserved. So, as we have already noted, the availability of audio-recording does not remove the necessity for the writing of fieldnotes. Indeed, an overemphasis on audio-recording can distort one's sense of 'the field', by focusing data collection on places where social processes can be recorded by this means, and concentrating attention on the analysis of spoken action. It may be possible to overcome some of these limitations by using visual recording devices, but these too have limitations and drawbacks.

Photography and video-recording

Photography has long been used in anthropology; by contrast, it has only been employed more recently, for the most part, in sociology and some other disciplines (Collier and Collier 1986; Ball and Smith 1992, 2001; Harper 1993, 2000, 2006). Ethnographic film also has a long history (see Marks 1995). Video-recording is more recent but is now widely used. Despite this, there is still a tendency to think of written language as the privileged medium of scholarly communication, and there are some tensions in the use of visual materials in 'a discipline of words' (Ball and Smith 1992: 5).

The collection and use of visual materials has gained particular currency from the increasing influence of cultural analysis in the social sciences. Visual materials, and representations of material culture, are key aspects of such research. This includes the semiotic analysis of photographs, films, and television programmes; the analysis of architectural space; the ethnography of design, and the analysis of domestic goods and spaces (see Pink 2004a). There is clearly opportunity for more traditional ethnographic research to draw on and incorporate such analytic strategies. At the same time, decisions have to be taken about whether visual data and the analytic strategies they make possible are appropriate for the purposes of a particular inquiry, and whether use of the recording devices concerned is viable in the field being investigated.

We are used to thinking of photography, film, and video-recording as producing faithful, realistic images of the world about us; but such habits of our own culture should not blind us to the fact that these forms of representation are partial and conventional. Decisions have to be made about from where shots are to be taken, whether the camera should be fixed or mobile, whether a single focus is to be adopted or whether the focus should vary; and if so when and how. Where the position and focus are not fixed, operation of the camera is likely to be full-time, so that it will be difficult if not impossible to observe and take notes simultaneously. Yet complementary observation and note-taking will almost certainly be necessary. Here, as elsewhere, contextual features will need to be documented, since by no means everything will be 'in shot', and some of what *is* in shot will be obscured. A team approach may well be required, then.

Of course, 'visual data' do not have to be created *ex nihilo* by ethnographers. As we noted in Chapter 6, there are many situations where visual materials are integral to social action and social organization. Furthermore, reflexivity in the visual domain can also be extended to providing one's research hosts and informants with the means to record their own visual materials. They can thus become co-producers of 'data'. The availability of cheap and easy-to-use cameras not only means that ethnographers can use them extensively, but also means that participants can be encouraged to use them as well.[2] This may be a useful means for understanding how participants – literally and figuratively – view their world (see, for example, Allan 2005; Darbyshire *et al.* 2005). Such data can also be highly illuminating in making sense of how participants consume spaces and objects, or how they move in given environments. Participant-produced images can also be used as stimuli in the conduct of interviews.

Recent decades have transformed the use of visual materials: the advent of newer digital technologies have created the opportunity for ethnographic work that genuinely incorporates visual materials into an integrated ethnographic enterprise. In particular, digital cameras and digital camcorders, together with the opportunity to scan visual and documentary sources into digital databases, have transformed the opportunities available to ethnographers, both 'in the field' and beyond. While we do not wish to imply that 'anyone can do it' without training, or without an understanding of what they are undertaking, it is clearly possible for visual materials to be gathered and analysed in a way that was rarely possible for earlier generations.

Despite these developments in digital technology, transcription is still usually required for the purposes of analysis where audio- or video-recording is employed; even though the development of this technology now means that sounds and images from digital audio-recorders, cameras, and camcorders can be incorporated directly into fieldnotes, or even into research reports (see Chapter 9).

Transcription

Transcription is a time-consuming business, and this must be allowed for in planning research. There are no hard-and-fast rules, but the ratio of transcribing time to recorded time is always high: at least five to one. If the talk is multi-party, if there is background noise, and if video-recordings are being transcribed, then it may take a great deal longer. Also relevant is the *kind* of transcription required: the detailed formats often used by discourse analysts are a great deal more time-consuming to produce than those which are more common in ethnographic work.

We do not intend to provide detailed instructions as to the preparation of transcripts, but a number of general precepts can be noted. In the first place, a decision needs to be made about whether full transcription is necessary. An alternative is to treat the audio- or video-recording as a document, indexing and summarizing much of it, transcribing only what seems essential. This may save considerable time, but it risks relevant material being overlooked – especially since what will be judged relevant will

---

2 Disposable film cameras are a good means for generating images here, though what they produce is less easy to store and manage than digital photographs.

change over time, and what is on the recordings that has not been transcribed will probably be forgotten.

Even where full transcription is to be carried out, as already indicated a decision must be made about how detailed this should be. There are well-established conventions for the preparation of transcripts. Some of these have been developed for the purposes of conversation or discourse analysis. They use the typographical characters of the standard keyboard and printer to represent some basic features of speech – such as pauses, overlaps, and interruptions – as well as how words are pronounced, when the speaker speeds up or slows down, where emphasis is placed, and so on. These will be essential for some research purposes, less important for others. Decisions must be made about what is to be represented in the transcription. Obviously, the more detailed the transcription, the more time it will take to produce; furthermore, very detailed transcriptions are by no means easy to read. At the same time, it is important that relevant features of the talk are included; and even then recourse may well sometimes need to be made to the original recording for purposes of analysis. The planning and conduct of research using audio- and video-recorded data must therefore involve strategic decisions about the kind of data to be collected, and the degree of detail to be preserved in the transcription.[3] Of course, fixed decisions do not have to be made at the start, and initial judgements may need to be reviewed.

Transcribing the video part of video-records is even more challenging, and time-consuming than dealing with audio-recordings. Here, conventions have been developed for indicating direction of gaze, so as to coordinate this with the pattern of talk. Sketches and screenshots of physical actions taking place alongside talk have also been used. Other researchers have provided written commentaries on what is happening instead of, or in addition to, these devices. Once again, including information of this kind multiplies the time required to transcribe data. However, it allows non-verbal aspects of social interaction and situations to be taken into account in a way that would otherwise be difficult. Here, as elsewhere, what kind of transcription is required depends upon the phenomena being studied and the purposes of inquiry. At the same time, the costs in terms of time and resources must be taken into account.[4]

Analytic notes, memos, and fieldwork journals

While one is reading documents, writing up fieldnotes, or transcribing audiovisual materials, promising analytic ideas often arise. It is important to make note of these, as they may prove useful later when analysing the data. It is essential, though, to do this in a way that retains a clear distinction between analytic notes, on the one hand, and both the accounts provided by participants and the researcher's own descriptions of actions and situations, on the other. For example, analytic notes may be placed in square brackets or double parentheses; or, as we shall see, they may be put in a fieldwork journal.

It is also important to engage in the regular review and development of analytic ideas through writing analytic memos. These are not fully developed working papers

3 For further discussion of transcription, see Mishler (1991); Atkinson (1992b); West (1996); Lapadat (1999); Poland (2002).
4 For discussions of transcription issues relating to video data, see Goodwin (1981, 2001); Heath (1997, 2004) and Heath and Hindmarsh (2002).

but occasional written notes whereby progress is assessed, emergent ideas are identified, research strategy is sketched out, and so on. We quoted extracts from an analytic memo in Chapter 2 (pp. 27–8). It is all too easy simply to allow one's fieldnotes and other types of data to pile up day-by-day and week-by-week. The very accumulation of material usually imparts a satisfying sense of progress, which can be measured in physical terms as notebooks are filled, interviews completed, periods of observation ticked off, or different research settings investigated. But it is a grave error to let this work build up without regular reflection and review. Under such circumstances the sense of progress may prove illusory, and a good deal of the data collection could be unnecessarily aimless.

As we have emphasized, the formulation of precise problems, hypotheses, and an appropriate research strategy is an emergent feature of ethnography. This process of progressive focusing means that the collection of data must be guided by the developing clarification of topics for inquiry. The regular production of analytic memoranda will force the ethnographer to go through such a process of explication. Ideally, every period of observation should result in processed notes and the reflexive monitoring of the research process. As the memoranda accumulate, they will constitute preliminary analyses, providing the researcher with guidance through the corpus of data. If this is done there is no danger of being confronted at the end of the fieldwork with an undifferentiated collection of material, with only one's memory to guide analysis.

The construction of analytic notes and memos therefore constitutes precisely the sort of internal dialogue, or thinking aloud, that is the essence of reflexive ethnography. Such activity should help one avoid lapsing into the 'natural attitude' and 'thinking as usual' in the field. Rather than coming to take one's understanding on trust, one is forced to question what one knows, how such knowledge has been acquired, the degree of certainty of such knowledge, and what further lines of inquiry are implied.

As already noted, analytic notes and memoranda may be appended to the daily fieldnotes, or they can be incorporated into yet another form of written account, the fieldwork journal. Such a journal or diary provides a running account of the conduct of the research. This includes a record not only of the fieldwork, but also of the ethnographer's own personal feelings and involvement (Coffey 1999). The latter are not simply the basis for gratuitous introspection or narcissistic self-absorption. As we point out elsewhere in this book, feelings of personal comfort, anxiety, surprise, shock, or revulsion are of analytic significance. In the first place, our feelings enter into and colour the social relationships we engage in during fieldwork. Second, such personal and subjective responses will inevitably influence one's choice of what is noteworthy, what is regarded as strange and problematic, and what appears to be mundane and obvious. One often relies implicitly on such feelings; therefore, their existence and possible influence must be acknowledged and, if possible, explicated in written form. Similarly, feelings of anxiety can pose limitations on data collection, leading to a restricting tunnel vision. One of us (Atkinson 1992a) has reflected on how his personal feelings about general medicine and surgery clearly influenced the nature and balance of his published research on medical education.

There is a constant interplay between the personal and emotional on the one hand, and the intellectual on the other. Private response should be transformed, by reflection and analysis, into potential public knowledge. The fieldwork journal is the vehicle for this kind of transformation. At a more mundane level, perhaps, the carefully made fieldwork journal will enable the conscientious ethnographer painstakingly to retrace and explicate the development of the research design, the emergence of analytic themes, and the systematic collection of data. The provision of such a 'natural history' of the research can be a crucial component of the complete ethnography.

Up to now, we have focused on data processing, emphasizing the decisions involved, and how this should be integrally related to the process of data analysis. In the remainder of the chapter we will examine the means that can be employed for the storage, indexing, and retrieval of ethnographic data.

Data storage, indexing and retrieval

Ethnographers usually store observational data records chronologically. Likewise, interview transcripts and the like are normally kept as complete records of the individual interview, and stored in order. However, the process of analysis will often require active reorganization of the data into themes and categories – often breaking the texts up into discrete chunks or segments and identifying them in accordance with an indexing or 'coding' system. (This is less common in conversation and discourse analysis, where the focus is often on local patterns.)

The coding of the data in terms of categories provides an important infrastructure for later searching and retrieval. It can also play an active role in the process of discovery, as the Webbs noted in one of the earliest methodological texts:

> It enables the scientific worker to break up his subject-matter, so as to isolate and examine at his leisure its various component parts, and to recombine the facts when they have been thus released from all accustomed categories, in new and experimental groupings.
>
> (Webb and Webb 1932: 83)

Moreover, the selection of categories as a basis for organizing the data can be of some significance, as a later sociologist notes, referring to what became a classic ethnographic study:

> As I gathered my early research data, I had to decide how I was to organize the written notes. In the very early stage of exploration, I simply put all the notes, in chronological order, in a single folder. As I was to go on to study a number of different groups and problems, it was obvious that this was no solution at all.
>
> I had to subdivide the notes. There seemed to be two main possibilities. I could organize the notes topically, with folders for politics, rackets, the church, the family, and so on. Or I could organize the notes in terms of the groups on which they were based, which would mean having folders on the Nortons, the Italian Community Club, and so on. Without really thinking the problem through, I began filing material on the group basis, reasoning that I could later redivide it on a topical basis when I had a better knowledge of what the relevant topics should be.
>
> As the material in the folders piled up, I came to realize that the organization of notes by social groups fitted in with the way in which my study was developing. For example, we have a college-boy member of the Italian Community Club saying: 'These racketeers give our district a bad name. They should really be cleaned out of here.' And we have a member of the Nortons saying: 'These racketeers are

really all right. When you need help, they'll give it to you. The legitimate businessman – he won't even give you the time of day.' Should these notes be filed under 'Racketeers, attitudes toward'? If so, they would only show that there are conflicting attitudes toward racketeers in Cornerville. Only a questionnaire (which is hardly feasible for such a topic) would show the distribution of attitudes in the district. Furthermore, how important would it be to know how many people felt one way or another on this topic? It seemed to me of much greater scientific interest to be able to relate the attitude to the group in which the individual participated. This shows why two individuals could be expected to have quite different attitudes on a given topic.

(Whyte 1981: 309)

Whyte's comments here emphasize the importance of anticipating how the data might be used. Equally important, no system of filing or coding and retrieval can ever remove the necessity to remain sensitive to the immediate social context of speech and action.

The allocation of data to categories in ethnography has usually differed from the kind of coding typical in quantitative research, including content analysis (Krippendorff 1980; however see also Franzosi 2004). In ethnographic coding, there is no requirement that items of data be assigned to one and only one category, or that there be explicit rules for assigning them:

We code [the fieldnotes] inclusively, that is to say if we have any reason to think that anything might go under the heading, we will put it in. We do not lose anything. We also code them in multiple categories, under anything that might be felt to be cogent. As a general rule, we want to get back anything that could conceivably bear on a given interest. . . . . It is a search procedure for getting all of the material that is pertinent.

(Becker 1968: 245)

Indeed, Lofland (1971) argues that in the case of analytic categories it pays to be 'wild', to include anything, however long a shot.

The identification of categories is central to the process of analysis (although it should not be confused with analysis per se). As a result, the list of categories in terms of which the data are organized generally undergoes considerable change over the course of the research. In particular, there is typically a shift towards more abstract categories as the work develops (see Chapter 8).

In the past, ethnographers manipulated their data by means of the physical indexing and sorting of precious manuscript and typescript texts. Nowadays, many ethnographers use personal computers to facilitate the storage, indexing and retrieval of textual data for analytic purposes. To a considerable extent, the computer software for ethnographic data storage and retrieval recapitulates the procedures associated with earlier, manual approaches. We shall comment on manual techniques before going on to discuss computer-based applications. It is important not to assume that all ethnographic data must now be stored and searched on computer. For many researchers there will still be a place for simple manual procedures.

Organizing and reorganizing the data in terms of categories can be done in a number of ways. The simplest is 'coding the record'. Here data are coded, that is, assigned to categories, on the running record itself (or, better, a copy of it). Comments relating the data to descriptive or analytic categories are written in the margin, on the reverse, or on interleaved pages, depending on the format of the data themselves. This is quick, and preserves the sense of 'reading' the data. It is not, however, well adapted to subsequent procedures of searching and retrieving data segments. In a more sophisticated version of this strategy, an analytic index is produced. Here each data segment is indexed under a developing set of headings, stored on index cards or in a simple database program. Identically or similarly coded segments can thus be found in the original hard copy of the data when required. However, this does not make their comparison very easy.

An alternative method of data organization, used by many ethnographers in the past, is physical sorting. Multiple copies of the data are made, and each segment of the data is stored in folders representing all the categories to which it is deemed relevant. With this approach, ethnographers can find all the data collected together when they come to analyse and write up a particular theme. At the same time, the physical storage of multiple copies has limitations: not least the time taken to produce copies and the sheer space requirements of a large and complex data set.

There is little doubt that when handling small data sets, such simple procedures can serve users just as well as more complex data-handling software. However, the capacities of word-processing have become so commonplace that most of us now take for granted the remarkable flexibility that it provides in storing, manipulating, sharing and searching textual materials. We can input and store vast amounts of written and visual materials. Moreover, it is possible to use wordprocessing programs to copy segments of data and paste them into folders relevant to different analytic themes. However, ethnographers now have available to them specialized software for the management of texts and pictures. Initially, this was restricted to following more or less the same pattern as the coding and retrieval involved in physical sorting. In other words, it relied on the procedure of marking segments of data with codes, and then using the capacity of the software rapidly to search the data set(s) for all segments tagged with the same code. In this way, instances in the data can be collated and aggregated under thematic, analytic headings.

However, over the course of recent years, the software has evolved to develop functions that reflect more fully the array of opportunities that are presented by digital technology. Over the same period, digital technologies themselves have become more widespread, more affordable, and better adapted to the needs of field researchers. There is now a specialist literature that deals directly with the use of CAQDAS (Computer Aided Qualitative Data Analysis Software), and that provides practical advice on how to use it. In the course of this chapter, we shall discuss the use of such analytic software in general terms, rather than attempting to offer the kind of user's guide that other publications readily provide (see, for instance, Lee and Fielding 2004).

One advantage of coding software over manual methods was the capacity to search the data comprehensively, avoiding partial or improperly selective sampling of events and examples. The fact that such searches were virtually instantaneous, encouraged more thorough examination of the data. The advantages of CAQDAS coding were more far-reaching, however. Manual searching is not an effective way of combining multiple codes. The great virtue of code-and-retrieve software capabilities lay in the fact that one could attach several codes to particular stretches of data, with segments overlapping one another, and codes nesting within one another. This facilitates more complex forms of analysis.

In this way, the complexity of coding could reflect the sort of complexity that one would hope to find in qualitative data. After all, interview informants do not talk about just one topic at a time. Equally, observed social action does not present itself to the ethnographer one theme at a time. The social world – and therefore our data – is complex in its enactments. Data, therefore, need to be coded densely, and to be faithful to the many possible topics and themes that are discoverable. It has been the great strength of CAQDAS not only that data can be coded in complex ways, but also that the data can then be searched and retrieved in ways that respect that complexity. Even elementary Boolean logic (X and Y, X not Y, etc.) can permit the analyst to conduct sophisticated searches. Equally, the capacity to treat code words as synonyms, and hence to combine codings, can help the analyst build up from detailed, concrete codings to more generic, analytically productive concepts.

The basic ideas and procedures of CAQDAS embodied the ideas about ethnographic analysis that were reflected in grounded theorizing – or at least the versions of grounded theorizing that were widely current at the time it was originally developed (Glaser and Strauss 1967; Strauss 1987).[5] Indeed, the authors of the software were in some cases quite explicit about the conceptual relationship between the two. Although it is always unwise to imply that any computer software exercises agency in predetermining how analysts conceptualize their work, and although senior commentators in the field stress the independence of software from any single analytic paradigm, there is little doubt that the parallel evolution of the software with other methodological writing has meant that there is a mutual influence. For many researchers and their students, the development of CAQDAS has meant the implementation of a 'grounded theory' strategy, where grounded theorizing itself has been largely equated to an analysis based on data-coding.[6]

The availability of software has also allowed the searching of large data sets for 'indigenous' terms in the texts of fieldnotes or transcripts. In other words, it is possible to find every example of the use of a given word by participants or informants, or the presence of such a term in one's own (or another researcher's) fieldnotes. Again, the use of Boolean algebra allows the grouping of terms together thereby creating complex search strategies. The use, therefore, of bulk-indexing software, that had originally been developed for tasks like indexing legal and other official documents, was a potentially useful resource for ethnographic and other qualitative analysts. While the commercial qualitative analysis software often has such a facility incorporated within it, specialized text-retrieval software – such as Wordcruncher or ZiINDEX – should remain part of the digital resource-base of the contemporary ethnographer.

One key development in CAQDAS software has been an increasing emphasis on so-called 'theory-building'. Whereas code-and-retrieve is predicated on establishing the relationship between codes and data, theory-building goes beyond this, the software being designed to show relationships among codes. Even so, as Atkinson, among others, has pointed out, a great deal of what passes for 'analysis' in current ethnographic research is often based on a 'culture of fragmentation'. That is, it is assumed that the basis of analysis rests in the work of segmenting and disaggregating data. It has been described in terms of *decontextualizing* data from its original location (e.g. in the

---

5 Grounded theorizing is discussed in Chapter 8.
6 This is not the place for arcane disputes, but we should note that Lee and Fielding (1996) have challenged this observation. However, their grounds for doing so are not watertight, since they rely for evidence only on explicit references to the use of grounded theorizing.

fieldnotes) and *recontextualizing* them into analytically driven categories. Now this is unexceptional in and of itself, and it would be hard to quarrel with as one productive way of managing data. But this is not the only way of thinking about data and it is certainly not the only way of thinking about analysis and the generation of theory. Approaches that are more sensitive to the immediate contexts of action, and that resist the treatment of instances as being susceptible to simple aggregation, are characteristic of many forms of discourse and narrative analysis. While code-based analyses do not necessarily violate those analytic considerations, they can readily lead to an overemphasis on decontextualized instances.

Kelle (2004: 485) has pointed out that many of the functions of contemporary CAQDAS are under-used by most researchers. 'In the ongoing discussions of the 1990s it became apparent that enhanced strategies for hypothesis testing, quantitatively oriented typology construction and "qualitative comparative analysis" were only seldom applied by CAQDAS users' (see also Dotzler 1995). Consequently, in evaluating the actual impact of CAQDAS on research practice, it is important to distinguish between the claims entered on its behalf by developers and advocates, the functional possibilities inscribed in the software, and the actual uses to which it is put. We should not be surprised to discover that, in practice, software has not led inexorably to more sophisticated and complex analytic work with ethnographic data. Our own experience suggests that many students and researchers are in practice using software still to perform the sort of sorting and retrieval tasks that were done manually in previous generations. This is not a problem in itself, but it detracts from overheated claims to the effect that the software is encouraging 'theory-building'.

It is important to realize that CAQDAS is by no means confined to the management of textual materials like transcripts and fieldnotes. It is often also possible to include and code visual and sound data. Indeed, there is no reason in principle to exclude any data that can be rendered digitally from inclusion in the standard software strategies. Furthermore, some packages also provide for combining quantitative and qualitative data.

Conclusion

While it is impossible to render explicit all the data acquired in fieldwork, every effort must be made to record it. Memory is an inadequate basis for subsequent analysis. Of course, most kinds of data recording are necessarily selective and involve some interpretation, however minimal. There is no set of basic, indubitable data available from which all else may be inferred. What is collected or recorded, and how, will depend in large part on the purposes and priorities of the research, and the conditions in which it is carried out. Moreover, in using various recording techniques we must remain aware of the effects their use may be having, both on participants and on our analytic interpretations; and be prepared to modify the strategy in light of this. Similarly, there is no finally correct way to store information or to retrieve it for analysis. The various systems – including currently available software – differ in appropriateness according to one's purposes, the nature of the data collected, the facilities and finance available, the size and scope of the research project, as well as personal convenience.

As with other aspects of ethnographic research, then, recording, storing, and retrieving data must be viewed as part of the reflexive process. Decisions are to be made, monitored, and – if necessary – remade in the light of methodological, practical and ethical considerations. At the same time, however, these techniques play an important role in promoting the quality of ethnographic research. They provide a crucial resource in assessing typicality of examples, checking construct-indicator linkages, searching for negative cases, triangulating across different data sources and stages of the fieldwork, and assessing the role of the researcher in shaping the nature of the data and the findings. In short, they facilitate – but should not determine – the process of analysis, a topic to which we turn in the next chapter.

8 The process of analysis

In ethnography the analysis of data is not a distinct stage of the research. In many ways, it begins in the pre-fieldwork phase, in the formulation and clarification of research problems, and continues through to the process of writing reports, articles, and books. Formally, it starts to take shape in analytic notes and memoranda; informally, it is embodied in the ethnographer's ideas and hunches. And in these ways, to one degree or another, the analysis of data feeds into research design and data collection. This iterative process is central to the 'grounded theorizing' promoted by Glaser and Strauss, in which theory is developed out of data analysis, and subsequent data collection is guided strategically by emergent theory.[1] However, much the same interactive process is also involved in other kinds of ethnographic research, including those which are directed not towards the generation of theory but to other research products, such as descriptions and explanations.

Although this chapter outlines some general issues in analysis, it is important to recognize that there is no formula or recipe for the analysis of ethnographic data. There are certainly no procedures that will guarantee success. Some representations of analysis – notably vulgar accounts of grounded theorizing strategies – seem to imply that there is a standard set of steps that the ethnographer should go through in order to make sense of their data. It is vital to ignore any such implication. General guides to analysis – including this chapter – can only suggest some potentially fruitful ways of working, they cannot provide recipes. Indeed, the important thing to recognize is that, in order to produce an ethnographic study that is equally rich in data and concepts, it is not enough merely to manage and manipulate the data. Data are materials to think with.

Analysis is often seen as being about, or as involving, theory. Quite a lot of researchers – novice and experienced – find the thought of theory daunting. This is usually because they have encountered it primarily in courses that emphasize relatively abstract, and sometimes quite obscure, forms of theorizing – ones that sometimes seem to have only a tenuous relationship with the evidence they cite. There are also those who pick on the work of one or a small number of theorists and seek to interpret their data entirely through his or her work. However, while the ideas of, say, de Beauvoir, Bourdieu,

---

1 There is now a considerable literature on grounded theorizing. The original source was Glaser and Strauss (1967). Both authors have provided illuminating elaborations on their initial ideas: see, for example, Glaser (1978) and Strauss (1987). For short introductory accounts, see Charmaz and Mitchell (2001), Dey (2004) and Pidgeon and Henwood (2004). Generally speaking, we have used the phrase 'grounded theorizing' here, rather than the more common 'grounded theory', in order to make clear that it is an activity not a procedure, and to distinguish it from the product of this activity: grounded theory.

Bakhtin, Baudrillard, or Butler may prove helpful in some respects, and for some analyses, it is almost always a mistake to try to make a whole ethnography conform to just one theoretical framework.

Theorizing need not, and should not, be like this. It ought to involve an iterative process in which ideas are used to make sense of data, and data are used to change our ideas. In other words, there should be movement back and forth between ideas and data. So, analysis is not just a matter of managing and manipulating data. We must be prepared to go beyond the data to develop ideas that will illuminate them, and this will allow us to link our ideas with those of others; and we must then bring those ideas back to test their fit with further data, and so on.

This relationship between data and ideas is at the heart of grounded theorizing.[2] This was developed in reaction against a preoccupation of many empirical social scientists at the time, which still prevails in some quarters today, with hypothesis-testing, where ideas are taken from the literature and then tested against data. However, it was also a rejection of the contrasting conception of research as dredging through an inert mound of data to produce descriptions of what is there. The central injunction of grounded theorizing is that there should be constant interplay between data and ideas throughout the research process. Ideas are emergent from one's experience in the field, and from one's preliminary analytic reflections on the data. As this should make clear, emergence is a function of the analytic work one puts in: it does not 'just happen'.

This commitment to a dialectical interaction between data collection and data analysis is not easy to sustain in practice. It may well demand lengthy withdrawals from the field in order to process and analyse the data before returning to collect further data. In effect this may require the re-negotiation of access, where return is to the same setting. Furthermore, there is an at least potential tension between an ethnographic concern with thick description and grounded theorizing. The result of these practical and methodological problems can be that when it comes to concentrating on the analysis, very often it is found that the data required to check a particular interpretation are missing; that the typicality of crucial items of data cannot be assessed; or that some of the comparative cases necessary for developing and testing an emerging set of analytic ideas have not been investigated; and, moreover, that there is little or no time to rectify these failings. Here, as elsewhere, ethnographers are faced with a trade-off, so that judgements about how much analysis can be done alongside the main data collection must be made in light of the aims of the research and the nature of the contexts in which data are being collected.

The problem can be worsened by the influence of naturalism, with its emphasis on 'capturing' the social world in description (Hammersley 1992: ch. 1). Naturalism reinforces what Lacey (1976: 71) calls 'the "it's all happening elsewhere" syndrome', a common ailment in fieldwork, where the researcher feels it necessary to try to be everywhere at once and to stay in the setting for as long as possible. As a result of this, a great deal of data is collected but little time is left for reflection on the significance of the data and the implications for collecting further data. Likewise, the naturalistic

2 In some quarters, there is an assumption that 'grounded theory' is a particular theoretical perspective – as if it were the equivalent of symbolic interactionism, or phenomenology. This is a misperception, and is unhelpful. Grounded theorizing is a way of working with data (of any sort, including quantitative data) in order to generate and develop ideas.

commitment to 'tell it like it is' tends to force the process of analysis to remain implicit and underdeveloped.

Fieldwork is a very demanding activity, and the processing of data is equally time-consuming. As a result, engaging in sustained data analysis alongside data collection is often very difficult in practice. Some level of reflexivity can and should be maintained, however, even if it is not possible to carry out much formal data analysis before the main fieldwork has been completed. Some reflection on the data collection process and what it is producing is essential if the research is not to drift along the line of least resistance and to face an analytical impasse in its final stages.

Ethnographic research should have a characteristic 'funnel' structure, being pro-gressively focused over its course. Over time the research problem needs to be developed, and may need to be transformed; and eventually its scope must be clarified and delimited, and its internal structure explored. In this sense, it is frequently well into the process of inquiry that one discovers what the research is really about; and not uncommonly it turns out to be about something rather different from the initial foreshadowed problems. An extreme example is some research by Shakespeare (1994), which started from a concern with how members of a housing cooperative accounted for its history, but eventually came to focus on the discursive structure of the 'confused talk' displayed by people suffering from various kinds of dementia. Here we have a dramatic change in substantive focus and site of investigation, but throughout this research there was a continuing analytic concern with the interactional character of interview discourse. Usually, shifts in research focus are less severe than this, more along the lines illustrated by Bohannon (1981). He identifies the various stages of a research project on poor residents of inner-city hotels, illustrating the importance of preliminary analysis; and he reports how the research problem was progressively redefined:

> We did indeed begin this project with the 'notion' (it was actually more formal than that – it was a hypothesis that proved wrong) that elderly individuals living in run-down hotels in the center city have established support networks. By and large they have not. Their networks are shallow and transient. It is [generally] part of the life adjustment of these people to run from the commitment that a support network implies.
>
> (Bohannon 1981: 45)

Starting from a view centred on arguments about 'disorganization' or 'dislocation', Bohannon and his research team came to reformulate their research in terms of 'adaptation'. In the course of this they were able to argue that welfare policies predicated on the former were not soundly based.

Progressive focusing may also involve a gradual shift from a concern with describing social events and processes towards developing and testing explanations or theories. However, studies will vary considerably in the distance they travel along this path. Some remain heavily descriptive, ranging from narrative life histories of an individual, group, or organization to accounts of the way of life to be found in particular settings. Of course, these are in no sense pure descriptions: they are constructions involving selection and interpretation. But they may involve little attempt to derive any general theoretical lessons, the theory they employ remaining implicit, being used as a tool rather than forming the focus of the research. Such accounts can be of great value. They may provide us with knowledge of cultures hitherto unknown, and thereby shake our assumptions about the parameters of human life, or challenge our stereotypes. Herein lies the interest of much anthropological work and of sociological accounts revealing the ways of life of low-status or deviant groups, for example.

A variation on this theme is to show the familiar in the apparently strange (Goffman 1961; Turnbull 1973) or the strange in the familiar (Garfinkel 1967).[3] An interesting application of this latter idea is Rawlings' (1988) explication of her knowledge as a participant in a therapeutic community. She takes an apparently ordinary first few minutes of a community meeting and shows that in many respects they were far from ordinary, that their appearance as ordinary was an interactional accomplishment, albeit a routine one (Rawlings 1988; see also Vrasidas 2001). Alternatively, descriptive accounts may contrast present conditions with an ideal, pointing up the discrepancy. Decision-making procedures within a political institution may be compared with an ideal type of democracy, for example; or personnel selection practices in a business organization may be compared with its official policy. Such comparisons are the stock-in-trade of ethnographic work.

By no means all ethnography remains at this descriptive level, however. Often, there is an attempt to draw out explanations or theoretical models of one kind or another. Here, features of the nature or history of the phenomenon under study start to be organized under more general categories. They are presented as examples of, for instance, particular kinds of social orientation, discursive practice, interactional strategy, institutional form, and so on. Going further, typologies may be developed that identify orientations, strategies, etc., of various related kinds which can be found in very different sorts of setting (Lofland 1971, 1976). Finally, a whole range of analytic categories may be integrated into a model of some aspect of the social process (Glaser and Strauss 1967; Glaser 1978; Becker 1998; Lofland *et al.* 2006). And this may then be subjected to test and further revision.

This is a long road to travel and there are many way-stations along its course. Moreover, as with all journeys, something is left behind. Concrete descriptions usually cover many different facets of the phenomena they portray: they give a rounded picture and open up all manner of theoretical possibilities. The development of explanations and theories involves a narrowing of focus and a process of abstraction. Theorized accounts provide a much more selective representation of the phenomena with which they deal. On the other hand, assuming that the theoretical ideas are well founded, they begin to give us much more knowledge about why events occur in the patterned ways they do.

In general, as we have seen in earlier chapters, ethnographers deal with what is often referred to as 'unstructured' data. What this means is that the data are not already constituted or organized in terms of a finite set of analytic categories determined by the researcher, in the way that most survey research data are. Rather, they typically take the form of open-ended verbal descriptions in fieldnotes, of transcriptions of audio- or video-recordings, of images of one kind or another, of extracts of text from documents, and so on. And, often, the process of analysis involves, simultaneously, the development of a set of analytic categories that capture relevant aspects of these data, and the assignment of particular items of data to those categories.

---

3 The injunction 'to make the familiar strange and the strange familiar' goes back at least to Romanticism, the phrase being attributed to Novalis. The idea of making the familiar strange was also central to some versions of literary theory, notably Russian formalism.

There is a wide variety of approaches to analysis of this sort. This arises partly from the diverse purposes of social research. Someone concerned with how the sequencing of contributions to everyday conversation is organized is likely to adopt a very different approach compared with someone interested in, say, the strength of the ties among an elite group within a national society and how this affects their exercise of power. Closely related to such differences in topic or purpose, of course, are differences in theoretical approach. There are those who would dismiss the first topic as trivial, just as there are those who would regard the second as beyond the realm of rigorous investigation, at least given the current state of social scientific knowledge. Our approach here will be a catholic one, ruling out neither of these forms of research. However, we cannot cover the full range of varieties of qualitative analysis in detail. Instead, we will focus on what we take to be central to much of it.[4]

Generating concepts

Underpinning the process of analysis is the necessity to *know* one's data. Detailed and repeated readings are necessary. In Chapter 7 we discussed organizing data by means of coding and indexing. These are entirely dependent on close reading – they are not mechanical tasks. It is not good enough to skim a transcript or set of fieldnotes and to have a broad sense of 'what it's all about', cherrypicking bits of data for quotation. Thin descriptions and unconvincing analyses derive from cursory reading and inadequate acquaintance with the data.

The initial task in analysing qualitative data is to find some concepts that help us to make sense of what is going on in the case or cases documented by the data. Often we will not be sure why what is happening is happening, and sometimes we may not even understand what is going on. The aim, though, is not just to make the data intelligible but to do so in an analytical way that provides a novel perspective on the phenomena we are concerned with, builds on previous work, and/or promises to tell us much about other phenomena of similar types.

The development of analytical categories and models has often been treated as a mysterious process about which little can be said and no guidance given. One must simply wait on the theoretical muse, it is sometimes implied. While we would certainly not wish to deny or downplay the role of creative imagination in research, we should point out that it is not restricted to the emergence of analytical ideas, but is equally important in devising ways of developing and testing these. Moreover, in neither case does recognition of the role of imagination negate the fact that there are general strategies available.

Besides obscuring the importance of strategies for generating concepts and models, overemphasis on the role of creative imagination in the development of analytical ideas also leads us to forget the function that our existing knowledge of the social world, and our reading of relevant literature, can perform in this process. It is only when we begin to understand that the imagination works via analogies and metaphors that this becomes plain. Vaughan (2004) has elaborated on the role of 'analogical theorizing'

---

4   Among the approaches we do not cover here are semiotic, conversation, discourse and narrative analysis. For introductions to these, see Manning (2004), Clayman and Gill (2004), Potter (2004) and Cortazzi (2001), respectively. It is our view, though, that there is a great deal of scope for fruitful influence and borrowing between these approaches and ethnography.

in her historical ethnography of the *Challenger* accident, in which she developed an explanation sharply at odds with the one put forward at the time.

While it is rare for ethnographic analysis to begin from a well-defined theory, and indeed there are dangers associated with such a starting point, the process of analysis cannot but rely on the existing ideas of the ethnographer and those that he or she can get access to in the literature (see Chapter 6). What is important is that these do not take the form of prejudgements, forcing interpretation of the data into their mould, but are instead used as resources to make sense of the data. This requires the exercise of some analytic nerve, tolerating uncertainty and ambiguity in one's interpretations, and resisting the temptation to rush to determinate conclusions.

In the early stages the aim is to use the data to think with. One looks to see whether any interesting patterns can be identified; whether anything stands out as surprising or puzzling; how the data relate to what one might have expected on the basis of common-sense knowledge, official accounts, or previous theory; and whether there are any apparent inconsistencies or contradictions among the views of different groups or individuals, within people's expressed beliefs or attitudes, or between these and what they do. Some such features and patterns may already have been noted in previous fieldnotes and analytic memos, perhaps even along with some ideas about how they might be explained.

What sorts of pattern one is looking for depends, of course, on research focus and theoretical orientation. These will also affect how much data one collects and how one approaches the analysis. Some ethnographers, notably those employing conversation or discourse analysis, employ relatively small amounts of data; and are concerned with local patterns visible within particular data sets. More usually, though, ethnographers collect quite large amounts of data of various kinds from different sources (observational fieldnotes and/or transcripts from various sites; interview notes and/or transcripts from different people; published and unpublished, official and personal documents; material objects; etc.); and they seek relationships across the whole corpus. Here the aim is to compare and relate what happens at various places and times in order to identify stable features (of people, groups, organizations, etc.) that transcend immediate contexts.

Useful analytical concepts sometimes arise 'spontaneously', being used by partici-pants themselves. And, indeed, unusual participant terms are always worth following up, since they may mark theoretically important or interesting phenomena (Becker and Geer 1957; Wieder 1974a, 1974b; Becker 1993). Some forms of ethnography, especially those based on or influenced by 'ethnoscience', are devoted almost exclusively to the listing, sorting, and interpretation of such 'folk' terms. They are concerned with the more or less formal semantics of such inventories (see Tyler 1969; Spradley 1970). However, most ethnographies, while using folk types, attempt to do more than simply document their meaning. They are taken as evidence of knowledge, belief, and actions that can be located within more general institutional contexts and analytic frameworks.

Alternatively, concepts may be 'observer-identified' (Lofland 1971; Lofland *et al.* 2006) – these are categories developed by the ethnographer rather than by members themselves. In the generation of such classifications, the analyst may draw together under the aegis of a single type what for members is a diverse and unrelated range of phenomena. The formulation of such types can draw on general, common-sense knowledge and on personal experience. Equally, though, they can be generated by borrowing or adapting existing concepts from the literature. For instance, in their research on the transition of students from middle to high schools, Measor and Woods

(1983) found that a variety of stories about life at the high school circulated among middle-school students, the most common one being that new entrants 'get their heads flushed in the loo' by older students. These stories had a standard form and seemed to reappear each year. Measor and Woods came to regard such stories as myths, and drew upon anthropological literature to understand the role they played in students' lives.

Sometimes, ethnographers find it necessary to formulate new terms to capture and characterize observer-identified types. Hargreaves provides an example with his development of the notion of 'contrastive rhetoric'. This refers to an

> interactional strategy whereby the boundaries of normal and acceptable practice are defined by institutionally and/or interactionally dominant individuals or groups through the introduction into discussion of alternative practices and social forms in stylized, trivialized and generally pejorative terms which connote their unacceptability.
>
> (Hargreaves 1981: 309)

Hargreaves uses this notion to analyse talk in a school staff meeting (Hargreaves 1981: 314), but he notes that many parallel applications are to be found in the sociology of the mass media and of deviance. He also draws attention to the similarities with the 'atrocity stories' sometimes produced by those in subordinate positions in medical settings (Stimson and Webb 1975; Dingwall 1977a; Hafferty 1988; Allen 2001).

At this stage in their development, the concepts will not usually be well-defined elements of an explicit analytical model. Rather, they will probably take the form of a loose collection of 'sensitizing concepts' (Blumer 1954). These contrast with what Blumer calls 'definitive concepts', which 'refer precisely to what is common to a class of objects, by the aid of the clear definition of attributes or fixed bench-marks'. A sensitizing concept, on the other hand, lacks such specificity, and 'it gives the user a general sense of reference and guidelines in approaching empirical instances. Where definitive concepts provide prescriptions of what to see, sensitizing concepts merely suggest directions along which to look' (Blumer 1954: 7; see also Hammersley 1989b). Sensitizing concepts are an important starting point; they are the germ of the analysis, and they can provide a focus for further data, collection.

Reading through the corpus of data and generating concepts which make sense of it, are the initial stages of ethnographic analysis. Very often, the concepts used to start with will be relatively mundane ones. Later, more analytically significant ones may be added. For instance, in his analysis of teachers' talk in a school staffroom, Hammersley (1980, 1981, 1998) developed categories that ranged from the very concrete (teachers' talk about students, about teaching, about national political events, etc.) to rather more abstract and analytic ones (trading news about students, exchanging mutual reassurances, accounting for decline and crisis, defending teacher competence, etc.). Needless to say, the process of coding the data is a recurrent one; as new categories emerge, previously coded data must be read again to see whether they contain any examples of the new codes The immediate aim is to reach a position where one has a set of promising categories and has carried out a systematic coding of all the data in terms of those categories. As we saw in Chapter 7, while there is no software which will do the coding for us, there are various programs that facilitate the process of analysis by allowing rapid retrieval of data relevant to particular categories and combinations of categories.

Having acquired some categories for organizing the data, the next task is to begin to work on those which seem likely to be central to one's analysis, with a view to clarifying their meaning and exploring their relations with other categories. The central strategy here is what Glaser and Strauss (1967) call the 'constant comparative method'. In this procedure, the analyst examines each item of data coded in terms of a partic-ular category, and notes its similarities with and differences from other data that have been categorized in the same way. This may lead to vaguely understood categories being differentiated into several more clearly defined ones, as well as to the specification of subcategories. In this way, new categories or subcategories emerge and there may be a considerable amount of reassignment of data among the categories (see Dey 1993; Boeije 2002).

As this process of systematic sifting and comparison develops, so the mutual relationships and internal structures of categories will be more clearly displayed. However, as we have indicated, the development of analytical ideas rarely takes the purely inductive form sometimes implied by Glaser and Strauss (heuristically useful though their approach is). Theoretical ideas, common-sense expectations, and stereotypes often play a key role. Indeed, it is these that allow the analyst to pick out surprising, interesting, and important features in the first place. Blanche Geer's (1964) famous account of her 'first days in the field' is a classic exemplification of the place of assumptions and stereotypes in the development of analytic themes.

Where a category forms part of a typology or model developed by others, however loosely constructed, relations with other categories may be implied that can be tentatively explored in the data. Where the fit is good and the model is well developed, it may even be possible to set about testing it rigorously. However, only rarely are sociological models sufficiently well developed for hypotheses to be derived and tested in this way. Generally, the process of testing requires considerable further development of the theory or explanation, and also specification of what would be appropriate indicators for its concepts.[5]

Of course, the ethnographer need not limit him- or herself to a single theory as a framework within which to analyse the data. Indeed, there are advantages to be gained from what Denzin (1989) termed 'theoretical triangulation': approaching data with multiple perspectives and hypotheses in mind. Bensman and Vidich (1960) provide an interesting example of this from their classic community study of Springdale. They report that they subjected their data to theoretical perspectives derived from Redfield, Weber, Tönnies, Veblen, Merton, Lynd, Warner, Mills, Sapir, and Tumin. In each case they asked themselves: 'What in [these] theories would permit us to comprehend our data?' Here, theories were not simply taken as off-the-peg solutions to research problems, but were used to provide focus for the analysis and for further fieldwork. These authors go on to note that:

> When one set of theories does not exhaust the potentialities of the data, other sets
> can be employed to point to and explain the facts which remain unexplained. Thus,
> for any initial statement of the field problem a whole series of theories may be

5 For discussions of the nature of theory development in ethnography, indicating some areas of disagreement, see Woods (1985, 1987) and Hammersley (1987a, 1987b). As regards what constitutes theory in ethnography, see Hammersley (1992: ch. 1.)

successively applied, each yielding different orders of data and each perhaps being limited by the special perspectives and dimensions on which it is predicated.

(Bensman and Vidich 1960: 165–6)

Not all ethnographers accept the validity of this approach; some see different theories as mutually incompatible, or rule out some theoretical approaches as incompatible with ethnography (Fielding and Fielding 1986; Silverman 1993: 157). However, our view is that one should use whatever resources are available which help to make sense of the data.

As we have indicated, the approach to the analysis of data adopted here is close in character to what is often labelled as 'grounded theorizing'. However, what falls under that heading displays some important internal differences in approach.

Making sense of grounded theorizing

While grounded theorizing is a very general perspective on analysis and theory-production, its use has been explored primarily within one broad sociological tradition – that of pragmatist symbolic interactionism – and its analytic strategies have particular affinities with that intellectual style (Atkinson and Housley 2003). It has had much less impact on anthropology, for instance, despite the fact that the kinds of thought processes involved in both disciplines are very similar. Moreover, there has been considerable discussion and dispute about, as well as development of, grounded theorizing. We cannot review this in detail here. However, there does need to be clarity about the general thrust of grounded theorizing, and it does need to be related to contemporary issues in theory and epistemology.

It has proved necessary to revisit the core concerns of grounded theorizing in recent years because in some quarters it had become translated from a set of general precepts and perspectives into something resembling a set of formulae and protocols (see Atkinson *et al.* 2003). To some extent, this was a reflection of the way in which Strauss took forward his distinctive approach to data analysis and how it was represented in his work with Corbin, notably in their jointly authored introductory text (Strauss and Corbin 1990, and later editions). This stimulated a vituperative response from Glaser (1992, 1993), seeking to re-establish what he saw as the original orientation of grounded theorizing.

It seems to us that a reading of the initial formulation in *The Discovery of Grounded Theory* (Glaser and Strauss 1967) can dispel many subsequent misunderstandings. The authors clearly intended to convey a general stance toward the development of fruitful ideas, concepts and theories that were generated through a close exploration of data. They were not advocating a rigid set of procedures intended to be used as a template for any and every project. Moreover, they were *not* advocating a uniquely 'qualitative' approach: their general stance would apply to the exploratory study of any form of data. They *were* advocating a move away from sterile reliance on pre-existing theory, or theory abstracted from any empirical research (with which sociology is still infested); and from forms of research, including ethnographic in character, that did not focus on theory development. In his own subsequent work and teaching, Strauss certainly never tried to simplify data through analytic procedures: he was always concerned with the elaboration of research questions and an appreciation of the complexity of social life and of sociological data. The more introductory treatments of the approach, and some secondary treatment of it, however, presented the idea of grounded theorizing as if it were driven exclusively by a somewhat mechanistic desire to *code* data, as if the desire were to reduce social complexity through a form of content analysis. Glaser's own manifest sense of betrayal, in response to this, illustrates most vividly, if nothing else, that there are multiple interpretations of the status and implications of grounded theorizing. Paradoxically, perhaps, while Glaser accused Strauss of rendering grounded theorizing improperly formulaic, Glaser himself wanted to use the strategy to produce generic concepts that were independent of the contexts of their discovery, or of the agents who produced them (the researchers), while Strauss typically stressed that theory is always grounded in the work of the analysts themselves and does not simply reside 'in the data'.

As this makes clear, grounded theorizing clearly cannot and should not be treated as a single orthodoxy. Nor are all aspects of it beyond question. Recent reviews have sought to free it from inappropriately mechanistic applications. Charmaz (2006) points out that there are different versions nested within the general approach (quite apart from the divergence of opinion between Glaser and Strauss themselves). She also points out that in practice the idea of grounded theorizing should be understood as a flexible, heuristic (Charmaz 2005, 2006; Charmaz and Mitchell 2001). She and Clarke (2005) also point out that there are changes and developments in the conceptualization of grounded theorizing, even in the work of Strauss and his own collaborators. Nor are current views of it immune to fundamental questioning (Dey 1999).

Clarke's (2005) work on grounded theorizing explicitly addresses the 'postmodern' turn in the social sciences, and in qualitative research particularly. Like us, she does not think that postmodernist ideas are radically divorced from the pragmatist thought that inspired interactionist and grounded-theory ideas in the first place (see Atkinson and Housley 2003; Delamont and Atkinson 2004). She does, however, address contemporary manifestations of that tradition, those that emphasize the multiplicity of social representations (including visual and narrative forms). She bases her approach on what she calls 'situational analysis', taking her conceptual framework beyond interactionism, to incorporate social-worlds analysis, discourse analysis, and actor-network theory. The situation, in all its social complexity, is treated as the unit of analysis. This approach is articulated through three main analytic strategies, all based on the notion of *mapping*. They are:

1   Situational maps as strategies for articulating the elements in the situation and examining relations among them.
2   Social worlds/arenas maps as cartographies of collective commitments, relations and sites of action.
3   Positional maps as simplification strategies for plotting positions articulated and not articulated in discourses.

(Clarke 2005: 86)

Here 'discourse' is treated in terms of narrative, visual and historical. These mapping exercises generate complex systems of relations between the elements and layers of the social situation.

As an extension of the original Straussian version of grounded theory and its variants, Clarke's (2005) approach emphasizes the adaptability of its root metaphors and analytic perspectives. In linking the general approach to postmodernism (broadly defined) she also shows that it is itself adaptable to new theoretical insights. Clarke is, of course, not the only methodologist to have done this. Denzin's intellectual trajectory has brought him from a 'classic' interactionist stance in his earliest methodological work (Denzin 1970), indeed one significantly influenced by positivism, towards a postmodern, performative mode of ethnography (e.g. Denzin 1997, 2003).

Our own perspective is informed by these approaches, but we do not express our general approach to analysis in terms of any single model or system. Rather, we believe that, within the scope of a book like this, it is more fruitful to concentrate on the kinds of concepts that can be derived, and the sort of analysis that can be generated. The general principle remains: the most important lessons to be learned about ethnographic analysis derive from the necessity of thinking not only *about* one's data, but also *with and through* the data, in order to produce fruitful ideas.

An emphasis on action

It is, of course, important to have a sense of the sort of ideas that one should be developing, or of the kinds of social phenomena about which ideas may be developed. While the focus of ethnographic inquiry can, of course, vary greatly, an important feature is a concern with action, with what people do and why. This emphasis on social action demands analysis of the socially shared means whereby people construct their social worlds through engagement in concerted social activities. The interest is in how people construct situations, and thereby their own identities, within institutional contexts which they must take into account in pursuing their goals and interests. Those institutional contexts are, of course, constituted through the actions of these and many other actors, in response to what they define as their own and others' needs, interests, values, etc.

It is a central assumption of ethnography that, in order to understand what people are doing and why, one needs to understand the meanings involved: how they interpret and evaluate the situations they face, and their own identities. For example, occupations, professions and other specialisms have esoteric knowledge and practices that are the repositories of *situated meanings*. Similarly, subcultures are defined in large measure by their local meaning-systems. For instance, in his classic study of horse-racing, Marvin Scott (1968) poses the question 'What is a horse?' This alerts us to the fact that while in some ways the meaning of 'horse' is self-evident, for those closely interested in the racing game, the meanings attached to that deceptively simple category can vary subtly. In much the same way, a subculture such as that of bikers (McDonald-Walker 2000) depends on local significance being attached to particular objects and events.

Much emphasis has therefore come to be placed, rightly, on ethnographers seeking to understand the meanings that are generated in, and that generate, social action; and to avoid imposing their own meanings. However, this is not as simple a contrast as it might seem, given that any understanding must draw on the resources available to the interpreter: they cannot be derived solely from what is being interpreted.[6] It should also be noted that emphasis on the role that meaning plays in social action has sometimes

---

6 This is one of the important points emphasized by Gadamer's philosophical hermeneutics: see Warnke (1987) and Dostal (2002).

led to an overemphasis on the collection and representation of data derived from interviews. As we have noted, interviews and conversations are important aspects of all fieldwork, but they cannot substitute for proper observation and examination of socially organized action.

Analysis, therefore, needs to pay serious attention to the means and methods whereby social actors perform social life and how they achieve orderly conduct. This may include the identification of *routine* activities. For instance, in organizational settings, we can document typical patterns of work, typical problems and typical solutions, characteristic strategies, and so on. The analysis, therefore, will, at a minimum, be a search for cases and instances of such activity types, their characteristic trajectories and their typical consequences. Such analyses might be undertaken in terms of the repertoires of *strategies* that actors use to achieve their ends.

Analysis of routine practices can also lead, in some social contexts, to the analysis of what we might call 'performances', such as *rituals*. These may be religious, but they need not be: there are secular rituals (see, for example, Tota 2004). Julius Roth's ethnography of everyday life in a tuberculosis hospital led to a classic paper on rituals of purity among medical and nursing staff (Roth 1963); virtually all of Erving Goffman's work can be thought of as a series of studies of the rituals of everyday interaction, including one series of essays explicitly devoted to this theme (Goffman 1972). More specifically, Cahill (1994) has pointed out the role that interactional ritual and ceremony play in routine behaviour in public places, and others have documented its role in medical encounters (Silverman 1984, 1996; Strong 2001). Coming from a different angle, Glaser and Strauss (1971) provide a sociological account of status passage, a rich series of ritual sites, reminiscent of the anthropological treatment of rites of passage. Anthropological literature, of course, suggests many kinds of ritual and related performances (Hughes-Freeland 1998). What these all have in common is the sense of repeated forms of activity, carried out with some degree of self-consciousness, in which the repetitious and formulaic character of the action itself has a degree of intrinsic significance. Atkinson's account of an opera company describes an 'opening night' of a new production; this has a somewhat ritualized air, and follows a recognizable pattern of events and celebrations (Atkinson 2006a).

In addition to focusing on the performance of routine actions and rituals, analysis must also, of course, give attention to unusual, deviant and problematic events and situations. One will pay attention to *failed performances*, *unexpected outcomes* or *crises*. These types of event may be numerically rare, but they often provide illumination of more mundane phenomena, by throwing the latter into sharp relief and by providing important information based on how social actors respond to them. As most accounts of grounded theorizing and other forms of ethnographic analysis agree, extreme, deviant and unusual cases are important in helping us to understand the limits of the normal and the unremarkable, and in mapping the types and variety of actions in any given social setting.

Understanding patterns of action can also involve an understanding of *rules*. This does not just mean the 'official' rules of bureaucracies and other organizations (significant though they may be in context), but the more general and usually informal rules or norms that guide everyday conduct. These may be articulated by social actors to one another (often in the course of socialization), but they are often observable by inference, as one studies the local management of conduct, or responses to perceived rule infraction.

The identification of rules does not imply that action is tightly rule-governed. Socially shared rules are, as we have already suggested, *guides* to action that social actors interpret in context, in accordance with local circumstances. Indeed, the analysis of rules and their pracrtical interpretation has been a major theme in the interactionist and ethnomethodological literature. Wieder's (1974a) study of a halfway house for ex-prisoners provides a classic account of how rules and norms are enacted and enunciated within the local organizational culture. Understanding social action means generating a systematic interpretation of the variety of rules, norms or conventions that constitute a given cultural setting; it also means gathering data and documenting how those rules are interpreted and acted on in practical, concrete situations.

This understanding of rules as guides implies the importance of *decisions*. The practicalities of decision-making are important in many organizational and professional contexts. Studies of policing, for example, need to be able to document the local circumstances under which police officers make decisions. For example, such decisions might include which members of the public to stop and search, which parts of a neighbourhood to survey most intently, which traffic violations to bother with and which to overlook, what times of the day and night to be particularly vigilant and what times to be more relaxed. In this context, as in others, decision-making is vital to the everyday performance of work: nobody can be equally alert to every possible infraction on every possible occasion (even under conditions of 'zero tolerance'). There is a substantial and long-established research literature on the practicalities of decision-making in a wide range of professional situations; from health professionals making decisions about diagnosis and choice of treatment to coroners deciding cause of death or judges determining what would be an appropriate sentence.

Of course, the analysis of actions includes the analysis of spoken actions. We have acknowledged that *talk* is an important aspect of ethnographic data collection. Viewed from the perspective of ethnographic analysis, we recognize that most forms of action involve talk, and that we can understand this talk only as it is involved in action. This means that it is not sufficient to reproduce extracts of talk as illustrative quotes, they need detailed analysis. It is also not adequate to treat them as if they were substitute or proxy data for what people do. It is a seriously inadequate form of ethnographic analysis to present interview material as if it provided direct evidence about the events that are recounted, or the norms that are enunciated. Equally, it is not adequate to treat interview or conversational data as if they give the analyst unmediated access to a social actor's personal experiences and feelings (Atkinson and Silverman 1997). Rather than using interview materials as handy illustrations, or as lazy substitutes for the proper analysis of observed action, they should be analysed systematically and coherently in the context of unfolding courses or patterns of action.

So, the proper analysis of talk has to recognize that social actors *do* things with words. As Coffey and Atkinson (1996) suggest, there is no need to privilege either participant observation or interviewing as the prime source of data, once one recognizes that spoken discourse always takes place within forms of action or performance. We need, therefore, to examine talk for its speech-act functions. In their everyday talk, as also in their interview responses, people are *performing* social actions. They are, for instance, offering *justifications* or *excuses* for themselves or others; they are providing *explanations* for events and actions; they attribute *motives* to their own and others' actions, and so on. The detailed analysis of field data, therefore, needs to examine the forms and functions of talk. This includes the analysis of stories and narratives. There is now a very substantial literature on 'narrative analysis' and we do not intend to recapitulate it all here.[7] What we *will* say is that it is necessary to recognize that narratives should be studied within the context of an overall ethnographic strategy. Narratives should not be treated as if they occupied a different, special and privileged analytic space.

The sort of analysis we have in mind is illustrated by treatments of scientists' accounts of scientific discoveries (Gilbert and Mulkay 1984; Atkinson *et al.* 1997). These analyses do not treat these narratives as if they were transparent accounts of how the science was done, or reliable versions of how the discoveries were made. Rather, they are examined for the *accounting devices* that the scientists used to explain their own and others' success, to attribute 'chance' and 'skill' to research groups' efforts, and to reconcile two versions of scientific success – the inexorable revelation of truth on the one hand, and local, personal circumstances on the other. A similar style of analysis is provided by Voysey Paun (2006) in her analysis of parents' accounts of life with a disabled child. She shows how parental accounts construct narratives of normal parenting and normal family life.

As we have already indicated, such analyses always need to be incorporated within broader ethnographic understandings. It is necessary to understand, for instance, how particular kinds of stories function within specific organizational or cultural contexts. Within settings of work, for example, one should be able to identify different genres of personal story and anecdote: *atrocity stories*, especially those recounting ghastly blunders, are often circulated in order to socialize novices into an occupational or local culture (Dingwall 1977a; Hafferty 1988). Managers use stories to make sense of organizational life, and they are told within particular organizational contexts (Czarniawska 2004). Moreover, these often correspond to broader types or genres of story: success stories, victim stories, hard-luck stories. Earlier, we mentioned the sorts of myths circulating among schoolchildren that were identified by Measor and Woods (1983), which are analogous to widely circulated 'urban legends' and similar kinds of modern folk-lore.

It is vital to keep in mind the extent to which situated stories draw on socially shared formats. While there are different types and functions of narratives, they relate to culturally appropriate conventions: either conforming to them or breaching them in significant ways. Even the most 'private' and 'personal' of experiences are couched in socially shared cultural forms. This has been vividly confirmed by the analysis of sexual stories by Plummer (1995), who demonstrates how accounts of rape and 'coming out' are constructed using conventional means. A thoroughgoing analysis, therefore, will examine talk, whether coming from 'naturally occurring contexts' or interviews, in order to discover the shared formats of narrative, and the conventions of genre. It will relate these forms and functions to the social situations in which they are produced and shared, the social positions of the tellers, and the composition of the audience(s).

In developing categories that make sense of the data, then, the focus must be on actions, the meanings that underpin or infuse them, and the wider situations that these actions both respond to and shape. And all these different aspects are intimately related.

---

7 See Atkinson and Delamont (2006) for a major collection of papers on the entire field; see Riessman (1993) for an authoritative introduction, and Riessman (2002) for an overview of the area.

Developing typologies

Very often the categories that have emerged in the analysis will be used simply to produce a description and/or explanation of the case or cases investigated. But sometimes ethnographers attempt to develop more systematic typologies that hold out the prospect of application to data from other situations. Here, a more or less exhaustive set of sub-types of some general category is identified. A very common pattern is the specification of various strategies which some category or group of actors adopt, or could adopt, to deal with a problem that they face routinely. However, typologies can have other sorts of foci too. For instance, Karp (1993) develops a typology of responses by patients to the prescription of antidepressant drugs. These are: resistance, trial, commitment, conversion, disenchantment, and deconversion. Rather than seeing these as alternative strategies he treats them as phases through which most patients go in their 'depressive careers', though of course there is the possibility of patients taking diverse routes through this set of responses. Karp explicitly draws a parallel with Robbins (1988) work which identifies stages of recruitment, conversion, and deconversion of people to a variety of religious groups.

These are the sorts of relationships among categories that ethnographers look out for. And once having produced typologies like these they may become interested in why particular strategies are adopted by particular sorts of people in particular circumstances, or why particular kinds of people follow particular career patterns.

Typologies in ethnographic accounts vary considerably in the degree to which they have been systematically developed. In 1970, Lofland complained that in this respect much ethnographic research suffered from 'analytic interruptus'. In their development of categories, Lofland suggested, many analysts fail 'to follow through to the implied logical conclusion . . . to reach [the] initially implied climax' (1970: 42). Taking the example of typologies of strategies, Lofland argues that the investigator must take the time and trouble:

1   To assemble self-consciously all [the] materials on how a [problem] is dealt with by the persons under study;
2   To tease out . . . variations among [the] assembled range of instances of strategies;
3   To classify them into an articulate set of . . . types of strategies; and
4   To present them to the reader in some orderly and preferably named and numbered manner.

(Lofland 1970: 42–3)

Elsewhere, he provided an extended discussion of the varieties of typology and how they might be developed (Lofland 1971; see also Lofland *et al.* 2006).

Lazarsfeld and Barton (1951) go even further in their recommendations for the systematic development of typologies. An initial set of categories differentiating a particular range of phenomena can be developed into a systematic typology, they argue, by specifying the dimensions underlying the discriminations it makes. Not only does this force clarification and perhaps modification of the categories already identified, but in addition it throws up other categories that may also be of importance.

We can illustrate this by reference to Glaser and Strauss's typology of 'awareness contexts'. They developed this concept to characterize the different kinds of social situation found among terminally ill hospital patients, their families, and medical personnel. The idea refers to the differential distribution of knowledge and understanding of the dying person's condition, from situations of 'closed awareness', when the patient is not informed of the diagnosis and prognosis, to 'open awareness', where the knowledge is shared openly by all parties. The idea of an awareness context is thus closely linked to the dynamics of information control characteristic of many medical encounters. However, in the following extract the notion is treated as a more general formal category. In such a formulation it is clearly applicable to a much wider range of social settings approximating to the general type of 'information games' (cf. Scott 1968; Lyman and Scott 1970). It is, for instance, directly applicable to the substantive issue of 'coming out' among homosexuals, and the management of the revelation or concealment of such an identity (Plummer 1975: 177–96). Glaser and Strauss (1964) write:

> We have singled out four types of awareness context for special consideration since they have proved useful in accounting for different types of interaction. An open awareness context obtains when each interactant is aware of the other's true identity and his own identity in the eyes of the other. A closed awareness context obtains when one interactant does not know either the other's identity or the other's view of his identity. A suspicion awareness context is a modification of the closed one: one interactant suspects the true identity of the other or the other's view of his own identity, or both. A pretense awareness context is a modification of the open one: both interactants are fully aware but pretend not to be.
>
> (Glaser and Strauss 1964: 669)

By identifying the dimensions underlying this typology, along the lines suggested by Lazarsfeld and Barton (1951), we find that there are rather more possibilities than Glaser and Strauss's initial typology allows (see Figure 1). Furthermore, some of these new possibilities look fruitful, such as cell X, where one party pretends while the other suspects, and cells Y and Z, where one pretends or suspects while the other does not

PARTY B

PARTY A	Knows	Pretends not to know	Suspects	Doesn't know
Knows			Suspicion	Closed
Pretends not to know		Pretence	X	Y
Suspects	Suspicion			Z
Doesn't know	Closed			

Figure 1 Typology of awareness contexts

know. Glaser (1978) warns us against what he calls the 'logical elaboration' of categories, and he is right to do so. Typologies should not be extended beyond their analytic value. Nonetheless, specification of the dimensions underlying a typology encourages us to think seriously and systematically about the nature of each category and its relationships with others. It may help us to spot previously unconsidered possibilities, or unsuspected relationships among categories.

Concepts and indicators

There is little point in developing highly systematized typologies, and models, if they provide little purchase on one's data. The development of an effective typology is not a purely logical or conceptual exercise: there must be constant recourse to the material one is analysing. As the categories of the analysis are being clarified and developed in relation to one another, so also must the links between concepts and indicators be specified and refined. Sensitizing concepts must be turned into something more like definitive concepts.[8] We should note that the links involved here are functional ones: what serves as concept and what as indicator will vary on different occasions.

In moving between data and concepts we must take great care to note plausible alternative links to those made in the emerging analysis, and these need to be investigated. While in no sense is it necessary, or even possible, to lay bare all the assumptions involved in concept-indicator linkages, it is important to make explicit and to examine those assumptions to which strong challenges can be made.

We can illustrate this by reference to Willis's classic research on the adaptations of working-class boys to school. He argues that the 'lads' he studied displayed a counterculture, an 'entrenched, general and personalized opposition to "authority"'. In supporting this claim he uses descriptions of the behaviour of the 'lads' as well as quotations from group interviews such as the following comments about teachers:

Joey: ... they're able to punish us. They're bigger than us, they stand for a bigger establishment than we do, like, we're just little and they stand for bigger things, and you try to get your own back. It's, uh, resenting authority I suppose.

Eddie: The teachers think they're high and mighty 'cos they're teachers, but they're nobody really, they're just ordinary people ain't they?

Bill: Teachers think they're everybody. They are more, they're higher than us, but they think they're a lot higher and they're not.

Spanksy: Wish we could call them first names and that ... think they're God.

Pete: That would be a lot better.

PW: I mean you say they're higher. Do you accept at all that they know better about things?

Joey: Yes, but that doesn't rank them above us, just because they are slightly more intelligent.

---

8 This is a controversial proposal: there are those who argue that sensitizing concepts render definitive concepts unnecessary in ethnographic research; see Williams (1976). However, it is unclear to us how sensitizing concepts can be adequate for the later stages of analysis; see Hammersley (1989a, 1989b).

Bill: The ought to treat us how they'd like us to treat them . . . .

Joey: . . . the way we're subject to their every whim like. They want something doing and we have to sort of do it, 'cos, er, er, we're just, we're under them like. We were with a woman teacher in here, and 'cos we all wear rings and one or two of them bangles, like he's got one on, and out of the blue, like, for no special reason, she says, 'take all that off'.

PW: Really?

Joey: Yeah, we says, 'One won't come off', she says, 'Take yours off as well.' I said, 'You'll have to chop my finger off first.'

PW: Why did she want you to take your rings off?

Joey: Just a sort of show like. Teachers do this, like, all of a sudden they'll make you do your ties up and things like this. You're subject to their every whim like. If they want something done, if you don't think it's right, and you object against it, you're down to Simmondsy (the head), or you get the cane, you get some extra work tonight.

PW: You think of most staff as kind of enemies . . . ?
           – Yeah.
           – Yeah.
           – Most of them.

Joey: It adds a bit of spice to yer life, if you're trying to get him for something he's done to you.

                                                              (Willis 1977: 11–12)

In assessing the way in which Willis links the concept of counterculture with the various indicators he uses, we need to consider whether, for example, students' expressions of opposition to teachers reflect a general opposition to 'authority' as such, or only to particular types of authority. And, indeed, in the course of doing this, we may need to clarify the concept of authority itself. Would it make any sense, for example, to argue that Joey, who seems to be the leader of the 'lads', has authority among them? Whether or not we use the concept of authority in a broad or narrow sense, we need to be clear about exactly what it is that the analysis claims the 'lads' are rejecting.

Another question we might ask is whether the 'lads' are opposed to all aspects of teachers' authority or only to those teacher demands that they regard as overstepping its legitimate boundaries. For example, the 'lads' complain about rules relating to their personal appearance, a complaint also reported in an earlier study by Werthman (1963), dealing with members of urban gangs in the United States. However, whereas Willis takes such complaints as an indicator of a general antipathy towards authority, Werthman interprets them as signifying the boundaries around what the boys he studied regarded as a teacher's legitimate area of control. Clearly, such alternative interpretations have serious implications for the character and validity of the analysis produced (see Hammersley 1990: ch 3).

While the nature of the alternative interpretations that must be considered will vary between studies, we can point to a number of issues that must be borne in mind when examining concept-indicator links. These correspond to the dimensions we discussed in Chapter 2 in relation to sampling within cases.

Social context

The issue of context is at the heart of the conflicting interpretations of student behaviour to be found in the work of Willis and Werthman. For Willis (1997), opposition characterized the contacts of the 'lads' with all forms of authority. For Werthman (1963), on the other hand, the behaviour of gang members towards teachers varied across contexts according to the actions of the teacher and how these were interpreted. We shall focus our discussion here on one of the most important elements of context: the audience to which the actions or accounts being used as data were directed. One important possible audience is, of course, the ethnographer. This is most obvious in the case of interviewing, an interactional format in which researchers play a key role through the questions they ask and their responses to answers, however non-directive the interview is. In interviews the very structure of the interaction forces participants to be aware of the ethnographer as audience. Interviewees' conceptions of the nature and purposes of social research, of the particular research project, and of the personal characteristics of the interviewer may, therefore, act as a strong influence on what they say, and how they say it.

This can be both a help and a hindrance in the production of relevant data and valid interpretations of them. 'Well-trained' informants and respondents can act as highly effective research assistants in reporting relevant data, data of which the ethnographer might not otherwise become aware. They can also make the data collection process much more efficient, since they can select out what is relevant from the mass of irrelevant data that is available to them.

There are also dangers here, though. The more 'sophisticated' the interviewee the greater the tendency for him or her to move away from description into analysis. While there is no such thing as pure description, it is essential to minimize the inference involved in descriptions used as data in order to provide for the possibility of checking and rechecking, constructing and reconstructing, interpretations of them. If the interviewee gives heavily theorized accounts of the events or experiences he or she is describing, however interesting or fruitful the theoretical ideas are, the database has been eroded.

Spradley (1979) provides a particularly good example of this problem, that of Bob, an informant he worked with in the course of his study of tramps. Bob had spent four years on skid row; he was also a Harvard graduate, and had gone on to do postgraduate work in anthropology. Spradley recounts:

> On my next visit to the treatment center I invited Bob into my office. We chatted casually for a few minutes, then I started asking him some ethnographic questions. 'What kind of men go through Seattle City Jail and end up at this alcoholism treatment center?' I asked. 'I've been thinking about the men who are here,' Bob said thoughtfully. 'I would divide them up first in terms of race. There are Negroes, Indians, Caucasians, and a few Eskimo. Next I think I would divide them on the basis of their education. Some have almost none, a few have some college. Then some of the men are married and some are single.' For the next fifteen minutes he proceeded to give me the standard analytic categories that many social scientists use.
>
> (Spradley 1979: 53)

Where the researcher is particularly interested in the categories in terms of which participants view the world, this sort of account is of limited value. We must be careful, then, in analysing our material, to be alert for the effects of audience in terms of people's views of the researcher's interests, and also perhaps what they are and are not likely to disclose to such an audience.

Even when the ethnographer is acting as observer, he or she may be an important audience for the participants, or at least for some of them. Informal questioning often forms part of participant observation, and Becker and Geer (1960) have pointed to the importance of distinguishing between solicited and unsolicited statements when assessing evidence. However, as we noted in Chapter 5, such a distinction is too crude. We cannot assume that unsolicited statements are uninfluenced by the researcher's presence. The same applies to other actions. It is now a central tenet of the sociological literature that people seek to manage impressions of themselves and of settings and groups with which they are associated (Goffman 1959). In a study of an Indian village community, Berreman (1962) discovered the extent to which his data were the product of impression management by the villagers only when he was forced to change his interpreter. This change modified his relationship with them, and produced different kinds of data.[9]

Sometimes participants will actually tell an ethnographer that they have been presenting a front. Bogdan and Taylor (1975) quote the comment of an attendant in a state institution for the 'mentally retarded' made to an ethnographer at the end of the first day of fieldwork: 'Yeah, we didn't do a lot of things today that we usually do. Like if you wasn't here we woulda snitched some food at dinner and maybe hit a couple of 'em around. See before we didn't know you was an OK guy' (Bogdan and Taylor 1975: 89). Of course, such admissions do not necessarily indicate that full access has finally been granted. While over the course of an extended stay in a setting participants generally acquire increasing trust in the ethnographer and find it more and more difficult to control the information available to him or her, members' creation and management of their personal fronts can prove a persistent problem. Thus, Punch (1979) reports how, at a party he attended some months after completing intensive and long-term fieldwork on police work in Amsterdam, one of his informants revealed to him, under the influence of alcohol, that he had been kept well away from evidence of police corruption. In the case of observational data too, then, one must be aware of the possible effects of the ethnographer as audience.

However, this concern with reactivity, with the effects of the researcher on the nature of the data he or she collects, can be somewhat misleading. Much as quantitative researchers seek to minimize reactivity through standardization, under the influence of naturalism ethnographers sometimes regard any effects of their presence or actions on the data simply as a source of bias. It is true that it can be a threat to the validity of inferences. However, participants' responses to ethnographers may also be an important source of information. Data in themselves cannot be valid or invalid; what is at issue are the inferences drawn from them. The point is that the ethnographer must try continually to be aware of how his or her presence may have shaped the data.

Similar considerations even apply in interpreting documents and data produced through secret research. Here too we must bear in mind the ways in which audience considerations may have shaped the actions and accounts produced. In secret participant observation, assuming that his or her cover has not been 'blown', the ethnographer

---

9 On the issues surrounding anthropologists' use of interpreters, and their neglect, see Borchgrevink (2003). Of course, the problem of negotiating language differences is not limited to anthropologists: see Temple and Young (2004).

cannot be an audience, as such. However, he or she may be an important audience in one or another participant identity, and other audiences will also shape what is and is not said or done in particular contexts. Similarly, we must remember that documents are always written for some audience, perhaps for several different ones simultaneously. This will affect the nature of the document, through what is taken as relevant, what can be assumed as background knowledge, what cannot or should not be said, and what must be said even if it is untrue. In the same way, in open participant observation and interviewing, consideration of the effects of audience must be extended beyond the role of the ethnographer.[10]

The significance of audience is heightened by the fact that the participants in a setting rarely perceive themselves as a homogeneous grouping. Different categories, groups, or factions are often involved, in relation to whom different fronts need to be maintained. And even within these divisions there will be more informal networks of communication that include some participants and exclude others, as Hitchcock (1983) shows in the case of a primary school's staff:

> On many occasions throughout the fieldwork, staff's comments would be prefaced by such statements as 'I know it's unprofessional of me talking like this . . .', 'I don't suppose I should really be telling you this', '. . . don't tell him I said this for goodness sake'. On other occasions when staff told me things these prefaces were not present; it was rather assumed that I wouldn't 'blow the scene' by telling someone else what had been said about them. That is, I was 'trusted' to keep things quiet or to keep what was said to myself.
>
> (Hitchcock 1983: 30)

Different things will be said and done in different company, then. In particular we must interpret differently what is done 'in public' and what is done 'in private', since the category to which an action belongs may have important consequences for how it relates to actions and attitudes in other contexts. At the same time, whether something is 'private' or 'public' is not always obvious, and there is a subtle shading between the two. One may have to know a setting very well in order to be able to recognize the public or private status of actions and even then it is easy to be mistaken. Indeed, what was public and what was private may get redefined retrospectively.

Even in the case of interviews, the ethnographer may not be the most significant audience, as we noted in Chapter 5. To one degree or another, and whatever assurances of confidentiality the ethnographer gives, interviewees may regard what they say as 'public' rather than 'private'; they may expect it to be communicated to others, or recorded for posterity. Krieger (1979) provides an example from her research on a radio station. Reflecting on interviewees' confidence or trust, she remarks:

> I came to think it reflected an expectation that this telling in the interview situation was more than to one person, it was a telling to the world at large, and not only a bid for recognition by that world, but also perhaps for forgiveness.
>
> (Krieger 1979a: 170–1)

---

10 One of the strengths even of open participant observation, of course, is that in 'natural' settings other audiences are generally much more powerful and significant for participants than the ethnographer, and their effects are likely to swamp those of the researcher.

Analysing data for the effects of audience is not, then, simply a matter of assessing the impact of the researcher, but also one of assessing the impact of any other audience the actor might be addressing, consciously or subconsciously. This applies to all forms of data and it is a crucial consideration if misleading inferences are to be avoided.

Time

What people say and do is produced in the context of a developing sequence of social interaction. If we ignore what has already occurred or what follows we are in danger of drawing the wrong conclusions. However, the temporal context of actions includes not only the host of events that occur before and after them but also the temporal framework in terms of which the people involved locate them. Within cultural settings, actors have 'moral careers': they pass through formal and informal stages and identity transformations – from novice to old hand, from outsider to insider. While these patterns are never single-stranded, and are often contested, they frequently represent an important consideration shaping action.

If we take seriously the idea that social identities are made, and that they are temporal processes, then we need to be able to analyse the socially organized ways in which identities are brought into being: how social actors 'become' inmates in a total institution; how learners acquire the knowledge and skills to perform as competent members of some kind; the pathways that people or objects traverse through complex organizations; the steps taken in arriving at organizational decisions, diagnoses as dispositions. These are all organized in terms of temporal order. The reconstruction of such trajectories is a powerful way of ordering ethnographic analyses.

Glaser and Strauss (1968) provide a striking example in their study of how dying patients are dealt with by hospital staff. They note how staff construct and reconstruct conceptions of the dying trajectories of patients, and how these play a key role in shaping their attitudes to the treatment of patients. Moreover, deviations from expected patterns can cause problems. How hospital staff react to signs of improvement in a patient, then, is dependent on the temporal context, in terms of which they read those signs. Relevant here are not only what has happened in the past, but also estimates of what is likely to happen in the future. Nor is this restricted to the staff; patients' families may not always welcome signs of improvement in their condition, for example because these are seen as part of a painful and lingering death (Wright 1981).

Ball (1983) has pointed out that many organizations are characterized by short- and long-term temporal cycles. Most universities and schools, for example, have terms whose beginnings and endings are important benchmarks for staff and students. Moreover, the different terms are not equivalent; they form part of a longer cycle based on the year – the autumn term is very different in many ways from the spring term, for example. For students, the years form part of an even larger cycle, their first year as freshers being very different in status from their final year as seniors. Data, of whatever kind, recorded at different times need to be examined in light of their place within the temporal patterns, short or long term, that structure the lives of those being studied.[11]

Individuals, organizations and groups have their various temporal frameworks. The past is always being constructed through acts of memory. Memory is not merely

11 For more on such patterns, see Roth (1963), Zerubavel (1979, 1981), and Coffey (1994).

a mental process of recall. It is a collective achievement (Connerton 1989; Middleton and Edwards 1990; Tota 2004) . Social actors create their sense of the past and their own biographies through *acts* of memory. The past is evoked through narrative performances. In analysing members' accounts of their own and others' lives, therefore, we need to be attentive to the ways in which the past is repeatedly constructed. Past, present and future are created and re-created together as actors share memories, plans or projects. The ethnography of the past, or of memory, therefore, is not an imaginative reconstruction of past events by the analyst, but rather an ethnography of how actors *create* pasts for themselves and for others.

From this point of view there are considerable advantages to be gained from combining interviews with participant observation. Each may provide information about temporal contexts whose implications for interpreting data can be assessed. The dangers of neglecting the effects of time are particularly great where reliance is placed upon a single data source, especially interviews or documents. Not only may what is said at one point in an interview be influenced by the interviewee's interpretation of what has been said earlier and what might be asked later, but also it is affected by what has happened to the person prior to the interview and what is anticipated in the near future. Where interviews are used alone, it is wise to give over some interview space to casual conversation about current events in the interviewee's life. Indeed, this may be a useful way of opening the interview to build rapport. Equally important, however, the analysis of interview data must take account of the temporal organization of what is said, and when, over the course of the interview itself.

Once again, it is not a matter of accepting or rejecting data, but rather of knowing how to interpret them; there is a great temptation to assume that actions, statements, or interview responses represent stable features of the person or of settings. This may be correct, but it cannot be assumed. Actions are embedded in temporal contexts and these may shape them in ways that are important for the analysis.

Personnel

Who is doing or saying things is an equally important consideration when it comes to assessing the relationship between concept and evidence. People's identities or social locations (that is, the patterns of social relationships in which they are enmeshed) can have two kinds of effect on the nature of the accounts or actions they produce. First, social locations determine the sort of information available to people. They clearly affect what it is possible for people to see and hear 'at first hand'; they also determine what people will get to know about, and how they will come to know things 'second hand'. Moreover, *how* they come to know things will affect *what* they 'know'.

The other way in which identities affect actions and accounts is through the particular perspectives that people in various social locations tend to generate, and that will filter their understanding and knowledge of the world, and shape their actions within it. In particular, the interpretation of information available to a person is likely to be selected and slanted in line with his or her prevailing interests and concerns. There may even be a strong element of wish-fulfilment involved. One must be aware of the possible effects of social identity on all kinds of data, including ethnographers' own observational reports: we too occupy particular locations and what we observe, what we record, and how we interpret it will be influenced by these.

The implications of identity for the accounts people provide vary somewhat depending upon whether the ethnographer is using these as a source of information or as data about people's perspectives or discursive practices. In the first case, the social location of the informant may be an important source of knowledge, but it is also a potential source of bias: it is a threat to validity that must be monitored. This kind of consideration must underlie the selection of informants and the interpretation of the data they provide, as well as the treatment of data from other sources. In using people's accounts for analysing their perspectives or discursive repertoires, on the other hand, social location is no longer a source of bias, it is a focus for the analysis. Here the aim is precisely to document how people see, make sense of, and talk or write about particular social locations. Of course, as we saw in Chapter 5, these two forms of analysis are complementary. And in the case of observational data produced by the ethnographer, their interaction is the essence of reflexivity.

Our discussion in this section has been designed to show that the relationships between concepts and indicators must be assessed by considering alternative interpretations of the data, and by following through the implications of particular interpretations to see if these are confirmed. And it is important here to take account of the dimensions of social context, time, and the people involved. However, some ethnographers have proposed more direct ways of testing these relationships. We will discuss two commonly mentioned strategies here: respondent validation and triangulation (see Seale 1999).

Respondent validation

A recognition of the importance of actors' social locations leads directly to the issue of 'respondent validation', a notion that has an uncertain and sometimes contested place in ethnographic analysis (Emerson and Pollner 1988; Bloor 1997). Some ethnographers have argued that a crucial test for their accounts is whether the actors whose beliefs and behaviour they are describing recognize the validity of those accounts (Lincoln and Guba 1985). The aim is therefore to 'establish a correspondence between the sociologist's and the member's view of the member's social world by exploring the extent to which members recognize, give assent to, the judgements of the sociologist' (Bloor 1978: 548–9).

In his own research on the decision rules employed by ENT (ear, nose, and throat) specialists, Bloor (1978) sent each specialist he studied a report describing his or her assessment practices. This was accompanied by a letter that asked each specialist to 'read through the report to see how far it corresponded with his own impressions of his clinic practice'. Bloor then discussed the reports in interviews with the doctors. He argues that for the most part the exercise was successful: 'some respondents endorsed my description of their practices, and where they did not the nature of the exercise was such as to enable me to correct the analysis so that this assent was no longer withheld' (Bloor 1978: 549). Using a different strategy, in his study of Beachside Comprehensive School, Ball (1981, 1984) held two seminars for the school's staff at which he presented some of his findings. His experience was rather less happy and fruitful, and suggests that while there is merit in the strategy, it is far from being problem-free. Rather more dangerous but, it seems, nevertheless productive in many respects, was Zulaika's feeding back his findings on Basque political violence in his natal village of Itziar at an open community meeting (Zulaika 1995).

The value of respondent validation lies in the fact that the participants involved in the events documented in the data may have access to additional knowledge of the context – of other relevant events, of temporal framework, of others' ulterior motives, for example – that is not available to the ethnographer. They may be part of information networks that are more powerful than those accessible to the ethnographer. In addition, they have access to their own experience of events, which may be of considerable importance. Such additional evidence may materially alter the plausibility of different possible interpretations of the data. Thus, Moffatt (1989: 329) reports how the conclusions of his research on students at Rutgers University were modified by their responses when he taught preliminary versions in his anthropology classes there.

At the same time, it is important to recognize the limitations of respondent validation. The information people receive through their networks may be false. Equally, we cannot assume that anyone is a privileged commentator on his or her own actions, in the sense that the truth of their account is guaranteed. As Schutz (1964) and others have noted, we can grasp the meanings of our actions only retrospectively. Moreover, these meanings are reconstructed on the basis of memory; they are not given in any immediate sense. Nor will the evidence for them necessarily be preserved. Much social action operates at a subconscious level, leaving no memory traces. Thus, in the case of Bloor's (1978) specialists, we cannot assume that they were consciously aware of the decision rules they used, or even that, infallibly, they could recognize them when someone else documented them. In short, while people are well-placed informants on their own actions, they are no more than that; and their accounts must be analysed in the same way as any other data, with close consideration being given to possible threats to validity.

This is reinforced once we recognize that it may be in a person's interests to misinterpret or misdescribe his or her own actions, or to counter the interpretations of the ethnographer. Both Bloor and Ball point out that participants generally interpret data in the light of different concerns from, and sometimes by criteria at odds with, those of the ethnographer. Bloor (1978) acknowledges, for instance, that:

> I had expected the specialists to respond to the reports in a manner similar to that of an academic colleague when one asks him to criticize a draft paper one has written. I became aware of having made this assumption when it was violated – I suspected that some of the specialists had not read the report in the expected critical spirit. They had read the report, I felt, in the way that we today might read a nineteenth century religious tract – with a modicum of detached, superficial interest, with a feeling that it displayed a certain peculiar charm perhaps, but without being so moved by its content as to feel the necessity to define one's own beliefs and practices in accordance with it or in contrast to it. They were unversed in the conventions of academic sociological criticism and they were perhaps only marginally interested in the content of the reports.
>
> (Bloor 1978: 550)

As with the accounts they provide in other circumstances, then, people's reactions to the ethnographer's analysis will be coloured by their social position and their perceptions of the research act. In the case of Bloor's doctors, they had only a marginal interest; Ball's school teachers, on the other hand, displayed a keener commitment. But this, too, was directly related to their social locations, and was at odds with that of the researcher:

many of the staff had apparently read my chapter solely in terms of what it had to say about them or their subject. There was little or no discussion of the general issues I was trying to raise or the overall arguments of the chapter . . . . I had taken as my task as ethnographer the description and analysis of large scale trends which extended as I saw them across the whole school, an overview. The staff responded from their particular view of the school, from the vantage point of the position they held.

(Ball 1984: 18–19)

Ball's teachers interpreted his work as critical, and queried the validity of his findings.[12]

Such feedback can, then, be highly problematic. Whether respondents are enthusiastic, indifferent, or hostile, their reactions cannot be taken as direct validation or refutation of the observer's inferences. Rather, such processes of so-called 'validation' should be treated as yet another valuable source of data and insight. At the same time, the consequences of feeding back data and analyses must be taken into account, both for the researcher and for others. This practice is sometimes advocated on ethical grounds, but a commitment to openness should be tempered by a sense of political realism.

Triangulation

In effect, respondent validation represents one kind of triangulation: the checking of inferences drawn from one set of data sources by collecting data from others. More specifically, data-source triangulation involves the comparison of data relating to the same phenomenon but deriving from different phases of the fieldwork, different points in the temporal cycles occurring in the setting, or the accounts of different participants (including the ethnographer) differentially located in the setting. This last form of triangulation can be extended indefinitely by showing each participant the others' accounts and recording his or her comments on them (Adelman 1977). This is very time-consuming but, besides providing a validity check, it also gives added depth to the description of the social meanings involved in a setting.

The term 'triangulation' derives from a loose analogy with navigation and surveying. For someone wanting to locate their position on a map, a single landmark can only provide the information that they are situated somewhere along a line in a particular direction from that landmark. With two landmarks, however, exact position can be pinpointed by taking bearings on both; one's position is at the point on the map where the two lines cross. In social research, if we rely on a single piece of data there is the danger that undetected error in our inferences may render our analysis incorrect. If, on the other hand, diverse kinds of data lead to the same conclusion, we can be a little more confident in that conclusion. This confidence is well founded to the degree that the different kinds of data have different likely directions of error built into them.

There are a number of other kinds of triangulation besides that relating to participants' accounts. Earlier, we mentioned theoretical triangulation, but there is also the possibility of triangulating between different researchers. While team research has sometimes been used by ethnographers, often the data generated by different observers have been designed to be complementary, relating to different aspects of a setting or different settings, rather than intended to facilitate triangulation. Nevertheless, team research

---

12 Scarth (1986: 202–3) reports a similar experience.

offers the opportunity for researcher triangulation. Of course, to maximize its potentialities the observers should be as different as possible, for example adopting very different roles in the field.[13]

Rather more common is method triangulation. Here, data produced by different data collection techniques are compared. To the extent that these techniques involve different kinds of validity threat, they provide a basis for checking interpretations. Ethnography often involves a combination of techniques and thus it may be possible to assess the validity of inferences between indicators and concepts by examining data relating to the same concept from participant observation, interviewing, and/or documents.

In triangulation, then, links between concepts and indicators are checked by recourse to other indicators. However, triangulation is not a simple test. Even if the results tally, this provides no guarantee that the inferences involved are correct. It may be that all the inferences are invalid, that as a result of systematic or even random error they lead to the same, incorrect, conclusion. What is involved in triangulation is not the combination of different kinds of data per se, but rather an attempt to relate different sorts of data in such a way as to counteract various possible threats to the validity of our analysis.

One should not, therefore, adopt a naively 'optimistic' view that the aggregation of data from different sources will unproblematically add up to produce a more accurate or complete picture. Although few writers have commented on it, differences between sets or types of data may be just as important and illuminating. Lever (1981) provides a valuable insight into this. Researching sex differences in children's play, she collected data by means of questionnaires and diaries, and found that these produced rather different results. She argues that this reflects varying effects of stereotyping according to 'the nature of the method or the posing of the question'; that this was why the children's statements of what they 'usually do', collected in her questionnaire, showed stronger sex differences than the information about what they 'actually do', collected in diaries. In short, Lever (1981: 205) proposes that 'abstract or unconditional inquiries yield responses that more closely correspond to a person's perceptions of social norms than inquiries of a concrete or detailed nature'. This is, of course, by no means the only way of responding to discrepancies between different sources of data, and sometimes it may be hard to bring data from different sources into a clear relationship (Perlesz and Lindsay 2003; Ribbens McCarthy *et al.* 2003).

In our view, the key point is, once again, that data must never be taken at face value. It is misleading automatically to treat some as true and some as false. Rather, what is involved in triangulation is a matter not of checking whether data are valid, but, at best, of discovering which inferences from those data seem more likely to be valid. Incidentally, it is worth noting that the sort of remarks offered in the past by Zelditch (1962) on the suitability of different methods for field research, and by Becker and Geer (1957) on participant observation and interviewing, can be read in this light. These articles, and others like them, are normally cited either to advocate one method against another, or to commend the combination of different methods; but even more than this they lend weight to the idea of reflexive triangulation.

What we have outlined here is the traditional conception of triangulation, introduced into the literature by the psychologist Donald Campbell and colleagues (Campbell and Fiske 1959; Webb *et al.* 1966). Some qualitative researchers have rejected this technique,

---

13 An early example of this was the work of Smith and Geoffrey (1968).

on various grounds. For example, it is sometimes claimed that different methods involve discrepant epistemological or ontological assumptions, so that the data they produce is necessarily incommensurable. Relatedly, there may be objection to the very concept of validity that is assumed by triangulation, in which research accounts are intended to correspond to the characteristics of real phenomena that exist independently of them (Blaikie 1991; Erzberger and Kelle 2003; Flick 2004). Our own view is that the nature of different methods, and particularly of the assumptions they involve, must always be borne in mind, but that the kinds of scepticism or relativism which motivate rejection of the conventional notion of validity, and thereby the original notion of triangulation, are unsustainable. The critics often promote different interpretations of 'triangulation', for example where the emphasis is on the complementarity of data from different sources. While we agree that these can be valuable, we do not see them as in conflict with the traditional use of triangulation (Hammersley 2007b).

Theories and the comparative method

Ethnographers have sometimes been reluctant to admit that one of their concerns is the production of causal models. This stems in part, no doubt, from the positivist connotations of the term 'causality', and perhaps also from a recognition of the extreme difficulty of assessing the validity of theoretical claims about causal relations. Nevertheless, theories implying causal relationships, not always clearly marked or expressed, are common in ethnographic work. It is important that the presence and significance of such theories are recognized and that they are explicated as fully as necessary and, at some point, systematically developed and tested.[14]

There is only one way of testing causal relations – the comparative method – though there are different ways of using it. By assessing the patterning of social events under different circumstances, we can assess the scope and the strength of the relationships posited by a theory. One version of the comparative method is the experiment. Here, at its simplest, a particular factor is varied across situations that are identical in all respects considered relevant. By holding constant factors involved in plausible rival theories, and by varying the cause specified in the theory being tested, the existence and strength of the presumed causal relation can be checked. Experiments are, in some ways, the most powerful means of assessing the validity of claims about causal relations. However, one can never be certain that all relevant variables have been controlled; and there are some serious disadvantages to the experimental method, notably its tendency to provide low ecological validity (its artificial character), as well as the political and ethical limits on its use. Given this, it is important to emphasize that experiments are not the only way in which the comparative method can be used to test causal hypotheses, even though they are taken as the ideal by positivism.

The positivist emphasis on the experiment as the model of scientific inquiry goes hand in hand with what Becker (1970) has called the 'single study model', which prescribes that all research should be devoted to the rigorous testing of theoretical hypotheses. While ethnography can certainly be used to test theories, by no means all

---

14 For explicit discussion of causality in the context of ethnographic and qualitative work, see Becker (1998) and Maxwell (2004a). For a more general guide to the explication of causal models, see Hage and Meeker (1988).

ethnographies are, or need to be, directed to this goal. As we saw earlier, instead they often provide relatively concrete descriptions or rather more developed typologies and models. And there is no obligation on the part of an ethnographer to engage in systematic theory-testing in any particular study. At the same time, it should be said that theories do require rigorous testing, and that many theoretical models developed in ethnographic research still await such treatment. In this respect, ethnography as a whole suffers from an even more serious form of 'analytic interruptus' than that which Lofland (1970) diagnosed (Hammersley 1985, 1987a, 1987b).

There has been some ethnographic work that has grappled explicitly with the problems of testing theories. The procedural model usually adopted here is that of analytic induction (see Becker 1998: ch. 5). This involves the following steps:

1   An initial definition of the phenomenon to be explained is formulated (for example, addiction to opiate drugs, embezzlement, etc.).
2   Some cases of this phenomenon are investigated, documenting potential explanatory features.
3   A hypothetical explanation is framed on the basis of analysis of the data, designed to identify common factors across the cases.
4   Further cases are investigated to test the hypothesis.
5   If the hypothesis does not fit the facts from these new cases, either the hypothesis is reformulated or the phenomenon to be explained is redefined (so that the negative cases are excluded).
6   This procedure of examining cases, reformulating the hypothesis, and/or redefining the phenomenon is continued until new cases continually confirm the validity of the hypothesis, at which point it may be concluded that the hypothesis is correct (though this can never be known with absolute certainty).

This process is represented in Figure 2.

There are relatively few clear examples of analytic induction in use. The classic ones are Cressey's (1950) work on 'financial trust violation' and Lindesmith's (1947) work on drug addiction. The notion of analytic induction was originally developed by Znaniecki (1934) in explicit opposition to statistical method. He claimed that it was the true method of the physical and biological sciences, and asserted its superiority on the grounds that it produces universal not probabilistic statements. However, Znaniecki's argument is not convincing. As Robinson (1969) pointed out, he drew too sharp a distinction between analytic induction and statistical method; and in fact the capacity of his version of analytic induction to produce universal statements derives from being concerned only with necessary, and not with sufficient, conditions. Besides the inclusion of sufficient as well as necessary conditions, there is another element we might add to analytic induction. The geneticist William Bateson is reported to have advised his students: 'Treasure your exceptions!' He argued that they are 'like the rough brickwork of a growing building which tells that there is more to come and shows where the next construction is to be' (quoted in Lipset 1980: 54). Both Cressey (1950) and Lindesmith (1947) do this, but they do not seem actively to have searched for exceptions. While no number of confirming instances can ever guarantee the validity of a theory, we can increase the chances of our acceptance of it being well founded if we adopt this strategy.

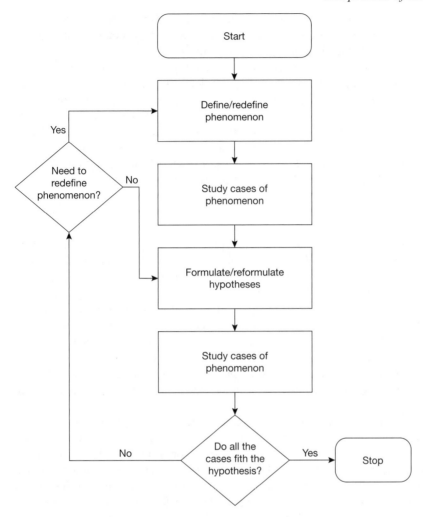

Figure 2 The process of analytic induction. Source: Hammersley (1989b: 170)

Analytic induction, developed to cover both necessary and sufficient conditions, and to include the search for negative evidence, seems a plausible reconstruction of the logic of theoretical science, not just of ethnographic work concerned with the production of theory. In this sense Znaniecki (1934) was almost certainly correct in the claims he made for it. In some respects it corresponds to the hypothetico-deductive method. But it differs from this, most importantly, in making clear that the testing of theoretical ideas is neither the starting point nor always the end point in the process of scientific inquiry: it follows on from the generation of theoretical ideas, a task whose importance is seriously underplayed by most accounts of the hypothetico-deductive method, and it usually indicates the need for further development and refinement of the theory, rather than giving it the imprimatur of truth.[15]

15 Some accounts of the hypothetico-deductive method recognize this; see, for example, Hempel (1966).

At the same time, however, we need to recognize what is presupposed by analytic induction. It assumes that social phenomena are governed by deterministic, albeit conditional, laws; such that if conditions X, Y and Z occur, then event A will be produced in all circumstances. There are objections to this from several directions; and among ethnographers in particular the concept of deterministic laws is often rejected on the grounds that it denies the manifest capacity of people to make decisions about how to act. As we saw in Chapter 1, this is a key element of naturalism, and also of many forms of constructionism. In one of the most influential discussions of this issue, Matza (1969) argues that while people can behave in a manner that is predictable by laws, human life proper involves a transcendence of determining conditions.[16] There are important and difficult issues that remain unresolved here.

Types of theory

We have emphasized that by no means all ethnographic work is, or need be, concerned explicitly with the refinement and testing of theories. Equally, we should note the range of different types of theory with which ethnographers may be concerned. For example, in sociology there is a well-established, though by no means always clearly expressed, distinction between macro and micro levels of analysis. Macro theories are those that apply to large-scale systems of social relations. They may trace linkages across the structure of a national society or even in relations among different nation-states. Micro-focused research, by contrast, is concerned with analysing more local forms of social organization, whether particular institutions or particular types of face-to-face encounter. What we have here, then, is a dimension along which the scale of the phenomena under study varies.[17]

While in many respects ethnography is better suited to research on micro theory, it can play an important role in developing and testing macro theories (see, for example, Willis 1977, 1981; Burawoy *et al.* 2000). Macro theories necessarily make claims about processes occurring in particular places and times that can be tested and developed through ethnographic inquiry. There have also been attempts to integrate macro and micro levels in various ways or to show that there is in fact only one level, not two (see Knorr-Cetina and Cicourel 1981). Usually, what is required here is multi-site ethnographic studies (see, for example, Burawoy *et al.* 2000; Hannerz 2003; Scheper-Hughes 2004).

Cross-cutting the macro–micro dimension is the distinction that Glaser and Strauss (1967) made between substantive and formal theory. While macro–micro relates to variation in the scope of the cases under study, the substantive–formal dimension concerns the generality of the categories under which cases are subsumed.[18] Formal categories subsume substantive categories. Thus, for example, the substantive study of taxi-drivers and their 'fares' can be placed under more formal categories such as 'service encounters' or 'fleeting relationships' (Davis 1959). Similarly, the study of a particular society can be used as an initial basis for theory about a general type

---

16 For a discussion of the history and current status of analytic induction in the light of these problems, see Hammersley (1989a).

17 The macro–micro distinction is by no means a straightforward one: see Hammersley (1984a).

18 For a discussion of the development of formal as opposed to substantive theory, see Glaser and Strauss (1967) and Glaser (1978).

of social formation; thus, Britain may be taken as an instance of capitalist, industrial, or even postmodern society.

Given these two dimensions, we can identify four broad types of theory; and, indeed, examples of all of these can be found in the work of ethnographers, stretching back across the history of this kind of work. Analyses of the structure, functioning, and development of societies in general, such as those of Radcliffe-Brown (1948) and Harris (1979), are macro-formal. Studies of particular societies, for instance Malinowski (1922) or Chagnon (1997), fall into the macro-substantive category. Micro-formal work consists of studies of more local forms of social organization. Examples would be Goffman on the 'presentation of self' (1959) and 'interaction ritual' (1972) and Glaser and Strauss (1971) on 'status passage'. Finally, there is micro-substantive research on particular types of organization or situation: for instance, Strong (2001) on 'doctor–patient interaction' or Hobbs (1988) on detectives and the informal economy in the East End of London. All these types of theory are worthwhile, but it is important to keep clearly in mind the kind of theory one is dealing with, since each would require the research to be pursued in a different manner. At the same time, what are involved here are differences in emphasis, rather than mutually exclusive foci.

So, ethnographers are not simply interested in generating accounts of particular settings and circumstances. The ethnographic imagination is always grounded in the local practicalities of everyday life in particular social settings. But the analytic gaze does not have to remain fixed on local circumstances. We must repeatedly ask ourselves how we are to make sense of local cultures and actions in terms that relate to wider analytic perspectives. This does not necessarily mean that we always have to relate the 'micro' to the 'macro' level. Indeed, that is often a short cut to inadequate analysis of local systems themselves. Rather, it means making sense of local action in terms that are applicable across a wider – a generic – range of phenomena. We develop analyses by making connections among the conceptual categories of our local data, and also by relating them explicitly to generic ideas that transcend them.

Consider, by way of an example, Michael Herzfeld's ethnographic study of craft workers in the Cretan town of Rethemnos. At the local level, Herzfeld (2004) describes the relationships between master craftsmen and their apprentices. This, however, is transformed into a much broader account of how masculinity is performed; and this is related to Herzfeld's (1985) own earlier account of the 'poetics of manhood' among sheep-stealing men on the same island of Crete. Equally, the ways in which the core of the craft is kept from apprentices, rather than explicitly shared with them, could be extended to a much wider domain of apprenticeship in the professions and other craft occupations, in which apprentice workers are required to pass through extended rites of passage, performing only menial tasks rather than being admitted directly to the 'mystery' of the craft itself. This not only makes links across a wide range of societies and social forms, but also provides a rather different perspective on the notion of apprenticeship from the romanticized version that is sometimes associated with the influential notion of 'community of practice' (Lave and Wenger 1991; Hammersley 2005).

Conclusion

In this chapter we have looked at the process of analysis in ethnography, tracing it from foreshadowed problems and the initial examination of a body of data, through the generation of concepts of various kinds, to the development of typologies and theories. In addition, we examined the relationship between concepts and indicators in ethnographic research, and the development and testing of theoretical ideas by means of the comparative method. We stressed that there are different sorts of theory and that theories are not the only product of ethnographic work; equally common and important are descriptions and explanations. We must not forget, however, that typically all the various products of ethnographic work, whatever their other differences, involve the production of text: ethnographic analysis is not just a cognitive activity but a form of writing. This has some important implications, as we shall see in the next chapter.

9 Writing ethnography

The disciplines of reading and writing

Writing ethnography is a key part of the entire research process. It is now widely recognized that 'the ethnography' is produced as much by how we write as by the processes of data collection and analysis. Ethnography is inescapably a textual enterprise, even if it is more than that. Furthermore, written language is an analytical tool not a transparent medium of communication. We can never reduce writing to a simple set of skills or prescriptions. What is needed is an appreciation of texts as the products of reading and writing. This calls for a widening of the ethnographer's traditional range of interests. One needs to think about more than 'research methods', as conventionally defined, or just the substantive focus of inquiry. The contemporary ethnographer must also take some account of contributions from literary theory, rhetoric, text linguistics, and related fields. We need to do so in order to inform our craft skills as producers of ethnographies, not in order to transform ethnography into a branch of literary studies. The principle of reflexivity that runs throughout this book implies a recognition of the extent to which researchers shape the phenomena that they study. In ethnography that principle is not confined to the practicalities of field work and data collection, it also applies to the writing we perform in order to transform our experience of a social world into a social science text.

Writing is, therefore, closely related to analysis. There are always many ways we could write about the social phenomena with which our research is concerned. As we shall outline later in this chapter, there are different genres of ethnographic writing, involving different kinds of ethnographic representation. There are different styles, different theories, and different audiences. Each way of constructing 'the ethnography' will bring out different emphases. Each mode of writing can produce complementary or even contrasting analyses. While ethnographic texts do not have an arbitrary relationship to the ethnographic field, it is important to recognize as early as possible that there is no single best way to represent any aspect of the social world. The world does not arrange itself into chapters and subheadings for our convenience.

Our understanding of writing is inextricably linked to reading. We write in the light of what and how we read. The individual scholar does not create his or her discipline afresh. The textual conventions of the past cannot be escaped entirely; nor would there by any advantage in achieving such an escape. The scholarly texts and the language, concepts, images, and metaphors of predecessors help to define the discursive space within which each new ethnography is produced and read. Hence it follows that the disciplines of writing are inextricable from the disciplines of reading. Ethnographers write, certainly, but their writing is shaped by what they have read. The good ethnographer cannot hope to succeed without a habit of wide reading. The ethnographer ideally develops a broad, comparative perspective on the literature.

In their original formulation of 'grounded theory', Glaser and Strauss (1967) commended the creative use of written sources in the production and elaboration of concepts: it is necessary to approach 'the literature' in a catholic and creative fashion. One of the most important disciplines for the ethnographer developing craft skills is, therefore, to read the work of others. Furthermore, we need to cultivate the capacity to read for the rhetoric and forms of writing employed by others, not just to read for content. And what is read need not be confined to the work of other ethnographers, or other social scientists. There are, after all, many genres through which authors explore social worlds. The domains of fiction and non-fiction alike provide many sources and models for written representations. An acquaintance with the anatomy of a wide variety of texts will encourage an appreciation of how to make novel and insightful texts of one's own.

Wide and eclectic reading can also encourage the development of 'sensitizing concepts' (Blumer 1954). The creative ethnographer will not wish to wait until the 'writing-up' phase of the research before exploring possible sources and models. Indeed, the disciplines of reading should inform the research from its earliest phases. The sources may be drawn from diverse origins. Erving Goffman's work is a distinguished example. His most successful studies generated highly original and productive insights on the basis of quite diverse written sources. Careful consideration of one of Goffman's major texts, such as *Asylums* (1961), will help illuminate just how adept he was at drawing together diverse ideas and observations, both 'fictional' and 'factual', 'serious' and 'popular'. For instance, in the essay 'The inmate world', Goffman's citations and quotations include: J. Kerkhoff, *How Thin the Veil: A Newspaperman's Story of his Own Mental Crack-Up and Recovery*; Ellie A. Cohen, *Human Behavior in the Concentration Camp*; Eugen Kogon, *The Theory and Practice of Hell*; Brendan Behan, *Borstal Boy*; Sara Harris, *The Wayward Ones: The Holy Rule of St Benedict*; Herman Melville, *White Jacket*; T.E. Gaddis, *Birdman of Alcatraz*; and a host of social science sources. There is no need for anyone to aspire to emulate Goffman's style in order to recognize and learn from his genius for using such resources in the construction of texts at once readerly and scholarly.

The general point was made many years ago by Davis (1974), who pointed to a number of thematic parallels between classic works of fiction and sociological writing. Davis noted that, like many other storytellers, sociologists construct narratives of tragedy, irony, and humour. The important issue in Davis's analysis is to remind us that there is no absolute difference between the way a social scientist writes and the way a more 'literary' author tackles a similar topic. For instance, when we read Goffman's *Asylums* and then turn to one of its literary analogues, such as *One Flew Over the Cuckoo's Nest*, we can start to recognize how each author uses the possibilities of written language to convey the experiences of inmates. Each author constructs a version of that sort of social world. Each does so under different auspices, for different purposes, and for different audiences. But if we wish to gain control over the resources of style, then it will repay us to read critically both works, and others like them. Likewise, the ethnographer interested in everyday life in medical institutions will find plenty of productive themes, parallels, and contrasts within literary sources. It is an excellent intellectual exercise to read the literary and the sociological or anthropological together. That exercise makes one more aware of one's own work as a writer, as well as sharpening awareness of textual possibilities. There is a good deal to be learned from a comparative reading of, say, Thomas Mann's (1996) *The Magic Mountain* and Betty MacDonald's (1948) *The Plague and I*, together with Julius Roth's (1963) ethnography of everyday life in a TB sanatorium, and perhaps also Susan Sontag (1979) on images of tuberculosis.

The sociologist or anthropologist of contemporary society may fruitfully explore the many ways in which modern industrial society has been represented: from realist novels to the 'new journalism' (Agar 1980; Denzin 1997). The ethnographer of a great city like London or Chicago will find many literary themes and images to explore, as will the student of small towns and rural 'communities'. The point has been made quite explicitly by Cappetti (1993) in relation to Chicago. She starts from the well-known affinities between the sociological representations of Chicago in the early decades of the twentieth century and the work of various literary figures. It was not an accident that the same Chicago fostered urban ethnography and realist fiction that often focused on similar subject matter and shared similar values. There was direct overlap between the sociological and literary circles. James Farrell, author of the *Studs Lonigan* trilogy, read sociology at Chicago, while Chicago sociologists were encouraged to pay attention to realist fiction (see Atkinson 1982).

An informed understanding of the genres and styles of literary or academic representation, therefore, forms a useful part of the ethnographer's craft knowledge. It is of crucial importance to recognize that crafting the ethnographic text is integral to the work of ethnography. 'Writing up' is not a mechanical exercise that can be performed routinely at the end of the 'real' research. In the rest of this chapter we explore a number of key issues to which the ethnographer needs to pay attention. The topics we discuss are relevant to any ethnographic text. Implicitly, we focus on texts of the scale of a monograph or doctoral dissertation, though much of what we say applies also to the construction of ethnographic journal papers.

We are assuming here that the ethnographer is engaged in a sustained attempt to translate their data into a text of social science *argument,* demonstrating relationships between data and concepts or theory. As we shall have occasion to point out later in the chapter, this does not seem to be the case for all social scientists. There are some who appear almost to have given up on analysis, and some who seem bent on using social science as a pretext for creative writing that has little to do with any canons of rigour and evidence. While the latter are interesting exercises in their own right, we do not believe that they substitute for the hard and serious work of social science.

Styles of ethnographic writing

Ethnographic writing can often be a frustrating business. One of the major problems is that the social world does not present itself as a series of separate analytic themes. As we have seen, we have to disentangle the multiple strands of social life in order to make analytic sense of them, before we reintegrate them into the synthesis of an ethnographic account. That work of synthesis is partly accomplished through writing. But it is not easy to produce a linear text from the host of data, impressions, memories and ideas that inhabit the ethnography. Starting and finishing the text, constructing a coherent account that does justice to the complexities of everyday life, ordering themes and events, providing adequate details and evidence – these are all issues that need to be resolved in constructing an ethnography. There is, of course no single, right way to do it. Indeed, everything we suggest in this chapter implies that the would-be author is always faced with choices. There are, however, some practical kinds of advice that can be offered. In this section, therefore, we outline some approaches and some general considerations that can help the reader make informed choices.

The kinds of textual approaches that are possible include *thematic* and *chronological* arrangements. The sort of analysis that we outlined in Chapter 9 readily yields a series of analytic themes, of greater and lesser generality. As a consequence, the ethnographic text – or at least the data-led chapters – can readily be organized along such thematic lines. The choice of themes, and the relative priority assigned to them, is always going to be one of the most significant decisions that the ethnographer needs to make. And it is not an easy one, or one that can be made successfully at the beginning of the writing process. Rather, it requires continual reflection on different possibilities, in light of trying to work with them. It is not a process in which the writer is fully in control. Instead, it is more like finding one's way through, or creating a path that leads, to a worthwhile destination.

One source of major organizing themes is *emic* categories; in other words, significant indigenous cultural categories. The organizing themes of the ethnographic account will, in this approach, be based on folk models: the terms, images and ideas that are current in the culture itself. The ethnography is, therefore arranged in terms of these key, characteristic categories. For example, in studying the online cultures associated with weight loss and dieting, one might use as organizing categories the various identities that participants take on in what they write: whether as owners of or contributors to web-sites. These would include identities involved in the active promotion and encouragement of anorexia and bulimia nervosa, concerned with providing or seeking detailed advice on accessing laxatives and effective purging, and/or with supplying motivational pictures of emaciated models and anorexic young women. The emic identity categories available here include: 'ana' and 'pro-ana' (derived from 'anorexia'); 'mia' (derived from 'bulimia'); 'buddy' (someone who will assist with weight loss); and 'fat' (a frequently self-ascribed negative identity) (see Hammersley and Treseder 2007).

Clearly, emic themes are not the only ones that we can use to organize ethnographic texts. There are also 'etic' categories that reflect the analyst's social science ideas. For instance, one might (hypothetically) identify major themes in terms of such notions as 'negotiated order', 'cultural bricolage', or 'habitus'. These are not indigenous terms (or are so only in very specialized social worlds). They summarize key analytic issues that the ethnographer has used to organize her or his findings, and to link them to significant theoretical arguments. The text's major parts – such as chapters or substantial sections – can be identified in terms of such key etic concepts, or in terms of ones that are more specific to the particular area of enquiry. For instance, Strong's (2001) classic ethnography of clinical encounters draws on a series of formal analytic themes. The main chapters of the monograph are called: 'Natural Parenthood', 'Collegial Authority', 'A Joint Venture', 'Medical Control' and 'Ease and Tension in the Alliance'. These chapter titles alone set the analytic tone and style, in which Strong pursues a sociological analysis of the *forms* that the clinical encounter can take.

In practice, many ethnographers will find themselves interweaving categories of both sorts. For instance, Agar's (1973) account of urban heroin users provides one example where members' terms are used to carry a good deal of the text's themes. However, these are embedded within observer-identified categories and typologies.

One such category is the focus of Agar's chapter on 'Events in Process'. At the same time, this is subdivided into sections that include 'Copping', 'Getting Off', 'The Bust', 'The Burn' and 'The Rip-Off'; all terms used by the heroin users themselves. Their use is entirely in keeping with Agar's general analytic stance, which emphasizes the elucidation of emic categories in identifying actions, events and processes.

While ethnographic texts are sometimes organized in terms of themes that pick out different aspects of the social phenomena that are the focus of inquiry, they may also be organized in terms of chronologies and trajectories. In other words, the text, or key parts of it, may follow a temporal rather than a thematic organization. These forms of textual organization are especially valuable if the ethnographic analysis is couched primarily in terms of careers, key processes and developmental cycles. Paul Rock's (1973) monograph on debt collection follows such a broadly temporal frame, although not exclusively, including the following chapter headings: 'Entering the Career', 'The Debt-Collector', The Solicitor', 'The County Court', 'Execution', 'The Judgement Summons Hearing and Committal Orders', 'The Bailiff's Working Personality', 'The Prison', 'The Debtor as Inmate' and 'Typifications of Debtors'. Obviously this is not a simple chronology. Implicitly it follows more than one trajectory – the career of the debt-collector, the trajectory of a debt, and the career of the debtor. In combination, they provide a mode of organizing the text that is faithful to a style of analysis that stresses processes of 'becoming', of process, and of moral careers. The ethnography describes trajectories and is itself organized in terms of those trajectories.

These are all ways of giving large-scale textual shape to the ethnographic monograph or doctoral thesis. They are not – as we have tried to show – pure types. Many ethnographic texts combine these organizing principles. These are not general models to be copied slavishly, then. The would-be author of a monograph certainly should not be sitting down and agonizing over which approach to use, as if they represented different textual 'paradigms'. But authors do need to think, recurrently, about how they are going to shape their work into a social science text, and what the main themes and chapters are going to be.

If those decisions can cause problems for authors, then the relationship between data and other textual materials can also prove troublesome: How should we weave together ethnographic evidence with more general analytic commentary? In the next section we turn to a discussion of this recurrent dilemma.

Types and instances

In our discussion of analysis in Chapter 8 we have already suggested that one way of thinking about data and theory is to explore the relationships between *types* and *cases*. Whether we talk in terms of analytic induction, grounded theorizing or developing pattern explanations we are essentially employing the same kind of procedures and the same mode of thought. We now want to suggest that this approach provides a useful way of thinking about aspects of writing. Indeed, there has been a long tradition of ethnographic writing in which the relationships between types and cases has driven the written style.

One contrast here is between *ideal types* and *actual types*. The notion of the ideal type is a very familiar one in sociology, and historically it is associated with Max Weber. The ideal type is an analytic construct. It does not, and is not intended to, correspond in every detail to all observed cases. It is intended to capture key features of a social phenomenon. It provides, as it were, a 'grammar' of a type of social institution or social process. A grammar does not represent all the possible utterances of a language, nor does it list or generate all the possible idiosyncrasies a speaker might display. It provides a somewhat idealized version of the language. In the same way, the social scientist's concepts can be idealizations. An influential example of an ideal type in the work of Max Weber is the notion of *bureaucracy*. This is not meant to describe all of the features of every formal organization. It serves as a model of one kind of organizational form against which actual organizations can be compared. Among the contributions of later sociologists, Erving Goffman's notion of the *total institution* is of a similar type. He used it to characterize key features that are common to such institutions as prisons, mental hospitals, military establishments, monastic foundations, boarding schools and the like. While they obviously differ in many ways, these organizations tend to have: a common timetable, strong boundaries, rituals designed to mark entry and leaving, and so on (Goffman 1961; see also Perry 2007).

Ideal types can be developed in relation to processes as well as organizations. The classic idea of the *rite of passage* is a case in point. When van Gennep (1960) first developed a grammar of such rituals, he proposed a basic, underlying structure that can be used to capture the common properties that make rituals of birth, marriage, death and other life-course transitions (such as religious initiations) essentially similar. A closely allied concept is that of *status passage*, which also allows us to draw out the common properties of many individual and collective transitions across a wide range of social and cultural settings. For example, in their work on the transfer of pupils from one age-specific school to another, Measor and Woods (1983) drew on this ideal type, linking it to another one concerned with beliefs: myths.

These, and many ideas like them, are familiar across the social sciences. And such ideal types are often used to structure the writing and representation of ethnographic research. We find – often implicitly – in much classic ethnographic writing that there is a constant interplay between the concrete and the abstract, the local and the generic, the substantive and the theoretical. Local, ethnographic descriptions are treated as exemplifications of generic, ideal-typical constructs. This is analogous to the use of individual 'cases' in legal studies to exemplify general legal principles, or of medical 'cases' to illustrate particular illnesses. This is why we find so many ethnographic authors using the textual strategy of *vignettes* and data *extracts*. These are normally derived from segments of interview transcripts, sequences from fieldnotes or transcripts, or similar data-types. The ethnographic text that uses this writing strategy, therefore, has a recurrent pattern. There is a repeated dialogue between the generic and the specific. Consequently the text is 'busy' and has a variegated texture.

It is not necessary for the conceptual framework of an ethnography be entirely novel. However, the successful text shows how the ideas on which it draws are being developed, tested, modified, or extended through contact with data from the particular cases investigated. According to Lofland, a successful ethnography involves a text that 'specifies constituent elements of the [analytic] frame, draws out implications, shows major variations, and uses all these as the means by which the qualitative data are organized and presented'. Further, it should be 'eventful': endowed with 'concrete interactional events, incidents, occurrences, episodes, anecdotes, scenes and happenings someplace in the real world' (Lofland 1974: 106, 107). The analytic claims need to be 'grounded' or anchored in the particularities of observed social life. At the same time, successful ethnographies are not overburdened with the repetitive rehearsal of incidents and illustrations. In other words, there should be a dynamic balance, a constant interplay between the concrete and the analytic, the empirical and the theoretical. It is part of the ethnographer's craft skill to try to strike a balance between the two, and that of the reader to evaluate the adequacy of the textual presentation. It is, however, the successful presentation of the local and the generic, the empirical and the abstract, that allows the reader to evaluate the ethnography's status and its claims.

In other words, many successful ethnographic texts embody the principles of 'grounded theorizing' and 'analytic induction' not by describing analytic procedures explicitly, but by *showing* those principles in the dialogue between ideas and data, generic frames and concrete exemplars. This is simultaneously an analytic and a textual approach. Many of the generic ideas can be thought of as metaphors, and the use of persuasive rhetoric in general is an important aspect of ethnographic writing.

Ethnography and rhetoric

Whatever their chosen styles, then, ethnographers need to have some awareness of the rhetorical devices that have been used in the production of ethnographic texts. There has been considerable scholarly interest in what conventions can be identified and how they are deployed in ethnographic writing. The discipline of anthropology has figured most prominently in this scrutiny of the ethnographic text, but this has reflected a much wider scholarly preoccupation with the 'rhetoric of inquiry' in both the natural and the social sciences. The ethnographer necessarily uses various figures of speech (tropes). These are used to construct recognizable and plausible reconstructions of social actors, actions, and settings. They are also used to convey many of the analytic themes as well. Very often, key concepts in sociology and anthropology are, in the broadest sense, metaphorical, in that they draw on imagery, analogy, and other devices.

Metaphor and synecdoche

As author of an ethnography, one's task is not to try to avoid metaphorical usage (it is virtually impossible to do so anyway). The scholarly or scientific authenticity of a text is not enhanced by the elimination of analogy and simile. The graphic use of metaphorical descriptions must always be part of the ethnographer's repertoire. But equally this is no recommendation of absolute licence. A recognition of the power of figurative language should lead also to recognition of the need for disciplined and principled usage. If deployed without due reflection, metaphors may prove, like the apprentice sorcerer's accomplices, helpers that get out of hand, running away with and finally overwhelming their hapless originator. The reflective ethnographer, then, will need to try out figures of speech: testing them against the data, searching not just for their power to organize data under a single theme, but also for their extensions and limitations. They may be productive of new, often unanticipated, insights, but they can also mislead. The writer of ethnography will therefore need to try out and explore the value of various figures of speech, gauging their relevance to the issues at hand, sensing the range of connotations, allusions, and implications. Noblit and Hare (1988) usefully summarize a number of criteria that may be brought to bear on the choice and evaluation of metaphors. These include economy, cogency, and range.

'Economy' refers to the simplicity with which the concept summarizes; 'cogency' to the efficiency of the metaphor, without 'redundancy, ambiguity and contradiction'; 'range' refers to the capacity of the metaphor to draw together diverse domains (Noblit and Hare 1988: 34).

The productive exploration of ethnographic fieldwork and data, therefore, can involve experimentation and reflection on metaphorical usage, though the processes are not necessarily susceptible to conscious and rational control. They are often the products of our 'divergent' rather than 'convergent' thought processes. Nonetheless, metaphorical insight can be facilitated. The ethnographic author should be willing to try out a range of possible concepts and analogies. The fruitful search is not for the 'best' set of ideas, but for a diversity of possible organizing themes and tropes. These can then be assessed for the extent to which they capture the desired dimensions or categories; the appropriateness of connotations; their value in suggesting new lines of analysis and comparison. There is a direct continuity between metaphorical thought and the development of 'generic' concepts, as advocated by Lofland *et al.* (2006). They link and juxtapose; they help to make the 'familiar' seem 'strange'; and vice versa.

The master-trope of the metaphor is complemented by that of *synecdoche*. This is a form of representation in which the 'part' stands for the 'whole'. It is not, therefore, just a source of allusion; it is an inevitable feature of descriptions. In principle, it is not possible to provide a description of anything that lists every conceivable attribute and detail; nor would this be desirable. In practice, most descriptions do not even approximate to an exhaustive listing. As we have just indicated, what we treat as 'data' are necessarily synecdochal. We select particular features and instances, identify them as somehow characteristic or representative of places, persons, or events. We endow particular fragments of observed or reported life with significance, precisely in the way we choose and present them as 'examples', 'illustrations, 'cases', or 'vignettes'.

The criteria that may be brought to bear are varied. Aesthetic criteria undoubtedly interact with more logical issues. The principled use of synecdoche will almost certainly be regulated by craft judgements rather than by rigid formulae. Issues of economy and redundancy will always arise. The question of economy reflects the fact that we cannot include every detail and every scrap of knowledge. Not only are time and space at a premium in the production of any written account, so too is the reader's attention. Descriptions and exemplifications that are too dense, too detailed, or too protracted will not normally lead to a usable text. Comprehensiveness and comprehensibility compete to some extent. For the most part there is a trade-off between the two, and the ethnographer needs to construct accounts through partial, selective reporting. The relationship between the 'part' and the 'whole' needs to be a valid one, of course. The choice of exemplification or illustration must reflect adequate analysis of the data, in terms of concepts and indicators. The synecdoche is, therefore, the complement of the metaphor. Both use natural language to produce 'telling' accounts. The metaphor transforms and illuminates while the synecdoche describes and exemplifies.

Narratives

In recent decades some social scientists have become increasingly preoccupied with the structure and functions of narrative. At the same time, they have come to realize that narratives are among their own stock-in-trade. Richardson (1990a, 1990b) and others have pointed out that the narrative mode is simultaneously crucial to the organization of everyday life (in the form of mundane stories and accounts of personal experience) and to the organization of ethnographic accounts themselves. The ethnographer draws on and elicits narratives as 'data' and recasts them in the sociological or anthropological narratives of scholarly writing. The narrative mode is especially appropriate to the character of ethnographic inquiry: it furnishes meaning and reason to reported events through contextual and processual presentations. It creates particular kinds of order, for example relating to intentions and unintended consequences. It reflects the fundamental importance of the temporal ordering of human experience (Adam 1990).

In narrating events, we show how people act and react in particular social circumstances. In doing so we reveal and reconstruct those social actors as 'characters' or social 'types'. Equally, we can display the patterning of action and interaction, its predictable routines, and the unpredictable surprises or crises. Through it, we can 'show' the reader both the mundane and the exotic.

Further, the overall 'significance' of the ethnographic monograph may be conveyed through its narrative structures:

> Beyond the fragmentary narratives of persons and circumstances are the meta-narratives that shape the ethnography overall. The ethnographic monograph, for instance, may be ordered in terms of large-scale narratives. It may take the form of a story of thwarted intentions; a display of order in chaos; or disorder in a rational organization. It can set up a reader's expectations only to deny them. It can transform the reported events of everyday life into the grand mythologies of human tragedy or triumph. The ethnography itself can become a morality tale; a high drama; a picaresque tale of low-life characters; a comedy of manners; a rural idyll. It may draw explicitly on literary parallels and archetypes.
>
> (Atkinson 1992b: 13)

The transformation of material from 'the field' into 'the text' is partly achieved by means of the narrative construction of everyday life. Given this, the ethnographer needs to recognize the crafts of storytelling and learn to develop them critically. As Richardson (1990a) argues, the narrative mode is to be valued as a basic tool in the ethnographer's craft:

> If we wish to understand the deepest and most universal of human experiences, if we wish our work to be faithful to the lived experiences of people, if we wish for a union between poetics and science, or if we wish to use our privileges and skills to empower the people we study, then we should value the narrative.
>
> (Richardson 1990a: 133–4)

The point for the practising ethnographic author is, therefore, the need to recognize the analytic power of the narrative: to recognize and use narrative reconstructions in a disciplined manner.

In constructing ethnographic texts, therefore, we are sometimes involved in the construction of meta-narratives. We produce narratives based on the narratives of the social actors we have studied. This intellectual and aesthetic work has been called 'storying other people's stories'. It is not necessary to assume that such storying is the main goal of ethnographic research, or to lose sight of other analytic goals, in order to recognize the importance of narrative elements in ethnographic monographs and other texts.

Irony and topos

Irony is a key figure of speech that has been employed a great deal by social scientists – ethnographers among them – and it has been commented on quite widely. An ironic tone is highly characteristic of the social scientist's stance. The interpretative cultural scientist frequently trades in implicit or explicit contrasts. The constant dialectic between the Ethnographer, the Reader, and the Others (who are represented in the text) is replete with possibilities for irony.

We trade in the complex and sometimes difficult contrasts between the 'familiar' and the 'strange', between the 'taken for granted' and the explicitly theorized, between intentions and 'unintended consequences' of social action. The ethnographer's insights are often produced out of the contrasts between competing frames of reference or rationality. Conventional morality may be contrasted with the situated moralities of particular cultures and subcultures. The significance of local cultures is established through (often implicit) contrasts with cosmopolitan or mainstream social arrangements.

There is a sense in which successive ethnographic monographs display an unconscious version of Popperian falsification: they confront received wisdom and undermine it with counter-examples; they contradict 'official' versions of the social world; they display local order where disorder is expected; they document situated moralities that differ from mainstream morality. Each ethnographic 'case' confronts and contests established theories and received ideas. Although theory-testing is sometimes assumed not to be normal part of the ethnographic enterprise, and most commentators stress inductive rather than deductive logic, the recurrent irony of ethnographic analysis and writing implicitly transforms the ethnographic tradition into a succession of critical cases that test and extend current thinking. In that sense, therefore, ethnographic texts implicitly conform to a style of theory-testing as well as theory-generation.

Sometimes in tension with the use of irony in ethnographic and other scholarly accounts is the appeal to *topoi*. The *topos* in classical rhetoric may be translated as a 'commonplace'. It is a rhetorical device whereby the hearer's or reader's agreement or affiliation is solicited through the use of widely shared opinion or well-known instances. In scholarly writing the work of the topos is often accomplished by means of the 'taken-for-granted reference'. Such citations of the literature are part of the stock-in-trade of the academic author. They are not necessarily used to establish or falsify a specific finding or point of detail. Rather, they are used to establish standard reference points; indeed, they are sometimes recycled repeatedly in order to support a conventional assertion rather than for the specific content of the original work cited. They are used to endorse 'what everyone knows' in the discipline and become part of the encoding of scholarly credit. Ethnographic writing has many classic references that are used for such purposes: for instance, Geer (1964) on first days in the field, Becker (1967b) or Gouldner (1968) on partisanship, or Mills (1940) on vocabularies of motive.[1]

---

1 For discussions of some of these, and reassessments, see Atkinson *et al.* (2003). A process of distortion is often involved in the recycling of 'standard references': see Hammersley (2000: ch. 3).

The ethnographer may, of course, use the topos of the standard reference in order to demonstrate the comparative, generic and intertextual nature of the work. This helps construct the archetype. It keys the particular ethnographic text to a background of shared knowledge. It can create the appearance of universal frames of reference that transcend the local particularities of the ethnographic field. The topoi of the ethnographic genre must be treated with great care, however. First, the taken-for-granted reference may reproduce errors from text to text, from scholarly generation to generation. Second, an uncritical appeal to 'commonplace' wisdom (whether social-scientific or lay) may rob the ethnography of analytic cutting-edge and novelty. One should not resort to common sense and common knowledge as mere reflex. There needs to be a constant tension between novel insight and received wisdom. It is part of the ethnographic author's literary or rhetorical repertory. And like all the other resources, it is to be used in a disciplined manner.

Audiences, styles, and genres

A reflexive awareness of ethnographic writing should take account of the potential audiences for the finished textual products. Ethnographers are, after all, enjoined to pay close attention to the social contexts in which actors construct their everyday accounts. We note whether accounts are solicited or volunteered, to whom they are made, with what effect (intended or unintended), and so on. Ethnographers have not, however, always carried over such an attitude into thinking about their own published accounts. There are potentially many audiences for social research: fellow research workers, hosts, students, and teachers in the social sciences; professionals and policy-makers; publishers, journal editors, and referees. There is also that amorphous audience the 'general public'. Audiences may expect and appreciate different forms and styles of writing: an academic monograph, a learned journal article, a popular magazine article, a polemical essay or pamphlet, a methodological or theoretical paper, or an autobiographical account of the research experience.

Audiences differ in the background assumptions, knowledge, and expectations they bring to the ethnographic text. Some will be well versed in the particulars of the setting and may have specific interests deriving from that. Others will be more thoroughly conversant with sociological or anthropological perspectives, but have little or no know-ledge of the field. Some readers will draw on theoretical and methodological perspectives that are in sympathy with the ethnography; some will start from a position of incom-prehension or hostility, and may need to be won over by the author. Some readers address themselves directly to practical and evaluative considerations. Some will prove impatient with the details of 'the story', while others will read precisely for the details and the vignettes, skipping over the explicitly theoretical or methodological discussions.

We can never tailor our ethnographies to match the interests of all our potential audiences simultaneously. No single text can accomplish all things for all readers. A sense of audience and a sense of style or genre will guide the author towards multiple spoken and written accounts. And indeed such awareness may itself lead to new analytic insights. As Schatzman and Strauss (1973) suggested, the act of writing can provide a source of discovery in its own right. Just as the ethnographer has grappled with problems of strangeness, familiarity, and discovery 'in the field', so a consideration of audience and style can lead to parallel insights.

Richardson (1990b) provides an excellent account of audience and style for ethnographic work. She describes how a major piece of research she had conducted led to the production of various different versions, each aimed at a different kind of audience, and couched in different styles. Her work as an author included publications for academic sociologists on the one hand, and a popular book, aimed at the 'trade' market, on the other. Her spoken accounts of the research included appearances on chat shows as a consequence of her popular writing. Each text implies a different version of the social phenomena it describes. In writing for different audiences, and in different styles, we are not simply describing 'the same thing' in different ways; we are subtly changing what we describe as well as how we do so. Exemplifying this, Wolf (1992) outlines alternative textual strategies in the production of her own research. She contrasts three different texts that she produced on the basis of her fieldwork in Taiwan. These had different styles, implied different readers, and took a different authorial point of view.

The majority of ethnographers will be thoroughly familiar with one dimension of stylistic contrast (usually aimed at the same sort of audience): that is, the contrast between 'realist' and 'confessional' accounts (van Maanen 1988). As van Maanen points out, it has been quite common for ethnographers to publish 'the ethnography' as a relatively impersonal, authoritative account, and then to produce one or more accounts of 'how I did it'. These latter autobiographical confessions are often published 'elsewhere', separate from the realist account, either in collections of such essays, or safely tucked away in an appendix to the main monograph.[2]

This is not the only difference in style and genre, however. The genre of, say, urban 'street' ethnography has tended to be different in style and tone from ethnographies of complex organizations. Equally, the 'classic' ethnographies of social or cultural anthropology differ from many of their contemporary counterparts. Moreover, anthropology has developed genres that reflect the intellectual traditions associated with particular geographical regions (Fardon 1990).

Van Maanen (1988) also goes on to identify a third variety of ethnographic writing (besides what he refers to as realist and confessional tales) the 'impressionist' tale, in which the ethnographer employs more overtly literary devices in the evocation of scenes and actions. These genres have become amplified, and to some extent transcended, by recent developments in ethnographic writing – which we elaborate on below – in which sociologists, anthropologists and others have engaged in more overtly literary and 'experimental' styles of textual production.

Our aim here is not to try to produce a definitive map of ethnographic styles, nor to suggest that each ethnography should be located within one or other genre. It is, however, important to recognize that how we write reflects directly on what we write about. The ethnographic text is part of the general process of reflexivity, in that it helps to construct the social phenomena it accounts for. It is, therefore, of profound importance that the ethnographer should recognize and understand what textual conventions he or she is using, and what receptions they invite on the part of readers.

Consideration of audience must also take account of the fact that our monographs, papers, and more popular texts may be read by our hosts or informants themselves. Neither the sociologist nor the anthropologist can assume that 'They' will never see the results of the research. If that was true of the non-literate cultures studied by many anthropologists in the past, it can no longer be assumed. One collection of autobiographical accounts by North American anthropologists (Brettell 1993) contains

---

2 For a listing of many of these 'natural histories of research', see Hammersley (2003b).

reflections on precisely that point. It documents, from geographically and socially diverse research settings, the politics of readers' receptions, when they are themselves the 'subjects' of the research. Sheehan (1993) describes, for instance, how an awareness that her work would certainly be read by her elite intellectual informants in Ireland was present in the course of the fieldwork itself and of how she wrote about it. This sense of 'audience' was particularly significant for Sheehan, given that 'those I wrote about would also be, in some instances, the same people authorized to critique the publications resulting from my research' (Sheehan 1993: 76). The response of key informants, such as 'Doc', to Whyte's *Street Corner Society* (1981; see also Whyte 1992), together with the politicized response when minority groups respond to their representation in ethnographic texts (Rosaldo 1986), sharpens our awareness of the complex relations of reading and writing that echo and amplify the social relations of 'fieldwork' itself.

Writing and representations

Up to this point, we have not mentioned one of the most significant factors that shaped ethnographic writing towards the end of the twentieth century. A 'crisis of representation' originated in American cultural anthropology in the 1980s. The particular publication that sparked this, and caused anthropologists to scrutinize their texts, was a collection of papers edited by Clifford and Marcus (1986), entitled *Writing Culture*. In some ways the effect of the book was based more on the general thrust of the volume as a whole rather than the detailed arguments and exemplars of the individual chapters. In essence, the collective message of the book's authors was focused on the authority of the ethnographic text. They questioned the established modes of ethnographic writing that embodied a single authorial voice and thereby, it was argued, a privileged ethnographic gaze. The consequence was – in some quarters – a radical reappraisal of how ethnographies are written.

Prior to this, Boon (1983) had suggested that the standard contents of anthropological monographs function to subsume the variety of human societies under the rubric of a single analytic paradigm. It was also argued that the characteristic style of the 'realist' sociological ethnography (van Maanen 1988) silences the voices of 'Others': the researched exist only as the muted objects of the ethnographer's scrutiny, being brought in to speak within texts only when they have something to say that supports the ethnographer's own 'story'. The ethnographic author thus reproduces the authority of the observer as a dominating form of surveillance and reportage (see Denzin 1997).

Similar arguments have also been entered by feminist critics of 'malestream' writing in the social sciences. As Devault (1990) and Stanley and Wise (1983) have argued, the feminist standpoint may subvert and transgress time-honoured modes of writing and representation that implicitly reproduce dominant modes of thought and discourse. Devault (1990) discusses Krieger's stream-of-consciousness ethnographic text on a women's community (Krieger 1983) as an example of a sociological work that self-consciously challenges some of the dominant conventions of ethnographic realist writing.

One consequence of this moment of supposed crisis was the advocacy of more open and 'messy' texts. In other words, rather than having a single narrative or a single authorial viewpoint, ethnographic texts would have more variegated textures, combining different kinds of writing style, and shifting viewpoint. These 'alternative' textual formats include ethno-drama, in which research findings are transformed into dramatic enactments, fictionalized narratives, and poems.[3]

Such transgressions of conventional realism in ethnographic texts have been advocated by a number of authors in the pursuit of 'postmodern' aesthetics and ethics in ethnographic representation. The postmodern turn attempts to celebrate the paradoxes and complexities of field research and social life. Various postmodern ethnographies have been produced (for example, Dorst 1989; Rose 1989) that employ a striking variety of textual devices in a highly self-conscious way. Work in this vein clearly foregrounds ethnography as a literary activity. Textual experimentation and the exploration of 'alternative' literary forms are the key features. These writerly ethnographic texts are self-consciously artful compositions (see Brady 2005; Denzin 2005; Hartnett and Engels 2005; Richardson and St Pierre 2005; Stewart 2005).

Such avant-garde approaches need cautious appraisal. We certainly do not advocate gratuitous textual experimentation. Furthermore, there are tensions within this movement. Whereas the conventional ethnography tended to be a fairly impersonal one, in which the ethnographer/author was relatively distanced from the text, recent alternative texts place the author firmly in the foreground. Here the principle of reflexivity has been taken to a textual extreme, in which the voice of the author is a dominant one. Key exemplars include the collection of papers edited by Ellis and Bochner (1996). Yet, as we noted, the crisis of representation was precipitated by a recognition of the fact that conventional ethnographic accounts imposed a particular kind of authorial perspective. The development of more self-consciously literary forms not only have failed to escape doing the same, but also have sometimes made the ethnographer even more central than in the older texts. There should, we believe, be a proper balance between a totally impersonal authorial style that elides the agency of the observer-author and an exaggeratedly literary form in which the author seems more important than the rest of the social world.

These new textual forms also run the danger of transforming the canons of rigour for ethnographic research into essentially aesthetic matters. While matters of style are always important, and the enduring ethnographies normally have a certain elegance of expression, the aestheticization of social research interposes new and extra dimensions of evaluation. At their best, such texts are interesting; at their worst they are strongly reminiscent of elementary exercises in 'creative writing' classes. Indeed, they substitute one highly conventional style (the classic realist ethnography) for another (the heavily autobiographical 'new' ethnography). In doing so they create the danger that a certain facility at creative writing can count for more than careful fieldwork and data analysis.

The genre of *autoethnography* is almost exclusively concerned with the 'voice' of the individual author, and in some cases it has been extended into fiction (Ellis and Bochner 2000). This genre of work – which is simultaneously analytic and textual – treats the ethnographer as simultaneously the subject and the object of observation. Hence the authorial voice is an autobiographical one. The emphasis in these texts is on the exploration of personal experience. As Anderson (2006) and Atkinson (2006b) have pointed out, the autoethnographic genre is not necessarily as new as its advocates and proponents claim. Moreover, the central place accorded to 'experience' in some

---

3 In some quarters, newer literary turns have become part of a new orthodoxy, and a few journals – notably *Qualitative Inquiry* and *Qualitative Studies in Education* - regularly feature 'papers' in alternative forms.

of the more recent texts displaces the key issues of social action and social organization. The social is transformed into the personal. While reflexivity implies the unavoidable implication of the observer in what she or he observes, there is, we believe, little justification for substituting self-absorption for a thoroughgoing sociological or anthropological imagination. Ironically, the published corpus of autobiographical work tends to reinforce our long-held view that social worlds of 'others' are almost invariably more interesting and more illuminating than the authors' own reflections. Anderson (2006) makes a case for *analytic autoethnography*, in which reflection is used to develop analytic insights, while arguing against the more self-indulgent approaches. We too believe that personal reflection should always be a part of theoretical and methodological development, and not the opportunity to put the ethnographer's self ahead of the 'others' about whom she or he writes.

Writing and responsibility

It is clear that the contemporary ethnographer, whatever his or her main discipline, cannot remain innocent about the conventions of ethnographic reporting. There is sufficient guidance available – of value to the novice and the old hand alike – to help in making principled decisions and choices (for example, Becker 1986; Richardson 1990b; Wolcott 2001). A thorough awareness of the possibilities of writing is now an indispensable part of the ethnographer's methodological understanding. One cannot 'write up' an ethnography as if it were a mechanical exercise, or as if the written text were a transparent medium of communication. How we write about the social world is of fundamental importance to our own and others' interpretations of it. To a considerable extent, the 'interpretations' of interpretative social science are couched in the poetics of ethnography itself. It is by no means novel, but illuminating nonetheless, to note that the very term 'ethnography' is used to describe the research process on the one hand, and its textual product on the other.

The well-informed ethnographer needs to recognize the reflexive relationship between the text and its subject matter. A grasp of the rhetoric, or the 'poetics', of ethnographic writing is of fundamental importance. It would, however, be quite wrong to conclude that problems of rhetoric are the only issues involved. The relationship between the ethnographic text and its subject matter may not be entirely straightforward, but it is not totally arbitrary. A recognition of the conventionality of writing does not entitle us to adopt a radically 'textual' approach. There are social actors and social life outside the text, and there are referential relationships between the one and the other. The ethnographer who engages in the arduous work of field research, data analysis, and scholarly writing will not be persuaded that the texts that constitute his or her 'data' and the texts of monographs, dissertations, papers, and the like are not referential. Indeed, it is a naive response to equate the recognition that our texts are constructed with the view that their relationship to the social phenomena they describe is arbitrary.

Hammersley (1993, 1998) suggests that the contemporary emphasis on rhetoric should not blind us to the more familiar preoccupations with scientific adequacy. We should certainly not privilege the rhetorical over the methodological. The two are inextricably linked, no doubt, but they have to be developed in partnership. An understanding of textual practices should not result in a textual free-for-all. There is no doubt that many ethnographies are successful (in terms of readers' critical response) by virtue of their style and persuasive use of rhetoric. On the other hand, persuasion is not the whole story. The critical reader of ethnography – as of any genre of scholarly writing – needs to be alert to the quality of the sociological or anthropological argument and the appropriate use of evidence in its support. In essence, therefore, Hammersley proposes that we should not, as readers, be unduly swayed or seduced by the readability of the ethnographic text. It is not enough that it prove 'evocative' or 'rich' in its descriptive detail, nor that it engage our sympathetic affiliation with the main characters, nor yet that it arouse our emotional responses to the reported scenes. It is equally important that the ethnography should display and demonstrate the adequacy of its empirical and theoretical claims. It is important that the ethnography sustain its authoritative status as a work of scholarly research.

Although there is a complex relationship between rhetoric and science, the author of the ethnography cannot rely purely on the readability and plausibility of his or her writing. It is necessary to maintain a proper regard for the canons of evidence. The claims (for accuracy, generalizability, etc.) need to be presented in a manner that is sufficiently explicit for the reader to be able to evaluate them. Indeed, prior to that, it is a requirement that the reader should be able to establish what claims are being made by the author in the first place, and why he or she believes that they are important and new.

In other words, we need to be able to recognize and evaluate the complex relationships between the various explicit and implicit messages that go into the whole ethnographic text. Some of these were identified earlier. The 'realist' text is not the only model that is available. It is important to recognize the value of textual experimentation, but this must be tailored to ethnographic purposes.

Ethnographies in the digital age

For the most part, in this chapter we have written about writing in the conventional sense of words on a page (paper or electronic). However, the developments in digital technology that we have mentioned in previous chapters have implications for the character of ethnographic (and other) research reports. For example, this technology allows the integration of audio and visual materials with written text. It is possible to accompany monographs with a DVD that contains still or moving images that exemplify key issues. Kersen Boom's (1995) ethnography of Indian dance was organized in precisely that manner. A more flexible approach is possible through the development and use of websites. Written text can thus be illustrated by placing visual and audio materials on websites that parallel the written text, and the written text can contain keys to particular web-pages, where relevant illustrative materials and data sets can be displayed. The advantage of the website over the DVD is, of course, that the former can be more easily updated. It also provides a more flexible and interactive environment that can be explored more freely by the reader.

So, using the internet as a platform, the digital ethnographer can now aim to integrate text, images, documents, sound files, and other data types within a single environment, and to link them in extremely flexible ways. In addition to text, in other words, still and video images can be drawn in, as can audio material. Moreover, the digital sound version of an interview can be stored and manipulated within the hypermedia environment, provided it is recorded or copied digitally. Indeed, if one records an interview using a digital camcorder, one can have the transcript and the recording available simultaneously. In other words, the hypermedia environment allows one to collate ethnographic material from a variety of sources. It allows the ethnographer to exploit the capacities of digital recording in different media. There is clearly no need to incorporate visual materials gratuitously, just because the available technology is cheap, but there is no doubt that digital imaging is a resource that can and should be used more often and more systematically by ethnographers. We live in visual cultures, and we base much of our claim for ethnographic research on the value of participant *observation*. While 'observation' in this context means far more than just watching, of course, it ought to remind us that the visual aspects of culture, and the observational aspects of research, should not be overlooked. Within the hypermedia environment, therefore, visual data have equal weight with textual or spoken data. They do not have to be relegated to the role of mere illustrative materials.

Since hypermedia software allows one to create links between different texts, different media and different data sets, it follows that it is not necessary to fragment the data. One's hypermedia environment can, therefore, retain the interview materials, the video recordings, the sound recordings, the photographs, and the documentary sources completely. One can navigate across documents and texts, or within them. Since the data set is always present, there is no end to the explorations and navigations that can be made. All links can be labelled and annotated. Analytic commentary, in different levels of detail and sophistication, can be linked directly with data sources and with each other. Moreover, there is no need to maintain a separate 'review of the literature', as appropriate references, glosses and commentaries can be linked to data. Moreover, the true benefit of digital technology finally emerges when the reader's engagement with the ethnography and its associated data can be interactive. In this context, the use of digital technology transcends its use merely as a way of collecting, archiving and displaying data. It becomes a way of transforming the ways in which ethnographers, their informants, their data, and their readers relate to one another.

The general principles of hypermedia ethnography have been described elsewhere, and we are not going to recapitulate either the technical details or the practicalities of implementation (Dicks *et al.* 2005). The underlying idea of *hypertext* is by no means novel. The notion, as developed by authors like Landow (1997), is based simply on the idea of linking texts and loci in texts. In the literary world, for instance, vast corpora of texts could be linked. Linkage could be based on inter-textual references, allusions and so on, usage of the same tropes, links from texts to critical apparatus, and so on. Hypertext can also be used to create narrative texts that depart from the conventional linear structure of most novels, biographies or histories. A hypertext work of fiction can be followed in a multiplicity of ways, by following links in various directions, that allow the reader to create unique versions of the text. The hypertext work, or the corpus of materials linked in hypertext, therefore constructs a multiplicity of connections, allowing multiple pathways for readers.

The developers of hypermedia ethnography point out that its value does not lie merely in a system of data management, nor even in the fact that it can incorporate digital data in various modes – textual, audio and visual. The true value, and the true sense in which this is an exploitation of digital technology, lies in the fact that hypermedia ethnography dissolves the distinctions between 'recording, 'analysing' and 'writing': 'Conventional approaches to CAQDAS have tended to naturalise the divisions between data management, analysis and representation, and thus there has been a tendency to neglect the potential of digital technology to transform all stages of the research pro- cess' (Coffey 2006: 18). In other words, most current uses of computer technology have little effect on data collection, and they do not impinge directly on the processes whereby ethnographers 'write up' the results of their analysis. This is set to change.

The complete realization of hypermedia ethnography is currently limited by various constraints. Multiple sources of data, especially visual data, are extremely greedy of computer memory, and although memory is cheaper and cheaper, and personal computers able to handle more and more information, practical limits can soon be reached. Equally important, the full integration of data storage, analysis and representation can create an extremely complicated environment in which the 'reader' needs to navigate. Without lots of guidance and on-screen help, readers can readily get lost in hyperspace: any user who has navigated even simple networks like citation searches will know that as one traces out a pathway of citations-to-citations-to-citations, one can lose one's bearings, and experience digital vertigo.

Although there have been some practical demonstrations of hypertext ethnography, and web-based materials are not uncommon, there are significant costs involved. The work of creating a hypertext ethnographic environment is labour-intensive, as well as being greedy of digital storage. One does need to acquire some skills, notably in editing, beyond those which ethnographers normally possess. Websites have to be maintained. It is easy to establish these facilities in the first flush of enthusiasm, and to maintain them during the life of a funded project. Ensuring their longevity is, however, more problematic. Yet, 'dead' digital environments will have no great advantage over the traditional medium of print. This is not an issue confined to ethnographic research. The investment of time and human resources involved in web-based research and pedagogic resources is already creating a resourcing time-bomb for research groups and research funders.

Conclusion

In this chapter we have considered some of the many issues involved in 'writing up' ethnographic research.[4] In many ways, what we have tried to indicate is a way of navigating across the complex environment created by philosophical, literary, and technological challenges to conventional forms of writing. We have stressed the importance of actual and potential relations with readers. Those relations are a particular case of a more general set, which relate to ethical as well as practical and methodological considerations. In the next chapter we turn to the issues of research ethics, as these concern ethnographic work.

---

4 We have not addressed here the task of disseminating research (see Hughes 2003; Barnes *et al.* 2003), or even what is involved in the process of publication. Furthermore, there are some who define the role of ethnographer more broadly in this respect than we do, to include bringing about particular kinds of change (see Gitlin *et al.* 1989; Scheper-Hughes 1995). At the same time, dissemination and the public role of the researcher have also been topics for empirical investigation (Fenton *et al.* 1998; Hammersley 2006b).

10 Ethics

In Chapter 1 we argued that, contrary to the views of some recent writers on qualitative research, the immediate goal of ethnography should be the production of knowledge – rather than, for example, the pursuit of political goals, serving evidence-based policy-making, or the improvement of professional practice. In this specific sense for us social research is not inevitably, *and should not be*, political; even though there are various other senses in which it could reasonably be described as necessarily political (see Hammersley 1995: ch. 6). Another way of putting this is to say that the only value which is intrinsic to the activity of research is truth: the aim should be to produce true accounts of social phenomena; though these should also be relevant to human concerns and have some news value. However, even if this position is adopted, it does not mean that all other values can be ignored in the course of doing research. Clearly, there are ways of pursuing inquiry that are unacceptable on other grounds.

To say that the goal of research is the production of knowledge, then, is not to say that this goal should be pursued at all costs. There are ethical issues surrounding social research, just as there are with any other form of human activity. In this chapter we will look at the particular forms they take in ethnography, and at the variety of arguments deployed in relation to them. We will concentrate primarily on issues to do with the behaviour of the researcher and its consequences for the people studied, or for others belonging to the same or similar groups and organizations.[1] Towards the end, we will look at the issue of ethical regulation, and the ways in which this introduces additional complexities into the decisions that ethnographers must take, and in some respects puts barriers in the way of this kind of work.

The issues

Most of the ethical issues we will discuss apply to social research generally, but the particular characteristics of ethnography give them a distinctive accent. We shall consider them under five headings: informed consent, privacy, harm, exploitation, and consequences for future research.

---

1 There are, of course, additional and equally important ethical matters, concerning relations with funding agencies – Willmott (1980); Pettigrew (1993) – and relationships within teams of researchers or between supervisors and research students – Bell (1977) – etc. For discussions of a wide range of ethical issues reflecting various perspectives, see Beals (1969); Diener and Crandall (1978); Barnes (1979); Beauchamp *et al.* (1982); Punch (1986); Homan (1991), Mauthner *et al.* (2002), van den Hoonard (2002), Christians (2005), Farrell (2005).

Informed consent

It is often argued that people must consent to being researched in an unconstrained way, making their decision on the basis of comprehensive and accurate information about it; and that they should be free to withdraw at any time. The most striking deviation from this principle in the context of ethnographic work is covert participant observation, where an ethnographer carries out research without most, or perhaps even all, of the other participants being aware that research is taking place. Examples include Homan's (1978) work on old-time pentecostalists, Holdaway's (1983) study of the police, Goode's (1996) use of bogus personal ads to investigate courtship, Calvey's (2000) work on bouncers, and Scheper-Hughes's (2004) study of organ-traffickers. Some commentators argue that such research is never, or hardly ever, justified; that it is analogous to infiltration by *agents provocateurs* or spies (Bulmer 1982: 3). Such objections may arise from the belief that this kind of work contravenes human rights of autonomy and dignity. Equally, they may stem from fears about its consequences. For instance, it has been suggested that 'social research involving deception and manipulation ultimately helps produce a society of cynics, liars and manipulators, and undermines the trust that is essential to a just social order' (Warwick 1982: 58). By contrast, other writers argue that there are occasions when covert research is legitimate. They point to the differences in purpose between covert research and spying, or note that spying is a necessity in inter-governmental and other forms of social relations. They also emphasize the extent to which we all restrict the disclosure of information about ourselves and our concerns in everyday life: we do not tell the whole truth to everyone all the time. Indeed, it has been suggested that the deception involved in covert participant observation 'is mild compared to that practised daily by official and business organizations' (Fielding 1982: 94). On a more positive note, it seems likely that some settings would not be accessible to open research, at least not without a great deal of reactivity – though, as we noted in Chapter 3, there is often some uncertainty surrounding this.[2]

While the issue of informed consent is raised most sharply by covert participant observation, it arises in other forms of ethnographic work too. Even when the fact that research is taking place is made explicit, it is not uncommon for participants quickly to forget this once they come to know the ethnographer as a person. Indeed, ethnographers seek to facilitate this by actively building rapport, in an attempt to minimize reactivity. Certainly, it would be disruptive continually to issue what Bell (1977: 59) refers to as 'some sociological equivalent of the familiar police caution, like "Anything you say or do may be taken down and used as data."'

Furthermore, even when operating in an overt manner, ethnographers rarely tell *all* the people they are studying *everything* about the research. There are various reasons for this. One is that, at the initial point of negotiating access, an ethnographer often does not know what will be involved, certainly not in any detail; even less, what the consequences are likely to be. Furthermore, even later, once the research problem and strategy have been clarified, there are reasons why only limited information may be provided to participants. For one thing, the people being studied may not be very interested in the research, and an insistence on providing information could be very

---

2 Much the same dispute about covert operations has long taken place within journalism, though the practice of covert data collection is probably much more common in that occupational context. See, for example, Leigh (2006).

intrusive. Equally important, divulging some sorts of information might affect people's behaviour in ways that will invalidate any conclusions from the research. For instance, to tell teachers that one is interested in whether they normally talk as much to girls as to boys in the classroom could produce false results, since they may make an effort (consciously or unconsciously) to equalize their interactions.[3]

Besides often failing to provide all of the information that might be considered necessary for informed consent, even ethnographers whose research is overt sometimes engage in active deception. Participants may be given a false impression, for example that the ethnographer agrees with their views or finds their behaviour ethically accept-able when he or she does not. This is integral to the kind of toleration that, is prob-ably essential to ethnographic work (Hammersley 2005a). This will often be a matter of researchers not mentioning their own views; but sometimes it may even involve them indicating agreement or acceptance despite their real beliefs, as in the case of Fielding's research on an extreme right-wing organization or Taylor's investigation of a ward in an institution for the 'mentally retarded' (Fielding 1982: 86–7; Taylor 1991).

Roth (1962) has argued that all research falls on a continuum between the completely covert and the completely open, and it is worth emphasizing that within the same piece of research the degree of openness may vary considerably across the different people in the field. For example, in his research on Bishop McGregor School, Burgess (1985d) informed the teachers that he was doing research; while the students were told only that he was a new part-time teacher, though they found out about the research subsequently by asking him questions (Burgess 1985d: 143ff). In much the same way, Lugosi (2006) describes how concealment, of various degrees and kinds, along with some disclosure, was unavoidable throughout his research on a bar patronized largely by a gay and lesbian clientele.

The eliciting of free consent is no more straightforward and routinely achieved than the provision of full information. Ethnographers often try to give people the opportunity to decline to be observed or interviewed, but this is not always possible, at least not without making the research highly disruptive, or rendering it impossible. For example, Atkinson's research on the bedside teaching of medical students in hospitals took place with the knowledge and consent of the specialists concerned, but not with that of either the students or the patients he observed (Atkinson 1981a, 1984, 1997). In the context of research on the police, Punch comments that 'In a large organization engaged in constant interaction with a considerable number of clients' it is physically impossible to obtain consent from everyone and seeking it 'will kill many a research project stone dead' (Punch 1986: 36). Involved here are also difficulties raised by the fact that, because ethnographers carry out research in natural settings, their control over the research process is often limited: they simply do not have the power to ensure that all participants are fully informed or that they freely consent to be involved.

Above and beyond this, there is the question of what constitutes free consent, of what amounts to a forcing of consent. For example, does an attempt to persuade someone to be interviewed or observed constitute a subtle form of coercion, or does this judgement depend upon what sorts of argument are used? It has also been proposed

---

3 By contrast, in action research this may not matter. Indeed, the aim may be to see how far behaviour can be changed. See Kelly's (1985) discussion of this aspect of the Girls into Science and Technology project.

that some people, in some roles, for example those in public office, do not have the right to refuse to be researched, and therefore do not need to be asked for their consent (Rainwater and Pittman 1967). While almost all ethnographers would accept the principle of informed consent, there is considerable disagreement about what this requires in particular cases, and about when (if ever) it can be waived.

Privacy

In everyday life we draw distinctions between public places (such as airports and parks) and private places (like the bedroom or the bathroom), as well as between information that is for public consumption and that which is secret or confidential. A frequent concern about ethnographic research is that it involves making public things that were said or done in private. This may be seen as breaching a matter of principle, but it is also sometimes feared that making the private public may have undesirable long-term consequences. For example, it has been suggested that all social research 'entails the possibility of destroying the privacy and autonomy of the individual, of providing more ammunition to those already in power, of laying the groundwork for an invincibly oppressive state' (Barnes 1979: 22). Like informed consent, however, the concept of privacy is complex. What is public and what private is rarely clear-cut. Is the talk among people in a bar public or private? Does it make any difference if it is loud or *sotto voce*? Similarly, what about mobile phone conversations carried out in public places, or discussions in online chat rooms? Are religious ceremonies public events if anyone is able to attend? It is not easy to answer these questions, and in part the answer depends upon one's point of view and the particular context.

In everyday life, we seem to draw the distinction between public and private differently depending upon whom is involved, and this is often reflected in the practice of researchers. For instance, it is quite common for educational researchers to ask children about their friendships, but it is more rare to investigate friendship patterns among adults; and, in part, this probably stems from the assumption that children's private lives are legitimately open to scrutiny in a way that those of adults are not, especially professional, middle-class adults. This is, of course, an assumption that is not beyond challenge.[4] Also, privacy seems to be defined in terms of specific audiences that are or are not regarded as having legitimate access to information of particular kinds. ('Not in front of the children' or, alternatively, 'Not in front of the adults'!) Sometimes, the invasion of privacy by researchers is justified on the grounds that since the account will be published for a specialized audience neither the people studied nor anyone else who knows them is likely to read it. But is this true? And, even if it is, does it excuse what has been done? Interestingly, some informants reacting to Scheper-Hughes's (1982) study of an Irish village, *Saints, Scholars and Schizophrenics*, complained that it had been written in a way that was accessible to them: 'Why couldn't you have left it as a dusty dissertation on a library shelf that no-one would read, or a scholarly book that only the 'experts' would read?' (Scheper-Hughes 1982: vii; see also Scheper-Hughes 2000). This offers an interesting sidelight on the desirability of popular or public social science designed to address a mass audience (see Burawoy 2005).

---

4 And, indeed, there are those who would not only resist such differential treatment but also seek to extend children's rights in research much further: see Grave and Walsh (1998).

Closely related to the issue of privacy is the idea advanced by some researchers that people have a right to control information relating to them, and that they must give their permission for particular uses of it by researchers (see, for example, Walker 1978; Lincoln and Guba 1989). Thus, Lincoln and Guba argue that 'when participants do not "own" the data they have furnished about themselves, they have been robbed of some essential element of dignity, in addition to having been abandoned in harm's way' (Lincoln and Guba 1989: 236). The idea that participants own any data pertaining to them has its most obvious application in relation to interviews, but it could in principle be extended to observational data as well. It is suggested that by assigning such ownership rights to people they can be protected from the consequences of information they regard as confidential or damaging being disclosed publicly by the researcher. However, there has been criticism of this view: as, on the one hand, facilitating the distortion of evidence by participants or making genuine research impossible, and, on the other, potentially being a strategy that puts pressure on people to supply information that they would not otherwise divulge (Jenkins 1980).

Particular problems regarding informed consent arise in the case of internet ethnography. Are publicly available websites, chat rooms, blogs, etc. a free source of data for researchers to use, or must they negotiate access? In participating in chat rooms or email exchanges, must ethnographers disclose their identities and purposes? How far are their responsibilities here similar to or different from those of other participants? There is now a considerable literature discussing these matters (see Sharf 1999; Markham 2005).

Harm

While ethnographic research rarely involves the sorts of damaging consequences that may be involved in, say, medical experiments on patients or physicists' investigations of nuclear fission, it can sometimes have consequences, both for the people studied and for others. These may arise as a result of the actual process of doing the research and/or through publication of the findings. At the very least, being researched can sometimes create anxiety or worsen it, and where people are already in stressful situations research may be judged to be unethical on these grounds alone. An example is research on terminal illness and how those who are dying, their relatives, friends, and relevant professionals deal with the situation. While there has been research in this area (for example, Glaser and Strauss 1968; Wright 1981; Seale 1998), it clearly requires careful consideration of its likely effects on the people involved. The research process may also have wider ramifications, beyond immediate effects on the people actually studied, for instance for broader categories of actor or for one or more social institutions. Thus, Troyna and Carrington (1989) criticize several studies for the use of research techniques which, they believe, reinforce racism: techniques such as asking informants about the typical characteristics of members of different ethnic groups. This sort of criticism may also be extended to sins of omission as well as sins of commission. For example, is a researcher behaving unethically if he or she witnesses racist or sexist talk without challenging it?[5]

5 For cases which raise these issues, see Hammersley (1980); Smart (1984: 155–6); Gallmeier (1991: 227); Griffin (1991: 116–18).

Harm may also arise within ethnographic research from the nature of the field relations that are established. At the very least, being researched can create stress and provoke anxiety, especially if the researcher is believed to be evaluating one's work, one's life or oneself. As we saw in Chapter 4, ethnographers usually seek to build rapport and trust, so that these effects may well lessen or disappear in the course of the fieldwork. At the same time, there are dangers that can arise from successfully establishing close relations with people in the field, for the researcher, for them, or for both. Irwin (2006) provides an extreme but illuminating illustration, raising questions about the desirability of complete immersion in the field by discussing her study of a tattoo shop, during the course of which she dated and married her key informant (then subsequently divorced him!).

Turning to the potentially harmful consequences of the publication of ethnographic accounts, these can come about in a variety of ways and may affect both the public reputations of individuals and their material circumstances. The classic example here is Vidich and Bensman's (1958) account of Springdale, a community in upper New York State. Not only were some readers able to identify this community, but also a few of the individuals described were recognizable too (notably those playing leading roles in local politics), and their behaviour was thereby opened up to public scrutiny.[6]

In the case of Maurice Punch's study of Dartington Hall, a progressive private school in Devon, the problems surrounding publication dogged the later stages of the research. Initially, the Trust which financed the school, whose members included an eminent British sociologist, funded Punch to do a follow-up investigation of ex-students. At the same time, Punch was registered for a PhD and was on the look-out for a progressive boarding school to study, and it was agreed he could use Dartington for this purpose. However, the history of the research turned into a catalogue of conflicts and recriminations. Early on, despite being funded by the Trust, Punch was refused access to the school's files by the joint headteachers, even though these were his only means of tracing former students. The major battle arose, however, over the eventual publication of a book from his thesis. Perhaps rather foolishly, Punch had signed a document which stated that he would not publish anything arising from the research without the written consent of the chairman of the Trust. As a result, once he had completed his dissertation there was a lengthy struggle, with threats of legal action, before he managed to get agreement for publication. Opposition to publication seems to have arisen in large part from the trustees' judgement that the research showed Dartington in a bad light. Punch provides his own summary of the findings:

> First, it was argued that this type of 'anti-institution', with its nebulous guidelines for action, is difficult to operationalize at a day-to-day level because so many of its concepts are imprecise and because they conflict with institutional imperatives for cohesion and continuity. Second, I felt that the ideal of 'non-interference' by staff was often compromised by the staff's manipulation of the student society. But, in turn, the pupils could subvert the freedom offered to them with collective behaviour, and by powerfully enforced group norms and sanctions, that were the

---

6 For discussions of the ethical issues raised by this case, see Becker (1964b); Vidich *et al.* (1964). And for discussion of the advantages and disadvantages of giving pseudonyms to the people and places researched, see Homan (1991: 142–8) and Walford (2002).

antithesis of the school's most cherished values. And third, there was evidence to suggest that some of the former pupils found it difficult to adjust to the wider society, remained dependent on the school and networks of former pupils, were somehow undermotivated in terms of conventional achievements, and rather than taking an active part in changing the world, seemed to opt out into a peripheral, artistic subculture.

(Punch 1986: 61–2)

It is not difficult to understand that the trustees might disagree with these findings, and why they wished that such a book not be published, especially given the increasingly hostile political environment in which the school found itself. And the trustees' fears were perhaps confirmed by the appearance in a national newspaper a week before the book's publication of the headline: 'An academic time-bomb in the form of a highly critical book is to explode under Dartington Hall progressive school next Thursday'.[7]

The reporting of research data or findings by the mass media has also been a significant factor in other studies. Morgan's research on women factory workers was picked up by national daily newspapers (Morgan 1972), and the Banbury restudy was described in a local newspaper under the headline: 'New probe into "snob town"' (Bell 1977: 38). Clearly, such publicity can damage the reputations of individuals, organizations, and locations, as well as hurting the feelings of those involved. Whether the responsibility for this lies with the researcher is an interesting, and difficult, question.

What is significant in cases such as these, of course, is not just whether the information published and publicized is true, but what implications it carries, or what implications it *may be taken to carry*, about the people studied and others like them. And there is considerable potential for problems arising from these implications built into the very nature of social research, as Becker (1964b) points out, drawing on the ideas of Everett Hughes:

> The sociological view of the world – abstract, relativistic, generalizing – necessarily deflates people's view of themselves and their organizations. Sociological analysis has this effect whether it consists of a detailed description of informal behavior or an abstract discussion of theoretical categories. The members of a church, for instance, may be no happier to learn that their behavior exhibits the influence of 'pattern variables' than to read a description of their everyday behavior which shows that it differs radically from what they profess on Sunday morning in church. In either case something precious to them is treated as merely an instance of a class.
>
> (Becker 1964b: 273)

The problem becomes even more serious, however, in the case of 'those who believe they possess the truth complete and undefiled', as Wallis (1977: 149) points out, reflecting on his study of scientologists. He managed to publish his book and avoid being prosecuted for libel only through lengthy negotiation and some modification of the text. In a response to his work, a representative of the Church of Scientology complained that Wallis, faced 'with a social movement of phenomenal growth and increasing impingement on society in areas of social reform' had chosen 'to paint, in

---

7 Subsequently, Punch's attempt to publish an account of the story behind the research was initially blocked by appeal to the British libel laws: Punch (1986: 49–69).

dark tones, a small square in the lower left-hand corner of the canvas' (Gaiman 1977: 169). It should be said, though, that responses to research reports on the part of those whose behaviour is described within them are not always negative, and are often minimal or non-existent.

The potential for damage caused by the publication of research findings is not restricted to effects on what is publicly known or on the reputations of people or organizations. Also relevant is the use that may be made of the information. An extreme case from many years ago is Condominas anthropological account of Sar Luk, a mountain village in South Vietnam, published in French in 1957. This was subsequently translated illegally by the US government and used by its army in the Vietnam War as part of 'ethnographic intelligence'. The information produced by Condominas does not seem to have been directly implicated in the South Vietnamese army's destruction of Sar Luk, but it is clear that the publication of information about this village had at least potentially deadly consequences for the people living there, even though Condominas may not reasonably have been able to anticipate this (see Barnes 1979: 155–6).

Even the existence of a PhD thesis in a university library can sometimes cause problems, as Wolf discovered in the case of his research on 'outlaw bikers':

> A few years . . . after I'd stopped riding with the Rebels, the Calgary police brought a member of the Rebels' Calgary chapter to court in an attempt to revoke his firearms acquisition certificate. A member of the Calgary police force claimed the status of 'expert witness' and acted as 'a witness for the crown prosecutor'. 'Expert witness' means that the individual is considered capable of offering the court an 'informed opinion' on a judicial matter by virtue of his or her overall knowledge and familiarity with the situation. When the lawyer for the defendant asked on what grounds the police officer could claim any knowledge of the Rebels, the officer was able to justify his eligibility as an expert witness by virtue of having read my thesis. The Calgary Rebel eventually won his court case and retained his legal right to possess firearms; however, he came up to Edmonton to settle a score with me.
>
> (Wolf 1991: 220)

While Wolf escaped retaliation, the Calgary Rebel and his associates made clear that they were against the publication of a book on the basis of his thesis: 'No way that you're going to publish that book!' Wolf comments: 'it was an interesting ethical complication: it was a dangerous personal complication. However, these were not the brothers with whom I had made my original pact, and I have decided to go ahead and publish' (1991: 221).

A more mundane example is Ditton's (1977) study of 'fiddling and pilferage' among bread salesmen. He opens the preface to his book in the following way:

> I am lucky enough to have a number of friends and colleagues. Probably not as many of the former . . . now that this book has been published. I don't expect that many of the men at Wellbread's will look too kindly on the cut in real wages that this work may mean to them, and my bakery self would agree with them.
>
> (Ditton 1977: vii)

It might be argued that Ditton's exposure of the 'fiddling and pilferage' among sales staff working for a particular bakery caused harm not only to the fortunes and reputations of those who worked for that bakery but also perhaps to those working for other bakeries. At the same time, like many other ethical issues in ethnography, this one is by no means unambiguous.

Finch (1984) raises a more general issue about harm in relation to her own work on playgroups and clergymen's wives. She argues that it is difficult even for feminists 'to devise ways of ensuring that information given so readily in interviews will not be used ultimately against the collective interests of women' (Finch 1984: 83). Of course, it is not always clear what is in whose interests, and some would argue that the value of scientific knowledge, or the public right to know, outweighs such considerations; but many ethnographers insist on the importance of trying to ensure that the knowledge produced by research is used for good, and not bad, ends. How far this can be done, and how well grounded judgements about what is good and bad are, no doubt varies considerably. Furthermore, ethnographers will usually have little control over the consequences of publishing their work, though in most cases these will be small or unimportant from many points of view.[8]

Exploitation

Sometimes it is claimed that research involves the exploitation of those studied: that people supply the information which is used by the researcher and yet get little or nothing in return. One of the teachers in the school that Beynon (1983: 47) studied summed this up, commenting: 'When you first arrived we thought "Here's another bloke getting a degree on our backs!" We resented the idea that we were just fodder for research.' And it is suggested by some commentators that, typically, researchers investigate those who are less powerful than themselves, and for this reason are able to establish a research bargain that advantages them and disadvantages those they study. This is a problem that can even arise in those situations where the researcher has an intellectual and emotional commitment to the people concerned and seeks to establish a non-hierarchical relationship with them, as Finch (1984) makes clear in the case of feminists studying other women.

Cannon (1992) found this to be an especially acute problem in her research on women with breast cancer. In dealing with it she encouraged the women themselves to reflect on the interview process, how and when it helped and did not help them, and left them substantially in control of the interviews (Cannon 1992: 162–3). Nonetheless, she felt guilt that her research might make their situations worse:

> Most of the women I interviewed felt ill, or at least were experiencing a certain amount of discomfort at the time of the interview; they disliked being in the hospital and my clinic-based interviews meant that I asked them to stay longer than

---

8 Harm may come not only to those studied but also to field researchers themselves. To a large extent, of course, they must take responsibility for their own safety, and there is now a small literature dealing with risk and danger in ethnographic and other research (Lee 1995; Lyng 1998; Lee-Treweek and Linkogle 2000; Jacobs 2002). However, research directors and research supervisors need to incorporate into their research plans and protocols reasonable consideration for the safety of students and research assistants in the field, while yet recognizing both that it is easy to overestimate risks, and at the same time impossible to avoid them completely.

necessary; my questions required them to go way back to when they first found an abnormality in their breast, something which, to most women with secondary spread, seemed far away and hardly relevant to the more immediately life-threatening problems they now had.

(Cannon 1992: 172)

At the same time, she was able to offer the women support, both physical and emotional, so much so that with some of them she became an important part of their social networks up to and including the point of death.

Here, as in many other cases, there were benefits as well as costs for those involved in the research, but these are never easy to assess. As a result, there are problems surrounding judgements about what exactly constitutes exploitation. The concept implies a comparison between what is given and what is received, and/or between what is contributed to the research by each side. And yet, of course, most of the benefits and costs, and the relative contributions, cannot be measured, certainly not on any absolute scale. Whether or not exploitation is taking place is always a matter of judgement, and one that is open to substantial reasonable disagreement.

The argument about the exploitative potential of ethnographic research leads commentators to make a variety of recommendations: that researchers should give something back, in the way of services or payment; that participants should be empowered by becoming part of the research process; or that research should be directed towards studying the powerful and not the powerless. Such proposed remedies do not always avoid the problem, however; and they are controversial in themselves. Indeed, they can sometimes compound the difficulties. Much depends upon the circumstances. Howarth (2002: 25) found that, despite what she assumed was prior agreement, informants reacted angrily to the payment she offered, on the grounds that it was exploitative: they accused her of racism and blocked her exit from the room. It is also worth noting that there are occasions when services of one kind or another are demanded by participants, or payment. For example, Scheper-Hughes (2004) reports her experience in seeking to get information about organ trafficking:

Nervously chewing sunflower seeds and spitting them out rapid-fire in our direction, Vladimir boldly demanded a 'fair price' – '200, OK, 100 dollars' – for an interview. When I slipped him a crisp $20.00 bill Vlad nodded his head.

(Scheper-Hughes 2004: 47–8)

Consequences for future research

Social researchers, and especially ethnographers, rely on being allowed access to settings. Research that is subsequently found objectionable by the people studied and/or by gatekeepers may have the effect that these and other people refuse access in the future. If this were to happen on a large scale, ethnographic research would become virtually impossible. This was one of the main arguments used by Fred Davis (1961a) in his criticism of Lofland and Lejeune's secret study of a branch of Alcoholics Anonymous (Lofland and Lejeune 1960, Lofland 1961); and by Erickson (1967) against the covert study of an apocalyptic religious group in *When Prophecy Fails* (Festinger *et al.* 1956). Of course, what is at issue here is not so much ethical responsibilities to the people studied but rather to colleagues, present and future. As we saw earlier, though, there may be good reasons routinely to expect a negative reaction from at least some of the people studied. For instance, Becker has claimed that there is an 'irreconcilable conflict between the interests of science and the interests of those studied', and that any good study is likely to provoke a hostile reaction (Becker 1964b: 276). This may be an exaggeration, but it does point to the fallacy of assuming that the researcher and the people studied will usually see the research in the same way. As in life generally, there may well be conflicting interpretations and clashes of interest; and there are no simple general solutions to such conflicts. The upshot of this is that while the individual ethnographer may have an ethical obligation to colleagues not to 'spoil the field', it may not always be possible to meet this obligation; and sometimes the courses of action required to meet it may be undesirable on other grounds.

Diverse perspectives

As we have indicated, these five ethical issues are subject to diverse points of view. Building on our discussion so far, we can identify four contrasting positions which have had an impact on thinking about the ethical issues surrounding ethnographic research. These by no means exhaust the possibilities, but they do indicate the range of perspectives to be found in the literature.[9]

First, there is what we might call *ethical absolutism*. There are commentators who argue that there are certain sorts of research strategy that are simply illegitimate, and should never be employed by researchers. For example, deception is often proscribed, and the establishment of fully informed consent with participants insisted on. Similarly, strict rules are laid down by some about what constitutes invasion of privacy, and it is argued that researchers must take no action which infringes it. Warwick's (1982) criticism of Humphreys' (1970) study of homosexual encounters in public lavatories comes close to this position. Such views are usually justified by appeal to political or religious commitments and/or to the existence of certain inalienable human rights. Interestingly, though, Shils (1959) offers a version drawing on a sociological theory about the role of the sacred in modern societies. An interesting example of an application of this approach in an ethnographic study is Benjamin's (1999) anthropological study of a Jewish community in Curaçao, in which he gave participants substantial control over the conduct of the research and its publication. A similar stance is sometimes taken in the sphere of childhood studies (see Grave and Walsh 1998; Farrell 2005).

Second, there are those who argue that what is and is not legitimate action on the part of researchers is necessarily a matter of judgement in context, and depends on assessment of the relative benefits and costs of pursuing research in various ways. We might call this *ethical situationism*. This point of view usually places particular emphasis on the avoidance of serious harm to participants, and insists on the legitimacy of research and the likelihood that offence to someone cannot be avoided. It leaves open to judgement the issue of what the benefits and costs of particular research strategies are in particular cases, and how these should be weighed. No strategy is proscribed absolutely, though some may be seen as more difficult to justify than others (see Becker 1964b; Simons and Usher 2000).

9 For discussions that take a different line on the divergent ethical perspectives to be found among researchers, see Mauthner *et al.* (2002) and Christians (2005).

A third position is *ethical relativism*. This implies that there is never a single determinate answer to the question of what is and is not legitimate behaviour on the part of a researcher. This is because judgements about the good and the bad are always dependent on commitment to a particular value perspective, and there is a plurality of values and cultures to which human beings can be committed. This position often leads to arguments to the effect that participants must be fully consulted or closely involved in the research, and that nothing must be done by the researcher that transgresses their moral values; on the principle that 'When in Rome one must do as the Romans'. Lincoln and Guba (1989) seem to adopt this position.

Finally, there are various forms of what we might call *Machiavellianism*. Here, ethical considerations are not given any priority, at least when carrying out certain sorts of research. A striking example of this is to be found in the writings of conflict methodologists. They argue that insistence on the establishment of informed consent would be counterproductive in the study of many large economic or state organizations, since those in control of them would have no scruples about manipulating the research for their own ends. It is suggested that in such contexts covert research may be essential (Lehman and Young 1974; Lundman and McFarlane 1976).

Douglas (1976) generalizes this argument, claiming that conventional views about the ethics of social research are based on a defective theory of society, one which assumes a moral consensus and widespread conformity to that consensus. He argues that deceptive methods are essential to do good social science because the social world is characterized by evasiveness, deceitfulness, secrecy, and fundamental social conflicts (Douglas 1976).

Douglas and the conflict methodologists argue, then, that researchers must be prepared to engage in unethical practices because this is often the only way that they will get the information they require (see also Hammersley 2007a). While those who pursue this line of argument may not assume that the end always justifies the means, they do believe that sometimes means which are ethically suspect from one point of view, such as deception, can be justified because they promise to produce a greater good, for example knowledge that could lead to social policies which will remedy social injustice.

The disagreements among these four positions are not just about values and their implications for action; they also relate to factual assumptions about the nature of the societies in which research is carried out, the sort of research that needs to be done and its relative value. Questions are also raised about whether the same ethical standards should be applied to all those involved in research, or whether standards should be applied differentially. For instance, should the members of an extreme right-wing political organization which engages in racial harassment be accorded the same ethical consideration as members of a democratically elected government? And should either of these be treated in terms of the same ethical norms as patients on a cancer ward? Indeed, sometimes different ethical stances may be taken towards different groups of people *within the same study*. Back and Solomos (1993: 189), for example, report adopting a 'profoundly inconsistent' ethical stance, being more open about their purposes and findings to black than to white informants. Some of these examples also indicate the fact that researchers do not operate in situations of complete freedom: those they study not only may have different needs and interests that should be taken into account, but also will have differential power to protect themselves and to pursue their interests in relation to researchers and others.

Taking a view

Our own position is closest to the second of the four views we outlined above, what we referred to as ethical situationism, though we accept elements of all of them. In our judgement there are dangers in treating particular procedures as if they were intrinsically ethical and desirable, whether this involves ensuring fully informed consent, giving people control over data relating to them, feeding back information about the research findings, or publishing information on the basis of 'the public's right to know'. What is appropriate and inappropriate depends upon the context to a large extent, and sometimes actions that are motivated by genuine ethical ideals can cause severe problems, not just for researchers but for the people they are studying as well.

Take the example of feeding back the findings of research to participants. This is now widely seen as an obligation on ethical grounds, because it is important to be open about one's research findings. The experience of Kelly in researching a city centre youth work project illustrates such a commitment and its dangers. She engaged in overt participant observation, but because of the high turnover in clientele not all of the young people were aware that she was a researcher. Also, some of those who were aware of her role did not realize the sort of information she was collecting and would publish. As a result, when an interim report was circulated there was a strong negative reaction which affected not only the research itself but also relationships between staff and clients (Davies and Kelly 1976; Cox *et al.* 1978). What this case illustrates is that by being open in this way researchers may upset the informational economy of the groups and organizations they are studying: for instance, through making information previously known only to a few available to all, or by making public and 'official' what had formerly only been private and informal. Similar problems arise in indigenous communities within which cultural knowledge is differentially distributed, for example by age or gender. Indeed, whereas, in the past, open publication of this knowledge by an anthropologist probably would not have made it widely available within the community itself, this is now no longer the case, given the global character of modern communication.

In much the same way, the justification of research and of the publication of findings on the grounds of a public right to know can be dangerous if it is not tempered by other considerations. As Shils (1959) points out:

> good arguments can be made against continuous publicity about public institutions. It could be claimed that extreme publicity not only breaks the confidentiality which enhances the imaginativeness and reflectiveness necessary for the effective working of institutions but also destroys the respect in which they should at least tentatively be held by the citizenry.
>
> (Shils 1959: 137)

Even Becker, whose views differ sharply from those of Shils, argues that one should refrain from publishing anything that will cause embarrassment or distress to the people studied if it is not central to the research or if its importance does not outweigh such consequences (Becker 1964b: 284). And, in fact, researchers frequently acquire confidential information that they do not use. In her study of gender and schooling in a rural English setting, Mason (1990: 106) reports becoming 'aware of details of covert practices such as "moonlighting", "taxdodging", and various details of "gossip"', which she was asked to keep confidential. Similarly, in attending case conferences for his research on haematologists, Atkinson (1995) came across suspicions about the description and staging of some tumours relating to patients who were being enrolled in a multi-site clinical trial. It seemed that these were being described in ways designed to make them conform to the particular clinical requirements of the trial. This did not relate to a central part of the research, nor was wholesale professional misconduct involved, and the details have never been published. However, this illustrates the sort of ethical dilemmas that can arise through becoming party to inside information.

Sometimes, though, the researcher may decide that even data and/or findings that are centrally relevant to the research must be suppressed for ethical reasons. The anthropologist Evans-Pritchard provides an example of such self-censorship in his book *Witchcraft, Oracles and Magic among the Azande*: he excluded information about a particular association devoted to the practice of magic, because of the consequences publication would have for its members. 'Europeans generally feel so strongly against this association and so fiercely punish its members that I refrain for the present from publishing an account of its rites, for some of them would offend European sentiments' (Evans-Pritchard 1937: 511, quoted in Barnes 1979: 40). Similarly, in their study of a college basketball team, Adler and Adler (1991: 179) report practising 'a degree of self-censorship, avoiding discussing potentially discrediting aspects of the setting'.

Underlying the treatment of any procedures as absolute ethical requirements are assumptions about how social settings *ought to be* that may neglect *how they actually are*. Moreover, views about how they ought to be may well differ for those with different cultural backgrounds or political commitments.[10] At the same time, it seems to us that there are values which most people, across most societies, would subscribe to in one form or another, and that these should guide researchers' judgements about what is and is not acceptable behaviour. And the values and feelings of those being studied must also be considered. However, it is important to recognize that it may not always be possible or desirable to avoid acting in ways that run contrary to these values. Values often conflict, and their implications for what is legitimate and illegitimate in particular situations is, potentially at least, always a matter for reasonable dispute. There is also the problem of the uncertain validity of our factual knowledge about what the consequences of different possible courses of action will and will not be, and thus about whether particular actions are likely to have undesirable effects.

For these reasons, what constitutes harm is a matter of judgement and may be contentious. A good illustration of this is provided by Homan's research on the prayer behaviour of oldtime pentecostalists. In response to criticism of his covert research strategy, he argued that had he informed the congregations he was observing about his research he would have interfered with their worship in a way that was less justifiable than their being observed by a researcher without knowing it. Whether or not one agrees with him, it is clear that conflicting principles are involved here, and perhaps also disagreements about the consequences of adopting covert and overt research strategies (see Homan and Bulmer 1982). Similarly, in the case of Ditton's (1977) research on bakery staff, whether one regards the latter as having suffered harm as a result of his research is a matter for debate. On the one hand, their incomes may have

---

10 For an interesting discussion of the difficulties involved in cultural differences in ethical judgements, see Shweder (2003).

been reduced as a result, and their reputations damaged, though it is not clear whether this actually occurred. On the other hand, the behaviour they were engaged in could be described as unethical and as harming others. Given this, should they not take responsibility for their actions? The response might be to ask why the particular people Ditton studied should have to face responsibility for their actions when others do not. After all, many businesses operate on the basis that there will be a certain level of theft on the part of employees. And one can raise questions about the levels of remuneration offered to bread workers compared to managing directors and shareholders of bakery firms. Moreover, the latter may also engage in criminal malpractice, perhaps on a greater financial scale, and without this being exposed to public scrutiny. In this example, as in many others, there is plenty of scope for debate about whether the research caused harm, how serious this was, and whether it was legitimate.

The same potential indeterminacy surrounds other ethical issues. An example is the confidentiality of information:

At times, in the course of conversations, teachers will say, 'and this is confidential'. But we might ask: what is actually held by the informant to be confidential – everything that is said, the name involved, or the occurrence of a particular episode? Further questions can also be raised: to whom is information confidential? To me and to the secretary who transcribes the tape? Or does it mean that sufficient confidentiality has been observed if pseudonyms are used? . . .

There are, nevertheless, some materials that are always confidential to the researcher and permanently lost from view. For example, in the middle of a taped conversation with a teacher I was requested to 'shut that bloody machine off'. At this point the individual told me about something that he had not done. The teacher indicated that the information should never be used. . . . Such situations pose a major dilemma for me. If the informant did not intend the information to influence my interpretation why did he tell it at all? In some respects this appears to be an invitation to incorporate this material in some way, but if it is done without giving data and sources, the assertions may look ungrounded. This kind of situation also presents many other problems. First, the researcher colludes with the other person involved in the conversation if no material is used. Second, in this instance the data that are being witheld would dramatically change a public account of a situation, so in this sense the researcher is involved in some deception.

(Burgess 1988a: 152)

Beynon (1983: 42) recounts a similar experience, though a different response: ' "Shall I tell you the truth about this place and will you keep it to yourself?", queried Mr Jovial. I could hardly reply that even inconsequential chat constituted potentially usable data! "Please do," I replied, feeling thoroughly devious.' As with confidentiality, so with honesty. The latter is certainly an important value, but this does not imply that we should always be absolutely honest. In everyday life most of us do not tell the whole truth and nothing but the truth in all circumstances. We are circumspect about whom we tell what, and we may even lie on occasion: not only to protect our own interests but to protect those of others too, sometimes even those to whom we are lying. What is at issue is not 'to deceive or not to deceive' in abstract, but what and how much to tell whom on what occasion. In research, as in everyday life, considerations about the likely effects of divulging various sorts of information and their desirability or undesirability arise and must be taken into account (see Baez 2002). In our view, an element of not telling the whole truth, even of active deception, may be justifiable so long as it is not designed to harm the people researched, and so long as there seems little chance that it will do so. However, by no means all ethnographers would agree with this.

As we noted earlier, there is also scope for disagreement about whether a particular research project involves exploitation of the people studied. The demands made on participants by research can vary a good deal, but so also can assessments of the level and significance of those demands. In the case of ethnography the impact of the research may seem to be minimal, in the sense that often all that is required is that participants carry on much as normal. However, being observed or interviewed can sometimes be a source of anxiety and strain. And while there are potential benefits from research for participants, for instance the chance to talk at length to someone about one's problems, how valuable these are found may vary considerably. Ultimately, it is the responsibility of ethnographers to ensure that they do not exploit the people they study, but this is necessarily a matter of judgement, and one that is open to challenge.

In this context, it is also important to remember that the possibility of dishonesty, manipulation, exploitation, and the causing of harm does not lie only on one side of the researcher-researched relationship. Wax (1952) notes how researchers may be seen as easy prey, as fair game whose sympathies and desire for information can be exploited for gifts and favours. Adler and Adler (1991) provide an example, describing how the drug dealers they were studying gradually began to take advantage of them:

> Money they gave us to hold, they knew they could always rely on having re-
> turned. Money we lent them in desperate times was never repaid, even when they
> were affluent again. Favors from us were expected by them, without any further
> reciprocation than openness about their activities.
>
> (Adler and Adler 1991: 178)

A more extreme case is that of Wallis (1977), who found himself subjected to intimidation when it became clear that he would not toe the line. This involved

> the activities of a staff member of the Scientology organization who visited my
> university . . ., presenting himself as a student wishing to undertake some study
> or research into Scottish religion. He asked to attend my classes and lectures and
> inquired whether I could put him up at my home for a few days! This naturally
> aroused my suspicion, and I shortly recalled having seen him in a staff member's
> uniform when I had taken the Communication Course at the Scientology
> headquarters. However, I took no action at this stage, not knowing precisely how
> to react. During his short stay in Stirling he made visits to my home in my absence
> and, unknown to me at that time, presented himself to students and others as a
> friend of mine in order to make inquiries concerning whether or not I was involved
> in the 'drug scene'. After a couple of days I confronted him with my knowledge
> of his background.
>   At this point he changed his story, claiming now to be a defector from
> Scientology, come to sell me information. I informed him that I was not buying
> information and gave him to understand that I believed his present story as little
> as his earlier one. . . .

In the weeks following his visit a number of forged letters came to light, some of which were supposedly written by me. These letters, sent to my university employers, colleagues and others, implicated me in a variety of acts, from a homosexual love affair to spying for the drug squad. Because I had few enemies and because this attention followed so closely upon the receipt of my paper by the Scientology organisation, it did not seem too difficult to infer the source of these attempts to inconvenience me.

(Wallis 1977: 157–8)

Scientologists also wrote to the body which was funding Wallis's research, complaining of his unethical behaviour and threatening legal action.

So, ethnographers must weigh the importance and contribution of their research against the chances and scale of any harm that is likely to be caused (to the people involved, to others, or to future access), against the values of honesty and fairness, against any infringement of privacy involved, and against any likely consequences for themselves and other researchers. But this must be done on the basis of a realistic view of human relations, not an idealized one; and there will be conflicting indications, difficult judgements, and probably disagreements. Ethical issues are not matters on which simple and consensual decisions can always be made. It is our view, however, that the most effective strategies for pursuing research should be adopted unless there is clear evidence that these are ethically unacceptable. In other words, indeterminacy and uncertainty should for the most part be resolved by ethnographers in favour of the interests of research, given that this is their primary task.

The issue of ethical regulation

Up to now, we have written as if it were the individual researcher, or research team, alone who made decisions about what is and is not, would and would not be, ethical in carrying out a particular project. While there is an important sense in which this is where the prime responsibility always resides, there are others who can make consequential judgements about this. This includes gatekeepers and funding bodies, and, increasingly, institutional review boards or university ethics committees. As we noted in Chapter 2, before beginning to negotiate access or collect data, it will often be necessary for the researcher to get the agreement of such bodies. Many social science associations have long had ethical codes, but for the most part it is only relatively recently, outside the United States, that full-blown ethical regulation has come to operate.[11]

Of course, different attitudes and strategies can be adopted to deal with ethical regulation. These range from automatic compliance, at one pole, to outright refusal to cooperate, at the other. Neither of these extremes is probably sensible, or perhaps ethical, in most circumstances. But ethnographers must weigh up how to deal with any conflicts between their own ethical judgements and those of ethical regulators, and between the demands of regulation and the methodological or practical requirements of their research.

---

11 For references to examples of professional codes, see the appendix to this chapter. Some of the questions now being raised about current ethical regulation were also raised when professional ethics codes were established: see Becker (1964a); Freidson (1964); Wax and Cassell (1981).

There are important questions to be asked, some of them of an ethical kind, about the justification for and consequences of the ethical regulation of social research that now takes place (van den Hoonaard 2002; Lincoln 2005; Hammersley 2006a). These stem from the fact that the regulation criteria have, to a large extent, been modelled on those developed for dealing with biomedical research. And the effects of this are compounded because ethical judgements about research cannot be separated from methodological and practical issues. Thus, it is often argued by ethical regulators that any risk of harm, or any cost, to participants must be weighed against the likely value of the research findings, which depends upon the effectiveness of the research design. In this way, ethics committees have become drawn into the role of determining what is good and bad research, and seeking to prevent the latter. Unfortunately, though, there is far from being any rational consensus among social researchers about either ethical or methodological issues, with the result that the decisions of ethics committees can have only limited intellectual legitimacy.

Ethical regulation of biomedical research arose out of, and is often justified by appeal to, abuses by medical researchers in the first half of the twentieth century. One example was the misuse of medical science by Nazi doctors and scientists, and their unspeakable 'experiments' on Jews, communists, homosexuals, Slavs and Roma in concentration camps. Another was the Tuskegee experiment, in which treatment for syphilis was withheld in the case of some black men in order to study the course of the disease. In fact, neither of these cases is entirely straightforward in their own terms. Both took place within legal frameworks, and so we should take care not to assume, unthinkingly, that ethical (any more than legal) regulation can prevent atrocities. As social scientists, we should be aware that ethical codes and their implementation are themselves cultural phenomena and reflect ideas about what it is and is not appropriate to do, and to whom, that are prevalent at the time. They are embedded within social frameworks of assumptions about what constitutes appropriate conduct, and also about what constitutes appropriate *research*. Nor should we assume that we have now gained some god-given omniscience about such matters. The Tuskegee case, in particular, is open to conflicting interpretations (Shweder 2004; see also Cave and Holm 2003), and the frequent appeals to it in the research ethics literature have come to take on the character of atrocity stories: simplified and exaggerated accounts designed for the purposes of justification.

Equally important, though, is that modes of regulation that are appropriate to biomedical research are by no means necessarily suitable for social research. What is involved in the practice of research, the people studied, the circumstances and purposes of inquiry, and the likely consequences, are all rather different in the two cases. Standard considerations about harm, informed consent, and so on, therefore need to be reinterpreted, and given different weight, in social research. In the case of ethnographic inquiry there are particular problems arising from the fact that fieldwork is carried out in settings over which the researcher does not have control, deals with many people simultaneously, and because research design in this context is not determined at the outset but develops over time.

An illustration of the problems concerns the issue of giving participants the right to withdraw from the research at any stage, a requirement which forms part of the protocol of many ethics committees. At first sight this may seem like a basic right which overrides the interests and convenience of the researcher. But ethnographers are normally dealing with social actors as members of an organization or setting, not as separate individuals. In concrete terms, how can it make sense for the would-be ethnographer, who has carefully negotiated access to, say, a research laboratory, with all the reasonable undertakings and assurances that might be expected, to accept that the research can be brought to a complete halt if one person decides to withdraw?

There is always considerable variation in the nature of the relations an ethnographer has with different participants in the field, and this will often reflect the extent to which the latter are willing to be involved in the research. They can certainly refuse to be interviewed, for example. However, giving them the right to prevent the researcher observing meetings in which they participate – which is required by the common demand, on the part of ethics committees, for opt-in consent to observation – effectively renders ethnographic research impossible.

While we would not want to place huge weight on it, there is an important sense in which social scientists, like journalists, play a key role in public accountability: they provide information for citizens about what goes on behind public facades. While ethics committees frequently acknowledge this in principle, in their deliberations it tends to be buried beneath standard concerns about, for example, procedures for ensuring informed consent. And, in fact, such committees are not usually in a position to judge what is and is not legitimate in terms of research practice in particular studies: their members rarely have the necessary background knowledge and experience in the kind of research proposed, or sufficiently detailed understanding about the setting in which the research is to be carried out.

As Crow *et al.* (2006) have indicated, there are optimists and pessimists regarding the consequences of current forms of ethical regulation. However, there is a growing body of informal evidence about the difficulties that it is posing for ethnographic work, for example leading researchers to drop some parts of an intended research plan, notably those involving participant observation, that are judged likely to be an obstacle to approval, or at least to cause substantial delay in obtaining it. There is also the likelihood of systematic deception in the representation of research to ethics committees, and occasionally the complete abandonment of particular projects in the face of the time and resources that would be required to get the agreement of relevant ethical regulators. A more creative strategy was employed by Scheper-Hughes (2004) in her research on human organ trafficking. She writes:

> As I could see no way of having my research pass through the Univeristy of California's Human Subjects Protection Committee, I applied for an exceptional dispensation . . . requesting that, for the purpose of this study, I be viewed as a human rights investigative reporter with the same rights as my colleagues in the Berkeley School of Journalism. Permission was eventually granted.
>
> (Scheper-Hughes 2004: 44–5)

We are in danger of allowing ethical concerns that are quite proper in general terms to transform the entire research process into a formulaic one, such that there are only a very limited number of permissible research designs, determined not by their validity but by their capacity to yield research protocols that can be checked against a set of simple (but often inappropriate) criteria. This is an issue for all social scientists. However, for the reasons we have explained, it represents a particularly severe challenge for ethnographic work.

Conclusion

We have discussed some key ethical issues surrounding ethnographic research, and outlined the rather different views about them to be found in the literature. We have also presented our own view that, while ethical considerations are important, they cannot be satisfactorily resolved by appeal to absolute rules, and that the effective pursuit of research should be the ethnographer's main concern. It is the responsibility of the ethnographer to try to act in ways that are ethically appropriate, taking due account of his or her goals and values, the situation in which the research is being carried out, and the values and interests of the people involved. In other words, as researchers, and as consumers of research, we must make judgements about what is and is not legitimate in particular cases. And we should be prepared to support our judgements with arguments if and when challenged. We must also recognize that others may disagree, even after we have presented our arguments, and not just because they have ulterior motives. It is important that the ethical issues surrounding research are discussed publicly, since this will feed into the deliberations of individual researchers and research teams. However, we do not believe that the forms of ethical regulation increasingly operating on social research today are desirable.

Reflexivity carries an important message in the field of ethics, as it does in relation to other aspects of ethnography. Some discussions of the ethics of social research seem to be premised on the idea that social researchers can and should act in an ethically superior manner to ordinary people, that they have, or should have, a heightened ethical sensibility and responsibility. An example is the frequent injunction that they should abide by 'the highest ethical standards', as if what this entailed were obvious, and as if doing it had no methodological consequences. There is also a tendency to dramatize matters excessively, implying a level of likely harm or moral transgression that is far in excess of what is typically involved.[12] Yet the ethical problems surrounding ethnographic research are, in fact, very similar to those that are relevant to other human activities. For example, what and how much to disclose of what one knows, believes, feels, etc., can be an issue for anyone at any time. And what is judged to be appropriate or desirable can vary a good deal. Above all, in everyday life ethical issues are subject to the same uncertainties and disagreements, the same play of vested interest and dogmatic opinions, and the same range of reasonable but conflicting arguments. All that can be required of ethnographers is that they take due note of the ethical aspects of their work and make the best judgements they can in the circumstances. They will have to live with the consequences of their actions; and, inevitably, so too will others. But, this is true of all of us in all aspects of our lives; it is the human condition.

This is not quite the last word. What we have discussed up to now are the ethical considerations that should restrain researchers' actions in the pursuit of inquiry, and the limits to these. But there can be exceptional occasions when a researcher should stop being a researcher and engage in action that is not directed towards the goal of producing knowledge. There is in fact always much action engaged in by ethnographers in the field that is not directly concerned with knowledge production. By its very nature, ethnography forces one into relationships with the people being studied, and one may do things because of those relationships, over and above any connection they

---

12 An example, in our view, is Warwick's (1982: 50) criticism of Laud Humphreys' (1970) study of homosexual activity in public lavatories as an infringement of the freedom of the men concerned.

have with the research. However, sometimes there will be actions that are needed because of those relationships, or because of obligations arising from other roles, which are not compatible with continuing to act as a researcher, or at least which must be carried out at the expense of the research. An example might be taking action if one witnesses physical abuse of disabled residents by those employed to care for them, though even here the decision may be a difficult one (see Taylor 1991: 245–6).

Becoming a researcher does not mean, then, that one is no longer a citizen or a person, that one's primary commitment to research must be sustained at all costs. However, in our view situations where these other identities should override that of researcher are very rare; and decisions to suspend or abandon the research role must arise from considerations that outweigh the value of the research very heavily. Account must also be taken of the usually very limited capacity of the researcher to help. A common example of this sort of action is the engagement of researchers in advocacy on the part of those they are studying. And frequently associated with the commitment to advocacy, it seems to us, is an underestimation of the difficulties involved, an overestimation of the likelihood of success, and a neglect of the danger of making the situation worse (see Hastrup and Elsass 1990).

Most of the time, then, the temptation to abandon the researcher role should be resisted. Certainly, we have little sympathy with attempts to redefine that role to make the researcher into a political activist. Like absolutist conceptions of research ethics, this often seems to be based on a conception of the researcher as in some sense above the world being studied, and thereby able to partake of god-like knowledge and powers. Against this, it is salutary to remind ourselves that the ethnographer is very much part of the social world he or she is studying, and is therefore subject to specific purposes, constraints, limitations, and weaknesses; like everyone else.

Appendix

Current social science research ethics codes include the following:

Association of Social Anthropologists (ASA) *Ethical Guidelines* http://www.theasa.org/ethics.htm

British Sociological Association (BSA) *Statement of Ethical Practice* http://www.britsoc.org.uk/about/ethic.htm

Social Research Association (SRA) *Ethical Guidelines* http://www.the-sra.org.uk/ethics.htm

American Sociological Association (ASA) *Code of Ethics* http://www.asanet.org/ethics.htm

American Anthropological Association (AAA) *Code of Ethics* http://aaanet.org/committees/ethics/ethicscode.pdf

British Psychological Society (BPS) *Code of Conduct: Ethical Principles and Guidelines* http://www.bps.org.uk/about/rules5.cfm

British Educational Research Association (BERA) *Revised Ethical Guidelines for Educational Research* (2004) http://www.bera.ac.uk/publications/pdfs/ethical.pdf

Epilogue
A distinctive analytic mentality

As we have tried to make clear in this book, there is an important sense in which ethnography is not just a set of methods but rather a particular mode of looking, listening, and thinking about social phenomena. In short, it displays a distinctive analytic mentality. This does not imply prior commitment to any single set of very specific ideas about the nature of the social world and how it can be understood. Rather, what is involved in this mentality is more along the following lines. A commitment:

1   not to jump to quick conclusions, even though this will delay the forming of hypotheses about what is going on, and even though the aim is eventually to reach some sort of conclusion;
2   to pay detailed attention to appearances, while not taking them at face value;
3   to seek to understand other people's views without treating what they say as either obviously true or obviously false;
4   to examine the circumstances in which people act, including much that they may not be aware of themselves, yet without losing sight of what they *do* attend to.

As our brief list makes clear, this orientation involves some difficult tensions. But while these are a source of recurrent troubles for ethnographers, they are also part of the dynamic of ethnographic work, they are what drives it forward in interesting directions. In this epilogue, we will look at some of the key tensions within the ethnographic mentality in more detail.

Getting the view from inside and from outside

One tension is between what we might call participant and analytic perspectives. Ethnographers typically insist on the need to understand the perspectives of the people being studied in order to explain, or even *to describe accurately*, the activities in which those people engage. In this respect, ethnographers are opposed to any approach which assumes that researchers can immediately know what people are doing and why, as well as those approaches which insist that we must start from some set of prior theoretical categories in describing people's behaviour. Instead, ethnographers insist on the value, for the purposes of inquiry, of suspending their own immediate inferences, common-sense assumptions and theoretical presuppositions, as far as possible, so as to try to take full account of what people say about their world and what they do. This emphasis on understanding people's own perspectives has a long history. The need for it is particularly obvious where one is studying a society that is very different from one's own – since much of what is seen and heard will not be immediately intelligible. However, it is equally, if not more, important to adopt this stance in studying familiar settings, where the tendency to assume that one already knows what is going on, and why, as well as who is involved and for what purposes, is particularly strong. While our inferences about these matters may of course be sound, this cannot be assumed. Those inferences must be suspended so as to avoid the danger of serious misunder-standing of people's intentions and motives; and, also, so as to open up ways of looking at familiar phenomena that are different from the ones that we use routinely ourselves, or those that follow from a particular theoretical perspective.

At the same time, there is also usually an emphasis within ethnographic work on developing an *analytic* understanding of people's perspectives and activities, one that will usually be different from, and perhaps even in conflict with, how the people studied see themselves and their world. There are several aspects to this. Ethnographers usually seek to take account of the perspectives of *several* categories or groups of actors involved in the situations they are studying, without treating any as auto-matically true, and especially without relying on conventional hierarchies of credibility (Becker 1967a). There is a recognition that there will usually be multiple perspectives, perhaps even in sharp conflict with one another on key points, and that all of these can be a source of insight.

Equally important, ethnographers will often take note of behaviour that is below people's level of consciousness: in other words, which is routinely ignored or not even noticed for practical purposes. Ethnographers also often seek to locate what people do in a wider socio-historical context than they may be aware of themselves. And what drives these differences between participant and analytic understandings is that ethnog-raphers are usually trying to understand people's actions, and the social institutions in which these are implicated, in such a way as to contribute to academic knowledge about the social world, rather than to further the practical enterprises in which the people they study, or others, are involved.[1]

The tension between participant and analytic perspectives is highlighted if we think of the ethnographer as simultaneously concerned to make the strange familiar, so as to *understand* it, and to make the familiar strange, so as to avoid *misunderstanding* it. The first of these commitments requires that we always begin from the assumption that people's behaviour is intelligible and rational – even if at first sight it seems non-sensical, pointless, or simply evil. From this stems ethnographic opposition to treating ordinary people's accounts as necessarily ideological and misleading, by contrast with the true understanding that can be generated by scientific work. There is also a wider sense of making the strange familiar in that what are sought are convincing explanations for what initially appears puzzling, as well as for what seemed so obvious as not to need explanation. Here there is a rejection of any proposal that human actions or social forms are simply inexplicable, or mysterious, in character.

On the other side, the commitment to making the familiar strange means that there is a refusal to take at face value what appears familiar or obvious, suspending those background assumptions that immediately give apparent sense to what we experience. This is governed partly by the aim of minimizing the danger of reliance on assumptions

---

1 This is not to deny that ethnographic method is sometimes used in more 'applied' or 'critical' forms of research, and within practitioner inquiries, where this contrast may not be so sharp.

that, though practically effective for the most part, are false. It also stems from the aim, already mentioned, of producing an *analytic* understanding of what is being studied, rather than simply reproducing participant understandings. Sometimes, too, there is a concern to avoid normalizing alien perspectives, to resist the tendency to assume that other people's lives can be immediately comprehended in *our* terms.

Given this important tension within the ethnographic mentality, it is important to note that, in recent years, there has been a recurrence of quite fundamental questioning about the very possibility of understanding other people. In the past, in the context of historical work, this was formulated in terms of the question 'Is it necessary to *be* Caesar in order to understand him?' If this were a literal requirement, then, of course, understanding others' actions would be impossible. While this question formulates understanding in largely psychological terms, the same problem arises if one construes it in cultural terms, asking how far it is possible genuinely to understand other cultures. Those who assume that there is a common human nature underlying diverse cultures can hope that this will facilitate such understanding. But many reject the idea that there is any common human nature; and/or ask how we could ever produce an account of its character that is not itself simply an expression of our *own* cultural assumptions.

These issues take on particular significance in the context of a world where most social scientists still belong to the West, and where Western societies are implicated in a process of globalization that seems to entail the obliteration, or at least substantial reconstruction, of other cultures. However, it is also an issue that arises *within* Western societies, for example concerning how far men can understand women, or white middle-class women can understand, say, poor Hispanic women, or whether heterosexuals can understand gays, able-bodied people comprehend people with disabilities, and so on.

One, not uncommon, way of dramatizing this problem is to formulate it as the problem of understanding 'the Other'. However, this misleadingly presents other people as a single metaphysical entity. Furthermore, there is a sense in which any process of understanding reduces the strange to the familiar, and we should not assume that this necessarily involves distortion. Indeed, the very notion of 'distortion' may imply a misleading conception of the goal of ethnography: as if its aim could be to capture and represent cultures or other social phenomena 'in their own terms'. Yet, surely, all knowledge, including that produced through ethnography, can only be about some aspects of the phenomena studied: it is aimed at answering some particular set of questions, rather than, literally, holding a mirror up to the world.

Can we ever get beyond our own cultural assumptions so as to achieve a proper understanding of what is initially alien to us? Interestingly, this question can be extended in an even more radical direction: Can we ever really claim to understand ourselves? After all, even our understandings of ourselves will be constituted in and through our particular background cultural assumptions. Others will see us differently, and who is to say that there is any single fully comprehensive account that is true? Questions running in the opposite direction include: do we need to get beyond all of our cultural assumptions in order to be able to understand people belonging to other cultures; must we assume that our background culture is a prison-house from which there is no escape?

These are difficult issues, but there seems no more reason to assume that all understanding is impossible than there is to believe that anyone has direct, absolutely valid knowledge about anything, even about themselves. We can recognize that social inquiry is an uncertain business, in the sense that we can never be entirely sure about the validity of any knowledge claims, without adopting a complete scepticism which is, in any case, self-refuting – to say that we can know nothing is itself to make a knowledge claim. We can recognize that, as ethnographers, we may be able to understand others better than they can understand themselves, in certain respects, because we are able to examine what they say and do in more detail than they do themselves, or because we can see them in a wider context and compare them with others in ways that, currently at least, they cannot. But, at the same time, we should not dismiss their own understandings of themselves as fanciful or ideological, since they will have access to some kinds of knowledge that are not available to us.

Equally difficult problems arise with the notion of analytic understanding. There is sometimes a tendency within ethnography, and outside of it as well, to see any analytic understanding as in some sense a cultural imposition, a form of symbolic violence; and this is especially true if it conflicts with participants' own understandings. But even if we put this aside, on the grounds that, as we have seen, 'understanding from within' is itself problematic, we must ask: on what grounds do we choose one form of analytic understanding over another? In the past, the answer to this would have been: by appeal to the evidence. However, not only has there been increasing questioning of what counts, and should count, as evidence, but it is also clear that many forms of analytic understanding are incommensurable – not least because they are addressing different questions and, as a result, rely on different presuppositions. This means that evidence cannot easily be used to judge among them, since each requires evidence of different kinds. Some commentators have concluded from this that there exist multiple analytic perspectives that must all be equally valued, or which can be evaluated only in particular contexts for particular purposes, or judged in aesthetic, political or ethical terms rather than according to whether they represent the world accurately. Others, however, see particular analytic approaches as providing us with important knowledge about the world, even though no approach can tell us everything there is to know, and even though what knowledge any study offers is always fallible. This is the position we take.

The particular versus the general

There is a second set of important, and closely related, tensions. Ethnographers are usually suspicious of rapid moves from statements about particular situations to broader claims, whether in the form of generalizations about some large population or inferences to some general theory. At the same time, while they usually study only a few cases, and cases that are themselves relatively small in scale, they are also almost inevitably concerned with drawing general conclusions of *some* kind. What is distinctive to their orientation is that they want to do this in ways that still respect the particularity of the cases they study.

Ethnographers differ in how they deal with this tension, and in how much thought they give to it. Some seek, *through* the detailed study of particular instances, to develop general, theoretical accounts of types of social phenomena that preserve particularity as far as possible through the density of the analysis. An example is grounded theorizing, in which data are collected in ways that are specifically designed to generate theories but where those theories are intended to capture all that is relevant in the particular cases studied. Other ethnographers select cases for study in ways that they believe enable them to draw general conclusions about some larger population, because these cases are typical or atypical in key respects, because they represent the leading edge of a changing trend, and so on. Yet others aim at producing thick descriptions whose general value is to be judged by readers when they use those descriptions to understand new situations in which they are interested or involved.

At face value, ethnography is weak as a basis for producing general conclusions. As regards theoretical inferences, by contrast with experimental research it cannot physically control variables so as to reveal associations that are likely to indicate causal relations. Nor is it able to make use of the techniques for statistical control employed by survey researchers. And, in relation to empirical generalizations from a sample to an extant population, it is not usually able to employ statistical sampling theory, which can allow survey researchers to produce findings that have a high, and specifiable, probability of being representative of that population.

However, these various means employed by other forms of research to deal with the issue of generality have themselves been subjected to considerable criticism. In the case of experimental method, there is the problem that what the subjects do is shaped by the experimental situation and by the experimenter, and therefore may not be indicative of what they would do in more normal circumstances. As regards survey research, the weakness of statistical control as against physical control is widely recognized, and there is the problem that very often the data on which the analysis is based consists of what people say in response to highly structured questions. Here, the problem arises of how reliable are inferences from such data to people's orientations and actions in ordinary contexts.

Of course, in everyday life, we all draw general conclusions from particular cases; albeit, if we are sensible, tentatively. What ethnographers do builds on this. Moreover, it is often possible for ethnographers to engage in comparative analysis, so as to provide some evidence about what causes what. And examining the details of the processes by which things happen also provides indications about what causal mechanisms may be in play. Much the same is true of generalization from cases studied to some larger population. As Schofield (1990) has elaborated, there are means by which ethnographers can make reasonable judgements about this. Ethnography cannot provide a definitive solution to the problem of generalization, but then neither can any other form of social research.

Process versus structure

A third set of tensions arises because ethnographers tend to emphasize the processual character of human social life while yet at the same time seeking to generate theoretical ideas that, of necessity, involve 'fixing' the phenomena under study as belonging to particular categories. Stress on the importance of studying social life as a process arose, to a large extent, from opposition to attempts to understand it in terms of fixed, determinate relationships among variables, in the way that many quantitative researchers do. Thus, much general social science has been concerned with identifying key variables, measuring them, and then investigating what are taken to be stable associations among them, whether through experimental control or statistical analysis. And the aim has been to produce causal models of these relationships that purport to hold true over time and across contexts. By contrast, ethnographers tend to emphasize the contingent character of human social life, the extent to which it does not take the form of repeated patterns or standard forms. They have drawn attention to how similar paths can lead to quite different destinations, and how very different paths may result in the same outcome. From their point of view, outcomes are not only never entirely predictable, but sometimes what happens is quite surprising, not being anticipated by anyone, and not even open to being captured in terms of some probability.

Emphasis on the processual character of human social life gives priority to detailed narratives, descriptions of the roles that various people play, accounts of the local contexts in which patterns of action occur, and so on. However, at the same time, ethnographers rarely wish to limit themselves to providing mere chronicles of events. Like historians, they usually want to *interpret* what is happening, to make sense of it and explain it. And, in order to do this, they cannot avoid employing analytic categories that presume general patterns. Indeed, the pressure to do this is even greater than it is in the case of historians, since the particular events ethnographers study do not usually carry much *intrinsic* interest for wider audiences, they are only of interest precisely as examples of more general categories of event. So, using such categories is essential if the research is to produce findings with any news value.

Once again, there is no simple, magic solution to this problem, for ethnographers or for anyone else. It remains the case, though, that ethnography serves as an important corrective to interpretations of social phenomena, in both everyday thinking and the social sciences, which assume that they can be understood in terms of universal or standard patterns of causal relationship, of whatever kind.

Discovery versus construction

The final tension we will discuss operates between a view of research as *discovery* and one which treats it as necessarily a matter of *construction*. On the first interpretation, ethnographers go into the field in order to find out what happens there so that they can document it. Indeed, often there is an emphasis on the value of ethnography in documenting what *really* goes on, behind official fronts. If, on the other hand, we interpret ethnography as a process of *constructing* accounts of the world, then we must acknowledge that, at least in some ways, what it produces will reflect the cultural background and the interpretive work of the ethnographer.

In the past, ethnographers generally saw their task as discovery, even while empha-sizing the extent to which the people they study construct the social world through various sense-making practices and the courses of action these produce. By contrast, much ordinary social science, then as now, was seen by ethnographers as operating behind the screen of prior hypotheses and structured research instruments that prevented the researchers concerned from *learning directly* about the social world. It was argued that their background assumptions were being protected from the correction that would result if they were to engage in direct contact with the world. Ethnography was treated as an antidote to this: exposing researchers to the world and thereby enabling them to find out what really goes on and why.

However, in recent times some of the assumptions on which this commitment to discovery is based have come to be questioned by many ethnographers. The idea that it is possible to get into direct contact with the world has been challenged, on the grounds that any process of observation is assumption-laden: we cannot but make sense of what we experience in terms of some set of concepts, and we cannot derive those concepts simply from 'the things themselves'. Furthermore, in seeking to understand, we are likely to reduce the strange to the familiar, tending to make sense of what we experience in terms of our existing categories, wherever possible. From this point of view, to talk of suspending one's background assumptions, in order to allow direct contact with reality and discovery of the truth, can be seen as a form of bad faith; as falsely claiming some superior means of acquiring knowledge. It might also be argued that it ignores the extent to which what one finds, and even what counts as a 'finding' or a 'discovery', is itself determined by background cultural expectations; and is therefore to some degree an expression of the ethnographer's individual and institutional self as much as it is a representation of the world.

More fundamentally, some of those who argue that what is involved is construction rather than discovery assume that there simply is no single reality which it is the task of researchers to represent. In other words, it is not only that we can never get access to reality, but also that the 'reality' that ethnographers document is no less a construction than the accounts produced by the people that they study. The very assumption that there is some single, available world in which we all live is rejected in favour of the idea that there are multiple realities. And yet, of course, to claim that there are multiple realities is itself to claim that one knows something about the multiplex character of reality.

In our view, it is impossible to do ethnography, or any other kind of research, without assuming that there is a reality that can be investigated and about which we can gain knowledge. However, ethnographers have always been acutely aware of the diverse cultural perspectives that exist within the social world, and of how these shape our understandings and actions. The principle of reflexivity, which we have emphasized throughout this book, underlines the fact that ethnographers themselves are part of the social world, and must work within whatever cultural perspectives are available to them. At the same time, this principle also insists that we can always learn to understand the world in new ways, and thereby come to better understandings of it. While we cannot prove in some absolute sense what is true and what false, and while there will sometimes be accounts amongst which it is hard to adjudicate with any confidence, this does not mean that just any account is as valid as any other.

Conclusion

We have suggested that much ethnographic research is guided by a distinctive analytic orientation; yet one which contains some important, unresolved, and perhaps unresolvable, tensions. We believe that these can be highly productive if they are held in balance. Of course, we do not wish to make exaggerated claims for the value of ethnography, as against other approaches to social research. Moreover, we acknowledge that its value is restricted to facilitating the production of knowledge: it is not an effective means for advocacy, empowerment, or bringing about socio-political change. But the value of the knowledge that ethnography can provide must not be underestimated; and there is a genuine danger of this in a world where the primary emphasis is on doing rather than knowing, and therefore on the rhetorical power of words rather than on their representational capacity. A reflexive ethnography implies a commitment to the value of understanding human social life; even while recognizing the limits to such understanding and to its power in the world.

References

Abell, J., Locke, A., Condor, S., Gibson, S. and Stevenson, C. (2006) 'Trying similarity, doing difference: the role of interviewer self-disclosure in interview talk with young people', *Qualitative Research*, 6, 2: 221–44.

Abraham, J. (1989) 'Testing Hargreaves' and Lacey's differentiation-polarisation theory in a setted comprehensive', *British Journal of Sociology*, 40, 1: 46–81.

Adam, B. (1990) *Time and Social Theory*, Cambridge: Polity.

Adelman, C. (1977) 'On first hearing', in C. Adelman (ed.) *Uttering, Muttering: Collecting, Using and Reporting Talk for Social and Educational Research*, London: Grant McIntyre.

Adkins, L. (2002) 'Reflexivity and the politics of qualitative research', in T. May (ed.) *Qualitative Research in Action*, London: Sage.

Adler, P.A. and Adler, P. (1987) *Membership Roles in Field Research*, Newbury Park, CA: Sage.

Adler, P.A. and Adler, P. (1991) *Membership Roles in Field Research*, Newbury Park, CA: Sage, 2nd edn.

Adler, P.A. and Adler, P. (1994) 'Observational techniques', in N.K. Denzin and Y.S. Lincoln (eds) *Handbook of Qualitative Research*, 1st edn, Thousand Oaks, CA: Sage.

Agar, M. (1973) *Ripping and Running: A Formal Ethnography of Urban Heroin Addicts*, New York: Seminar Press.

Agar, M. (1980) *Professional Stranger*, New York: Academic Press.

Aggleton, P. (1987) *Rebels without a Cause: Middle-Class Youth and the Transition from School to Work*, London: Faber.

Allan, A. (2005) 'Using photographic diaries to research the gender and academic identities of young girls', in G. Troman, B. Jeffrey, and G. Walford (eds) *Methodological Issues and Practices in Ethnography*, Amsterdam: Elsevier.

Allen, D. (2001) 'Narrating nursing jurisdiction: "atrocity stories" and "boundary-work"', *Symbolic Interaction*, 24, 1: 75–103.

American Anthropological Association (AAA) (1998) *Code of Ethics*, http://aaanet.org/committees/ethics/ethicscode.pdf

American Sociological Association (ASA) (1997) *Code of Ethics*, http://www.asanet.org/ethics.htm

Anderson, E. (2006) 'Jelly's place: an ethnographic memoir', in D. Hobbs and R. Wright (eds) *The Sage Handbook of Fieldwork*, London: Sage.

Anderson, L. (2006) 'Analytic autoethnography', *Journal of Contemporary Ethnography*, 35, 4: 375–95.

Anderson, J. (2002) 'Reconsidering environmental resistance: working through Secondspace and Thirdspace approaches', *Qualitative Research*, 2, 3: 301–21.

Anteby, M. (2003) 'The "moralities" of poaching: manufacturing personal artifacts on the factory floor', *Ethnography*, 4, 2: 217–39.

Arensberg, C.M. and Kimball, S.T. (1968) *Family and Community in Ireland*, Cambridge, MA: Harvard University Press (first published in 1940).

Ashmore, M. (1989) *The Reflexive Thesis*, Chicago, IL: University of Chicago Press.

Association of Social Anthropologists (ASA) (1999) *Ethical Guidelines*, http://www.theasa.org/ethics.htm

Atkinson, J.M. (1978) *Discovering Suicide: Studies in the Social Organization of Sudden Death*, London: Macmillan.

Atkinson, P. (n.d.) 'Trophies', unpublished analytic memo, Department of Sociology, University College Cardiff.

Atkinson, P. (1976) 'The clinical experience: an ethnography of medical education', unpublished PhD thesis, University of Edinburgh.

Atkinson, P. (1981a) *The Clinical Experience*, Farnborough, UK: Gower.

Atkinson, P. (1981b) 'Transition from school to working life', unpublished memorandum, Sociological Research Unit, University College, Cardiff.

Atkinson, P. (1982) 'Writing ethnography', in H.J. Helle (ed.) *Kultur und Institution*, Berlin: Dunker & Humblot.

Atkinson, P. (1984) 'Wards and deeds', in R.G. Burgess (ed.) *The Research Process in Educational Settings*, Lewes, UK: Falmer.

Atkinson, P. (1992a) 'The ethnography of a medical setting: reading, writing and rhetoric', *Qualitative Health Research*, 2, 4: 451–74.

Atkinson, P. (1992b) *Understanding Ethnographic Texts*, Newbury Park, CA: Sage.

Atkinson, P. (1995) *Medical Talk and Medical Work*, London: Sage.

Atkinson, P. (1997) *Clinical Experience: The Construction and Reconstruction of Medical Reality*, Aldershot, UK: Ashgate.

Atkinson, P. (2006a) *Everyday Arias: An Operatic Ethnography*, Lanham, MD: AltaMira.

Atkinson, P. (2006b) 'Rescuing autoethnography', *Journal of Contemporary Ethnography* 35, 4: 400–4.

Atkinson, P. and Coffey, A. (2002) 'Revisiting the relationship between participant observation and interviewing', in J.F. Gubrium, and J.A. Holstein (eds) *Handbook of Interview Research* Thousand Oaks, CA: Sage.

Atkinson, P. and Delamont, S. (eds) (2006) *Narrative Analysis*, 4 vols, London: Sage.

Atkinson, P. and Housley, W. (2003) *Interactionism: An Essay in Sociological Amnesia*, London: Sage.

Atkinson, P.A. and Silverman, D. (1997) 'Kundera's *Immortality*: the interview society and the invention of the self', *Qualitative Inquiry*, 3: 304–25.

Atkinson, P., Batchelor, C. and Parsons, E. (1997) 'The rhetoric of prediction, skill and chance in the research to clone a disease gene', in M.A. Elston (ed.) *The Sociology of Medical Science and Technology*, Oxford: Blackwell.

Atkinson, P., Coffey, A. and Delamont, S. (1999) 'Ethnography: post, past and present', *Journal of Contemporary Ethnography*, 28, 5: 460–71.

Atkinson, P., Coffey, A. and Delamont, S. (2003) *Key Themes in Qualitative Research: Continuities and Change*, Walnut Creek, CA: AltaMira.

Atkinson, P., Coffey, A., Delamont, S., Lofland, J. and Lofland, L. (eds) (2001) *Handbook of Ethnography*, London: Sage.

Back, L. (2004) 'Politics, research and understanding', in C. Seale, G. Gobo, J.F. Gubrium and D. Silverman (eds) *Qualitative Research Practice*, London: Sage.

Back, L. and Solomos, J. (1993) 'Doing research, writing politics, the dilemmas of political intervention in research on racism', *Economy and Society*, 22, 2: 178–99.

Baez, B. (2002) 'Confidentiality in qualitative research: reflections on secrets, power and agency', *Qualitative Research*, 2, 1: 35–58.

Ball, M.S. (2005) 'Working with images in daily life and police practice: an assessment of the documentary tradition', *Qualitative Sociology*, 5, 4: 499–521.

Ball, M.S. and Smith, G.W.H. (1992) *Analyzing Visual Data*, Newbury Park, CA: Sage.

Ball, M.S. and Smith, G. (2001), 'Technologies of realism? Ethnographic uses of photography and film', in P. Atkinson, A. Coffey, S. Delamont, J. Lofland and L. Lofland (eds) *Handbook of Ethnography*, London: Sage.

Ball, S.J. (1980) 'Initial encounters in the classroom and the process of establishment', in P. Woods (ed.) *Pupil Strategies*, London: Croom Helm.

Ball, S.J. (1981) *Beachside Comprehensive*, London: Cambridge University Press.

Ball, S.J. (1983) 'Case study research in education: some notes and problems', in M. Hammersley (ed.) *The Ethnography of Schooling: Methodological Issues*, Driffield, UK: Nafferton.

Ball, S.J. (1984) 'Beachside reconsidered: reflections on a methodological apprenticeship', in R.G. Burgess (ed.) *The Research Process in Educational Settings*, Lewes, UK: Falmer.

Ball, S.J. (1994) 'Political interviews and the politics of interviewing', in G. Walford (ed.) *Researching the Powerful in Education*, London: UCL Press.

Barbera-Stein, L. (1979) 'Access negotiations: comments on the sociology of the sociologist's knowledge', paper presented at the Seventy-Fourth Annual Meeting of the American Sociological Association, Boston, MA, August.

Barnes, C. (2003) 'What a difference a decade makes: reflections on doing "emancipatory" disability research', *Disability and Society*, 18, 1: 3–17.

Barnes, J.A. (1979) *Who Should Know What? Social Science, Privacy and Ethics*, Harmondsworth: Penguin.

Barnes, V., Clouder, D.L., Hughes, C., Purkiss, J. and Pritchard, J. (2003) 'Deconstructing dissemination: dissemination as qualitative research', *Qualitative Research*, 3, 2: 147–64.

Barrett, R.A. (1974) *Benabarre: The Modernization of a Spanish Village*, New York: Holt, Rinehart & Winston.

Beals, R. (1969) *Politics of Social Research: An Inquiry into the Ethics and Responsibilities of Social Scientists*, Chicago, IL: Aldine.

Beauchamp, T.L. *et al.* (eds) (1982) *Ethical Issues in Social Science Research*, Baltimore, MD: Johns Hopkins University Press.

Bechofer, F., Elliott, B. and McCrone, D. (1984) 'Safety in numbers: the use of multiple interviewers', *Sociology*, 18, 1: 97–100.

Becker, H.S. (1964a) 'Against the code of ethics', *American Sociological Review*, 29, 3: 409–10.

Becker, H.S. (1964b) 'Problems in the publication of field studies', in A.J. Vidich, J. Bensman and M.R. Stein (eds) *Reflections on Community Studies*, New York: Wiley.

Becker, H.S. (1967a) Comment reported in R.J. Hill and K. Stones Crittenden (eds) *Proceedings of the Purdue Symposium on Ethnomethodology*, Institute for the Study of Social Change, Department of Sociology, Purdue University, IN.

Becker, H.S. (1967b) 'Whose side are we on?', *Social Problems*, 14: 239–47.

Becker, H.S. (1970) 'Life history and the scientific mosaic', in H.S. Becker, *Sociological Work*, Chicago, IL: Aldine.

Becker, H.S. (1971) Footnote to M. Wax and R. Wax, 'Great tradition, little tradition, and formal education', in M. Wax, S. Diamond and F. Gearing (eds) *Anthropological Perspectives on Education*, New York: Basic Books.

Becker, H.S. (1986) *Writing for Social Scientists*, Chicago, IL: University of Chicago Press.

Becker, H.S. (1993) 'How I learned what a crock was', *Journal of Contemporary Ethnography*, 22, 1: 28–35.

Becker, H.S. (1998) *Tricks of the Trade: How to Think about Your Research While You're Doing It*, Chicago, IL: University of Chicago Press.

Becker, H.S. and Geer, B. (1957) 'Participant observation and interviewing: a comparison', *Human Organization*, 6: 28–34.

Becker, H.S. and Geer, B. (1960) 'Participant observation: the analysis of qualitative field data', in R.N. Adams and J.J. Preiss (eds) *Human Organization Research: Field Relations and Techniques*, Homewood, IL: Dorsey Press.

Belk, R. (1995) *Collecting in a Consumer Society*, London: Routledge.

Bell, C. (1977) 'Reflections on the Banbury restudy', in C. Bell and H. Newby (eds) *Doing Sociological Research*, London: Allen & Unwin.

Benjamin, A.F. (1999) 'Contract and covenant in Curaçao: reciprocal relationships in scholarly research', in N.M.P. King, G.E. Henderson and J. Stein (eds) *Beyond Regulations: Ethics in Human Subjects Research*, Chapel Hill, NC: University of North Carolina Press.

Bensman, J. and Vidich, A. (1960) 'Social theory in field research', *American Journal of Sociology*, 65: 577–84.

Benson, O. and Stangroom, J. (2006) *Why Truth Matters*, London: Continuum.

Beoku-Betts, J. (1994) 'When black is not enough: doing field research among Gullah women', *National Women's Studies Association Journal*, 6, 3: 413–33.

Berger, P. and Luckmann, T. (1967) *The Social Construction of Reality*, London: Allen Lane.

Berlak, A.C., Berlak, H., Bagenstos, N.T. and Mikel, E.R. (1975) 'Teaching and learning in English primary schools', *School Review*, 83, 2: 215–43.

Berreman, G. (1962) *Behind Many Masks: Ethnography and Impression Management in a Himalayan Village*, Monograph 4, Society for Applied Anthropology, Ithaca, NY: Cornell University Press.

Bettelheim, B. (1970) *The Informed Heart*, London: Paladin.

Beynon, J. (1983) 'Ways-in and staying-in: fieldwork as problem solving', in M. Hammersley (ed.) *The Ethnography of Schooling: Methodological Issues*, Driffield, UK: Nafferton.

Blackwood, E. (1995) 'Falling in love with an-Other lesbian: reflections on identity in fieldwork', in D. Kulick and M. Wilson (eds) *Taboo: Sex, Identity and Erotic Subjectivity in Anthropological Fieldwork*, London: Routledge.

Blaikie, N.W.H. (1991) 'A critique of the use of triangulation in social research', *Quality and Quantity*, 25, 2: 115–36

Bloor, M. (1978) 'On the analysis of observational data: a discussion of the worth and uses of inductive techniques and respondent validation', *Sociology*, 12, 3: 545–52.

Bloor, M. (1997) 'Techniques of validation in qualitative research: a critical commentary', in G. Miller and R. Dingwall (eds) *Context and Method in Qualitative Research*, London: Sage.

Blumer, H. (1954) 'What is wrong with social theory?', *American Sociological Review*, 19: 3–10.

Blumer, H. (1969) *Symbolic Interactionism*, Englewood Cliffs, NJ: Prentice Hall.

Boeije, H. (2002) 'A purposeful approach to the constant comparative method in the analysis of qualitative interviews', *Quality and Quantity*, 36: 391–409.

Bogdan, R. and Taylor, S. (1975) *Introduction to Qualitative Research Methods*, New York: Wiley.

Bohannon, P. (1981) 'Unseen community: the natural history of a research project', in D.A. Messerschmidt (ed.) *Anthropologists at Home in North America: Methods and Issues in the Study of One's Own Society*, Cambridge: Cambridge University Press.

Boon, J. (1983) 'Functionalists write too: Frazer, Malinowski and the semiotics of the monograph', *Semiotica*, 46, 2–4: 131–49.

Booth, C. (1902–3) *Life and Labour of the People in London:* London: Macmillan.

Borchgrevink, A. (2003) 'Silencing language: of anthropologists and interpreters', *Ethnography*, 4, 1: 95–121.

Borden, I. (2002) *Skateboarding, Space and the City: Architecture and the Body*, Oxford: Berg.

Bourdieu, P. (1979) *Algeria 1960: The Disenchantment of the World, the Sense of Honour, the Kabyle House or the World Reversed*, Cambridge: Cambridge University Press.

Bowen, E. (1954) *Return to Laughter*, London: Gollancz.

Brady, I. (2005) 'Poetics for a planet: discourse on some problems of being-in-place', in N.K. Denzin and Y.S. Lincoln (eds) *Handbook of Qualitative Research*, 3rd edn, Thousand Oaks, CA: Sage.

Brettell, C.B. (ed.) (1993) *When They Read What We Write: The Politics of Ethnography*, Westport, CT: Bergin & Garvey,

Brewer, J. with Magee, K. (1991) *Inside the RUC: Routine Policing in a Divided Society*, Oxford: Clarendon Press.

British Educational Research Association (BERA) (2004) *Revised Ethical Guidelines for Educational Research*, http://www.bera.ac.uk/publications/pdfs/ETHICA1.PDF

British Psychological Society (BPS) (2006) *Code of Conduct: Ethical Principles and Guidelines*, http://www.bps.org.uk/about/rules5.cfm

British Sociological Association (BSA) (2002) *Statement of Ethical Practice*, http://www.britsoc.org.uk/about/ethic.htm

Brown, P. (1987) *Schooling Ordinary Kids*, London: Methuen.

Buchli, V. (ed.) (2002) *The Material Culture Reader*, Oxford: Berg.

Bulmer, M. (1980) 'Why don't sociologists make more use of official statistics?', *Sociology*, 14, 4: 505–23.

Bulmer, M. (ed.) (1982) *Social Research Ethics: An Examination of the Merits of Covert Participant Observation*, London: Macmillan.

Bulmer, M. (1984) *The Chicago School of Sociology*, Chicago, IL: University of Chicago Press.

Burawoy, M. (2005) 'Presidential address: For public sociology', *American Sociological Review*, 70, 1: 4–28. Reprinted in *British Journal of Sociology*, 56, 2.

Burawoy, M., Blum, J.A., George, S., Gille, Z., Gowan, T., Haney, L., Klawiter, M., Lopez, S.H., Riain, S. and Thayer, M. (2000) *Global Ethnography: Forces, Connections, and Imaginations in a Postmodern World*, Berkeley, CA: University of California Press.

Burgess, R.G. (1984a) *In the Field: An Introduction to Field Research*, London: Allen & Unwin.

Burgess, R. G. (ed.) (1984b) *The Research Process in Educational Settings*, Lewes, UK: Falmer.

Burgess, R.G. (ed.) (1985a) *Issues in Educational Research: Qualitative Methods*, Lewes, UK: Falmer.

Burgess, R.G. (ed.) (1985b) *Strategies of Educational Research: Qualitative Methods*, Lewes, UK: Falmer.

Burgess, R.G. (ed.) (1985c) *Field Methods in the Study of Education*, Lewes, UK: Falmer.

Burgess, R.G. (1985d) 'The whole truth? Some ethical problems of research in a comprehensive school', in R.G. Burgess (ed.) *Field Methods in the Study of Education*, Lewes, UK: Falmer.

Burgess, R.G. (1985e) 'In the company of teachers: key informants and the study of a comprehensive school', in R.G. Burgess (ed.) *Strategies of Educational Research: Qualitative Methods*, Lewes, UK: Falmer.

Burgess, R.G. (1988a) 'Conversations with a purpose: the ethnographic interview in educational research', in R.G. Burgess (ed.) *Studies in Qualitative Methodology, vol. 1, Conducting Qualitative Research*, Greenwich, CT: JAI Press.

Burgess, R.G. (ed.) (1988b), *Studies in Qualitative Methodology, vol. 1, Conducting Qualitative Research*, Greenwich, CT: JAI Press

Burke, K. (1964) *Perspectives by Incongruity*, Bloomington, IN: Indiana University Press.

Butler, T. and Robson, G. (2003) *London Calling: The Middle Classes and the Remaking of Inner London*, Oxford: Berg.

Cahill, S. (1994) 'Following Goffman, following Durkheim into the public realm', in S. Cahill and L.H. Lofland (eds) *Research in Community Sociology: Supplement 1, The Community of the Streets*, Greenwich, CT: JAI Press.

Calvey, D. (2000) 'Getting on the door and staying there', in G. Lee-Treweek and S. Linkogle (eds) *Danger in the Field: Risk and Ethics in Social Research*, London: Routledge.

Campbell, D.T. and Fiske, D.W. (1959) 'Convergent and discriminant validation by the multitrait-multimethod matrix', *Psychological Bulletin*, 56, 2: 81–105.

Campbell, J. (1992) 'Fieldwork among the Sarakatsani, 1954–5', in J. De Pina-Cabral and J. Campbell (eds) *Europe Observed*, London: Macmillan.

Cannon, S. (1992) 'Reflections on fieldwork in stressful situations', in R.G. Burgess (ed.) *Studies in Qualitative Methodology, vol. 3, Learning about Fieldwork*, Greenwich, CT: JAI Press.

Cappetti, C. (1993) *Writing Chicago: Modernism, Ethnography and the Novel*, New York: Columbia University Press.

Carey, J.T. (1972) 'Problems of access and risk in observing drug scenes', in J.D. Douglas (ed.) *Research on Deviance*, New York: Random House.

Cassell, J. (1988) 'The relationship of observer to observed when studying up', in R.G. Burgess (ed.) *Studies in Qualitative Methodology, vol. 1, Conducting Qualitative Research*, Greenwich, CT: JAI Press.

Cave, E. and Holm, S. (2003) 'Milgram and Tuskegee – paradigm research projects in bioethics', *Health Care Analysis*, 11, 1: 27–40.

Chagnon, N.A. (1997) *Yanomamö: The Fierce People*, 5th edn, Fort Worth, TX: Harcourt Brace College (first published 1968).

Chambliss, W. (1975) 'On the paucity of original research on organized crime', *American Sociologist*, 10: 36–9.

Chandler, J. (1990) 'Researching and the relevance of gender', in R.G. Burgess (ed.) *Studies in Qualitative Methodology, vol. 2, Reflections on Field Experience*, Greenwich, CT: JAI Press.

Charmaz, K. (2005) 'Grounded theory in the 21st century: a qualitative method for advancing social justice, in N.K. Denzin and Y.S. Lincoln (eds) *Handbook of Qualitative Research*, 3rd edn, Thousand Oaks, CA: Sage.

Charmaz, K. (2006) *Constructing Grounded Theory*, London: Sage.

Charmaz, K. and Mitchell, R.G. (2001) 'Grounded theory in ethnography', in P. Atkinson, A. Coffey, S. Delamont, J. Lofland and L. Lofland (eds) *Handbook of Ethnography*, London: Sage.

Chase, (2005) 'Narrative inquiry: Multiple lenses, approaches, voices', in N.K. Denzin and Y.S. Lincoln (eds) 3rd edn.

Christians, C.G. (2005) 'Ethics and politics in qualitative research', in N.K. Denzin and Y.S. Lincoln (eds) *Handbook of Qualitative Research*, 3rd edn, Thousand Oaks, CA: Sage.

Cicourel, A. (1967) *The Social Organization of Juvenile Justice*, New York: Wiley.

Cicourel, A. (1976) *The Social Organization of Juvenile Justice*, 2nd edn, London: Heinemann.

Cicourel, A. and Kitsuse, J. (1963) *The Educational Decision Makers*, New York: Bobbs-Merrill.

Clarke, A. (2005) *Situational Analysis: Grounded Theory after the Postmodern Turn*, Thousand Oaks, CA: Sage.

Clayman, S.E. and Gill, V.T. (2004) 'Conversation analysis', in M. Hardy and A. Bryman (eds) *Handbook of Data Analysis*, London: Sage.

Clifford, J. and Marcus, G. (eds) (1986) *Writing Culture: The Poetics and Politics of Ethnography*, Berkeley, CA: University of California Press.

Coffey, A.J. (1993) 'Double entry: the professional and organizational socialization of graduate accountants', unpublished PhD thesis, University of Wales College of Cardiff.

Coffey, A.J. (1994) 'Timing is everything: graduate accountants, time and organizational commitment', *Sociology*, 28, 4: 957–74.

Coffey, A.J. (1999) *The Ethnographic Self*, Thousand Oaks, CA: Sage.

Coffey, A., Renold, E., Dicks, B. and Mason, B. (2006) 'Hypermedia ethnography in educational settings: possibilities and challenges', *Ethnography and Education*, 1, 1: 15–30.

Coffey, A.J. and Atkinson, P. (1996) *Making Sense of Qualitative Data: Complementary Research Strategies*, Thousand Oaks, CA: Sage.

Coffey, A.J. and Atkinson, P. (2004) 'Analysing documentary realities', in D. Silverman (ed.) *Qualitative Research: Theory, Method and Practice*, 2nd edn, London: Sage.

Collier, J. and Collier, M. (1986) *Visual Anthropology: Photography as a Research Method*, revised edn, Albuquerque, NM: University of New Mexico Press.

Connerton, P. (1989) *How Societies Remember*, Cambridge: Cambridge University Press.

Cook-Gumperz, J. (ed.) (2006) *The Social Construction of Literacy*, 2nd edn, Cambridge: Cambridge University Press.

Cooper, B. and Dunne, M. (2000) *Assessing Children's Mathematical Knowledge: Social Class, Sex and Problem-Solving*, Maidenhead: Open University Press.

Corsaro, W.A. (1981) 'Entering the child's world – research strategies for field entry and data collection in a preschool setting', in J.L. Green and C. Wallat (eds) *Ethnography and Language in Educational Settings*, Norwood, NJ: Ablex.

Corsino, L. (1984) 'Underinvolvement and dynamics of personality: notes on bias in field research situations', unpublished manuscript. (Adapted from 'The making of a campaign organization', doctoral dissertation, University of Massachusetts, Amherst, 1978.)

Cortazzi, M. (2001) 'Narrative analysis in ethnography', in P. Atkinson, A. Coffey, S. Delamont, J. Lofland and L. Lofland (eds) *Handbook of Ethnography*, London: Sage.

Cox, A., Cox, C., Brandon, D. and Scott, D. (1978) 'The social worker, the client, the social anthropologist and the "new honesty"', occasional paper, Youth Development Trust, c/o Duncan Scott, Department of Social Administration, University of Manchester.

Coxon, A.P.M. (1988) 'Something sensational . . .: the sexual diary as a tool for mapping detailed sexual behaviour', *Sociological Review*, 36, 2: 353–67.

Coxon, A.P.M. (1996) *Between the Sheets: Sexual Diaries and Gay Men's Sex in the Era of AIDS*, London: Cassell.

Cressey, D. (1950) 'The criminal violation of financial trust', *American Sociological Review*, 15: 738–43.

Crow, G., Wiles, R., Heath, S. and Charles, V. (2006) 'Research ethics and data quality: the implications of informed consent', *International Journal of Social Research Methodology*, 9, 2: 83–95.

Crowley, D. and Reid, S.E. (eds) (2002) *Socialist Spaces: Sites of Everyday Life in the Eastern Bloc*, Oxford: Berg.

Currer, C. (1992) 'Strangers or sisters? An exploration of familiarity, strangeness, and power in research', in R.G. Burgess (ed.) *Studies in Qualitative Methodology, vol. 3, Learning about Fieldwork*, Greenwich, CT: JAI Press.

Curtis, J.E. and Petras, J.W. (eds) (1970) *The Sociology of Knowledge*, London: Duckworth.

Czarniawska, B. (2004) 'The uses of narrative in social science research', in M. Hardy and A. Bryman (eds) *Handbook of Data Analysis*, London: Sage.

Dalton, M. (1959) *Men Who Manage: Fusions of Feeling and Theory in Administration*, New York: Wiley.

Darbyshire, P., MacDougall, C. and Schiller, W. (2005) 'Multiple methods in qualitative research with children: more insight or just more?', *Qualitative Research*, 5, 4: 417–36.

Davies, M. and Kelly, E. (1976) 'The social worker, the client, and the social anthropologist', *British Journal of Social Work*, 6, 2: 213–31.

Davies, R.M. and Atkinson, P.A. (1991) 'Students of midwifery: "Doing the obs" and other coping strategies', *Midwifery*, 7: 113–21.

Davis, F. (1959) 'The cabdriver and his fare: facets of a fleeting relationship', *American Journal of Sociology*, 65, 2: 158–65.

Davis, F. (1961a) 'Comment on "Initial interactions of newcomers in Alcoholics Anonymous"', *Social Problems*, 8: 364–5.

Davis, F. (1961b) 'Deviance disavowal: the management of strained interaction by the visibly handicapped', *Social Problems*, 1: 120–32.

Davis, F. (1974) 'Stories and sociology', *Urban Life and Culture*, 3, 3: 310–16.

Dean, J.P., Eichorn, R.I. and Dean, L.R. (1967) 'Fruitful informants for intensive interviewing', in J.T. Doby (ed.) *An Introduction to Social Research*, 2nd edn, New York: Appleton-Century-Crofts,.

Deegan, M.J. (2001) 'The Chicago School of ethnography', in P. Atkinson, A. Coffey, S. Delamont, J. Lofland and L. Lofland (eds) *Handbook of Ethnography*, London: Sage.

Delamont, S. (1984) 'The old girl network: reflections on the fieldwork at St Luke's', in R.G. Burgess (ed.) *The Research Process in Educational Settings*, Lewes, UK: Falmer.

Delamont, S. (2004a) 'Leaving the dim-moon city of delight: terminating your fieldwork', in C. Pole (ed.) *Fieldwork*, 4 vols, London: Sage.

Delamont, S. (2004b) 'Participant observation', in C. Seale, G. Gobo, J.F. Gubrium and D. Silverman (eds) *Qualitative Research Practice*, London: Sage.

Delamont, S. and Atkinson, P.A. (1995) *Fighting Familiarity*, Cresskill, NJ: Hampton.

Delamont, S. and Atkinson, P. (2004) 'Qualitative research and the postmodern turn', in M. Hardy and A. Bryman (eds) *Handbook of Data Analysis*, London: Sage.

Den Hollander, A.N.J. (1967) 'Social description: problems of reliability and validity', in D.G. Jongmans and P.C.W. Gutkind (eds) *Anthropologists in the Field*, Assen, Netherlands: Van Gorcum.

Denzin, N.K. (1970) *The Research Act in Sociology: A Theoretical Introduction to Sociological Method*, 1st edn, Chicago, IL: Aldine.

Denzin, N.K. (1971) 'The logic of naturalistic inquiry', *Social Forces*, 50: 166–82.

Denzin, N.K. (1989) *The Research Act: A Theoretical Introduction to Sociological Methods*, 3rd edn, Englewood Cliffs, NJ: Prentice Hall.

Denzin, N.K. (1997) *Interpretive Ethnography: Ethnographic Practices for the 21st Century*, Thousand Oaks, CA: Sage.

Denzin, N.K. (2003) *Performance Ethnography: Critical Pedagogy and the Politics of Culture*, Thousand Oaks, CA: Sage.

Denzin, N.K. (2005) 'Emancipatory discourses and the ethics and politics of interpretation', in N.K. Denzin and Y.S. Lincoln (eds) *Handbook of Qualitative Research*, 3rd edn, Thousand Oaks, CA: Sage.

Denzin, N.K. and Giardina, M.D. (eds) (2006) *Qualitative Inquiry and the Conservative Challenge*, Walnut Creek, CA: Left Coast Press.

Denzin, N.K. and Lincoln, Y.S. (eds) (2005) *Handbook of Qualitative Research*, 3rd edn, Thousand Oaks, CA: Sage.

Derrida, J. (1976) *Of Grammatology*, Baltimore, MD: Johns Hopkins University Press (first published in French in 1967).

Devault, M.L. (1990) 'Women write sociology: rhetorical strategies', in A. Hunter (ed.) *The Rhetoric of Social Research: Understood and Believed*, New Brunswick, NJ: Rutgers University Press.

Dews, P. (1987) *Logics of Disintegration: Post-Structuralist Thought and the Claims of Critical Theory*, London: Verso.

Dexter, L. (1970) *Elite and Specialized Interviewing*, Evanston, IL: Northwestern University Press.

Dey, I. (1993) *Qualitative Data Analysis: A User-Friendly Guide for Social Scientists*, London: Routledge.

Dey, I. (1999) *Grounding Grounded Theory: Guidelines for Qualitative Inquiry*, San Diego, CA: Academic Press.

Dey, I. (2004) 'Grounded theory', in C. Seale, G. Gobo, J.F. Gubrium and D. Silverman (eds) *Qualitative Research Practice*, London: Sage.

Dicks, B., Mason, B., Coffey, A. and Atkinson, P. (2005) *Qualitative Research and Hypermedia: Ethnography for the Digital Age*, London: Sage.

Diener, E. and Crandall, R. (1978) *Ethics in Social and Behavioral Research*, Chicago, IL: University of Chicago Press.

Dingwall, R. (1977a) 'Atrocity stories and professional relationships', *Sociology of Work and Occupations*, 4, 4: 371–96.

Dingwall, R. (1977b) *The Social Organization of Health Visitor Training*, London: Croom Helm.

Ditton, J. (1977) *Part Time Crime: An Ethnography of Fiddling and Pilferage*, London: Macmillan.

Dodds, G. and Tavernor, R. (2001) *Body and Building: Essays on the Changing Relation of the Body and Architecture*, Cambridge, MA: MIT Press.

Dodge, M. and Geis, G. (2002) 'Fieldwork with the elite: interviewing white-collar criminals', in T. May (ed.) *Qualitative Research in Action*, London: Sage.

Dorst, J.D. (1989) *The Written Suburb: An Ethnographic Dilemma*, Philadelphia, PA: University of Pennsylvania Press.

Dostal, J. (ed.) (2002) *The Cambridge Companion to Gadamer*, Cambridge: Cambridge University Press.

Dotzler, H. (1995) 'Using software for interpretive text analysis: results from interviews with research teams', paper presented at *SoftStat '95: Eighth Conference on the Scientific Use of Statistical Software*, Heidelberg, Germany, 26–30 March.

Douglas, J.D. (1967) *The Social Meanings of Suicide*, Princeton, NJ: Princeton University Press.

Douglas, J.D. (1976) *Investigative Social Research*, Beverly Hills, CA: Sage.

Dumit, J. (2004) *Picturing Personhood: Brain Scans and Biomedical Identity*, Princeton, NJ: Princeton University Press.

Easterday, L., Papademas, D., Schorr, L. and Valentine, C. (1977) 'The making of a female researcher', *Urban Life*, 6, 3: 333–48.

Economic and Social Research Council (ESRC) (2005) *Research Ethics Framework*, available at: http://www.esrcsocietytoday.ac.uk/ESRCInfoCentre/Images/ESRC_Re_Ethics_Frame_tcm 611291.pdf

Edensor, T. (1998) *Tourists at the Taj: Performance and Meaning at a Symbolic Site*, London: Routledge.

Edgerton, R.B. (1965) 'Some dimensions of disillusionment in culture contact', *Southwestern Journal of Anthropology*, 21: 231–43.

Ellis, C. and Bochner, A. (eds) (1996) *Composing Ethnography*, Walnut Creek, CA: AltaMira.

Ellis, C. and Bochner, A. (2000) 'Autoethnography, personal narrative, reflexivity: researcher as subject', in N.K. Denzin and Y.S. Lincoln (eds) *Handbook of Qualitative Research*, 2nd edn, Thousand Oaks, CA: Sage.

Emerson, R.M., Fretz, R.I. and Shaw, L.L. (eds) (1995) *Writing Ethnographic Fieldnotes*, Chicago, IL: University of Chicago Press.

Emerson, R.M. and Pollner, M. (1988) 'On the use of members' responses to researchers' accounts', *Human Organization*, 47: 189–98.

Emmison, M. and Smith, P. (2000) *Researching the Visual*, London: Sage.

English-Lueck, J.A. (2002) *Cultures @ Silicon Valley*, Stanford, CA: Stanford University Press.

Epstein, D. (1998) 'Are you a girl or are you a teacher? The "least adult" role in research about gender and sexuality in a primary school', in G. Walford (ed.) *Doing Research about Education*, London: Falmer.

Erben, M. (1993) 'The problem of other lives: social perspectives on written biography', *Sociology*, 27, 1: 15–25,

Erickson, K.T. (1967) 'A comment on disguised observation in sociology', *Social Problems*, 14, 4: 366–7.

Erzberger, C. and Kelle, U. (2003) 'Making inferences in mixed methods: the rules of integration', in A. Tashakkori and C. Teddlie (eds) *Handbook of Mixed Methods in Social and Behavioral Research*, Thousand Oaks, CA: Sage.

Evans, A.D. (1991) 'Maintaining relationships in a school for the deaf', in W.B. Shaffir and R.A. Stebbins (eds) *Experiencing Fieldwork: An Inside View of Qualitative Research*, Newbury Park, CA: Sage.

Evans, M. (1993) 'Reading lives: how the personal might be social', *Sociology*, 27, 1: 5–13.

Evans-Pritchard, E.E. (1937) *Witchcraft, Oracles and Magic among the Azande*, Oxford: Clarendon Press.

Everhart, R.B. (1977) 'Between stranger and friend: some consequences of "long term" fieldwork in schools', *American Educational Research Journal*, 14, 1: 1–15.

Fardon, R. (ed.) (1990) *Localising Strategies: Regional Traditions of Ethnographic Writing*, Edinburgh: Scottish Academic Press.

Farrell, A. (ed.) (2005) *Ethical Research with Children*, Maidenhead: Open University Press.

Feldman, M.S., Bell, J. and Berger, M.T. (2003) *Gaining Access: A Practical and Theoretical Guide for Qualitative Researchers*, Walnut Creek, CA: AltaMira.

Fenton, N., Bryman, A., Deacon, D. with Birmingham, P. (1998) *Mediating Social Science*, London: Sage.

Ferrell, J. and Hamm, M.S. (eds) (1998) *Ethnography at the Edge: Crime, Deviance and Field Research*, Boston, MA: Northeastern University Press.

Festinger, L., Riecken, H. and Schachter, S. (1956) *When Prophecy Fails*, St Paul, MN: University of Minnesota Press. Republished 1964, London: Harper & Row.

Fetterman, D. (ed.) (1984) *Ethnography in Educational Evaluation*, Beverly Hills, CA: Sage.

Fetterman, D. and Pittman, M. (eds) (1986) *Educational Evaluation: Ethnography in Theory, Practice and Politics*, Beverly Hills, CA: Sage.

Fielding, N. (1982) 'Observational research on the National Front', in M. Bulmer (ed.) *Social Research Ethics: An Examination of the Merits of Covert Participant Observation*, London: Macmillan.

Fielding, N. (ed.) (2003) *Interviewing*, 4 vols, London: Sage.

Fielding, N. and Fielding, J.L. (1986) *Linking Data*, Newbury Park, CA: Sage.

Finch, J. (1984) '"It's great to have someone to talk to": the ethics and politics of interviewing women', in C. Bell and H. Roberts (eds) *Social Researching: Politics, Problems and Practice*, London: Routledge & Kegan Paul.

Fine, G.A. (1993) 'Ten lies of ethnographers: moral dilemmas in fieldwork', *Journal of Contemporary Ethnography*, 22, 3: 267–94.

Fine, G.A. and Sandstrom, K.L. (1988) *Knowing Children: Participant Observation with Minors*, Newbury Park, CA: Sage.

Finlay, L. (2002) 'Negotiating the swamp: the operation and challenge of reflexivity in research practice', *Qualitative Research*, 2, 2: 209–30.

Finn, C.A. (2001) *An Archaeologist's Year in Silicon Valley*, Cambridge, MA: MIT Press.

Flick, U. (2004) 'Triangulation in qualitative research', in U. Flick, E. von Kardoff and I. Steinke (eds) *A Companion to Qualitative Research*, London: Sage.

Fonow, M.M. and Cook, J.A. (eds) (1991) *Beyond Methodology: Feminist Scholarship as Lived Research*, Bloomington, IN: Indiana University Press.

Fowler, D.D. and Hardesty, D.L. (1994) 'Introduction', in D.D. Fowler and D.L. Hardesty (eds) *Others Knowing Others: Perspectives on Ethnographic Careers*, Washington, DC: Smithsonian Institution Press.

Fox, R.C. (1964) 'An American sociologist in the land of Belgian medical research', in R.E. Hammond (ed.) *Sociologists at Work: Essays on the Craft of Social Research*, New York: Basic Books.

Franklin, K.K. and Lowry, C. (2001) 'Computer-mediated focus group sessions: naturalistic inquiry in a networked environment', *Qualitative Research*, 1, 2: 169–84.

Franzosi, R.P. (2004) 'Content analysis', in M. Hardy and A. Bryman (eds) *Handbook of Data Analysis*, London: Sage.

Freidson, E. (1964) 'Against the code of ethics', *American Sociological Review*, 29, 3: 410.

Freilich, M. (ed.) (1970a) *Marginal Natives: Anthropologists at Work*, New York: Harper & Row.

Freilich, M. (1970b) 'Mohawk heroes and Trinidadian peasants', in M. Freilich (ed.) *Marginal Natives: Anthropologists at Work*, New York: Harper & Row.

Friedman, M. (1991) 'The re-evaluation of logical positivism', *Journal of Philosophy*, 88, 10: 505–19.

Frosh, P. (2003) *The Image Factory: Consumer Culture, Photography and the Visual Content Industry*, Oxford: Berg.

Frosh, P., Phoenix, A. and Pattman, R. (2002) *Young Masculinities: Understanding Boys in Contemporary Society*, Basingstoke: Palgrave.

Gaiman, D. (1977) 'Appendix: a scientologist's comment', in C. Bell and H. Newby (eds) *Doing Sociological Research*, London: Allen & Unwin.

Gallmeier, C.P. (1991) 'Leaving, revisiting, and staying in touch: neglected issues in field research', in W.B. Shaffir and R.A. Stebbins (eds) *Experiencing Fieldwork: An Inside View of Qualitative Research*, Newbury Park, CA: Sage.

Gamst, F.C. (1980) *The Hoghead: An Industrial Ethnology of the Locomotive Engineer*, New York: Holt, Rinehart & Winston.

Garfinkel, H. (1967) *Studies in Ethnomethodology*, Englewood Cliffs, NJ: Prentice Hall.

Gatson, S.N. and Zweerink, A. (2004) 'Ethnography online: "natives" practising and inscribing community', *Qualitative Research*, 4, 2: 179–200.

Gee, J.P. (1996) *Social Linguistics and Literacies: Ideology in Discourse*, 2nd edn, London: Taylor & Francis.

Geer, B. (1964) 'First days in the field', in R.E. Hammond (ed.) *Sociologists at Work: Essays on the Craft of Social Research*, New York: Basic Books.

Geer, B. (1970) 'Studying a college', in R. Habenstein (ed.) *Pathways to Data*, Chicago, IL: Aldine.

George, V. and Dundes, A. (1978) 'The gomer: a figure of American hospital folk speech', *Journal of American Folklore*, 91, 359: 568–81.

Gewirtz, S. and Cribb, A. (2006) 'What to do about values in social research: the case for ethical reflexivity in the sociology of education', *British Journal of Sociology of Education*, 27, 2: 141–55.

Giallombardo, R. (1966) 'Social roles in a prison for women', *Social Problems*, 13: 268–88.

Gilbert, N. and Mulkay, M. (1984) *Opening Pandora's Box*, Cambridge: Cambridge University Press.

Gitlin, A.D., Siegel, M. and Boru, K. (1989) 'The politics of method: from leftist ethnography to educative research', *Qualitative Studies in Education*, 2, 3: 237–53,

Glaser, B. (1978) *Theoretical Sensitivity*, San Francisco, CA: Sociology Press.

Glaser, B. (1992) *Emergence Versus Forcing: Basics of Grounded Theory Analysis*, Mill Valley, CA: Sociology Press.

Glaser, B. (ed.) (1993) *Examples of Grounded Theory: A Reader*, Mill Valley, CA: Sociology Press.

Glaser, B. and Strauss, A. (1964) 'Awareness contexts and social interaction', *American Sociological Review*, 29: 669–79.

Glaser, B. and Strauss, A. (1967) *The Discovery of Grounded Theory: Strategies for Qualitative Research*, Chicago, IL: Aldine.

Glaser, B. and Strauss, A. (1968) *Time for Dying*, Chicago, IL: Aldine.

Glaser, B. and Strauss, A. (1971) *Status Passage*, Chicago, IL: Aldine.

Goffman, E. (1955) 'On face-work: an analysis of ritual elements in social interaction', *Psychiatry*, 18, 3: 213–31.

Goffman, E. (1959) *The Presentation of Self in Everyday Life*, New York: Doubleday.

Goffman, E. (1961) *Asylums: Essays on the Social Situation of Mental Patients and Other Inmates*, New York: Doubleday.

Goffman, E. (1963) *Behavior in Public Places*, Glencoe, IL: Free Press.

Goffman, E. (1971) *Relations in Public: Micro Studies of the Public Order*, New York: Basic Books.

Goffman, E. (1972) *Interaction Ritual*, Harmondsworth: Penguin.

Gold, R. (1958) 'Roles in sociological fieldwork', *Social Forces*, 36: 217 23.

Golde, P. (ed.) (1986) *Women in the Field: Anthropological Experiences*, 2nd edn, Berkeley, CA: University of California Press.

Goode, E. (1996) 'The ethics of deception in social research: a case study', *Qualitative Sociology*, 10, 1: 11–33.

Goode, E. (1999) 'Sex with informants as deviant behavior: an account and commentary', *Deviant Behavior*, 20: 301–24.

Goode, E. (2002) 'Sexual involvement and social research in a fat civil rights organization', *Qualitative Sociology*, 25: 501–34.

Goodwin, C. (1981) *Conversational Organization: Interaction between Speakers and Hearers*, New York: Academic Press.

Goodwin, C. (2001) 'Practices of seeing, visual analysis: an ethnomethodological approach', in T. van Leeuwen and C. Jewitt (eds) *Handbook of Visual Analysis*, London: Sage.

Goody, J. (ed.) (1968) *Literacy in Traditional Societies*, Cambridge: Cambridge University Press.

Goody, J. (1986) *The Logic of Writing and the Organization of Society*, Cambridge: Cambridge University Press.

Goody, J. (1987) *The Interface between the Written and the Oral*, Cambridge: Cambridge University Press.

Gouldner, A.W. (1954) *Patterns of Industrial Bureaucracy*, New York: Free Press.

Gouldner, A.W. (1968) 'The sociologist as partisan', *American Sociologist*, May: 103–16.

Graham, L. (1995) *On the Line at Subaru-Isuzu: The Japanese Model and the American Worker*, Ithaca, NY: ILR Press.

Grave, M.E. and Walsh, D.J. (1998) *Studying Children in Context: Theories, Methods and Ethics*, Thousand Oaks, CA: Sage.

Gregor, T. (1977) *Mehinaku: The Drama of Daily Life in a Brazilian Indian Village*, Chicago, IL: University of Chicago Press.

Gregory, F. M. (2003) 'The fabric or the building? Influences on homeowner investment', unpublished PhD thesis, Cardiff University.

Gregory, R. (1970) *The Intelligent Eye*, London: Weidenfeld & Nicolson.

Griffin, C. (1991) 'The researcher talks back: dealing with power relations in studies of young people's entry into the job market', in W.B. Shaffir and R.A. Stebbins (eds) *Experiencing Fieldwork: An Inside View of Qualitative Research*, Newbury Park, CA: Sage.

Guba, E. (1978) *Toward a Methodology of Naturalistic Inquiry in Educational Evaluation*, Los Angeles, CA: Center for the Study of Evaluation, UCLA Graduate School of Education.

Guba, E. (ed.) (1990) *The Paradigm Dialog*, Newbury Park, CA: Sage.

Gubrium, J.F. and Holstein, J.A. (1997) *The New Language of Qualitative Method*, New York: Oxford University Press.

Gubrium, J.F. and Holstein, J.A. (eds) (2002) *Handbook of Interview Research: Context and Method*, Thousand Oaks, CA: Sage.

Gubrium, J. and Silverman, D. (eds) (1989) *The Politics of Field Research: Beyond Enlightenment*, Newbury Park, CA: Sage.

Gupta, A. (2005) 'Narratives of corruption: anthropological and fictional accounts of the Indian state', *Ethnography*, 6, 1: 5–34.

Gurney, J.N. (1991) 'Female researchers in male-dominated settings: implications for short-term versus long-term research', in W.B. Shaffir and R.A. Stebbins (eds) *Experiencing Fieldwork: An Inside View of Qualitative Research*, Newbury Park, CA: Sage.

Gutting, G. (1989) *Michel Foucault's Archaeology of Scientific Reason*, Cambridge: Cambridge University Press.

Gutting, G. (ed.) (1994) *The Cambridge Companion to Foucault*, Cambridge: Cambridge University Press.

Gutting, G. (2001) *French Philosophy in the Twentieth Century*, Cambridge: Cambridge University Press.

Haack, S. (1993) *Evidence and Inquiry: Towards a Reconstruction in Epistemology*, Oxford: Blackwell.

Hafferty, F.W. (1988) 'Cadaver stories and the emotional socialisation of medical students', *Journal of Health and Social Behavior*, 29: 344–56.

Hage, J. and Meeker, B.F. (1988) *Social Causality*, Boston, MA: Unwin Hyman.

Halfpenny, P. (1982) *Positivism and Sociology*, London: Allen & Unwin.

Hammersley, M. (1980) 'A peculiar world? Teaching and learning in an inner city school', unpublished PhD thesis, University of Manchester.

Hammersley, M. (1981) 'Ideology in the staffroom? A critique of false consciousness', in L. Barton and S. Walker (eds) *Schools, Teachers and Teaching*, Lewes, UK: Falmer.

Hammersley, M. (1984a) 'Some reflections on the macro-micro problem in the sociology of education', *Sociological Review*, 32, 2: 316–24.

Hammersley, M. (1984b) 'The researcher exposed: a natural history', in R.G. Burgess (ed.) *The Research Process in Educational Settings*, Lewes, UK: Falmer.

Hammersley, M. (1985) 'From ethnography to theory: a programme and paradigm for case study research in the sociology of education', *Sociology*, 19, 2: 244–59.

Hammersley, M. (1987a) 'Ethnography and the cumulative development of theory', *British Educational Research Journal*, 13, 3: 73–81.

Hammersley, M. (1987b) 'Ethnography for survival?', *British Educational Research Journal*, 13, 3: 283–95.

Hammersley, M. (1989a) *The Dilemma of Qualitative Method: Herbert Blumer and the Chicago Tradition*, London: Routledge.

Hammersley, M. (1989b) 'The problem of the concept: Herbert Blumer on the relationship between concepts and data', *Journal of Contemporary Ethnography*, 18, 2: 133–59.

Hammersley, M. (1990) *Classroom Ethnography: Empirical and Methodological Essays*, Milton Keynes: Open University Press.

Hammersley, M. (1991) 'Staffroom news', reprinted as an appendix in M. Hammersley (1998) *Reading Ethnographic Research: A Critical Guide*, 2nd edn, London: Longman.

Hammersley, M. (1992) *What's Wrong with Ethnography?*, London: Routledge.

Hammersley, M. (1993) 'The rhetorical turn in ethnography', *Social Science Information*, 32, 1: 23–37. Reprinted in C. Pole (ed.) *Fieldwork*, vol. 4, London: Sage.

Hammersley, M. (1995) *The Politics of Social Research*, London: Sage.

Hammersley, M. (1998) *Reading Ethnographic Research: A Critical Guide*, 2nd edn, London: Longman.

Hammersley, M. (2000) *Taking Sides in Social Research: Essays on Partisanship and Bias*, London: Routledge.

Hammersley, M. (2002) *Educational Research, Policymaking and Practice*, London: Paul Chapman.

Hammersley, M. (2003a) 'Analytics are no substitute for methodology: a response to Speer and Hutchby', *Sociology*, 37, 2: 339–51.

Hammersley, M. (2003b) *Guide to Natural Histories of Research*. Available at: http://www.cf.ac.uk/socsi/capacity/Activities/Themes/Expertise/guide.pdf

Hammersley, M. (2003c) 'Recent radical criticism of interview studies: any implications for the sociology of education?', *British Journal of Sociology of Education*, 24, 1: 119–26.

Hammersley, M. (2004) 'Get real! A defence of realism', in H. Piper and I. Stronach (eds) *Educational Research: Difference and Diversity*, Aldershot, UK: Ashgate.

Hammersley, M. (2005a) 'Ethnography, toleration and authenticity: ethical reflections on fieldwork, analysis and writing', in G. Troman, B. Jeffrey and G. Walford (eds) *Methodological Issues and Practices in Ethnography*, Amsterdam: Elsevier.

Hammersley, M. (2005b) 'What can the literature on communities of practice tell us about educational research? Reflections on some recent proposals', *International Journal of Research and Method in Education*, 28, 1: 5–21.

Hammersley, M. (2006a) 'Are ethics committees ethical?', *Qualitative Researcher* 2, spring. Available at: http://www.cardiff.ac.uk/socsi/qualiti/QR_Issue2_06.pdf

Hammersley, M. (2006b) *Media Bias in Reporting Social Research? The Case of Reviewing Ethnic Inequalities in Education*, London: Routledge.

Hammersley, M. (2007a) 'Against the ethicists!', unpublished paper.

Hammersley, M. (2007b) 'Troubles with triangulation', in M. Bergman (ed.) *Advances in Mixed Methods Research: Theories and Applications*, London, Sage.

Hammersley, M. and Treseder, P. (2007) 'Identity as an analytic problem: who's who in 'pro-ana' web-sites?', *Qualitative Research*, 7, 3.

Haney, L. (2002) 'Negotiating power and expertise in the field', in T. May (ed.) *Qualitative Research in Action*, London: Sage.

Hannerz, U. (1969) *Soulside*, New York: Columbia University Press.

Hannerz, U. (2003) 'Being there . . . and there . . . and there! Reflections on multi-site ethnography', *Ethnography*, 4, 2: 201–16.

Hansen, E.C. (1977) *Rural Catalonia under the Franco Regime*, Cambridge: Cambridge University Press.

Hanson, N.R. (1958) *Patterns of Discovery*, London: Cambridge University Press.

Hargreaves, A. (1981) 'Contrastive rhetoric and extremist talk: teachers, hegemony and the educationist context', in L. Barton and S. Walker (eds) *Schools, Teachers and Teaching*, Lewes, UK: Falmer.

Hargreaves, D. (1967) *Social Relations in a Secondary School*, London: Routledge & Kegan Paul.

Hargreaves, D. (1977) 'The process of typification in the classroom: models and methods', *British Journal of Educational Psychology*, 47: 274–84.

Hargreaves, D., Hester, S. and Mellor, F. (1975) *Deviance in Classrooms*, London: Routledge & Kegan Paul.

Harper, D. (1993) 'On the authority of the image: visual sociology at the crossroads', in N.K. Denzin and Y.S. Lincoln (eds) *Handbook of Qualitative Research*, 1st edn, Thousand Oaks, CA: Sage.

Harper, D. (2000) 'Reimagining visual methods: Galileo to *Necromancer*', in N.K. Denzin and Y.S. Lincoln (eds) *Handbook of Qualitative Research*, 2nd edn, Thousand Oaks, CA: Sage.

Harper, D. (2006) 'What's new visually?', in N.K. Denzin and Y.S. Lincoln (eds) *Handbook of Qualitative Research*, 3rd edn, Thousand Oaks, CA: Sage.

Harris, M. (1979) *Cultural Materialism: The Struggle for a Science of Culture*, New York: Random House.

Hart, E. and Bond, M. (1995) *Action Research for Health and Social Care*, Buckingham: Open University Press.

Hartnett, S.J. and Engels, J.D. (2005) '"Aria in time of war": investigative poetry and the politics of witnessing', in N.K. Denzin and Y.S. Lincoln (eds) *Handbook of Qualitative Research*, 3rd edn, Thousand Oaks, CA: Sage.

Harvey, L. (1985) *Myths of the Chicago School*, Aldershot, UK: Gower.

Hastrup, K. and Elsass, P. (1990) 'Anthropological advocacy: a contradiction in terms?', *Current Anthropology*, 31, 3: 301–11.

Healy, K. (2001) 'Participatory action research and social work: a critical appraisal', *International Social Work*, 44, 1: 93–105.

Heath, C. (1981) 'The opening sequence in doctor-patient interaction', in P. Atkinson and C. Heath (eds) *Medical Work: Realities and Routines*, Farnborough, UK: Gower.

Heath, C. (1997) 'The analysis of activities in face to face interaction using video', in D. Silverman (ed.) *Qualitative Research: Theory, Method and Practice*, London: Sage.

Heath, C. (2004) 'Analysing face-to-face interaction: video, the visual and material', in D. Silverman (ed.) *Qualitative Research: Theory, Method and Practice*, 2nd edn, London: Sage.

Heath, C. and Hindmarsh, J. (2002) 'Analysing interaction: video, ethnography and situated conduct', in T. May (ed.) *Qualitative Research in Action*, London: Sage.

Heath, C. and Luff, P. (2000) *Technology in Action*, Cambridge: Cambridge University Press.

Hempel, C.G. (1966) *Philosophy of Natural Science*, Englewood Cliffs, NJ: Prentice Hall.

Henderson, K. (1998) *On Line and on Paper: Visual Representations, Visual Culture, and Computer Graphics in Design Engineering*, Cambridge: MA: MIT Press.

Henslin, J.M. (1990) 'It's not a lovely place to visit, and I wouldn't want to live there', in R.G. Burgess (ed.) *Studies in Qualitative Methodology, vol. 2, Reflections on Field Experience*, Greenwich, CT: JAI Press.

Herzfeld, M. (1985) *The Poetics of Manhood: Contest and Identity in a Cretan Mountain Village*, Princeton, NJ: Princeton University Press.

Herzfeld, M. (2004) *The Body Impolitic: Artisans and Artifice in the Global Hierarchy of Value*, Chicago, IL: University of Chicago Press.

Herzog, H. (2005) 'On home turf: interview location and its social meaning', *Qualitative Sociology*, 28, 1: 25–48.

Hess, D. (2001) 'Ethnography and the development of science and technology studies', in P. Atkinson, A. Coffey, S. Delamont, J. Lofland and L. Lofland (eds) *Handbook of Ethnography*, London: Sage.

Hewitt, J.P. and Stokes, R. (1976) 'Aligning actions', *American Sociological Review*, 41: 838–49.

Hey, V. (1997) *The Company She Keeps: An Ethnography of Girls' Friendships*, Buckingham: Open University Press.

Hine, C. (2000) *Virtual Ethnography*, London: Sage.

Hine, C. (ed.) (2005) *Virtual Methods: Issues in Social Research on the Internet*, Oxford: Berg.

Hitchcock, C. (1983) 'Fieldwork as practical activity: reflections on fieldwork and the social organization of an urban, open-plan primary school', in M. Hammersley (ed.) *The Ethnography of Schooling: Methodological Issues*, Driffield, UK: Nafferton.

Hobbs, D. (1988) *Doing the Business*, Oxford: Oxford University Press.

Hodkinson, P. (2004) 'Research as a form of work: expertise, community, and methodological objectivity', *British Educational Research Journal*, 30, 1: 9–26.

Hoffman, J.E. (1980) 'Problems of access in the study of social elites and boards of directors', in W.B. Shaffir, R.A. Stebbins and A. Turowetz (eds) *Fieldwork Experience: Qualitative Approaches to Social Research*, New York: St Martin's Press.

Holdaway, S. (1982) '"An inside job": a case study of covert research on the police', in M. Bulmer (ed.) *Social Research Ethics: An Examination of the Merits of Covert Participant Observation*, London: Macmillan.

Holdaway, S. (1983) *Inside the British Police: A Force at Work*, Oxford: Blackwell.

Holman Jones, S. (2005) 'Autoethnography: making the personal political', in N.K. Denzin and Y.S. Lincoln (eds) *Handbook of Qualitative Research*, 3rd edn, Thousand Oaks, CA: Sage.

Holstein, J.A. and Gubrium, J.F. (1995) *The Active Interview*, Thousand Oaks, CA: Sage.

Holstein, J.A. and Miller, G. (eds) (1989) *Perspectives on Social Problems*, vol. 1, Greenwich, CT: JAI Press.

Holstein, J.A. and Miller, G. (eds) (1993) *Reconsidering Social Constructionism: Debates in Social Problems Theory*, New York: Aldine de Gruyter.

Homan, R. (1978) 'Interpersonal communications in pentecostal meetings', *Sociological Review*, 26, 3: 499–518.

Homan, R. (1980) 'The ethics of covert methods', *British Journal of Sociology*, 31, 1: 46–59.

Homan, R. (1991) *The Ethics of Social Research*, London: Longman.

Homan, R. and Bulmer, M. (1982) 'On the merits of covert methods: a dialogue', in M. Bulmer (ed.) *Social Research Ethics: An Examination of the Merits of Covert Participant Observation*, London: Macmillan.

Howard, R.J. (1982) *Three Faces of Hermeneutics*, Berkeley, CA: University of California Press.

Howarth, C. (2002) 'Using the theory of social representations to explore difference in the research relationship', *Qualitative Research*, 2, 1: 21–34.

Hudson, C. (2004) 'Reducing inequalities in field relations: who gets the power?', in B. Jeffrey and G. Walford (eds) *Ethnographies of Educational and Cultural Conflicts: Strategies and Resolutions*, Amsterdam: Elsevier.

Hughes, C. (ed.) (2003) *Disseminating Qualitative Research in Educational Settings*, Maidenhead, Open University Press.

Hughes-Freeland, F. (ed.) (1998) *Ritual, Performance, Media*, London: Routledge.

Humphreys, L. (1970) *Tearoom Trade*, Chicago, IL: Aldine.

Hunt, L. (1984) 'The development of rapport through the negotiation of gender in fieldwork among the police', *Human Organization*, 43: 283–96.

Hunter, A. (1993) 'Local knowledge and local power: notes on the ethnography of local community elites', *Journal of Contemporary Ethnography*, 22, 1: 36–58.

Hurdley, R. (2006) 'Dismantling mantelpieces: narrating identities and materialising culture in the home', *Sociology*, 40, 4: 717–33.

Hurdley, R. (2007) 'Objecting relations: the problem of the gift', *Sociological Review*, 55, 1: 124–43.

Hustler, D., Cassidy, A. and Cuff, E.C. (eds) (1986) *Action Research in Classrooms and Schools*, London: Allen & Unwin.

Irwin, K. (2006) 'Into the dark heart of ethnography: the lived ethics and inequality of intimate field relationships', *Qualitative Sociology*, 29, 2, 155–75.

Jacobs, B. (2006) 'The case for dangerous fieldwork', in D. Hobbs and R. Wright (eds) *The Sage Handbook of Fieldwork*, London: Sage.

Jacobs, J.B. (1974) 'Participant observation in prison', *Urban Life and Culture*, 3, 2: 221–40.

James, N. and Busher, H. (2006) 'Credibility, authenticity and voice: dilemmas in online interviewing', *Qualitative Research*, 6, 3: 403–20.

Jenkins, D. (1980) 'An adversary's account of SAFARI's ethics of case study', in C. Richards (ed.) *Power in the Curriculum*, Driffield, UK: Nafferton.

Johnson, J. (1975) *Doing Field Research*, New York: Free Press.

Jordan, A. (2006) 'Make yourself at home: the social construction of research roles in family studies', *Qualitative Research*, 6, 2: 169–85.

Jowett, M. and O'Toole, G. (2006) 'Focusing researchers' minds: contrasting experiences of using focus groups in feminist qualitative research', *Qualitative Research*, 6, 4: 453–72

Jules-Rosette, B. (1978a) 'The veil of objectivity: prophecy, divination, and social inquiry', *American Anthropologist*, 80, 3: 549–70.

Jules-Rosette, B. (1978b) 'Towards a theory of ethnography', *Sociological Symposium*, 24: 81–98.

Julier, G. (2000) *The Culture of Design*, London: Sage.

Junker, B. (1960) *Field Work*, Chicago, IL: University of Chicago Press.

Kaplan, I.M. (1991) 'Gone fishing, be back later: ending and resuming research among fisherman', in W.B. Shaffir and R.A. Stebbins (eds) *Experiencing Fieldwork: An Inside View of Qualitative Research*, Newbury Park, CA: Sage.

Karp, D.A. (1980) 'Observing behavior in public places: problems and strategies', in W.B. Shaffir, R.A. Stebbins and A. Turowetz (eds) *Fieldwork Experience: Qualitative Approaches to Social Research*, New York: St Martin's Press.

Karp, D.A. (1993) 'Taking anti-depressant medications: resistance, trial commitment, conversion and disenchantment', *Qualitative Sociology*, 16, 4: 337–59.

Kearney, K.S. and Hyle, A.E. (2004) 'Drawing out emotions: the use of participant-produced drawings in qualitative inquiry', *Qualitative Research*, 4, 3: 361–82.

Keiser, R.I. (1970) 'Fieldwork among the Vice Lords of Chicago', in G.D. Spindler (ed.) *Being an Anthropologist*, New York: Holt, Rinehart & Winston.

Kelle, U. (2004) 'Computer-assisted qualitative data analysis', in C. Seale, G. Gobo, J.F. Gubrium and D. Silverman (eds) *Qualitative Research Practice*, London: Sage.

Kelly, A. (1985) 'Action research: what it is and what it can do', in R.G. Burgess (ed.) *Issues in Educational Research: Qualitative Methods*, Lewes, UK: Falmer.

Kemmis, S. and McTaggart, R. (2005) 'Participatory action research: communicative action in the public sphere', in N.K. Denzin and Y.S. Lincoln (eds) *Handbook of Qualitative Research*, 3rd edn, Thousand Oaks, CA: Sage.

Kendall, G. and Wickham, G. (2004) 'The Foucaultian framework', in C. Seale, G. Gobo, J.F. Gubrium and D. Silverman (eds) *Qualitative Research Practice*, London: Sage.

Kersenboom, S. (1995) *Word, Sound, Image: The Life of the Tamil Text*, Oxford: Berg.

Klukaid, H.V. and Bright, M. (1957) 'The tandem interview: a trial of the two-interviewer team', *Public Opinion Quarterly*, 21, 2: 304–12.

Klatch, R.E. (1988) 'The methodological problems of studying a politically resistant community', in R.G. Burgess (ed.) *Studies in Qualitative Methodology, vol. 1, Conducting Qualitative Research*, Greenwich, CT: JAI Press.

Knorr-Cetina, K.D. and Cicourel, A.V. (eds) (1981) *Advances in Social Theory and Methodology: Towards an Integration of Micro and Macro-Sociologies*, Boston, MA: Routledge & Kegan Paul.

Knox, C. (2001) 'Establishing research legitimacy in the contested political ground of contemporary Northern Ireland', *Qualitative Research*, 1, 2: 205–22.

Kolakowski, L. (1972) *Positivist Philosophy: From Hume to the Vienna Circle*, Harmondsworth: Penguin.

Kondo, D. (1990) *Crafting Selves*, Chicago, IL: University of Chicago Press.

Krieger, S. (1979) 'Research and the construction of a text', in N.K. Denzin (ed.) *Studies in Symbolic Interaction*, vol. 2, Greenwich, CT: JAI Press.

Krieger, S. (1983) *The Mirror Dance: Identity in a Women's Community*, Philadelphia, PA: Temple University Press.

Krippendorff, K. (1980) *Content Analysis*, Beverly Hills, CA: Sage.

Kuhn, T.S. (1996) *The Structure of Scientific Revolutions*, 3rd edn, Chicago, IL: University of Chicago Press.

Kulick, D. and Willson, M. (eds) (1995) *Taboo, Sex, Identity, and Erotic Subjectivity in Anthropological Fieldwork*, London: Routledge.

Kusow, A.M. (2003) 'Beyond indigenous authenticity: reflections on the insider/outsider debate in immigration research', *Symbolic Interaction*, 26: 591–9.

Labaree, R.V. (2002) 'The risk of "going observationalist": negotiating the hidden dilemmas of being an insider participant observer', *Qualitative Research*, 2, 1: 97–122.

Labov, W. (1969) 'The logic of nonstandard English', *Georgetown Monographs on Language and Linguistics*, 22: 1–31.

Lacey, C. (1970) *Hightown Grammar*, Manchester: Manchester University Press.

Lacey, C. (1976) 'Problems of sociological fieldwork: a review of the methodology of "Hightown Grammar"', in M. Shipman (ed.) *The Organization and Impact of Social Research*, London: Routledge & Kegan Paul.

Landes, R. (1986) 'A woman anthropologist in Brazil', in P. Golde (ed.) *Women in the Field: Anthropological Experiences*, 2nd edn, Berkeley, CA: University of California Press.

Landow G.P. (1997) *Hypertext 2.0: The Convergence of Contemporary Critical Theory and Technology*, Baltimore, MD: Johns Hopkins University Press.

Lapadat, J.C. (1999) 'Problematizing transcription: purpose, paradigm and quality', *International Journal of Social Research Methodology*, 3, 3: 203–19

Lather, P. (1986) 'Issues of validity in openly ideological research', *Interchange*, 17, 4: 63–84.

Lather, P. (1991) *Getting Smart: Feminist Research and Pedagogy with/in the Postmodern*, New York: Routledge.

Latour, B. and Woolgar, S. (1979) *Laboratory Life*, Beverly Hills, CA: Sage; republished 2nd edn, 1986, Princeton, NJ: Princeton University Press.

Lave, J. and Wenger, E. (1991) *Situated Learning: Legitimate Peripheral Participation*, Cambridge: Cambridge University Press.

Lazarsfeld, R.P., and Barton, A. (1951) 'Qualitative measurement in the social sciences: classification, typologies and indices', in D.R. Lerner and R.D. Lasswell (eds) *The Policy Sciences*, Stanford, CA: Stanford University Press.

Leach, E.R. (1957) 'The epistemological background to Malinowski's empiricism', in R. Firth (ed.) *Man and Culture: An Evaluation of the Work of Bronislaw Malinowski*, London: Routledge & Kegan Paul.

Lee, R.M. (1992) 'Nobody said it had to be easy: postgraduate field research in Northern Ireland', in R.G. Burgess (ed.) *Studies in Qualitative Methodology, vol. 3, Learning about Fieldwork*, Greenwich, CT: JAI Press.

Lee, R.M. (1995) *Dangerous Fieldwork*, Thousand Oaks, CA: Sage.

Lee, R.M. (2000) *Unobtrusive Methods in Social Research*, Buckingham: Open University Press.

Lee, R.M. and Fielding, N. (eds) (1991) *Using Computers in Qualitative Research*, London: Sage.

Lee, R.M. and Fielding, N. (1996) 'Qualitative data analysis: representations of a technology: a comment on Coffey, Holbrook and Atkinson', *Sociological Research Online*, 1, 4, http://www.socresonline.org.uk/socresonline/1/4/lf.html

Lee, R.M. and Fielding, N. (2004) 'Tools for qualitative data analysis', in M. Hardy and A. Bryman (eds) *Handbook of Data Analysis*, London: Sage.

Lee-Treweek, G. and Linkogle, S. (eds) (2000) *Danger in the Field: Risk and Ethics in Social Research*, London: Routledge.

Lehman, T. and Young, T.R. (1974) 'From conflict theory to conflict methodology: an emerging paradigm for sociology', *Sociological Quarterly*, 44, 1: 15–28.

Leigh, D. (2006) 'Scandal on tap', *Media Guardian*, 4 December, p. 1.

Lepenies, W. (1988) *Between Literature and Sociology*, Cambridge: Cambridge University Press.

LePlay, F. (1879) *Les Ouvriers Européens*, Paris: Alfred Maine et Fils.

Lerner, D. (1957) 'The "hard-headed" Frenchman: on se defend, toujours', *Encounter*, 8, March: 27–32.

Lever, J. (1981) 'Multiple methods of data collection: a note on divergence', *Urban Life*, 10, 2: 199–213.

Liebow, E. (1967) *Tally's Corner*, London: Routledge & Kegan Paul.

Lincoln, Y.S. (2005) 'Institutional review boards and methodological conservatism: the challenge to and from phenomenological paradigms', in N.K. Denzin and Y S. Lincoln (eds) *Handbook of Qualitative Research*, 3rd edn, Thousand Oaks, CA: Sage.

Lincoln, Y. S. and Guba, E. (1985) *Naturalistic Inquiry*, Beverly Hills, CA: Sage.

Lincoln, Y.S. and Guba, E. (1989) 'Ethics: the failure of positivist science', *Review of Higher Education*, 12, 3: 221–40.

Lindesmith, A. (1947) *Opiate Addiction*, Bloomington, IN: Principia Press.

Lipset, D. (1980) *Gregory Bateson: The Legacy of a Scientist*, Englewood Cliffs, NJ: Prentice Hall.

Llewellyn, M. (1980) 'Studying girls at school: the implications of confusion', in R. Deem (ed.) *Schooling for Women's Work*, London: Routledge & Kegan Paul.

Lofland, J. (1961) 'Comment on "Initial interactions of newcomers in AA"', *Social Problems*, 8: 365–7.

Lofland, J. (1967) 'Notes on naturalism', *Kansas Journal of Sociology*, 3, 2: 45–61.

Lofland, J. (1970) 'Interactionist imagery and analytic interruptus', in T. Shibutani (ed.) *Human Nature and Collective Behavior: Papers in Honor of Herbert Blumer*, Englewood Cliffs, NJ: Prentice Hall.

Lofland, J. (1971) *Analyzing Social Settings: A Guide to Qualitative Observation and Analysis*, Belmont, CA: Wadsworth.

Lofland, J. (1974) 'Styles of reporting qualitative field research', *American Sociologist*, 9, August: 101–11.

Lofland, J. (1976) *Doing Social Life: The Qualitative Study of Human Interaction in Natural Settings*, New York: Wiley.

Lofland, J. (1980) 'Early Goffman: style, structure, substance, soul', in J. Ditton (ed.) *The View from Goffinan*, London: Macmillan.

Lofland, J. and Lejeune, R.A. (1960) 'Initial interactions of newcomers in Alcoholics Anonymous', *Social Problems*, 8: 102–11.

Lofland, J. and Lofland, L.H. (1984) *Analysing Social Settings*, 2nd edn, Belmont, CA: Wadsworth.

Lofland, J., Snow, D.A., Anderson, L. and Lofland, L.H. (2006) *Analyzing Social Settings: A Guide to Qualitative Observation and Analysis*, 4th edn, Belmont, CA: Wadsworth.

Lofland, L.H. (1966) *In the Presence of Strangers: A Study of Behaviour in Public Settings*, Working Paper 19, University of Michigan, Ann Arbor, MI, Center for Research on Social Organization.

Lofland, L.H. (1973) *A World of Strangers: Order and Action in Urban Public Space*, New York: Basic Books.

Lugosi, P. (2006) 'Between overt and covert research: concealment and disclosure in an ethnographic study of commercial hospitality', *Qualitative Inquiry*, 12, 3: 541–61.

Lundman, R.J. and McFarlane, P.T. (1976) 'Conflict methodology: an introduction and preliminary assessment', *Sociological Quarterly*, 17: 503–12.

Lyman, S.M. and Scott, M.B. (1970) *A Sociology of the Absurd*, New York: Appleton-Century-Crofts.

Lynch, M. (2000) 'Against reflexivity as an academic virtue and source of privileged knowledge', *Theory, Culture and Society*, 17, 3: 26–54.

Lynch, M. and Woolgar, S. (eds) (1990) *Representation in Scientific Practice*, Cambridge, MA: MIT Press.

Lynd, R.S. and Lynd, H.M. (1929) *Middletown*, New York: Harcourt, Brace and World.

Lynd, R.S. and Lynd, H.M. (1937) *Middletown in Transition*, New York: Harcourt, Brace and World.

Lyng, S. (1998) 'Dangerous methods: risk taking and the research process', in J. Ferrell and M.S. Hamm (eds) *Ethnography at the Edge: Crime, Deviance and Field Research*, Boston, MA: Northeastern University Press.

Mac an Ghaill, M. (1991) 'Young, Gifted and Black: methodological reflections of a teacher/researcher', in G. Walford (ed.) *Researching the Powerful in Education*, London: UCL Press.

McCall, G.J. (2006) 'The tradition of fieldwork', in D. Hobbs and R. Wright (eds) *The Sage Handbook of Fieldwork*, London: Sage.

McCurdy, D.W. (1976) 'The medicine man', in M.A. Rynkiewich and J.P. Spradley (eds) *Ethics and Anthropology: Dilemmas in Fieldwork*, New York: Wiley.

MacDonald, B. (1948) *The Plague and I*, London: Hammond.

Macdonald, S. (2001) 'British social anthropology', in P. Atkinson, A. Coffey, S. Delamont, J. Lofland and L. Lofland (eds) *Handbook of Ethnography*, London: Sage.

Macdonald, S. (2002) *Behind the Scenes at the Science Museum*, Oxford: Berg.

McDonald, S. (2005) 'Studying actions in context: a qualitative shadowing method for organizational research', *Qualitative Research*, 5, 4: 455–73.

McDonald-Walker, S. (2000) *Bikers: Culture, Politics and Power*, Oxford: Berg.

McKie, L. (2002) 'Engagement and evaluation in qualitative inquiry', in T. May (ed.) *Qualitative Research in Action*, London: Sage.

Maines, D.R. (2001) *The Faultline of Consciousness: A View of Interactionism in Sociology*, New York: Aldine de Gruyter.

Makkreel, R. A. (1975) *Dilthey: Philosopher of the Human Studies*, Princeton, NJ: Princeton University Press.

Malinowski, B. (1922) *Argonauts of the Western Pacific*, London: Routledge & Kegan Paul.

Malinowski, B. (1967) *A Diary in the Strict Sense of the Term*, London: Routledge & Kegan Paul.

Mandell, N. (1988) 'The least-adult role in studying children', *Journal of Contemporary Ethnography*, 16: 433–67.

Mann, C. and Stewart, F. (2000) *Internet Communication and Qualitative Research: A Handbook for Researching Online*, London: Sage.

Mann, T. (1996) *The Magic Mountain*, New York: Vintage.

Manning, P.K. (1980) 'Goffman's framing order: style as structure', in J. Ditton (ed.) *The View from Goffman*, London: Macmillan.

Manning, P. K. (2004) 'Semiotics and data analysis', in M. Hardy and A. Bryman (eds) *Handbook of Data Analysis*, London: Sage.

Markham, A. (1998) *Life Online: Researching Real Experience in Virtual Space*, Walnut Creek, CA: AltaMira.

Markham, A. (2004) 'The internet as research context', in C. Seale, G. Gobo, J.F. Gubrium and D. Silverman (eds) *Qualitative Research Practice*, London: Sage.

Markham, A. (2005) 'The methods, politics, and ethics of representation in online ethnography', in N.K. Denzin and Y.S. Lincoln (eds) *Handbook of Qualitative Research*, 3rd edn, Thousand Oaks, CA: Sage.

Marks, D. (1995) 'Ethnographic film: from Flaberty to Asch and after', *American Anthropologist*, 97, 2: 337–47.

Mason, K. (1990) 'Not waving but bidding: reflections on research in a rural setting', in R.G. Burgess (ed.) *Studies in Qualitative Methodology, vol. 2, Reflections on Field Experience*, Greenwich, CT: JAI Press.

Matza, D. (1969) *Becoming Deviant*, Englewood Cliffs, NJ: Prentice Hall.

Mauthner, M., Birch, M., Jessop, J. and Miller, T. (eds) (2002) *Ethics in Qualitative Research*, London: Sage.

Maxwell, J.A. (2004a) 'Causal explanation, qualitative research, and scientific inquiry in education', *Educational Researcher*, 33, 2: 3–11.

Maxwell, J.A. (2004b) *Qualitative Research Design: An Interactive Approach*, Thousand Oaks, CA: Sage.

Mayhew, H. (1861) *London Labour and the London Poor*, London: Griffin Bohn.

Measor, L. (1983) 'Gender and the sciences: pupils' gender-based conceptions of school subjects', in M. Hammersley and A. Hargreaves (eds) *Curriculum Practice: Sociological Accounts*, Lewes, UK: Falmer.

Measor, L. (1985) 'Interviewing: a strategy in qualitative research', in R.G. Burgess (ed.) *Strategies of Educational Research: Qualitative Methods*, Lewes, UK: Falmer.

Measor, L. and Woods, P. (1983) 'The interpretation of pupil myths', in M. Hammersley (ed.) *The Ethnography of Schooling: Methodological Issues*, Driffield, UK: Nafferton.

Medawar, P. (1967) *The Art of the Soluble*, London: Methuen,

Mehan, H. (1974) 'Assessing children's school performance', in H.P. Dreitzel (ed.) *Recent Sociology*, no. 5, *Childhood and Socialization*, London: Collier Macmillan.

Merton, R.K. (1959) 'Introduction: notes on problem-finding in sociology', in R.K. Merton, L. Broom and L.S. Cottrell Jr (eds) *Sociology Today*, vol. 1, New York: Harper & Row.

Merton, R.K. (1972) 'Insiders and outsiders: a chapter in the sociology of knowledge', *American Journal of Sociology*, 78, 1: 9–47.

Middleton, D. and Edwards, D. (eds) (1990) *Collective Remembering*, London: Sage.

Miller, B. and Humphreys, L. (2004) 'Keeping in touch: maintaining contacts with stigmatized subjects', in C. Pole (ed.) *Fieldwork*, 4 vols, London: Sage.

Miller, D. (ed.) (1998) *Material Cultures: Why Some Things Matter*, Chicago, IL: University of Chicago Press.

Miller, D. (ed.) (2001a) *Car Cultures*, Oxford: Berg.

Miller, D. (ed.) (2001b) *Home Possessions*, Oxford: Berg.

Miller, S.M. (1952) 'The participant observer and 'over-rapport'', *American Sociological Review*, 17, 2: 97–9.

Mills, C.W. (1940) 'Situated actions and vocabularies of motive', *American Sociological Review* 5, 6: 439–52.

Mishler, E.G. (1991) 'Representing discourse: the rhetoric of transcription', *Journal of Narrative and Life History*, 1, 4: 255–80.

Mitchell, R.G. (1991) 'Secrecy and disclosure in fieldwork', in W.B. Shaffir and R.A. Stebbins (eds) *Experiencing Fieldwork: An Inside View of Qualitative Research*, Newbury Park, CA: Sage.

Moffatt, M. (1989) *Coming of Age in New Jersey*, New Brunswick, NJ: Rutgers University Press.

Morgan, D.H.J. (1972) 'The British Association Scandal: the effect of publicity on a sociological investigation', *Sociological Review*, 20, 2: 185–206.

Mungham, C. and Thomas, P.A. (1981) 'Studying lawyers: aspects of the theory, method and politics of social research', *British Journal of Law and Society*, 8, 1: 79–96.

Murphy, E., Dingwall, R., Greatbatch, D., Parker, S. and Watson, P. (1998) 'Qualitative research methods in health technology assessment: a review of the literature', *Health Technology Assessment*, 2, 16: 1–260. Available at: http: //www.hta.nhsweb.nhs.uk/execsumm/summ216.htm (accessed on 14 August 2002).

Nadel, S.F. (1939) 'The interview technique in social anthropology', in F.C. Bartlett, M. Ginsberg, E.J. Lindgren, and R.H. Thouless (eds) *The Study of Society*, London: Routledge & Kegan Paul.

Nader, L. (1986) 'From anguish to exultation', in P. Golde (ed.) *Women in the Field: Anthropological Experiences*, 2nd edn, Berkeley, CA: University of California Press.

Noblit, G.W. and Hare, R.D. (1988) *Meta-Ethnography: Synthesizing Qualitative Studies*, Newbury Park, CA: Sage.

Nygren, L. and Blom, B. (2001) 'Analysis of short reflective narratives: a method for the study of knowledge in social workers' actions', *Qualitative Research*, 1, 3: 369–84.

Oakley, A. (1981) 'Interviewing women: a contradiction in terms', in H. Roberts (ed.) *Doing Feminist Research*, London: Routledge & Kegan Paul.

Oboler, R.S. (1986) 'For better or worse: anthropologists and husbands in the field', in T.L. Whitehead and M.E. Conaway (eds) *Self, Sex, and Gender in Cross-Cultural Fieldwork*, Urbana, IL: University of Illinois Press.

O'Hear, A. (ed.) (1996) *Verstehen and Humane Understanding*, Cambridge: Cambridge University Press.

Okely, J. (1983) *The Traveller-Gypsies*, London: Cambridge University Press.

Olesen, V. (1990) 'Immersed, amorphous and episodic fieldwork: theory and policy in three contrasting contexts', in R.G. Burgess (ed.) *Studies in Qualitative Methodology, vol. 2, Reflections on Field Experience*, Greenwich, CT: JAI Press.

Olesen, V. (2005) 'Early millennial feminist qualitative research: challenges and contours', in N.K. Denzin and Y.S. Lincoln (eds) *Handbook of Qualitative Research*, 3rd edn, Thousand Oaks, CA: Sage.

Olesen, V. and Whittaker, E. (1968) *The Silent Dialogue: A Study in the Social Psychology of Professional Socialization*, San Francisco, CA: Jossey-Bass.

O'Reilly, K. (2000) *The British on the Costa del Sol: Transnational Identities and Local Communities*, London: Routledge.

O'Reilly, K. (2005) *Ethnographic Methods*, London: Routledge.

Ostrander, S.A. (1993) '"Surely you're not in this just to be helpful?": access, rapport and interviews in three studies of elites', *Journal of Contemporary Ethnography*, 22, 1: 7–27.

Owens, G.R. (2003) 'What! Me a spy? Intrigue and reflexivity in Zanzibar', *Ethnography*, 4, 1: 122–44.

Paechter, C. (1996) 'Power, knowledge and the confessional in qualitative research', *Discourse: Studies in the Politics of Education*, 17, 1: 75–84.

Painter, C. (ed.) (2002) *Contemporary Art and the Home*, Oxford: Berg.

Papanek, H. (1964) 'The woman fieldworker in a purdah society', *Human Organization*, 23: 160–3.

Parker, H.J. (1974) *View from the Boys: A Sociology of Downtown Adolescents*, 2nd edn, London: David & Charles.

Patrick, J. (1973) *A Glasgow Gang Observed*, London: Eyre Methuen.

Pattillo-McCoy, M. (1999) *Black Picket Fences: Privilege and Peril among the Black Middle Class*, Chicago, IL: University of Chicago Press.

Pearce, S. (ed.) (1994) *Interpreting Objects and Collections*, London: Routledge.

Pelto, P.J. and Pelto, G.H. (1978) 'Ethnography: the fieldwork enterprise', in J.J. Honigmann (ed.) *Handbook of Social and Cultural Anthropology*, Chicago, IL: Rand McNally.

Perlesz, A. and Lindsay, J. (2003) 'Methodological triangulation in researching families: making sense of dissonant data', *International Journal of Social Research Methodology*, 6, 1: 25–40.

Perlman, M.L. (1970) 'Intensive fieldwork and scope sampling: methods for studying the same problem at different levels', in M. Freilich (ed.) *Marginal Natives: Anthropologists at Work*, New York: Harper & Row.

Perry, N. (2007) 'Organizations as total institutions', in G. Ritzer (ed.) *The Blackwell Encyclopedia of Sociology*, vol. III, Oxford, Blackwell.

Peshkin, A. (1985) 'Virtuous subjectivity: in the participant-observer's I's', in D.N. Berg and K.K. Smith (eds) *Exploring Clinical Methods for Social Research*, Beverly Hills, CA: Sage.

Pettigrew, M. (1994) 'Coming to terms with research: the contract business', in D. Halpin, and B. Troyna (eds.), Researching Education Policy, London, Falmer.

Pettinari, C.J. (1988) *Task, Talk and Text in the Operating Room: A Study in Medical Discourse*, Norwood, NJ: Ablex.

Pettinger, L. (2005) 'Representing shop work: a dual ethnography', *Qualitative Research*, 5, 3: 347–64.

Pidgeon, N. and Henwood, K. (2004) 'Grounded theory', in M. Hardy and A. Bryman (eds) *Handbook of Data Analysis*, London: Sage.

Pieke, F.N. (1995) 'Witnessing the 1989 Chinese People's Movement', in C. Nordstrom and A.C.G.M. Robben (eds) *Fieldwork under Fire: Contemporary Studies of Violence and Survival*, Berkeley, CA: University of California Press.

Pinch, T. and Trocco, F. (2002) *Analog Days: The Invention and Impact of the Moog Synthesizer*, Cambridge, MA: Harvard University Press.

Pink, S. (2004a) *Home Truths: Changing Gender in the Sensory Home*, Oxford: Berg.

Pink, S. (2004b) 'Visual methods', in C. Seale, G. Gobo, J.F. Gubrium and D. Silverman (eds) *Qualitative Research Practice*, London: Sage.

Pink, S. (2006) *The Future of Visual Anthropology: Engaging the Senses*, London: Routledge.

Piper, H. and Stronach, I. (2004) 'Doing difference: beyond here there be monsters', in H. Piper and I. Stronach (eds) *Educational Research: Difference and Diversity*, Aldershot, UK: Ashgate.

Platt, J. (1981) 'On interviewing one's peers', *British Journal of Sociology*, 32, 1: 75–91.

Plummer, K. (1975) *Sexual Stigma: An Interactionist Account*, London: Routledge & Kegan Paul.

Plummer, K. (1995) *Telling Sexual Stories*, London: Routledge.

Plummer, K. (2000) *Documents of Life 2: An Invitation to a Critical Humanism*, London: Sage.

Plummer, K. (2001) 'The call of life stories in ethnographic research', in P. Atkinson, A. Coffey, S. Delamont, J. Lofland and L. Lofland (eds) *Handbook of Ethnography*, London: Sage.

Plummer, K. (2005) 'Critical humanism and queer theory: living with the tensions', in N.K. Denzin and Y.S. Lincoln (eds) *Handbook of Qualitative Research*, 3rd edn, Thousand Oaks, CA: Sage.

Podalsky, L. (2002) *Specular City: The Transformation of Culture, Consumption, and Space After Perón*, Philadelphia, PA: Temple University Press.

Poland, B.D. (2002) 'Transcription quality', in J.F. Gubrium and J.A. Holstein (eds) *Handbook of Interview Research*, Thousand Oaks, CA: Sage.

Pollard, A. (1985) 'Opportunities and difficulties of a teacher-ethnographer: a personal account', in R.G. Burgess (ed.) *Field Methods in the Study of Education*, Lewes, UK: Falmer.

Popper, K. (1972) *The Logic of Scientific Discovery*, London: Hutchinson.

Porter, T.M. (1995) *Trust in Numbers: The Pursuit of Objectivity in Science and Public Life*, Princeton, NJ: Princeton University Press.

Potter, J. (2004) 'Discourse analysis', in M. Hardy and A. Bryman (eds) *Handbook of Data Analysis*, London: Sage.

Potter, J. and Hepburn, A. (2005) 'Qualitative interviews in psychology: problems and possibilities', *Qualitative Research in Psychology*, 2: 281–307

Powdermaker, H. (1966) *Stranger and Friend: The Way of an Anthropologist*, New York: Norton.

Power, M. (1997) *The Audit Society: Rituals of Verification*, Oxford: Oxford University Press.

Prior, L. (1985) 'Making sense of mortality', *Sociology of Health and Illness*, 7, 2: 167–90.

Prior, L. (1989) *The Social Organization of Death*, London: Macmillan.

Prior, L. (1993) *The Social Organization of Mental Illness*, London: Sage.

Prior, L. (2003) *Using Documents in Social Research*, London: Sage.

Prior, L. (2004) 'Documents', in C. Seale, G. Gobo, J.F. Gubrium and D. Silverman (eds) *Qualitative Research Practice*, London: Sage.

Prior, L. and Bloor, M. (1993) 'Why people die: social representations of death and its causes', *Science and Culture*, 3, 3: 346–74.

Punch, M. (1979) *Policing the Inner City*, London: Macmillan.

Punch, M. (1986) *The Politics and Ethics of Fieldwork*, Beverly Hills, CA: Sage.

Radcliffe-Brown, A.R. (1948) *A Natural Science of Society*, New York: Free Press.

Rainbird, H. (1990) 'Expectations and revelations: examining conflict in the Andes', in R.G. Burgess (ed.) *Studies in Qualitative Methodology, vol 2, Reflections on Field Experience*, Greenwich, CT: JAI Press.

Rainwater, L. and Pittman, D.J. (1967) 'Ethical problems in studying a politically sensitive and deviant community', *Social Problems*, 14: 357–66. Reprinted in G.J. McCall and J.L. Simmons (eds) (1969) *Issues in Participant Observation: A Text and Reader*, Reading, MA: Addison-Wesley.

Rawlings, B. (1988) 'Local knowledge: the analysis of transcribed audio materials for organizational ethnography', in R.G. Burgess (ed.) *Studies in Qualitative Methodology, vol. 1, Conducting Qualitative Research*, Greenwich, CT: JAI Press.

Reed-Danahay, D. (ed.) (1997) *Auto/Ethnography: Rewriting the Self and the Social*, Oxford: Berg.

Reed-Danahay, D. (2001) 'Autobiography, intimacy and ethnography', in P. Atkinson, A. Coffey, S. Delamont, J. Lofland and L. Lofland (eds) *Handbook of Ethnography*, London: Sage.

Rees, C. (1981) 'Records and hospital routine', in P. Atkinson and C. Heath (eds) *Medical Work: Realities and Routines*, Farnborough, UK: Gower.

Reichenbach, H. (1938) *Experience and Prediction: An Analysis of the Foundations and the Structure of Knowledge*, Chicago, IL: University of Chicago Press.

Reichenbach, H. (1951) *The Rise of Scientific Philosophy*, Berkeley, CA: University of California Press.

Reid, S.E. and Crowley, D. (eds) (2000) *Style and Socialism: Modernity and Material culture in Post-War Eastern Europe*, Oxford: Berg.

Reynolds, L.T. and Herman-Kinney, N.J. (eds) (2003) *Handbook of Symbolic Interactionism*, Walnut Creek, CA: AltaMira.

Ribbens McCarthy, J., Holland, J. and Gillies, V. (2003) 'Multiple perspectives on "family" lives of young people: methodological and theoretical issues in case study research', *International Journal of Social Research Methodology*, 6, 1: 1–23.

Richardson, L. (1990a) 'Narrative and sociology', *Journal of Contemporary Ethnography*, 19: 116–35.

Richardson, L. (1990b) *Writing Strategies: Reaching Diverse Audiences*, Newbury Park, CA: Sage.

Richardson, L. and St Pierre, E.A. (2005) 'Writing: a method of inquiry', in N.K. Denzin and Y.S. Lincoln (eds) *Handbook of Qualitative Research*, 3rd edn, Thousand Oaks, CA: Sage.

Riddell, S. (1992) *Gender and the Politics of the Curriculum*, London: Routledge.

Riemer, J.W. (1977) 'Varieties of opportunistic research', *Urban Life*, 5, 4: 467–77.

Riessman, C.K. (1987) 'When gender is not enough: women interviewing women', *Gender and Society*, 1, 2: 172–207.

Riessman, C.K. (1993) *Narrative Analysis*, Newbury Park, CA: Sage.

Riessman, C.K. (2002) 'Analysis of personal narratives', in J.F. Gubrium and J.A. Holstein (eds) *Handbook of Interview Research*, Thousand Oaks, CA: Sage.

Robbins, T. (1988) *Cults, Converts and Charisma*, Newbury Park, CA: Sage.

Roberts, H. (ed.) (1981) *Doing Feminist Research*, London: Routledge & Kegan Paul.

Robinson, D.A. (1971) *The Process of Becoming Ill*, London: Routledge & Kegan Paul.

Robinson, W.S. (1969) 'The logical structure of analytic induction', in G.J. McCall and J.L. Simmons (eds) *Issues in Participant Observation: A Text and Reader*, Reading, MA: Addison-Wesley.

Rock, P. (1973) *Making People Pay*, London: Routledge & Kegan Paul.

Rock, P. (1979) *The Making of Symbolic Interactionism*, London: Macmillan.

Rohner, R. (1969) *The Ethnography of Franz Boas*, Chicago, IL: University of Chicago Press.

Rosaldo, R. (1986) 'From the door of his tent', in J. Clifford and G. Marcus (eds) *Writing Culture: The Poetics and Politics of Ethnography*, Berkeley, CA: University of California Press.

Rose, D. (1989) *Patterns of American Culture: Ethnography and Estrangement*, Philadelphia, PA: University of Pennsylvania Press.

Rosenhahn, D.L. (1973) 'On being sane in insane places', *Science*, 179: 250–8. Reprinted in M. Bulmer (ed.) *Social Research Ethics: An Examination of the Merits of Covert Participation Observation*, London: Macmillan.

Roth, J. (1962) 'Comments on "secret observation"', *Social Problems*, 9, 3: 283–4.

Roth, J. (1963) *Timetables*, New York: Bobbs-Merrill.

Rule, J.B. (1978) *Insight and Social Betterment: A Preface to Applied Social Science*, New York: Oxford University Press.

Ryan, P. (2006) 'Researching Irish gay male lives: reflections on disclosure and intellectual autobiography in the production of personal narratives', *Qualitative Research*, 6, 2: 151–68.

Sacks, H. (1975) 'Everyone has to lie', in M. Sanches and B. Blount (eds) *Sociocultural Dimensions of Language Use*, London: Academic Press.

Salvador, T., Bell, G. and Anderson, K. (1999) 'Design ethnography', *Design Management Journal*, 10, 4: 35–41.

Sampson, H. (2004) 'Navigating the waves: the usefulness of a pilot in qualitative research', *Qualitative Research*, 4, 3: 383–402.

Sampson, H. and Thomas, M. (2003) 'Lone researchers at sea: gender, risk, and responsibility', *Qualitative Research*, 3, 2: 165–89.

Sanders, T. (2006) 'Researching sex work: dynamics, difficulties and decisions', in D. Hobbs and R. Wright (eds) *The Sage Handbook of Fieldwork*, London: Sage.

Sanjek, R. (ed.) (1990) *Fieldnotes: The Makings of Anthropology*, Ithaca, NY: Cornell University Press.

Scarth, J. (1986) 'The influence of examinations on whole-school curriculum decision-making: an ethnographic case study', unpublished PhD thesis, University of Lancaster.

Scarth, J. and Hammersley, M. (1988) 'Examinations and teaching: an exploratory study', *British Educational Research Journal*, 14, 3: 231–49. Reprinted in M. Hammersley (1990) *Classroom Ethnography: Empirical and Methodological Essays*, Milton Keynes: Open University Press.

Schatzman, L. and Strauss, A. (1955) 'Social class and modes of communication', *American Journal of Sociology*, 60: 329–38.

Schatzman, L. and Strauss, A. (1973) *Field Research: Strategies for a Natural Sociology*, Englewood Cliffs, NJ: Prentice Hall.

Scheper-Hughes, N. (1982) *Saints, Scholars and Schizophrenics: Mental Illness in Rural Ireland*, 2nd edn, Berkeley, CA: University of California Press.

Scheper-Hughes, N. (1995) 'The primacy of the ethical: propositions for a militant anthropology', *Current Anthropology*, 36, 3: 409–20.

Scheper-Hughes, N. (2004) 'Parts unknown: undercover ethnography of the organs-trafficking underworld', *Ethnography*, 5, 1: 29–73.

Schofield, J.W. (1990) 'Increasing the generalizability of qualitative research', in E.W. Eisner and A. Peshkin (eds) *Qualitative Inquiry in Education: The Continuing Debate*, New York: Teachers College Press.

Schuman, H. (1982) 'Artifacts are in the mind of the beholder', *American Sociologist*, 17, 1: 21–8.

Schutz, A. (1964) 'The stranger: an essay in social psychology', in A. Schutz (ed.) *Collected Papers, vol. II*, The Hague: Martinus Nijhoff.

Scott, G.G. (1983) *The Magicians: A Study of the Use of Power in a Black Magic Group*, New York: Irvington.

Scott, M.B. (1968) *The Racing Game*, Chicago, IL: Aldine.

Scott, S. (1984) 'The personable and the powerful: gender and status in social research', in C. Bell and H. Roberts (eds) *Social Researching: Policies, Problems and Practice*, London: Routledge & Kegan Paul.

Scott, S. (2004) 'Researching shyness: a contradiction in terms?', *Qualitative Research*, 4, 1: 91–105.

Scourfield, J. and Coffey, A. (2006) 'Access, ethics and the (re-)construction of gender: the case of the researcher as suspected "paedophile"', *International Journal of Social Research Methodology*, 9, 1: 29–40.

Seale C. (1998) *Constructing Death: The Sociology of Dying and Bereavement*, Cambridge University Press.

Seale, C. (1999) *The Quality of Qualitative Research*, London: Sage.

Seale, C., Gobo, G., Gubrium, J.F. and Silverman, D. (eds) (2004) *Qualitative Research Practice*, London: Sage.

Sevigny, M.J. (1981) 'Triangulated inquiry – a methodology for the analysis of classroom interaction', in J.L. Green and C. Wallat (eds) *Ethnography and Language in Educational Settings*, Norwood, NJ: Ablex.

Shaffir, W.B. (1985) 'Some reflections on approaches to fieldwork in Hassidic communities', *Jewish Journal of Sociology*, 27, 2: 115–34.

Shaffir, W.B. (1991) 'Managing a convincing self-presentation: some personal reflections on entering the field', in W.B. Shaffir and R.A. Stebbins (eds) *Experiencing Fieldwork: An Inside View of Qualitative Research*, Newbury Park, CA: Sage.

Shakespeare, P. (1994) 'Aspects of confused speech', unpublished manuscript, Open University, Milton Keynes.

Shakespeare, P. (1997) *Aspects of Confused Speech: A Study of Verbal Interaction Between Confused and Normal Speakers*, Mahwah, NJ: Lawrence Erlbaum.

Sharf, B. (1999) 'Beyond netiquette: the ethics of doing naturalistic discourse research on the internet', in S. Jones (ed.) *Doing Internet Research*, Thousand Oaks, CA: Sage.

Sharrock, R. and Read, R. (2002) *Kuhn: Philosopher of Scientific Revolution*, Cambridge: Polity.

Shaw, I. (1999) *Qualitative Evaluation*, London: Sage.

Sheehan, E.A. (1993) 'The student of culture and the ethnography of Irish intellectuals', in C.B. Brettell (ed.) (1993) *When They Read What We Write: The Politics of Ethnography*, Westport, CT: Bergin & Garvey.

Sheridan, D. (1993) 'Writing to the archive: Mass Observation as autobiography', *Sociology*, 27, 1: 27–40.

Shils, E. (1959) 'Social inquiry and the autonomy of the individual', in D.P. Lerner (ed.) *The Human Meaning of the Human Sciences*, New York: Meridian.

Shweder, R.A. (2003) 'The idea of moral progress: Bush versus Posner versus Berlin', *Philosophy of Education Society Yearbook*, Champaign, IL: Philosophy of Education Society Publications, available at http: //www.ed.uiuc.edu/EPS/PES-yearbook/2003/2003toc.htm (accessed 1 February 2007).

Shweder, R.A. (2004) 'Tuskegee re-examined', *Spiked*, available at http: www.spiked-online.com/Articles/0000000CA34A.htm (accessed 18 February 2007).

Silverman, D. (1973) 'Interview talk: bringing off a research instrument', *Sociology*, 7, 1: 31–48.

Silverman, D. (1984) 'Going private: ceremonial forms in a private oncology clinic', *Sociology*, 18, 2: 191–202.

Silverman, D. (1993) *Interpreting Qualitative Data: Methods for Analysing Talk, Text and Interaction*, London: Sage.

Silverman, D. (1996) *Discourses of Counselling*, London: Sage.

Silverman, D. (ed.) (2004) *Qualitative Research: Theory, Method and Practice*, 2nd edn, London: Sage.

Silverstein, P.A. (2004) 'Of rooting and uprooting: Kabyle habitus, domesticity, and structural nostalgia', *Ethnography*, 5, 4: 553–78.

Simons, H. (1981) 'Conversation piece: the practice of interviewing in case study research', in C. Adelman (ed.) *Uttering, Muttering: Collecting, Using and Reporting Talk for Social and Educational Research*, London: Grant McIntyre.

Simons, H. and Usher, R. (eds) (2000) *Situated Ethics in Educational Research*, London: Routledge Falmer.

Sjoberg, G. and Nett, R. (1968) *A Methodology for Social Research*, New York: Harper & Row.

Skipper, J.K. and McCaghy, C.H. (1972) 'Respondents' intrusion upon the situation: the problem of interviewing subjects with special qualities', *Sociological Quarterly*, 13: 237–43.

Skolnick, J. (1966) *Justice without Trial: Law Enforcement in Democratic Society*, New York: Wiley.

Smart, C. (1984) *The Ties that Bind: Law, Marriage and the Reproduction of Patriarchal Relations*, London: Routledge & Kegan Paul.

Smigel, F. (1958) 'Interviewing a legal elite: the Wall Street lawyer', *American Journal of Sociology*, 64: 159–64.

Smith, D. (1987) *The Everyday World as Problematic: A Feminist Sociology*, Boston, MA: Northeastern University Press.

Smith, D. (1993) '"Literacy" and business: "social problems" as social organization', in J.A. Holstein and G. Miller (eds) *Reconsidering Social Constructionism: Debates in Social Problems Theory*, New York: Aldine de Gruyter.

Smith, J.K. (1989) *The Nature of Social and Educational Inquiry*, Norwood, NJ: Ablex.

Smith, J.K. and Heshusius, L. (1986) 'Closing down the conversation: the end of the quantitative–qualitative debate among educational inquirers', *Educational Researcher*, 15, 1: 4–12.

Smith, J.K. and Hodkinson, P. (2005) 'Relativism, criteria and politics', in N.K. Denzin and Y.S. Lincoln (eds) *Handbook of Qualitative Research*, 3rd edn, Thousand Oaks, CA: Sage.

Smith, L.M. and Geoffrey, W. (1968) *Complexities of the Urban Classroom: An Analysis Towards a General Theory of Teaching*, New York: Holt, Rinehart & Winston.

Snow, D. (1980) 'The disengagement process: a neglected problem in participant observation research', *Qualitative Sociology*, 3, 2: 100–22.

Social Research Association (SRA) (2003) *Ethical Guidelines*, http://www.the-sra.org.uk/ethics.htm

Sontag, S. (1979) *Illness as Metaphor*, London: Allen Lane.

Speer, S.A. (2002) 'Natural and contrived data: a sustainable distinction?', *Discourse Studies*, 4, 4: 511–25.

Spradley, J.P. (1970) *You Owe Yourself a Drunk: An Ethnography of Urban Nomads*, Boston, MA: Little, Brown.

Spradley, J.P. (1979) *The Ethnographic Interview*, New York: Holt, Rinehart & Winston.

Stanley, J. (1989) *Marks on the Memory: Experiencing School*, Milton Keynes: Buckingham, Open University Press.

Stanley, L. (1992) *The Auto/Biographical I: Theory and Practice of Feminist Auto/Biography*, Manchester: Manchester University Press.

Stanley, L. (1993) 'On auto/biography in sociology', *Sociology*, 27, 1: 41–52.

Stanley, L. (2001) 'Mass Observation's fieldwork methods', in P. Atkinson, A. Coffey, S. Delamont, J. Lofland and L. Lofland (eds) *Handbook of Ethnography*, London: Sage.

Stanley, L. and Wise, S. (1983) *Breaking Out*, London: Routledge & Kegan Paul.

Stein, M.R. (1964) 'The eclipse of community: some glances at the education of a sociologist', in A.J. Vidich, J. Bensman and M.R. Stein (eds) *Reflections on Community Studies*, New York: Wiley.

Stewart, K. (2005) 'Cultural poesis: the generativity of emergent things', in N.K. Denzin and Y.S. Lincoln (eds) *Handbook of Qualitative Research*, 3rd edn, Thousand Oaks, CA: Sage.

Stewart, K. and Williams, M. (2005) 'Researching online populations: the use of online focus groups for social research', *Qualitative Research*, 5, 4: 395–416.

Stimson, G.V. and Webb, B. (1975) *Going to See the Doctor: The Consultation Process in General Practice*, London: Routledge & Kegan Paul.

Strauss, A. (1970) 'Discovering new theory from previous theory', in T. Shibutani (ed.) *Human Nature and Collective Behaviour: Essays in Honor of Herbert Blumer*, Englewood Cliffs, NJ: Prentice Hall.

Strauss, A. (1987) *Qualitative Analysis for Social Scientists*, Cambridge: Cambridge University Press.

Strauss, A. and Corbin, J. (1990) *Basics of Qualitative Research: Grounded Theory Procedures and Techniques*, Newbury Park, CA: Sage.

Strauss, A. and Corbin, J. (1998) *Basics of Qualitative Research: Grounded Theory Procedures and Techniques*, 2nd edn, Newbury Park, CA: Sage.

Street, B.V. (1984) *Literacy in Theory and Practice*, Cambridge: Cambridge University Press.

Strenski, I. (1982) 'Malinowski: second positivism, second romanticism', *Man*, 17: 766–77.

Strong, P.M. (2001) *The Ceremonial Order of the Clinic: Parents, Doctors and Medical Bureaucracies*, Aldershot, UK: Ashgate. First published in 1979, London: Routledge & Kegan Paul.

Sturges, J.E. and Hanrahan, K.J. (2004) 'Comparing telephone and face-to-face qualitative interviewing: a research note', *Qualitative Research*, 4, 1: 107–18.

Styles, J. (1979) 'Outsider/insider: researching gay baths', *Urban Life*, 8, 2: 135–52.

Sudarkasa, N. (1986) 'In a world of women: fieldwork in a Yoruba community', in P. Golde (ed.) *Women in the Field: Anthropological Experience*, 2nd edn, Berkeley, CA: University of California Press.

Sudnow, D. (1965) 'Normal crimes: sociological features of the Penal Code in a Public Defender's office', *Social Problems*, 12: 255–76.

Sullivan, M.A., Queen, S.A. and Patrick, R.C. (1958) 'Participant observation as employed in the study of a military training program', *American Sociological Review*, 23, 6: 660–7.

Tang, N. (2002) 'Interviewer and interviewee relationships between women', *Sociology*, 36, 3: 703–21.

Tashakkori, A. and Teddlie, C. (eds) (2003) *Handbook of Mixed Methods in Social and Behavioral Research*, Thousand Oaks, CA: Sage.

Taylor, C., Wilkie, M. and Baser, J. (2006) *Doing Action Research: A Guide for School Support Staff*, London: Paul Chapman.

Taylor, S.J. (1991) 'Leaving the field: research, relationships, and responsibilities', in W.B. Shaffir and R.A. Stebbins (eds) *Experiencing Fieldwork: An Inside View of Qualitative Research*, Newbury Park, CA: Sage.

Temple, B. and Young, A. (2004) 'Qualitative research and translation dilemmas', *Qualitative Research*, 4, 2: 161–78.

Thomas, R.J. (1993) 'Interviewing important people in big companies', *Journal of Contemporary Ethnography*, 22, 1: 80–96,

Thomas, W.I. (1967) *The Unadjusted Girl*, New York: Harper & Row. First published 1923, Boston, MA: Little, Brown.

Thomas, W.L and Znaniecki, F. (1927) *The Polish Peasant in Europe and America*, New York: Knopf.

Thorne, B. (1983) 'Political activist as participant observer: conflicts of commitment in a study of the draft resistance movement of the 1960s', in R.M. Emerson (ed.) *Contemporary Field Research*, Boston, MA: Little, Brown.

Tobias, S. (1990) *They're Not Dumb, They're Different*, Tucson, AZ: Research Corporation.

Törrönen, J. (2002) 'Semiotic theory on qualitative interviewing using stimulus texts', *Qualitative Research*, 2, 3: 343–62.

Tota, A.L. (2004) 'Ethnographying public memory: the commemorative genre for the victims of terrorism in Italy', *Qualitative Research*, 4, 2: 131–59.

Toulmin, S. (1972) *Human Understanding*, Oxford: Clarendon Press.

Treseder, P. (2006) 'Diet as a social problem: an investigation of children's and young people's perspectives on nutrition and body image', unpublished PhD thesis, Open University, Milton Keynes.

Troustine, P. and Christensen, T. (1982) *Movers and Shakers: The Study of Community Power*, New York: St Martin's Press.

Troyna, B. (1994) 'Reforms, research and being reflexive about being reflective', in D. Halpin and B. Troyna (eds) *Researching Education Policy*, London: Falmer.

Troyna, B. and Carrington, B. (1989) 'Whose side are we on? Ethical dilemmas in research on "race" and education', in R.G. Burgess (ed.) *The Ethics of Educational Research*, Lewes, UK: Falmer.

Truzzi, M. (ed.) (1974) *Verstehen: Subjective Understanding in the Social Sciences*, Reading, MA: Addison-Wesley.

Turnbull, C. (1973) *The Mountain People*, London: Cape.

Tyler, S.A. (ed.) (1969) *Cognitive Anthropology*, New York: Holt, Rinehart & Winston.

Tyler, S.A. (1986) 'Post-modern ethnography: from document of the occult to occult document', in J. Clifford and G. Marcus (eds) *Writing Culture: The Poetics and Politics of Ethnography*, Berkeley, CA: University of California Press.

Valis, N. (2003) *The Culture of Cursilería: Bad Taste, Kitsch, and Class in Modern Spain*, Durham, NC: Duke University Press.

Van den Berg, H., Wetherell, M. and Houtkoop-Steenstra, H. (eds) (2003) *Analyzing Race Talk: Multidisciplinary Approaches to the Interview*, Cambridge: Cambridge University Press.

van den Hoonaard, W.C. (ed.) (2002) *Walking the Tightrope: Ethical Issues for Qualitative Researchers*, Toronto: University of Toronto Press.

Van Gennep, A. (1960) *The Rites of Passage*, Chicago, IL, University of Chicago Press.

van Maanen, J. (1988) *Tales of the Field*, Chicago, IL: University of Chicago Press.

van Maanen, J. (1991) 'Playing back the tape: early days in the field', in W.B. Shaffir and R.A. Stebbins (eds) *Experiencing Fieldwork: An Inside View of Qualitative Research*, Newbury Park, CA: Sage.

Vaughan, D. (2004) 'Theorizing disaster: analogy, historical ethnography, and the *Challenger* accident', *Ethnography*, 5, 3: 315–47.

Vidich, A.J. and Bensman, J. (1958) *Small Town in Mass Society*, Princeton, NJ: Princeton University Press.

Vidich, A.J., Bensman, J. and Stein, M.R. (eds) (1964) *Reflections on Community Studies*, New York: Wiley.

Voysey Paun, M. (2006) *A Constant Burden*, 2nd edn, Aldershot, UK: Ashgate.

Vrasidas, C. (2001) 'Interpretivism and symbolic interactionism: "Making the familiar strange and interesting again" in educational technology research', in W. Heinecke and J. Willis (eds) *Research Methods in Educational Technology*, Greenwich, CT: Information Age Publishing.

Walford, G. (1991) 'Researching the City Technology College, Kingshurst', in Walford (ed.) *Doing Educational Research*, London: Routledge.

Walford, G. (2002) 'Why don't researchers name their research sites?', in G. Walford (ed.) *Debates and Developments in Ethnographic Methodology, Studies in Educational Ethnography*, vol. 6, Amsterdam: JAI Press.

Walford, G. and Miller, H. (1991) *City Technology College*, Buckingham: Open University Press.

Walker, J.C. (1988) *Louts and Legends*, Sydney: Allen & Unwin.

Walker, R. (1978) 'The conduct of educational case studies: ethics, theories and procedures', in B. Dockerell and D. Hamilton (eds) *Rethinking Educational Research*, London: Hodder & Stoughton.

Wallis, R. (1977) 'The moral career of a research project', in C. Bell and H. Newby (eds) *Doing Sociological Research*, London: Allen & Unwin.

Warnke, G. (1987) *Gadamer: Hermeneutics, Tradition and Reason*, Cambridge: Polity.

Warren, C.A.B. (1974) *Identity and Community in the Gay World*, New York: Wiley.

Warren, C.A.B. (1988) *Gender Issues in Field Research*, Newbury Park, CA: Sage.

Warwick, D.P. (1982) 'Tearoom trade: means and ends in social research', in M. Bulmer (ed.) *Social Research Ethics: An Examination of the Merits of Covert Participant Observation*, London: Macmillan.

Wax, M.L. and Cassell, J. (1981) 'From regulation to reflection: ethics in social research', *American Sociologist*, 16, 4: 224–9.

Wax, R.H. (1952) 'Reciprocity as a field technique', *Human Organization*, 11: 34–7.

Wax, R.H. (1971) *Doing Fieldwork: Warnings and Advice*, Chicago, IL: University of Chicago Press.

Webb, E.J., Campbell, D.T., Schwartz, R.D. and Sechrest, L. (1966) *Unobtrusive Measures: Nonreactive Research in the Social Sciences*, Chicago, IL: Rand McNally.

Webb, S. and Webb, B. (1932) *Methods of Social Study*, London: Longmans Green.

Weber, F. (2001) 'Settings, interactions and things: a plea for multi-integrative ethnography', *Ethnography*, 2, 4: 475–99.

Werthman, C. (1963) 'Delinquents in schools: a test for the legitimacy of authority', *Berkeley Journal of Sociology*, 8, 1: 39–60.

West, C. (1996) 'Ethnography and orthography: a (modest) methodological proposal', *Journal of Contemporary Ethnography*, 25, 3: 327–52.

West, W.G. (1980) 'Access to adolescent deviants and deviance', in W.B. Shaffir, R.A. Stebbins and A. Turowetz (eds) *Fieldwork Experience: Qualitative Approaches to Social Research*, New York: St Martin's Press.

Westmarland, L. (2000) 'Taking the flak: operational policing, fear and violence', in G. Lee-Treweek and S. Linkogle (eds) (2000) *Danger in the Field: Risk and Ethics in Social Research*, London: Routledge.

Whitehead, T.L. (1986) 'Breakdown, resolution, and coherence: the fieldwork experiences of a big, brown, pretty-talking man in a West Indian community', in T.L. Whitehead and M.E. Conaway (eds) *Self, Sex, and Gender in Cross-Cultural Fieldwork*, Urbana, IL: University of Illinois Press/

Whitehead, T.L. and Conaway, M.E. (eds) (1986) *Self, Sex, and Gender in Cross-Cultural Fieldwork*, Urbana, IL: University of Illinois Press.

Whitten, N. (1970) 'Network analysis and processes of adaptation among Ecuadorian and Nova Scotian negroes', in M. Freilich (ed.) *Marginal Natives: Anthropologists at Work*, New York: Harper & Row.

Whyte, W.F. (1953) 'Interviewing for organizational research', *Human Organization*, 12: 15–22.

Whyte, W.F. (1981) *Street Corner Society: The Social Structure of an Italian Slum*, 3rd edn, Chicago, IL: University of Chicago Press.

Whyte, W.F. (1992) 'In defense of *Street Corner Society*', *Journal of Contemporary Ethnography*, 21, 1: 52–68.

Wieder, D. (1974a) *Language and Social Reality: The Case of Telling the Convict Code*, The Hague: Mouton.

Wieder, D. (1974b) 'Telling the code', in R. Turner (ed.) *Ethnomethodology*, Harmondsworth: Penguin.

Williams, M. (2006) *Virtually Criminal: Crime, Deviance and Regulation Online*, London: Routledge.

Williams, R. (1976) 'Symbolic interactionism: fusion of theory and research', in D.C. Thorns (ed.) *New Directions in Sociology*, London: David & Charles.

Willis, P. (1977) *Learning to Labour: How Working Class Kids Get Working Class Jobs*, Farnborough, UK: Saxon House.

Willis, P. (1981) 'Cultural production is different from cultural reproduction is different from social reproduction is different from reproduction', *Interchange*, 12, 2–3: 48–67.

Willmott, P. (1980) 'A view from an independent research institute', in M. Cross (ed.) *Social Research and Public Policy: Three Perspectives*, London: Social Research Association.

Wintrob, R.M. (1969) 'An inward focus: a consideration of psychological stress in fieldwork', in F. Henry and S. Saberwal (eds) *Stress and Response in Fieldwork*, New York: Holt, Rinehart & Winston.

Wolcott, H.F. (2001) *Writing Up Qualitative Research*, 2nd edn, Thousand Oaks, CA: Sage.

Wolf, D. (1991) 'High risk methodology: reflections on leaving an outlaw society', in W.B. Shaffir and R.A. Stebbins (eds) *Experiencing Fieldwork: An Inside View of Qualitative Research*, Newbury Park, CA: Sage.

Wolf, M. (1992) *A Thrice-Told Tale: Feminism, Postmodernism and Ethnographic Responsibility*, Stanford, CA: Stanford University Press.

Wolff, K.H. (1964) 'Surrender and community study: the study of Loma', in A.J. Vidich, J. Bensman and M.R. Stein (eds) *Reflections on Community Studies*, New York: Wiley.

Wolfinger, N. H. (2002) 'On writing fieldnotes: collection strategies and background expectancies', *Qualitative Research*, 2, 1: 85–95

Woods, P. (1979) *The Divided School*, London: Routledge & Kegan Paul,

Woods, P. (1981) 'Understanding through talk', in C. Adelman (ed.) *Uttering, Muttering: Collecting, Using and Reporting Talk for Social and Educational Research*, London: Grant McIntyre.

Woods, P. (1985) 'Ethnography and theory construction in educational research', in R.G. Burgess (ed.) *Field Methods in the Study of Education*, Lewes, UK: Falmer.

Woods, P. (1987) 'Ethnography at the crossroads: a reply to Hammersley', *British Educational Research Journal*, 13, 3: 297–307.

Wright, M. (1981) 'Coming to terms with death: patient care in a hospice for the terminally ill', in P. Atkinson and C. Heath (eds) *Medical Work: Realities and Routines*, Farnborough, UK: Gower.

Young, M. (1991) *An Inside Job: Policing and Police Culture in Britain*, Oxford: Clarendon Press.

Zelditch, M. (1962) 'Some methodological problems of field studies', *American Journal of Sociology* 67: 566–76.

Zerubavel, E. (1979) *Patterns of Time in Hospital Life*, Chicago, IL: University of Chicago Press.

Zerubavel, E. (1981) *Hidden Rhythms: Schedules and Calendars in Social Life*, Chicago, IL: University of Chicago Press.

Zimmerman, D.H. and Wieder, D.L. (1977) 'The diary: diary-interview method', *Urban Life*, 5, 4: 479–98.

Znaniecki, F. (1934) *The Method of Sociology*, New York: Farrar & Rinehart.

Zorbaugh, H. (1929) *The Gold Coast and the Slum*, Chicago, IL: University of Chicago Press.

Zulaika, J. (1995) 'The anthropologist as terrorist', in C. Nordstrom and A.C.G.M. Robben (eds) *Fieldwork under Fire: Contemporary Studies of Violence and Survival*, Berkeley, CA: University of California Press.

Index

225–7; motivations for 22–4; purposes of 162, 209; sampling of persons 37–8; selection of settings and cases 28–35; temporal variation 35–7; triangulation 183–4; web-based 208; *see also* covert research

researchers: ethical actions 228–9; expectations about 60–1, 64; field roles 79–86, 96; impression management 65, 66–73; insider-outsider position 86–7, 89; interviews 109; partners 78–9; personal characteristics 73–9; reactivity 101, 102, 120, 177; risk and danger 217n8; suspicion towards 63

resistance 64

respondent validation 181–3

rhetoric 197, 200–1, 205–6

Richardson, L. 198–9, 202

Riessman, C.K. 109

right of withdrawal 226–7

right-wing groups 34, 54, 72–3

rites of passage 196

rituals 137, 169, 196

Robbins, T. 172

Robinson, D. 127

Robinson, W.S. 186

Rock, Paul 195

Roth, Julius 169, 193, 211

routine activities 169

Royal Navy 104–5

Royal Ulster Constabulary (RUC) 65, 76

rules 25–6, 169–70

Ryan, P. 46, 49, 109

sampling 4, 34, 35–9, 234; context 39; interviewees 106; people 37–8; theoretical 33, 107; time 35–7

Sampson, H. 30, 41, 50

Sanders, T. 50

Schatzman, L. 23, 37, 143, 201

Scheper-Hughes, N. 89, 210, 212, 218, 227

Schofield, J.W. 234

schools 25–6, 35, 39, 78–9; boredom 103; case selection 33–4; Dartington Hall study 214–15; experience of researcher 71–2; field roles 86; gender differences 22; group interviews 113, 114; informal conversations with pupils 70–1; interview locations 114, 116; observational difficulties 82; parental consent for research 52–3; respondent validation 181, 182–3; 'sensitive' periods 52; teacher accounts 99, 101–2, 108

Schuman, H. 16, 17

Schutz, A. 8–9, 80, 182

science 11–12, 14–15, 24–5, 171; scientific knowledge 134; scientific method 5–6, 7; scientific papers 128

scientologists 215–16, 224–5

Scott, G.G. 83–4

Scott, Marvin 168

Scott, Sue 64

Scott, Susie 138

Scourfield, J. 61

self-censorship 222

self-disclosure 72–3, 109

self-presentation 66–73, 109

'sensitive' periods 52

'sensitizing concepts' 27, 124, 164, 174, 192

settings 28–32; access issues 39–40, 50; context 39; physical 135; preconceptions 80, 81–2; temporal variation 37

Sevigny, M.J. 86

sexual behaviour 127

sexual harassment 93

sexual scene 43–4

shadowing 39

Shaffir, W.B. 54–5, 61, 105

Shakespeare, P. 160

Sheehan, E.A. 203

Sheridan, D. 126

Shils, E. 219, 221

ships 30, 41, 50

shyness 138

Simmel, G. 36

Simons, Helen 111–12

'single study model' 185–6

situated vocabularies 145

'situational analysis' 167

Sjoberg, G. 123

Skipper, J.K. 115–16

Skolnick, J. 34

Smigel, F. 61

Snow, David 95

social action 133, 134–5, 137, 168–71, 182

social class 59, 88

social context 176–9

social control 138

social conversation 70–1

social facts 81, 109

social interaction 21–2, 91, 134, 137, 150, 179

social locations 180, 181, 182

social networks 47–8

social relations 59, 133, 134, 135

social skills 69

social workers 42, 145

social-worlds analysis 167

sociology 1, 2; Chicago school 2, 5, 9, 122, 138; ethical issues 215; grounded theorizing 166; macro/micro theories 188;